Jews for nothing

DOV AHARONI FISCH

Jews for nothing

on Cults, Intermarriage, and Assimilation

FELDHEIM PUBLISHERS
Jerusalem • New York

First published 1984
ISBN 0-87306-347-3

Phototypeset at the Feldheim Press

Philipp Feldheim Inc.
200 Airport Executive Park
Spring Valley, NY 10977

96 East Broadway
New York, NY 10002

Feldheim Publishers Ltd
POB 6525 / Jerusalem, Israel

Printed in Israel

To my mother
Shirley
who understood the value
of a rich and thorough Jewish education
and who spared no expense
and allowed no personal consideration
to interfere
with the devoted raising of a Jewish family
I dedicate this book

Where thanks are due

While it may have ultimately been my hand which committed this book to paper, it would be impossible for me to neglect to thank the many who helped make this project a reality. Perhaps my greatest debt of gratitude is to those who, by their dedication, sincerity, and example, helped inspire so many of my generation to return to the Jewish experience. Such a list of individuals would have to include: Rabbi Avigdor Miller, Rabbi Avraham Weiss, Rebbetzin Esther Jungreis, the Lubavitcher Rebbe, Rabbi Velvel Perl, Rabbi Shlomo Riskin, Rabbi Yaakov Dardac, Rabbi Meir Kahane, Rabbi Shlomo Carlebach, and Rabbi Shlomo Thaler. Although each has stressed different aspects of Judaism, these inspired teachers have combined to create an atmosphere which has totally re-Jew-venated my generation. They have written books. They have spoken words. And they have performed deeds.

I am also deeply indebted to a long-time friend, Bobby Brown, who taught me the meaning and value of Jewish books. He has accumulated one of the largest privately-owned Jewish libraries in the world, and—more significantly—he has himself become the embodiment of the lessons contained therein.

To those in Jewish activist circles who encouraged me to write this book, I am deeply grateful for their support. And those of my generation who have already begun to spread Jewish meaning—people like Mat Hoffman, Gershon Winkler, Mordechai Reich, Yisroel Cohen,

Dovid Deen, and Shelly Lang—I can only thank them for having created a new Jewish climate in which a book like this would be conceivable.

Moreover, I am deeply grateful to Rabbi Sholom Klass, Mrs. Irene Klass, and Arnie Fine who helped start me on the road to this book by opening the pages of the *Jewish Press* to me as early as 1971. Many of this book's key themes were first presented on that newspaper's pages. Together with a dedicated staff, they have created a great instrument in the effort to strengthen Jewish identity in the United States.

A special word of thanks goes, as well, to Yitzchok Feldheim, my publisher. The role he played in reviewing my manuscript, making solid criticisms, and suggesting valuable changes in the text was of major significance. Moreover, his great patience in waiting for me to make the final revisions prior to publication—even as I was balancing my schedule with my full-time studies at the Yeshiva University rabbinical seminary and doing youth and outreach work at New York's Lincoln Square Synagogue—was of great personal value. The result of his concern, time, and effort is hopefully reflected in the text. And the Feldheim team's expertise did not end in America with Yitzchok. Sara Rivka Cohen, who combed through the text in the Jerusalem office of my publishers, did a brilliant job in tightening the prose and sharpening the manuscript. I am deeply grateful to her for her role in preparing this book for publication.

Others who took time to look at parts of the manuscript include Dr. Abraham Stern of Yeshiva University, Rabbi Larry Gevirtz of the Jewish Community Relations Council task force on missionary activity in New York, Rabbi Nisson Wolpin of Agudath Israel's *Jewish Observer*, and Rabbi Pinchas Stolper of the Union of Orthodox Jewish Congregations. I wish to express my appreciation to them for taking the time to review sections of the manuscript and for favorable comments they made. Such encouragement was of great value, and it came at an important time in the manuscript's final development.

Finally, to my wife, Linda, who encouraged me to write, who sharpened my thinking and my prose, who backed me when I encountered obstacles, who paid the bills and kept the gas and electricity running during the period of my writing, and who superbly strengthened every paragraph in this book—with the lone exception of the current one—I express my deepest thanks. The Talmud tells a man to love his wife as himself and to respect her more than himself. Linda has surely made this the easiest rabbinical dictum to abide by in all of Judaism.

Contents

Introduction

This book is born of its generation.

As such, it is a book of confusion and questions. It reflects the challenges facing young Jews on the high school and college campuses of America. But it also seeks, gropes for answers.

The late 1960s saw a revolution of spirit capture the hearts and minds of young Americans. What may have appeared to be an essentially political upheaval was, in fact, something far wider in scope. Transcending the realm of politics, the revolution affected the spheres of traditional social, economic, and spiritual values as well. Young people learned to question accepted values and to demand answers to questions their parents had not dared to ask. As the ethic of inquiry gained force among the young, it encountered a stubborn barrier in the parental generation of acceptance.

I am a child of the sixties and seventies. Growing up in an

emancipated society—a society which extolled reason over superstition, inquiry over acceptance, and modernity over tradition—I was taught to confront blindly accepted notions. I was taught to think and to question. And the lessons I learned were taught to my contemporaries, as well.

But when we came home with our questions, we were often denied answers. Within the Orthodox Jewish community which nurtured and bred me, my generation found resistance to inquiry. Questions were brushed aside by rabbis outraged at their "free-thinking fifteen-year-olds." One does not ask questions about Christianity or about Marxism, we were brusquely told. A true Jew does not honor Bible criticism with a response, we learned. And so we stopped asking our rabbis the questions which so distressed them.

But, of course, the questions did not go away. "Emancipated" from the ghettoes of Eastern Europe, we went on to top-notch universities. (For me, Columbia University was the next stop.) There, we heard the questions again. Only, this time, the "questions" were not manifestations of inquiry but of cynicism. The questions were emerging not from the mouths of traditional students seeking answers but from the lecture-notes of professors advocating new ideas. And, for the young American Jew who had been denied answers three years earlier, there was now no response to the intellectual challenges posed by trained skeptics.

On campuses throughout the United States, there are religious departments whose professors teach courses aimed at dissecting the Bible. Hard questions are raised by advocates of nonacceptance, and the interested student must search endlessly for the rabbi who will provide the answers. "Judaic studies" courses are offered, and they are frequently taught by individuals who mock Jewish tradition and authentic Jewish values. For the student who can yet believe that there is a second side to the question, there is virtually nowhere to turn.

More significantly, most Jewish students do not have any background in traditional Judaism. Denied a yeshiva education by "enlightened" parents—or subjected to a Talmud

Torah/Bar Mitzva Factory, which really never taught Talmud or Torah—these young Jews cannot begin to cope with the attacks against traditional Judaism. Not only have they no avenue on which to travel in search of answers; they also have no desire, no reason, to look for answers in defense of Jewish tradition. They were raised in an open society by parents who insisted, "My child will go to public school—not a yeshiva—because I want him to have the freedom to make his own choice as to whether or not he will be religious." But because they were never exposed to the alternative viewpoint which contends that Jewish tradition has something to offer, that "freedom of choice," ironically, never materializes for most Jewish youths.

Nevertheless, while the young, alienated Jew is not racked by questions about Judaism, he is not free from dilemma either. Satisfied that Judaism is an ancient relic holding no truths or answers for the modern generation in which he lives, he searches elsewhere for answers. Piety is glaringly lacking in a religion of nursing-home owners, and spirituality is absent from a theology which extols the paganistic bar mitzva (replete, quite often, with go-go dancers, foul-mouthed comedians, ostentatious and boorish relatives, and bought-off rabbis). There is no God in the massive Temple whose catering halls, basketball courts, and indoor swimming pools take up 90 percent of the lavish structure. Judaism, a religion of shameful Portnoys, bagels, and sonorous ministers, is not for the young Jew.

But he yearns for spirituality. He longs for God, for Divinity, for other-worldly discipline. And, frequently convinced that such values are not to be found in Judaism, he gravitates towards the theological alternatives awaiting him on the campuses of America. Guru Maharj Ji, Hare Krishna, Rev. Sun Myung Moon, and Christian missionaries court young Jews passionately. They theologically wine and dine the young Jew. And, if their love affair with the Jewish soul culminates successfully, they never let go of their conquest.

I have seen young Jews leave their people and join foreign cults. I have heard the questions of those still struggling to maintain a faith which survived nearly four thousand years without struggle. I myself have asked — and have been asked — the questions. And I have wrestled with ideas which have challenged traditionally held beliefs.

This book is not only addressed to my generation. It seeks to communicate our concerns to the world of our fathers and mothers as well. Speaking to "religious" and "non-religious" Jews alike, it seeks to explore some of the main challenges to Judaism posed in our time. As the effort of a young Jew who continues to grapple with new ideas and to confront new questions, it remains humanly incomplete. But, by dealing head-on with those issues which beg for answers, I believe that it will chart important new ground. And, in a generation of search and inquiry, such an approach to the study of Judaism can no longer be avoided.

The problem facing us today is not that there are
Jews for Jesus or Jews for Reverend Moonie.
The problem is that there are so many sweet,
holy Yiddelehs *who are Jews for Nothing.*

(SHLOMO CARLEBACH)

1

THE CULTS

They sacrificed to powerless spirits, to non-gods, to gods whom they knew not, to new gods who had but recently arrived . . . (DEUTERONOMY 32:17)

Any consideration of the crises facing young American Jews today must begin with a look at the new and puzzling cults. In our lifetime, we have been witness to a major religious revival which has stormed America. By the tens of thousands, Americans of all walks of life have begun to re-evaluate long-held beliefs and to return to religion. National magazines have noted this trend in major cover stories; television networks have aired special news documentaries tracing this phenomenon; and the general culture of the past decade has begun to reflect this nation-wide movement.

While most of the revival has centered on the traditional faiths known to Americans, a significant theological counter-culture has emerged as well. Buoyed by a steady stream of gurus from the East, directed by pronouncements made by acknowledged youth culture heroes, and driven forward by a host of socio-political factors, the "cult explosion" has made its impact wherever young people are to be found.

Especially open to these exotic and foreign ideas have been teen- and college-age Jews raised in American suburbia. Although given "everything they could possibly want—and the best," these individuals have left their people and their communities to undertake a search for something they were not able to find back home. Some have gone on to Hare Krishna temples, where they have assumed new identities under Sanskrit names and shaven heads. Others have journeyed forth to the expanses of Tarrytown, New York, where they have discovered their own Moon, a fiery Korean preacher who claims to have been worshipped by Jesus and sent by God. Gurus have captured their imagination; Zen masters have picked their minds. Even a pudgy kid from India who lives in regal splendor with his airline-stewardess wife and his Mercedes-Benz limousines has succeeded in attracting some of the best of our young people.

For most Jewish families, the loss of a son or daughter to a cult is just that: a loss. Names change to incoherent Sanskrit, Bengali, Korean, and other forms. Lifestyles change. Most importantly, concepts change. In the vast majority of cults, young people are taught to distrust and hate their parents—the latter frequently being portrayed as servants of Satan or some other evil demon. Communication between parent and child becomes almost impossible. Phone calls are prohibited by cult leaders; mail is often delivered in a censored condition (if at all), and—if the parent persists in efforts to reach the captured member of the family—cult leaders arrange the transfer of their new human conquest to a different base of operations. Sometimes the transfer is from New York to San Francisco. Sometimes from New York to New Delhi.

Jewish parents have become frantic over the loss of sons and daughters to the new cults, and tens of thousands of others nervously fear what the future may hold for them. Throughout the United States, discussion of the cults has become a major topic of Jewish concern, and efforts to "save our children" can be found in just about every major Jewish community in America.

Why are young Jews leaving their faith, their heritage, and their people for the uncertain worlds of the East? Why have they given up the "good life" and deserted all their material luxuries for an opportunity to contract tuberculosis in a Krishna temple, to become celibate in a Children of God commune, or to simply sit for years meditating in a Zen Buddhism center on the nature of the noise produced by a person clapping with only one hand?

These are the questions Jewish parents are asking.

To find an answer—a real answer—we must go beyond external appearances. We must begin to consider what has really been given to young Jews in the last twenty years, and we must contrast that with what the cults have to offer. Indeed, we must begin to understand what the cults themselves are—not just in terms of their strange habits, weird clothes, and foreign dialects but also with regard to their philosophies, lifestyles, and teleological-eschatological paradigms.

This section will not deal with each and every cult ever reported to have existed in America. Many cults have not appreciably affected the Jewish community (though most have left one mark or another). Satanism, witchcraft, spiritualism, and their ilk have proven too bizarre or inane for even the most confused of our people. Other groups like Bahai, Meher Baba, and their sort seem to have passed by now. Indeed, one of the "vocational hazards" faced by every cult leader is the possibility that his new religion, which emerges on the American scene basking in the spotlight of media publicity, may shortly thereafter be sent packing in ignominious secrecy.

It is wholly probable that, one day, some of the cults discussed on the pages that follow will have disappeared from the American scene and that new theological aberrations will have arrived to take their places and to suck new minds and bodies away from the Jewish fold. Such a development would not be surprising because—even as the gurus and prophets come and go—the factors giving rise to their success and the sociopolitical elements enabling them to lure away intelligent, searching young people will remain the same.

Thus, we must consider the individual sects not only as isolated phenomena but also as inevitable outgrowths of certain conditions. The Hare Krishna, the Jesus freaks, and the Moonies must be compared no less than contrasted because it is that which they have in common which serves as the key to the great enigma of our time: Why do young people join those bizarre cults?

CHAPTER **1**

Jews for Jesus
Christians in Hebrew wrapping

And he shall speak peace to the
nations . . . (ZECHARIAH 9:10)

And he shall turn the heart of the fathers
to the children and the heart of the
children to their fathers . . . (MALACHI 3:24)

. . . .

Do not think that I came to bring peace
on the earth; I did not come to bring
peace but a sword. For I came to set a
man against his father, and a daughter
against her mother, and a daughter-in law
against her mother-in-law. (MATTHEW 10:34-35)

As vultures hovering and circling over thirsting bodies in the
desert, they come with their tracts to the spiritual wastelands of
suburbia, patiently waiting for the opportunity to snare yet
another Jewish soul thirsting for Divinity. They smile and
softly preach the gospel of peace. Sometimes they wear buttons
which proclaim "I Found It!" Other times they dress in shirts
which read: "Jews for Jesus." They are Christian missionaries,
and they will stop at nothing to win the soul of the young Jew.

The missionary bit is nothing new to our people. Having
been butchered by crusaders, burned by bishops, and defamed
by leaders of all Christian denominations for our manifold
"crimes" (such as causing the Black Death by poisoning the
wells of Europe, and killing Christian babies at Passover time),
we have come to know the Christian missionaries. They are in

THE CULTS | 22

pursuit of our souls, and they will kill us if they have to — but only for the lofty purpose of saving us, of course.

Naturally, today's Christian missionary does not stand in Stony Brook, Long Island with a huge wooden cross dangling from his neck and a sword at his hip. Times have changed, and two thousand years of Jewish survival have convinced even the stubbornest missionary that we will not leave our faith under the threat of death. So they have learned a new approach. Love.

Oh, how they spread love! They go to the fourteen-year-old Jew who has never opened a Bible (bar mitzva *haftorot* these days are memorized from records), and they show him the Jewish Bible. They turn to Exodus 21:24 and read the words of the "cruel, vengeful God of the Jews": "An eye for an eye." Then they take out a handy Christian Bible, turn to Matthew 5:44, and read, "But I say to you: Love your enemies, and pray for those who persecute you." The approach is effective, especially if the young victim is a sensitive, kind individual. And young Jews are certainly that.

The presentation must be more sophisticated for an older subject. Sooner or later most young Jews are bound to hear from a grandparent that the Oral Law (which is today embodied in the Talmud) was given by God to Moses at the same time that He revealed His Torah (Bible). And that Oral Law, which serves as the key to understanding the intent of the Torah (i.e., the Written Law), emphatically explains that Exodus 21:24 is not to be understood literally. Never in Jewish history did a rabbi authorize the execution of the barbaric *lex talionis* doctrine. The Talmud teaches that a monetary fine is to be imposed when one inflicts an injury which results in the loss of his victim's eyesight. Any Jewish child who has finished one year of yeshiva schooling knows this. But very few young Jews ever attend a Jewish parochial school.

Nevertheless, word leaks down, and sooner or later the "eye for eye" routine becomes a risky angle of argumentation for the Christian missionary who wants to go places. Moreover, even the Jew who has not studied in yeshiva knows that there is more to Christianity than "love thy neighbor." Two thousand years of crusades, inquisitions, pogroms, and holocausts are hard to cover up—even on Madison Avenue. So other approaches are necessitated.

For a number of decades, Christian missionary groups had been racking their brains in efforts to conceive a tactic which would increase the rate of Jewish conversions. Labor as they might, they were unable to break the ice. Jews were just turned-off to the entire Christian presentation. Even a Jewish ignoramus, when confronted by a Bible-toting preacher speaking of the merits of "Christian love" over "Jewish vengeance," might easily respond, "Sir, do you take me for a fool?" The missionaries tried everything, even offering parents free room, board, clothing, and education for their children—in return for their souls. But, while a few terribly pressured individuals gave in now and then, the overall missionary effort was a flop. Jews just wouldn't become Christians.

Much of the credit for the renewal of the missionary fervor—and for the marked success which has characterized the new version of Christian proselytizing—must go to a forty-eight-year-old Baptist minister named "Moishe Rosen." Ordained in 1957, Rosen began working for the American Board of Missions to the Jews (ABMJ). As a paid missionary, he was obligated to do street-preaching by his boss, Dr. Daniel Fuchs. First sent to a Jewish section in Los Angeles by the Board of Missions, Rosen set up shop in a small house provided by his organization. Despite the fact that he was paid to convert Jews, he found the job to be grueling at times, especially when knowledgeable Jews approached him and interrupted his preaching efforts on Los Angeles street corners. On one occasion, he pulled an especially adamant Jewish fellow aside and pleaded, "I know you don't agree with what I say, but for me this is a living. I'm paid for preaching. If I can't do it, if I fail, they'll fire me. I have a wife and two children. Let me preach. Let me do my work."[1]

THE CULTS | 24

As is evident, Rosen could be a very crass fellow. Indeed, during his earlier days he displayed the level of his Jewish knowledge by noting that, while Christian religious services are conducted in a decorous fashion, the synagogue is much noisier because "even gossip during prayers is sanctified according to the Talmud."[2]

After plugging away in Los Angeles, Rosen began to learn the tricks of his trade. And he perfected them. He found hecklers to be essential to his pitch because one good hothead "helped to build up the crowd." Moreover, he began to find that the easiest Jews to proselytize were the non-Orthodox ones. He explained this by noting that "what often passes for Judaism today has no more relation to authentic, biblical Judaism than Unitarianism has to New Testament Christianity."[3] Therefore, when dealing with such Jews, Rosen would claim that it was *he* who was the "authentic Jew." Soon, he would perfect his approach.

By 1965, Rosen was doing so well that the ABMJ decided to promote him. He was made "director of recruiting and training." Two years later, when the Board of Missions finally decided to relocate in New York City—the most heavily populated Jewish urban center in the world—Rosen came along and was made "missionary in charge of Headquarters District."[4] In Rosen's own words, "I was well on my way toward becoming a religious organization man."[5] In addition to attending regular meetings called by the Board of Missions for the purpose of planning "missionary strategy," Rosen actively served on the boards of other evangelistic agencies. Moreover, he was put in charge of a $168,000 building program. By 1970, he was influential indeed, supervising everything from fundraising drives to the designing of the ABMJ's kitchen facilities.

In time, Rosen found himself increasingly isolated from the street activity to which he had become accustomed earlier. He was rapidly becoming a "self-satisfied religious bureaucrat who was more concerned with running an efficient organization than with showing compassion to other human beings."[6] Dressed in a dark suit and thin tie, clean-shaven and with a crew cut, Rosen was a most fitting organization man. Deeply conservative, he held negative views on young radicals and disliked their counterculture.[7] More interestingly, he found the environment of the ABMJ—an agency geared toward "witnessing to Jews"—to be so uniformly un-Jewish as to impair his own sense of the prevailing Jewish mood. Though reading Jewish journals regularly, Rosen admitted feeling no commitment to the Jewish people.[8]

Out of touch with American youth, out of touch with the Jewish community he was seeking to proselytize, Rosen was symbolically "hit over the head" after a speech he made to a group at Columbia University. Berating "hippies, radicals, and revolutionaries," he was pulled aside by a fellow missionary after his talk and chastised.

"What you're doing is alienating a lot of people you should be trying to reach," he was scolded. "Do you know that a lot of hippies are Jewish?"[9]

Rosen was "crestfallen." Jolted into the realization that he was losing the touch he had begun to master in California, Rosen sought coaching from a young woman whom he knew to be familiar with the youth counterculture.[10] Soon after, he was writing his first brochures tailored to the Jewish hippies in their own lingo:

> Hey, you with the beard!
> We think you are Beautiful.
> God likes long hair and beards, too.
> He didn't want the Israelites to trim their beards.
> Can you imagine Moses or Elijah with a crew cut?[11]

Or Moishe Rosen.

Having discovered this unexplored approach to missionary activity, Rosen decided to leave his New York office and to travel to San Francisco, the center of the "hippie population." In early 1970 he flew to the West Coast to address students at Simpson Bible College, Conservative Baptist Theological Seminary, and Golden Gate Baptist Seminary.[12] He was soon able to win Dr. Fuchs's backing for a more permanent move to San

Francisco. In no time, Rosen had established new missionary headquarters in Corte Madera.

With the relocation, Rosen set his new campaign into motion with all the wisdom of a public-relations expert. He concluded that if he was to succeed he would have to throw out his dark suits and skinny ties and start wearing blue jeans.[13] Likewise, he decided at this time to synthesize a new missionary ideology, based on his earlier successes in confusing young Jews from non-observant homes by asserting that it was he who was the authentic Jew, not their rabbis. Summoning all the marketing skills he had developed during his youth when he was a sales manager of a Denver cemetery,[14] he decided to send forth individuals portraying themselves as "Jews made kosher by Jesus." Preying on the lack of Jewish knowledge evinced by young Jews raised in non-observant homes, Rosen would claim that his movement was not less Jewish than the typical Reform or Conservative Jewish temple. In the minister's words: "The promise of salvation [is] non-existent in much of contemporary Judaism. The Reform Jews, for example, have another version of the prayer book in which they have deleted all references to the personal Messiah and the rebuilding of the Temple."[15]

To help reinforce this deception, Rosen's evangelists occasionally would wear yarmulkes (skullcaps) or other Jewish symbols. Special "Jews for Jesus" T-shirts were designed, replete with the mandatory star of David. Even the literature produced was tailored to evoke Jewish feelings. One brochure was entitled "Christmas Is a Jewish Holiday" and featured on its cover the drawing of a Christmas tree adorned with a huge Jewish star. A second circular captured a Jew's attention by asking, in large letters, "Will Israel Survive?" and a third one was headlined: "*Lechayim!* To Life!" In every way possible, Jewish symbols were arrogated.

In every way possible. Rosen and his later imitators have left no stone unturned in seeking to ensnare unsuspecting Jews. They have published Jewish Arts Calendars and have re-issued under their own organizational logos other less fanciful calendars listing Jewish holidays and Friday evening candle-lighting times. Recording groups with names like "The Liberated Wailing Wall" and "The Israelites" have cut a wide assortment of discs bearing such titles as "Hineni," "Shema Yisroel," and "Kol Simcha." B'nai Yeshua, a Christian organization seeking to convert Jews on Long Island, has run Saturday evening *havdala* services. Others have published Passover *haggadot* and have conducted Passover *seder* services in an effort to create a comfortable setting maximally conducive to the proselytization of impressionable Jews.

In the most absurd implementation of this tactic to date, one Christian missionary outfit spent two years trying to trademark the term *Shechina.* The word, which Hebraically refers to the omnipresence of God, has been used by Jews for tens of centuries in their description of God's ever-present being. In kabbalistic mysticism, moreover, God's *Shechina* is of central significance. Nevertheless, B'nai Yeshua, Incorporated, fought a long battle to usurp the term and to gain sole right to its use. Only the good sense of the Trademark Trial and Appeal Board put an end to this outrage.

As the *Shechina* affair has indicated, there are no bounds to the arrogance of those prepared to boldly imitate the Rosen method. One New York group began a "Christian Brothers Carpet Cleaning Service," which left leaflets for unsuspecting homeowners in the city. When individuals hired the group to clean their carpets, they subsequently found that trained and verbose Christian missionaries were invariably dispatched by the company.

Even more savage has been the vulture-like attempt to prey on unsuspecting Jews immigrating to the United States from countries of persecution. In 1979 Rosen called for increased efforts to proselytize Iranian Jewish students who were then fleeing to America in a desperate attempt to avoid the Jew-hatred rampant under the Khomeini regime. In a similar vein, Rosen and his ilk have cooordinated a massive drive to reach Soviet Jewish immigrants before their co-religionists do. To achieve this goal, missionaries have placed large advertisements in Russian-language publications, offering Jewish immigrants everything from English classes to jobs. The distribution of missionary literature and Christian Bibles in Russian translation has become a common sight on street corners of neighborhoods like Brighton Beach, Brooklyn, where large numbers of Soviet Jewish immigrants have made their new homes.

Rosen has attempted to portray his tactics of deception in a pious light: "We have combined our penchant for pithy sayings with a knack for satire and irony in our broadside tracts . . . One technique we use in writing broadsides is to employ irony by taking a Jewish concept or slogan and 'reinterpreting' it in a Christian context."

Examples of such "irony" abound. Christian missionaries have gone so far as to use the name of Rebbetzin Esther Jungreis's "Hineni" organization and a near duplication of the Jewish Defense League logo. Such infringements are especially praiseworthy, according to Rosen, because they provoke lawsuits which attract attention in the Jewish press. "There would [be] no other way to get so much publicity on such a small amount of money," he beams.[16]

Coming from a clergyman, such a statement is also an "irony."

But it is consistent with Rosen's approach to religion. He portrays himself as an "authentic Jew" and claims his "faith is almost indistinguishable from Orthodox Judaism." But, beneath the yarmulke and *tzitzit*, he is a man who has "even been known to wear a clerical collar and vestments" when appearing before more liturgical churches.[17] Lowering his guard on another occasion when no media representatives were present, he took a group of "Jews for Jesus" to eat in a non-kosher Chinese restaurant.[18] Indeed, a leading member of his organization's ruling circle is a young man, Bruce Skoropinski, who is not Jewish but was in fact a student-body president at Simpson College.[19] Rosen has even made use of undercover spies when he felt it desirable to infiltrate Jewish groups.[20]

If Rosen and his "Jews for Jesus" seem less than kosher, it is not surprising. His Hebrew-Christian gambit is a fraud. One can no sooner be a Christian and a Jew simultaneously than he can be a Christian and a Moslem. The claim that a Jew need not give up his Jewishness in order to join Christianity is a carefully constructed ruse aimed directly at the enormous pool of young American Jews who were raised in assimilated, middle- and upper-class areas and who were denied the opportunity to receive a meaningful Jewish education by parents who preferred that their children go to public schools "like everyone else."

Significant, in this light, is Rosen's own book, whose jacket describes the group as "a dynamic Christian movement" which "presents effective evangelism techniques . . . which will enrich the spiritual life of every Christian." Bluntly, the jacket description of the book adds, "This organization is dedicated to spreading the Christian message." In his book, the Baptist minister writes that one of the key values of his proselytizing among Jews has been that "our experience has taught me the importance of mobilizing Christian young people for God's work."[21] Although he continues to claim that "Jews for Jesus" is for real, Rosen does not deny that the organization has been granted tens of thousands of dollars by the American Board of Missions to the Jews, a fiery, right-wing Christian outfit.[22]

Perhaps the key to understanding Rosen is his own confession: "I was a salesman before becoming an evangelist."[23]

RESPONDING TO THE CHALLENGE

While it is important to understand the roots of the "Jews for Jesus" scheme, the issues go deeper than the group itself. In the past few years, offshoots have appeared under such names as "B'nai Yeshua" and "Shechina '75." Using Hebrew words to describe themselves and Jewish symbols to portray their beliefs, these groups have worked day and night to obscure the differences between Judaism and Christianity. Their purpose is clear: by paving over the irreconcilable differences between the two faiths, they hope to facilitate mass conversions of alienated and unaffiliated young Jews who, at present, cannot bring themselves to leave the Jewish fold. The "Hebrew-Christian" concept, then, represents the best Madison Avenue can offer: one can rest assured that, while he may be giving up his soul to the Church, he is not exactly leaving the Jewish people. In purely eschatological terms, the "Jews for Jesus" idea is the best thing to happen to the Christian Church since the Inquisition.

Thus, it becomes more important than ever for Jews to understand that there *are* differences between the two religions, deep conceptual variances which sharply individuate Judaism and Christianity. The illusion of a common "Judeo-Christian" heritage is further debunked by a careful consideration of the irreconcilable scriptural differences between the Torah and the Christian Gospels.

To begin with, Judaism rejects as abhorrent the Christian contention that all mankind is stained, from the moment of birth, by the "Original Sin" committed by Adam and Eve in the Garden of Eden. While Christian dogma insists that every person is doomed to eternal damnation regardless of the perfection of his deeds — and that only by the grace of the Father, who sent "His only Son" to die for humanity's sins, can salvation be achieved through faith — Judaism maintains that every human being is born spiritually pure and that the path to salvation is within each person's reach. No intermediary is needed for a Jew to gain a portion in the World to Come; if a Jew performs deeds (*mitzvot*) — good, pure, holy deeds — he is assured eternal life. Moreover, those born non-Jews need only conduct themselves in the humane manner expected of the sons of Noah[24] to achieve a share in the World to Come. Judaism does not threaten members of other faiths with eternal damnation. It is too secure in itself and in its eternal truth to impose the ultimate penalty — eternal damnation — on those who, by no fault of their own, were born into families accepting divergent faith-systems.

Christianity is not so secure. For the Jew who does not convert, Jesus — who supposedly commanded his disciples to love their enemies — ominously warns that there will be no hope. Indeed, the Christian who lacks faith, though he may be saintly in deeds, must perish into hell—the victim of the ineradicable "Original Sin." Only the individual who has faith that Jesus died for his sins, in order to atone for his and all mankind's inheritance of "Original Sin," can gain salvation. Deeds are relegated to a secondary level, and many discard the significance of the law altogether. The important aspect is the faith that the Father sent "His Son" to atone for mankind by offering his blood on the altar of the cross.

To Jews, this entire notion of vicarious atonement is foreign. The Torah reports the requirement laid by God upon the Jewish people to perform *mitzvot*. "All the commandments which I command you this day shall you observe to do . . ."[25] In the words of Moses:

> And now, Israel, what does the Lord your God require of you but to fear the Lord your God, to walk in all His ways, and to love Him, and to serve the Lord your God with all your heart and with all your soul, *to keep the commandments of the Lord and His statutes* which I command you this day for your good?[26]

The entire notion of "Original Sin" is inconsistent with an objective reading of the Torah (known to Christians as the "Old Testament"). And that becomes terribly significant in light of Christian theology's contention that the entire value of the "New Testament" is rooted in its supposed compatibility with and fulfillment of the "Old Testament." If the Christian Gospels can be shown to seriously misinterpret the Torah, the entire theology of the Church crumbles. And so it does. How can "Original Sin" be attributed to the Adam-and-Eve incident—or any other affair—in light of the words of Ezekiel 18:19-20:

> Yet you say, "Why? Does not the son bear the iniquity of the father?" When the son has done what is lawful and right, and has kept all My statutes, and has done them, he shall surely live.
>
> The soul that sins, it shall die. The son shall not bear the iniquity of the father . . .[27]

The fact is that "Original Sin" is one of the problems Christian theologians must forever wrestle with. It is out of step with the entire theme of the "Old Testament." If all men were doomed — without exception — to spend eternity in hell, how did the righteous who lived before Jesus "atoned for mankind" manage? Did Abraham, Isaac, Jacob, Moses, Samuel, and David need Jesus to "atone for them"? Did Sarah, Rebeccah, Leah, Rachel, Miriam, and Deborah have no salvation despite their saintly lives? Of course the "Old Testament" never conceived so repugnant an idea as "Original Sin." There was always a difference between the nature of existence-after-death for the righteous and of that for the wicked. When the prophet Balaam prayed, "Let me die the death of the righteous,"[28] he was unknowingly presenting the Christian theologians of future centuries with a perplexing problem: if all men, righteous and wicked, experienced the same end, what in the world was Balaam talking about? Ultimately, the doctrine of "Original Sin" is one of the "deep mysteries" which had to be concocted to give historical and theological significance to the brutal killing of Jesus.

But "Original Sin" presents additional problems as well. According to the dogma, Jesus had to die in a manner in which his blood would be spilled in order to "atone for mankind." The whole significance of his crucifixion takes on special meaning to Christian theologians who — having concocted the "Original Sin" thesis — now assert that a blood offering was needed for atonement. Pointing to Leviticus 17:11, they note that "the life of the flesh is in the blood, and I have given it to you upon the altar to make an atonement for your souls." Therefore, contend the theologians, no one can ever gain atonement for any sins ("Original" or otherwise) without a blood-offering, and since the Holy Temple no longer stands (thus preventing us from preparing sacrifices for atonement) only Jesus' "blood-offering" can provide atonement for mankind.

This desperate rationale, again frantically concocted to give meaning to the barbaric murder of Jesus by the Romans, stands completely without basis. Everything in the Torah militates against the notion of corporal sacrifice. We are enjoined in Leviticus 18:21 never to allow any of our sons to die as sacrifices. When Abraham prepared to perform the will of God in Genesis 22 by sacrificing his son Isaac, an angel of God was dispatched to stop the ritual from being performed. Abraham had displayed his faith, and God taught mankind a lesson for all time: "Do not lay your hand on the lad."

But the question transcends these two cases. If atonement could never be achieved without a blood-offering (which is the Christian contention in contradistinction to Judaism's attitude, which posits atonement through prayer and repentance — and not exclusively through sacrifice), then how can Christian dogma explain away the incident described in Jonah 3? The people of Nineveh had sinned greatly and were marked for severe punishment. However, after being chastised by the prophet of God, the entire city, led by their king, fasted and repented. God saw their actions, and He forgave them.

Thus, the Torah clearly indicated the possibility of atonement without a blood-offering.[29] To Christian theologians, these matters remain "great mysteries." And mysteries they are.

Perhaps the most egregious misconstruction of Torah was perpetrated by Paul, when he carried the "Original Sin" doctrine to its ultimate conclusion: if belief that Jesus died for man's sins assures salvation, then what need is there to perform the law? True, God asserted again and again throughout the Torah that one gains salvation by performing deeds, by observing and performing the commandments. But Paul had a new faith to propagate, and — if Christianity was to have a chance to spread — it would have to clearly define its emphasis on faith.

Paul naively misunderstood a verse in Deuteronomy to mean that one who violates but one of God's laws is doomed. Therefore, he propounded that Jesus came to absolve mankind from the obligation to fulfill the law. (Or, in Paul's terms, "Christ redeemed us from the curse of the law."[30]) By faith alone, man could gain salvation. Aside from the fact that Paul's innovation (which has become accepted as normative Christianity) deviated from the very words of Jesus, Paul created a new notion in theology which became the basis of the conceptual differences between Judaism and Christianity. Jesus had said, "Do not think that I came to abolish the law or the prophets; I did not come to abolish but to fulfill. For truly I say to you, until heaven and earth pass away, not the smallest letter or stroke shall pass away from the law until all is accomplished. Whoever, then, annuls one of the least of these commandments, and so teaches others, shall be called least in the kingdom of heaven . . ."[31] (From this it would appear that Paul's fate after death is yet another of the great "mysteries" in Christian theology.)

To Judaism, the law was given by God to discipline man and to make him holy. The law is not a curse but a blessing; indeed, Jews begin their daily prayers by praising and blessing God for having granted us His Torah laws, and we conclude our day by thanking God for His laws which "are our life and lengthen our days." We rejoice in the laws every day, and every year we euphorically dance and sing on Simchat Torah—the holiday which marks the conclusion of our annual study of the Torah. The law uplifts man; it sanctifies the mundane. It lends to every act and aspect of holiness. Sexual relations between husband and wife—extolled by the law—become a holy and beautiful part of life. (How different from the Christian attitude which sees the body as a base receptacle for sin and which perceives all sexual relations to be smeared with an intangible sense of impurity! In Catholicism, the perfect priest must remain celibate; the ideal woman—ever since the description of the "immaculate conception"—must be a virgin.)

We believe that laws help liberate man from his animalistic instincts. The Jew who follows the laws of *kashrut* raises the meaning of food and eating to the holiest heights from the lowest depths. Every physical act, toned by the perfect Law, becomes a spiritual and sacred experience. The laws uplift man, and we proudly seek to live by them.

The Pauline theology, which sought to "liberate man" from

the "curse of the law," created a system of faith without accountability. Crusades, inquisitions, and hundreds of other bloody undertakings were decreed by the fathers of Catholicism and, later, Protestantism—all in the name of God![32] Concerned as they were with faith, they could not bear the Jewish people's rejection of Jesus' claims; unconcerned as they were with law, they stopped at nothing to make their feelings known.

It is to the Pauline rejection of the law that Judaism expresses its strongest disagreement. The crusaders and their spiritual descendants—for a thousand years—have conclusively proven that "morality" and "ethics" are highly subjective terms, open to wide variations of interpretation without the benefit of Divine guidance. Living by the law, we Jews have embodied those notions of justice, kindness, and charity which are so richly present throughout the pages of the Torah, while the symbols and leaders of Christianity have personified all the cruel, vengeful elements so easily construed from their Gospels. One compares the past two thousand years of Jewish life to the same period of Christian life, and one sees which system uplifts the finest elements in man.

Indeed, while Paul praised Jesus for sparing mankind from the obligations inherent in the Torah, the Christian Gospels would seem to have resulted in quite a different set of consequences. Which system is harder to live by—a Judaism which permits and praises marital relations or a Christianity which prefers celibacy but accepts marital sex, though debasing it as an expression of the lusts of "sinful flesh"?[33] Which system is harder to live by—a Judaism which permits divorce when, for any of the many possible reasons, something goes wrong in a marriage, or a Christianity whose unmarried Savior virtually outlaws divorce?[34] Which system is harder to live by—a Judaism which recognizes the inexorable need of a man to seek justice when a wrong is done or Christianity which threatens damnation to the individual who does not turn the other cheek when wronged? It is a testimony to the eternal wisdom of the Torah that its adherents have been in the forefront of the efforts to achieve justice and equality for every wronged individual. It is not a testimony to the Christian Gospels that it has served as the document in whose name bloody crusades, inquisitions, pogroms, and wars have been declared.

Indeed, it is the very record of the Christian world which has led Judaism to affirm, again and again, that we cannot accept the claims put forth on behalf of Jesus of Nazareth. The Torah, whose prophecies he came to "fulfill," predicted that the Messiah would speak peace to the nations[35] and that he would bring fathers and sons together.[36] But Jesus did the exact opposite. According to Matthew 10:34-5, he said: "Do not think that I came to bring peace on the earth; I did not come to bring peace but a sword. For I came to set a man against his father, and a daughter against her mother, and a daughter-in-law against her mother-in-law."[37]

It had been prophesied that the Messiah would be of the line of David. Because the Bible considers a person's descent *only* on the basis of the paternal line and *never* on the basis of the mother's ancestors, Jesus could claim Davidic lineage only on the basis of Joseph's descent. But if Jesus was born of a virgin then Jospeh was not his father and he could not claim roots extending back to David. Thus Jesus could not have been the individual of whom the "Old Testament" prophets spoke when they foretold the coming of a Messiah in the end of days. (Moreover, it is to be noted that Joseph's own lineage is in serious question. Two conflicting accounts are offered in Matthew 1:2-16 and Luke 3:23-28; they contradict each other so grievously that the effort to understand how a Divinely inspired "New Testament" could be so inconsistent constitutes yet another of the Church's "great mysteries.")

Jesus' teachings offered us nothing new. The "golden rule" for which he took credit was an outrageous example of misinterpretation, misquoting, and lack of biblical erudition. In Matthew 5:43-44, we read: "You have heard that it was said, 'You shall love your neighbor and hate your enemy.' But I say to you, 'Love your enemies, and pray for those who persecute you.' "

It is a point of fact that the "golden rule" to "Love your

neighbor as yourself" pre-dated Jesus and appeared in the Torah.[38] It is an incredible fact that the Christian Messiah was less acquainted with the Scriptures he had come to "fulfill" than are most fourth-grade yeshiva students. Nowhere in the Torah is it written that one should hate an enemy. On the contrary, it is written, "You shall not hate your brother in your heart."[39] How fascinating it is to compare the behavior of the people of the Torah with that of the people of the Christian Gospels! Who were the haters, and who showed love? Jesus did not exactly "turn the other cheek" when he threatened those of other faiths by warning, "Whoever shall deny me before men, I will also deny him before my Father who is in heaven."[40] And it was not exactly in consonance with the "golden rule" that Jesus expressed his unwillingness to help a non-Jewish woman (whom he compared to a dog simply because she was not of the "house of Israel").[41]

If Jesus lapsed, his disciples sank in an ocean of hate. Perhaps the ultimate proof of Christianity's bankruptcy as an uplifting system is to be found in its shameful failure to engender love in the ranks of its own leaders. The hate spewed forth by the fathers of the Catholic Church and Protestant Reformation—and reiterated by Christian leaders during the Nazi holocaust—can testify forever as our answer to those missionaries who would teach the Jewish people the "golden rule." Consider these thoughts penned by Martin Luther: "Set their synagogues on fire, and whatever does not burn up should be covered or spread over with dirt so that no one may ever be able to see a cinder or stone of it . . . Their homes should likewise be broken down and destroyed . . . They should be deprived of their prayer books and Talmuds . . . Their rabbis must be forbidden to teach under the threat of death."[42]

In his work "The Jews and Their Lies," Luther had this to say about "those miserable, wicked people":

> They are the real liars and bloodhounds . . . The sun never did shine on a more bloodthirsty and revengeful people . . . Wherever you see or hear a Jew teaching, do not think otherwise than that you are hearing a

poisonous Basiliskus who with his face poisons and kills people . . . The Devil has possessed these people with all his angels . . . Therefore know, my dear Christian, that next to the Devil you have no more bitter, more poisonous, more vehement an enemy than a real Jew . . .[43]

Luther, who was the father of the Protestant Reformation, was not alone. In fact, his attitude toward the Jews was not inconsistent with the teachings of the popes and saints of the Catholic Church, which represented the other branch of "Christian charity." Justin Martyr, one of the early saints, wrote his wish that Jewish towns be consumed in flames and that no Jew ever be able to go to Jerusalem.[44] Eusebius, Bishop of Caesarea, taught his uneducated followers that Jews crucify Christians every Purim.[45] Saint Ephraem referred to synagogues as whorehouses.[46] Saint Zeno, Bishop of Verona, expressed his disappointment in a raid by monks on Jewish homes, which culminated with the murder of many Jews and the burning of their bodies. Zeno felt that a great many more Jews could have been burned.[47] Saint Jerome, one of the most influential of the early Church fathers, called for the prosecution of all Jews refusing to accept Christianity, while the famed St. Augustine described Judas Iscariot as "the true image" of the Jew and added that Jews "forever will bear the guilt for the death of Jesus."[48] Augustine saw the Jews as living proof of the truth of Christianity, noting that their *eternal* wandering and *permanent* expulsion from the Land of Israel (sic) firmly proved that God had rejected them. Jews were not to be killed, said Augustine, because they had a role to play as the Church's "slave-librarian."[49]

Saint Ambrose, another of the leading early Church fathers and Bishop of Milan, endorsed the burning of synagogues.[50] He was one of the architects of Christian ethics, and ethical he seems when compared with the fourth-century "Bishop with the Golden Tongue," Saint John Chrysostom. The Golden Tongue—so named because of his widespread reputation as a lover of all humanity[51]—considered the Jews to be "the most

worthless of all men—they are lecherous, greedy, rapacious—
they are perfidious murderers of Christians, they worship the
devil, their religion is a sickness."[52] Sometimes Chrysostom's
"fervent love for all mankind" was expressed in this way: "The
Jews are the odious assassins of Christ and for killing God there
is no expiation possible, no indulgence or pardon. Christians
may never cease vengeance, and the Jews must live in servitude
forever . . . It is incumbent on all Christians to hate the
Jews."[53]

It is no wonder that he was known as the Golden Tongue.
Consider his description of the synagogue: "A criminal assembly of Jews . . . the refuge of devils, a gulf and abyss of
perdition . . . Whatever name even more horrible could be
found will never be worse than the synagogue deserves,"[54]
Moreover, he noted, "I hate the synagogue . . . I hate the Jews
for the same reason."[55] He could not have reacted otherwise for
as his Golden Tongue put it, "Debauchery and drunkenness
had brought them to the level of the lusty goat and the pig.
They know only one thing, to satisfy their stomachs, to get
drunk, to kill and beat each other up like stage villains and
coachmen."[56]

If Chrysostom was the Golden Tongue, then the beloved
Saint Gregory of Nyssa was the Golden Thesaurus as is evident
from this brief description of the Jews: "Slayers of the Lord,
murderers of the prophets, adversaries of God, haters of God,
men who show contempt for the law, foes of grace, enemies of
their father's faith, advocates of the devil, brood of vipers,
slanderers, scoffers, men whose minds are in darkness, leaven of
the Pharisees, assembly of demons, sinners, wicked men,
stoners, and haters of righteousness."[57]

Nor were the Church fathers content to confine their
feelings to sermons. From their mouths emerged the words
which unleashed crusades, blood libels, pogroms, and
inquisitions against the Jews. Indeed, actions such as those
taken by Pope Paul IV in the sixteenth century—who
compelled Jews to wear yellow badges, to reside in 'ghettoes,
and to refrain from speaking to Christians—would later serve

as policy-models for Adolph Hitler and the Nazis. Consider the implications of these words preached by Peter the Venerable, Abbot of Cluny: "I do not require you to put to death those accursed beings . . . They must be made to suffer fearful torments and be preserved for greater ignominy, for an existence more bitter than death."[58]

The Church conceived no end of ways and means to put into effect ideas like those expressed by this venerable abbot who was described as "one of the kindest and most genial natures to be met with . . . a model of Christian charity."[59] Ideas were sown in the minds of the uneducated masses, myths and slanders were contrived, and accusations were fabricated. Inspired by the words spoken by Jesus in John 8:44, Church fathers implanted in their followers' minds demonic images of the Jews. Afterwards, the images were brought to life. The feared Antichrist—the arch-enemy of God whom Christian theology predicted would come to do battle on behalf of Satan in the end of days—was portrayed as a Jew from the tribe of Dan; even St. Thomas Aquinas accepted this characterization.[60] Dramatic performances depicted the Jew as a devil with the beard and horns of a goat. Efforts were made by Christian authorities to force Jews in real life to wear horns on their hats. Caricatures associated Jews with horned beasts, pigs, frogs, worms, snakes, and scorpions.[61] Satan, on the other hand, was conceived as possessing Jewish attributes.

It was not long before the masses believed that Jews worshipped Satan in their synagogues and that frightening black-magic rituals were performed there. This popular notion gave rise to the "desecration of the host" slander. Believing that the wafers taken during church services carry with them a magical ability to transubstantiate into the body of Jesus, ecclesiastical leaders spread terrifying accounts of Satanic synagogue rituals in which Jews supposedly encircled a wafer stolen from a local church and stabbed it repeatedly. The Jews would offer prayers to their father, the Devil, and would then torture the wafer, stick pins in the wafer, and cut at the wafer, according to the frenzied reports. On some occasions, individuals claiming to have been present at the rites would assert that moans and cries emanated from the wafer, as Jesus anguished.[62] Indeed, it was asserted in more than one case that blood gushed out of the wafer. Here were the Jews "who killed Christ" re-enacting their crime of deicide centuries later! The masses rose up in arms against the Jews for "desecrating the host." Were it not for the immense suffering faced by the Jewish communities subjected to this grave calumny, the entire affair would seem laughable. If Jews rejected Christian doctrines and never believed in the notion of transubstantiation to begin with, why in the world would they play with wafers? Jews never believed in the "holy Eucharist," so they might just as well have preoccupied themselves with slices of cheese! The slander was vicious, barbaric, and—most significantly of all—an indication for all time that universal love and the "golden rule" are absent from the theology which Christian missionaries have tried to stuff down the throats of Jews for two thousand years.

Perhaps the most famous of all the Church-contrived slanders was the "ritual-murder charge," which accused the Jews of kidnapping Christian children, killing them, and using their blood for demonic rites. This tale was spread by Church leaders throughout the Middle Ages, and it became the most popular of tools employed by anti-Semites seeking to rouse passionate feelings against the Jews. Fabricated by a monk named Theobald, the blood libel first appeared on paper in the middle of the twelfth century, when Thomas of Monmouth, an English monk of the Benedictine order, penned an accusation against the Jews.[63] Charging that they were responsible for the death of a young boy from Norwich named William, Thomas claimed that the Jews had crucified the lad after snatching him. The slur against the Jewish people led to two things: "Blessed William of Norwich" was elevated as Christianity's first child martyr, and the Jewish community had to gird itself for an anti-Semitic rallying-cry which has yet to disappear.

In 1171, a blood-libel case erupted in France. Although no corpse was ever found to corroborate the accuser's claim that he had seen Jews throw an unidentifiable child into a river, fifty-one Jews were burned at the stake for the "crime." In 1255, the Jews of Lincoln were charged with having kidnapped, mocked, tortured, crucified, and disemboweled an eight-year-old boy. Eighteen Jews were executed; they gave their lives to make the name "Hugh of Lincoln" famous in Christian annals.[64] The ritual-murder accusation proved so effective in agitating large populations against the Jews that it was adopted by Russian Tsars and the Nazis in the modern era. Throughout Germany and Eastern Europe during the first half of this century, blood libels appeared and whipped communities into hysteria every Passover season, when word spread that Jews needed "Christian blood" to make their *matzot*. And this Christian contribution to mankind did not restrict itself to Europe.

On September 22, 1928, four-year-old Barbra Griffith disappeared in New York State. Mayor W. Gilbert Hawes suggested to state-trooper Cpt. H. M. McCann that representatives of the Jewish community be questioned. Trooper McCann interrogated Rabbi Berel Brennglass at great length, asking whether Jews needed to sacrifice a Christian child during the Rosh Hashana-Yom Kippur season. The controversy came to a close when Barbra showed up two days later, after finding her way out of a forest in which she had gotten lost.[65]

While the blood libel has lived on, other calumnies disappeared. But they also left in their trails thousands of Jewish martyrs, who died as victims of cruel hoaxes perpetrated by the Church. Probably the single most horrifying frenzy of them all was the tragic "well-poisoning" charge of the embattled fourteenth century. In 1348, the Black Death erupted in Europe, hitting Italy, France and eventually all of the continent save Poland and Bohemia.[66] The bubonic plague ran rampant, despite frantic efforts to control its spread, and as many as one-third of the people of Europe succumbed to its effects. It was not long before the Jews were blamed for the scourge. Charged with having "poisoned the wells" of Europe with spiders, frogs, lizards and other loathsome vermin, the Jews—who were already suffering from the plague on a level comparable to that of the Christian community—were forced to endure a holocaust which would not be equaled in scope for six hundred years.[67] By the hundreds and thousands, Jews were murdered by frenetic Christian mobs. In Germany, where the massacres were most intense, the Jewish community was nearly exterminated. "In over two hundred communities of Germany, Jewish inhabitants were put to the indescribable tortures of which the Catholic Church was such a subtle master, and finally put to death."[68] Six hundred were burned alive in Freiburg, the Jewish populace of Frankfort was decimated, and other communities met similar fates.

Despite the enormity of the holocaust, the massacres of 1348-1349 were not inconceivable. After centuries of Church-inspired crusades, European Jewry knew what they could expect from Christian neighbors. The First Crusade was launched by Pope Urban II in 1095 at Clermont. When the holy crusaders reached Jerusalem, they did not hesitate to kill the "infidels." Desperately in need of shelter, the Jews of Jerusalem gathered in the city's chief synagogue. This did not deter the crusaders, who set fire to the Jewish house of worship and burned all their victims alive. Even the few Jews who had escaped to the roof of the al-Aqsa mosque were targeted; crusaders climbed after them and beheaded the surviving remnant.[69] Reporting on his successful mission, Godfrey of Bouillon wrote to the pope, "If you want to know what has been done with the enemy found in Jerusalem, learn that in the Porch and in the Temple of Solomon, our people had the vile blood . . . up to the knees of their horses."[70]

In Europe, anti-Semitic massacres occurred at Speyer, Metz, Trier, and Cologne. In Rouen, every Jew refusing baptism was murdered; a similar pre-"Jew for Jesus" approach was tried at cities like Regensburg and Prague, where thousands of Jews chose martyrdom over baptism. The Jews of Ratisbon, Germany, were forced to the banks of the Danube; all those refusing to convert were subsequently drowned in the waters of the river. At Worms, the synagogue was pillaged, homes were looted, and death was meted out to all those refusing baptism (except for the children, who were seized and brought to

Christian regions where they were forcibly baptized and raised as Christians). The few survivors who had been promised shelter in the Bishop's castle were turned over to the mobs after they refused to convert. More than eight hundred died in Worms. The city of Mainz witnessed a similar disaster, as crusaders butchered more than 1,000 Jews who refused to convert.

The Second Crusade, which began in 1146, was not a more impressive example of "Christian charity" or of the "golden rule." A monk named Rudolph took charge and led the holy crusaders back to Cologne, Mainz, Worms, and Speyer, where they wiped out those Jews who had settled in the blood-stained cities over the course of the previous half-century. Once again, the crusaders fulfilled their religious obligation to kill a Jew, it having been taught that whoever killed a Jew who refused baptism had all his sins forgiven him.[71]

The Shepherds' Crusade of 1320, so named because of the large number of shepherds and swineherds who answered the first call to action on behalf of Christ, set their sights once more on the Jews. This time, no Jews in France were killed (the government having expelled the entire Jewish population from the land in 1306), but Jews were found elsewhere. Tragic massacres took place throughout Europe. And the shepherds and swineherds were not always alone. In many areas, local officials joined the crusaders in pillaging and murdering Jewish communities.[72]

As the French government showed, Jews could be persecuted even when crusades were not in progress. Nor were mass expulsions limited to her borders; under pressure from the Archbishop of Canterbury, the Jews of England had been expelled in 1290. Not till Oliver Cromwell came to power nearly four hundred years later was the order rescinded. Of course, there were not all that many Jews left in England by the end of the thirteenth century. In 1262 nearly two thousand Jews were murdered by mobs under the influence of Church leaders. All of London Jewry was arrested in 1279, and 280 of their number were publicly executed.[73] By the time they were expelled in

1290, the Jews of England could not have been plagued too severely by sentimental ties to "home."

The nature of Christian love and concern for Jewish souls took on a new appearance with the advent of the Inquisition. While the Grand Inquisition affected many European countries, the persecution in Spain was especially brutal. Spanish Christianity had finally overcome Mohammedan opposition, seizing the last symbol of challenge, Granada. With Christianity's religious supremacy firm, King Ferdinand and Queen Isabella undertook a major program aimed at sharing their beliefs with everyone. Under the influence of her Dominican confessor, Tomas Torquemada, Isabella determined that she was obligated by the dictates of her faith to cleanse Spain of all "heresy." Together with her royal husband, who saw financial advantages to such a theological adventure, she sought papal permission to institute an official program of inquiry (to be backed by all the necessary tools of fifteenth-century jurisprudence), whose goal would be to obliterate "heresy" within Spain. The pope acceded after some haggling over the final destination of the fortunes which would be seized from Inquisition victims.[74] By 1482 the stage was set for the first Inquisition; it would be conducted in Seville.

Carefully coordinated by the Dominicans, suggestions were circulated to facilitate the detection of secretive Jews, known as "Marranos" (i.e., "pigs"). Inquisitors were advised to take notice of individuals who did not light fires on Saturday. People seeking to purchase specially prepared meats or wines were to be carefully watched. In fact, any of a number of actions committed by an unsuspecting person might prove reasonable cause for an order to appear before an official tribunal for interrogation.[75] Once before the court, one would be expected to tell all: whether he was a Jew, whether he knew anyone who had performed any of the actions typical of a Jew, whether he knew of any hiding places of Jews. To expedite the witness's ability to assist the Grand Inquisition, Torquemada's men employed such legal aids as the rack. Not surprisingly, the Dominicans were able to induce many "confessions."

Confessions led to state-provided "atonement." From the rack, the Jewish infidel would be taken to the stake. There, in a great *auto-da-fé* ("act of faith"), he would be burned alive before a massive audience comprised of royalty and nobility, as well as of common folk. By means of the Inquisition's merciful execution (or "death without spilling blood," as it was officially called)[76], the Jew's soul would be freed from his heretical body. So considerate were these models of "Christian charity" that even dead Jews were given the opportunity to do penance. When evidence came before the tribunal that a deceased person had in fact been a Jew, the corpse would be exhumed, and it would be "put to death without spilling blood" at the fiery stake.

The Christian Inquisition's authority expanded in Spain, and the terror continued for a decade. Finally, in 1492, Torquemada's ultimate request was granted: Spanish Jewry was given four months' time to evacuate the land which had spawned them. The edict's deadline date—August 2, 1492—incredibly coincided with the traditional Jewish day of sorrow and mourning, Tisha b'Av.[77] By that day's conclusion, Spanish Jewry had been expelled. Historians have estimated the total number banished to be as many as 800,000 people; more moderate estimates place the total at 150,000.[78] In any event, 1492 was to be recorded in the Jewish national consciousness as yet one more reason that we cannot but be offended when a "Jew for Jesus" or any other Christian missionary approaches us with an offer to join his "religion of love."

This new Christian persecution was not limited to Spain. When King Manuel, who became monarch of Portugal in 1495, married the daughter of Ferdinand and Isabella, the Inquisition came to his country, followed by another edict of expulsion. The religious terror reached Italy, too, and the Jews were ultimately forced into specially designated residential areas called "ghettoes."[79] To make matters worse, inasmuch as these countries were the leaders in exploring the New World, the Inquisition eventually reared its head in the Americas. It was officially introduced in the West Indies in 1511; five years later, it was inaugurated in South America. While Inquisitors now had Moslems and Indians to contend with, Jews still bore the brunt of the persecution. The first burning of a Jew in the Americas occurred in 1574. Thereafter, many public executions were conducted. The 1639 *auto-da-fé* at Lima, Peru, saw 63 people condemned by the tribunal, with ten Marranos being burned alive.

Wherever Christian leadership could impose its will, it did. Indeed the roots of the Nazi holocaust are easily traced to the barbaric legislation enacted by the Church during the Middle Ages. Just as Pope Nicholas III was a spiritual ancestor of the Grand Inquisition by virtue of his decision that all Jews who refused to be baptized and to accept the Christian religion should be handed over to secular authorities for burning at the stake,[80] so were the Church fathers who participated at the Lateran Council of 1215 and at the 1565 Council of Milan the progenitors of the 1935 Nuremburg Laws enacted by the Nazis.

Over one thousand delegates participated at the Fourth Lateran Council in 1215. Among the laws they passed were many which later found their way into Hitler's legislative packages. Jews were forbidden to appear in public on certain days (like Easter), and they were prohibited from wearing their best raiment on Sundays. They were barred from holding public office, and all money they had earned by participating in such a vocation had to be turned over to Christians. This Church council also legislated that all Jews had to wear a distinctive "badge of shame" on all clothing.[81] While they did not go as far as the pious Saint Louis—who was born the year the Council met and who, upon maturation, urged every Christian to refrain from arguing with Jews and to simply defend the faith "by his sword, wherewith he should pierce the belly of the reviler as far as it will go"[82]—the delegates of the Fourth Lateran Council clearly paved the way for the Nazi laws of the twentieth century. Their shameful actions were repeated three centuries later when Pope Paul IV came to power.

Originally known as Cardinal Caraffa, Pope Paul IV assumed Catholicism's highest position in 1555. Within two months, he was promulgating laws which again forced Jews to wear a distinctive "badge of shame" and which confined the Jews to ghettoes. Declaring Jews "condemned by God to eternal slavery" in his papal bull *Cum nimis absurdum,* he ordered the liquidation of all Jewish holdings maintained outside the ghetto walls.[83] A decade later, the Council of Milan called for a boycott of Jewish commerce. Similarly, Christians were forbidden to request treatment from Jewish doctors, and Jews were barred from university positions and public office.[84] One is left nothing but astonished after considering the homology of the Christian edicts and the Nazi laws.

The connection between the Nazis and the Church is not only implicit but explicit. Aside from the infamous July 1933 Concordat which cemented the mutual understanding between Berlin and the Vatican, it is noteworthy that the German Catholic Center Party voted with the Nazis for the "Enabling Act" on March 23, 1933. As early as 1924, Hitler noted with gratification that, despite internal theological differences, Catholics and Protestants could sit together in unity within the ranks of the Nazi Movement:

> In the ranks of the movement, the most devout
> Protestant could sit beside the most devout Catholic,
> without coming into the slightest conflict with his
> religious convictions. The mighty common struggle which
> both carried on against the destroyer of Aryan
> humanity had, on the contrary, taught them mutually to
> respect and esteem one another.[85]

The Concordat helped Hitler win over the Christian community. Michael Cardinal Faulhaber praised Hitler, noting that he had achieved more in six months than all the parties and parliaments of Germany had in the previous sixty years. When Hitler reached his fiftieth birthday in 1939, Faulhaber called for special Church celebrations of the momentous event. Joining in these sentiments was Bishop Conrod Grober of Freiburg who approved of Nazi efforts to maintain a "pure race."

Hitler was not ungrateful. On one occasion, the SA and SS shock troops were dispatched to the Berlin Cathedral. They were sent not to disrupt but to assist in the celebration of Mass with the gentle cleric Father Marianus. While SA and SS "choirboys" lifted their voices on behalf of the Lord, Father Marianus compared "Christ's reviving the dead to life" to Hitler's efforts to revive German life. At the conclusion of the service, the entire congregation joined in singing the Horst Wessel hymn and intoning a blessing.

In 1935, Cardinal Bertram said, "The Catholic clergy and people stand positively for the present State administration." When Hitler turned fifty, this pious Cardinal not only expressed his admiration to Hitler but said he would urge Christians everywhere to pray for the Führer, too.[86] Even more pious was Pope Pius XII, who represented "Christian charity" to the world. When Myron Taylor, President Roosevelt's personal emissary to the Vatican, asked the Pontiff to speak out against the deportations and murders of Jews in Nazi lands, the Vatican replied that it would need proof of the charges.[87] This response was somewhat curious, coming a full year after the internationally publicized Kristallnacht riots, deportations, and killings. Harold Tittmann, Taylor's deputy, commented on an address by Cardinal Salotti which praised the "historical mission of Pius XII" by noting, "One looks in vain in the address for the recording of any action on his part in recent months that could be construed as moral leadership . . ."[88] On another occasion Tittmann wrote, "the Holy Father appears to be occupying himself exclusively with spiritual matters, charitable acts, and rhetoric, while adopting an ostrich-like policy toward these notorious atrocities."[89] Although Monsignor Montini, a close aide to Pius XII and a papal Undersecretary of State, defended the refusal by the Holy See to speak out when he told Tittmann, "the time may come when . . . the Holy Father will feel himself obliged to speak out," that time never came.[90] (The Good Monsignor, who performed such a valuable service to the Vatican by defending its policies and programs during this period, went on to become Pope Paul VI.)

There were others outside of Germany as well. In Slovakia, the government of the Catholic priest Tisso brutally persecuted the Jews. When a rabbi attempted to ask Archbishop Kametko to influence his former private secretary Tisso to have mercy and to prevent the planned expulsion of the Jews from the country, the Archbishop replied: "This is no mere expulsion. There—you will not die of hunger and pestilence; there—they will slaughter you all, old and young, women and children, in one day. This is your punishment for the death of our Redeemer. There is only one hope for you—to convert all to our religion. Then I shall effect the annulling of this decree."[91]

And children *were* killed, as was later revealed during the trials of the major war criminals: "They killed them with their parents, in groups, and alone. They killed them in children's homes and hospitals, burying them alive in graves, throwing them into flames, stabbing them with bayonets, poisoning them, conducting experiments upon them, extracting their blood for the use of the German army, throwing them into prison and Gestapo torture chambers and concentration camps where the children died from hunger, torture, and epidemic diseases. . . ."[92]

Another noteworthy cleric is Viorel Trifa of Rumania, who gained fame as the leader of the pro-Hitler Iron Guard.[93] During the early 1940s he addressed thousands of armed students in Bucharest and other parts of the country. Trifa's Iron Guard was Rumania's equivalent of the "Brownshirts,"[94] enforcing Nazi laws and conducting "spontaneous pogroms." Indeed, on November 26, 1940, Trifa personally directed a pogrom in Ploesti, according to eyewitness testimony.[95] In January, 1941, Trifa led a pogrom through Bucharest's Jewish quarter; the Iron Guardists burned down synagogues, demolished stores, and devastated private apartments.[96] Hundreds of Jews were murdered, their corpses were left naked in the streets, gold was extracted from their teeth, and multiple stab wounds left their bodies stained with blood. Final death tolls reached the thousands.[97] For his instigation and participation in this horrifying massacre, Trifa was later sentenced *in absentia* to life imprisonment by Rumania's Antonescu government.

But Trifa never served his sentence. He fled Rumania, spent time in Hitler's Germany, and —after a circuitous journey—he came to the United States of America, where he applied for entry rights. Denying that he had ever preached against the Jews and asserting that he had not been involved in the Iron Guard, he was admitted to the U.S. By 1952, Trifa was back in business in Michigan, later becoming the Archbishop of the Rumanian Orthodox Church in America, a position he held for over twenty-five years, and serving on the governing board of the National Council of the Churches of Christ—America's most prestigious Protestant body[98]—for a number of years.

When Jewish groups began protesting the National Council's harboring of a former Nazi collaborator, the Protestant umbrella-body refused to respond. Only after a group of young Jews led by Rabbi Avraham Weiss staged a demonstration which received major publicity in the *New York Times* did the Council of Churches agree to meet and discuss the matter.[99] Embarrassed by Trifa's own confession that he had served in the Iron Guard[100]—a confession conveniently made twenty years after his original interview with United States immigration authorities— the Protestant leaders debated the issue, focusing their attention not on Trifa's murderous past but on the need to counter charges that they were evading moral responsibility through legalisms.[101] Meanwhile, Serge Troubetzky, secretary of the Orthodox Church of America, praised the Iron Guard leader as a man who "has earned the devotion of his flock and trust of his fellow bishops."[102]

Repeatedly, the National Council of Churches was called on to deal with the issue. In a memorandum, William Weiler of the Council's office on Christian-Jewish relations referred to the issue as "an agonizing conflict which deeply affects our Christian family."[103] Yet the "Christian family" of the National Council of Churches still did not remove Trifa from its directorate.[104] How tragic it is that it took "the long arm of the law"—the judicial system of the United States—to solve the NCC's "agonizing conflict." Despite NCC equivocating, Trifa was found guilty as charged and ordered deported from the United States.

Indeed, the Protestant body's attitude toward the Jews has been criticized on other scores as well. Back in 1977, the NCC was jolted by a charge by the Anti-Defamation League of B'nai B'rith that the Council had shown pronounced anti-Israel prejudice by unilaterally circulating pro-Arab, anti-Israel propaganda publications and by sponsoring workshop discussions on the Middle East which deny expression of those viewpoints reflective of Jewish concerns on behalf of Israel's survival.

The anti-Israel charge was reiterated three years later when sixteen major American Jewish organizations refused to participate in an NCC conference on the Middle East, protesting that the program was disturbingly structured in a manner which reflected raw bias against Israel and support for the terrorist organization led by Yasser Arafat.[105] In a letter to Rev. Tracey K. Jones, Jr., chairperson of the Council's Middle East panel, the American Jewish organizations complained that the conference was organized around a format which presented "slanderous charges" that were "a gross and deliberate misrepresentation of fact and history."[106] Underlining the charges, the ADL condemned the "clear and consistent pro-Arab and pro-PLO stance which has marked the NCC attitude for many years." Later, a spokesman for the American Jewish Committee charged that the NCC was guilty of "persistent, unrelenting hostility and bias against Israel."[107] Perhaps the most dramatic indication of the virulent anti-Israel sentiment within the National Council of Churches came when the Rev. Isaac Rottenberg of the Reformed Church in America wrote a letter to the *New York Times* admitting that the NCC was guilty of conducting "a persistent anti-Israel propaganda campaign." Stating that "every NCC governing board meeting has been preceded by internal bureaucratic power plays aimed at criticizing Israel," Rottenberg went on to note that whenever "concerns were raised in the Council about anti-Semitism, the Holocaust, or the emergence of neo-Nazi movements, attempts have been made to trivialize them or to neutralize them."[108]

Days after his letter appeared in the *Times* , Rottenberg was fired from his post at the National Council of Churches.

When one considers that the Council's constituents include the Christian Methodist Episcopal Church, the Episcopal Church, the Lutheran Church in America, the National Baptist Convention of America, the Presbyterian Church in the United States, the United Methodist Church, and the United Presbyterian Church in the United States of America, it becomes all the more apparent that Christian attitudes have not changed all that much in two thousand years. It is not hard to imagine how the descendants of those murdered by Archbishop Trifa would react to a reading of the lofty preamble to the Council of Church's constitution:

> The National Council of the Churches of Christ in the United States of America is a cooperative agency of Christian communions seeking to fulfill the unity and mission to which God calls them. The member communions, responding to the gospel revealed in the Scriptures, confess Jesus, the incarnate Son of God, as Savior and Lord. Relying on the transforming power of the Holy Spirit, the council works to bring churches into a life-giving fellowship and into common witness, study and action to the glory of God and in service to all creation.

The Jewish people stand before God and man as a common witness, too. As a witness to two thousand years of Christian hate and persecution, culminating in the hesitation of the National Council of Churches to expel from its midst a man who instigated anti-Jewish pogroms, who led the pro-Hitler Iron Guard, who participated in the murder of Rumanian Jewry, and who was condemned *in absentia* to a life-sentence in Rumania. Tragically, the record of the Protestant body does little to dispel the image the Church has so brutally created for itself after two thousand years.

The two-thousand-year record of Christian hate toward the Jews is voluminous. Tomes have been written on the subject, but even the most documented studies have proven incomplete as new findings are announced. In this brief exposition, only fragments of the statements uttered by the most famous of the leading Church fathers have been recalled. Only the most painful of persecutions—those engendered by the "desecration of the host" slander, the blood libel, the "well-poisoning" myth, the Crusades, the Grand Inquisition, and the Nazi holocaust— have been recounted. Only the most famous of ecclesiastic conferences have been mentioned. Were the entire record committed to print, it would fill libraries. Sadly, the record of the "New Testament" as a "document of love" speaks for itself and is a refutation of the Christian missionaries' arguments such as no other. It constitutes the ultimate vindication of two thousand years of Jewish martyrdom at the hands of Christian leaders and missionaries whose tactics lacked the "polish" of the modern-day "Jews for Jesus."

Religion is not for God but for man. It is meant to uplift man, to raise his soul from the level of a beast to the level of an an angel, to sanctify him. When God gave the Jewish people His Torah at Mount Sinai, He laid down for eternity the purpose of Judaism: "Holy shall you be, for I the Lord am holy.[109] After four thousand years we Jews can look back on our history with pride—not only in the awe-inspiring deeds of our heroic ancestors, who courageously maintained themselves as a holy Jewish nation in the midst of a hostile world, but in our religion which gave rise to such people.

Christianity, too, must consider its condition, its record. Let no Jew ever again be subjected to missionary preachings about the need to convert to the "religion of love" which advocates "the golden rule" as embodied in "Christian charity." We have borne witness to the record. Who would have believed our story? We were despised, rejected, laden with sorrows, acquainted with grief. We were forced to bear grief and pain and death because of the sins of others. Children were kidnapped — and we were blamed. A bubonic plague struck—and we were punished. An economic crisis hit Germany, caused partly by the burden placed on her for her sins in World War I—and we were gassed and cremated. We were wounded, bruised, stricken, oppressed, afflicted, cut off from the land of our fathers. We were stricken, pierced, and murdered for crimes committed by others but blamed on us. And, through it all, the world looked upon us and asserted that the grief was our due, inflicted by God as a punishment. For nearly two thousand years we wandered through the Exile in sorrow, often with no alternative but to give up our lives in the sanctification of God's name. The world says we went as sheep to the slaughter, a callous judgment offered by those who were not there. In short, we have beheld the fulfillment of the bitter prophecy of Isaiah 53, in which he foretold what would happen to the Jewish people, the suffering servant of God. Let us rejoice in the knowledge that a visionary so Divinely inspired as to be able to so accurately predict the course of Jewish history has also foretold our future destiny:

> Violence shall no more be heard in your land . . .
>
> Your people also shall all be righteous; they shall inherit the land forever; they shall be the branch of My planting, the work of My hands . . .
>
> Behold, the Lord has proclaimed unto the end of the world, "Say to the daughter of Zion, 'Behold, your salvation comes . . .' "
>
> And they shall call them "the holy people, the redeemed of the Lord."[110]

It is perhaps one of the great injustices of modern history that the Church, ashamed of its past and unable to face up to the fact that it served as the tool of persecution of the Jewish people, has sought to redefine Isaiah 53. Twisting the entire chapter's tone out of context, Christians have read into that chapter a supposed prophecy that Jesus would come as Messiah. As we have already shown, Jesus contradicted prophecies of Zechariah, Isaiah, and Malachi by preaching dissonance between father and son and by announcing that he came not to bring peace but a sword.[111] Moreover, we have already discussed the fact that the prophecy that the true Messiah would be of Davidic descent was not fulfilled by Jesus.

Therefore, even if we were to refrain from responding to Christian distortions of Isaiah 53, we would be justified in our rejection of Christian claims. Yet we must respond to the perversion of Isaiah 53 out of respect for our martyrs, out of a sense of duty to prevent the Church from covering up its role in the suffering which was perpetrated for two thousand years.

When the prophet Isaiah spoke of a servant of God who would be despised, rejected, laden with sorrows, acquainted with grief, wounded, bruised, stricken, oppressed, afflicted, and cut off from the land of the living, he was obviously speaking of the Jewish people. Such an understanding of the prophecy is not based solely on a subsequent perception of the road of Jewish history. Isaiah 53 refers to the Jewish people—and it is interpreted accordingly—because Isaiah 52 refers to the Jewish people. And Chapter 53 comes after Chapter 52. The context of Chapter 53 is to be understood in the light of the verses leading up to it. An honest reading of Chapter 52 would indicate that Isaiah is speaking of the Jewish people. Consider the chapter's development:

> *My people* went down in time past into Egypt . . .
> (Verse 4)
> Now, therefore, what have I here, says the Lord, that
> *My people* is taken away for nothing? They that rule over
> them make them howl . . . (Verse 5)
> Therefore, *My people* shall know My name . . . (Verse 6)
> Break forth into joy, sing together, O waste places of
> Jerusalem: for the Lord has comforted *His people*; He has
> redeemed Jerusalem. (Verse 9)
> Behold, *My servant* shall prosper, he shall be exalted and
> extolled, and be very high. (Verse 13)

As Chapter 52 ends and Chapter 53 begins, Isaiah continues his prophecy, noting how bad times would get before they would get better. "Who would have believed our report?" asks Isaiah. Obviously, a good question coming *before* thousands of years of crusades, inquisitions, and holocausts. Who *would* have believed such a report? Indeed, during the actual Nazi holocaust, much of the world could not believe all the reports smuggled out of Germany concerning a systematic effort aimed at exterminating the Jews. Who would have believed Christianity capable of performing such inhuman horrors as the Inquisition? Who would have believed that the Jewish people would suffer as history proved?

Isaiah, speaking of the Jewish people, continues by noting that we were despised and rejected, filled with sorrows, and acquainted with grief. (Though speaking in past tense, he is prophesying, as Christians will also agree.) We were wounded because of others' sins, crises, and hang-ups. We bore griefs inflicted by others and suffered sorrows caused by others. And the very ones who persecuted us defended their actions by saying that we were being stricken, smitten by God for our sins.

A verse-by-verse examination of the chapter will clearly convince the most skeptical reader of the prophet's intention to foretell the course of Jewish history. Because Isaiah prophesied in poetic terminology, he referred to the Jews in the third-person singular: "My servant . . . he . . . him . . ." This literary device was nothing more than a continuation from the beginning of this prophecy (Chapter 52, verse 13) where Isaiah had referred to the Jews as "My servant . . . he shall be exalted" in verse 13. (For the cynic who will ask whether verse 13 might refer to Jesus as well, it should be recalled that Chapter 52 begins with references to "My people went . . . into Egypt," "My people is taken away . . ." "My people shall know My name," and ". . . the Lord has comforted His people. . . .")

Thus, the prophet's poetic use of the terms "My servant," "he," "him," and "his" was meant to convey the destiny *of the people*—Israel, the Jews. Only a Church desperately looking for veiled references to Jesus in the Torah could have so brutally perverted the context of Isaiah 53. And for good reason. If the Jews are the ones whose persecution Isaiah lamented, then the Church may very well represent the persecutors (of "My servant") whose shame and iniquities Isaiah forecast.

It should be noted, moreover, that the Jewish people are

frequently referred to as "My servant" by Isaiah. In Isaiah 41:8, the poetic prophet says, "But, you Israel are *My servant . . .* "[112] The following verse continues: "You whom I have taken from the ends of the earth, and called you from its corners, and said unto you, 'You are *My servant*,' I have chosen you and not cast you away."

In Isaiah 44:21, the prophet says, "Remember these, O Jacob and Israel; for you are *My servant*. I have formed you; you are *My servant*: O Israel, you shall not be forgotten by Me." There are numerous other examples of the Jewish people being called "My servant" in the Bible; to cite them all would be a matter of redundancy. In fact, there are countless other examples of the Jewish people being referred to in the singular form. Indeed, when God gave the Ten Commandments, He instructed the people in the second-person *singular*. Although the English language does not distinguish between singular and plural references in second-person, the Hebrew language does. The Jewish people, in the millions, were addressed in the singular form.

Not only is it self-evident that Isaiah 53 *does* refer to the Jewish people's suffering; it is equally evident that it does *not* refer to Jesus — a fact which keeps that chapter consistent with every other chapter in the Torah (or "Old Testament"). If Jesus was a Divinity — part of Christianity's Trinity of the Father, the Son, and the Holy Ghost — how could he be a "servant"? Christianity does not maintain that the Father, Son, and Holy Ghost are separate from each other; otherwise, Christianity would immediately collapse under the weight of Deuteronomy 6:4 — "Hear O Israel, the Lord is our God, the Lord is *One*." Rather, Christianity laboriously asserts that the three are really one and the same "Godhead." So Jesus could not be a "servant" of the Father because that would destroy the Unity of the Trinity. Once it is claimed that Jesus is the "servant" in Isaiah 53, then the question must be asked: "Whose servant?"

There are many other aspects of Isaiah 53 which describe a "servant" who could not have been Jesus. Only two of these points will be raised in this treatment of the chapter; again, extended treatment would amount to redundancy. Both points arise out of consideration of verse 9: ". . . he had done no violence, neither was any deceit in his mouth." When Jesus entered Jerusalem and started a riot by overturning tables,[113] his act was one of violence. For the purpose of this discussion, we shall not enter into the merits of his deed; let us simply take note that he did commit a violent act, which further knocks him out of Isaiah 53. Moreover, when he asserted that the Torah commands men to hate their enemies,[114] his mouth uttered deceitful words as we have already shown earlier in this chapter.

The claim that Jesus was the object of Isaiah 53 is one of the most unfortunate of all the many Christian perversions of the Torah. Perhaps Christianity would have been wiser to claim Judaism and the Torah to be meaningless *in toto*. But by claiming the "Old Testament" to be a valid document and the forerunner of the "New Testament," Christianity backed itself into a corner. If Jesus was the Messiah prophesied in the Torah, then he had to fulfill the prophecies made. He did not speak peace to the nations. He did not speak truth when he misrepresented the Torah, which was the authentic conceiver of "the golden rule." He was not of the line of David. He did not turn the hearts of the fathers to their sons and the hearts of the sons to their fathers; on the contrary, he said that he had come to set them apart.

He confused Jewish law and contradicted himself. On the one hand, he said that a man is not defiled by what enters his mouth[115]—which has been grasped by Christianity as permission to ignore the dietary laws of the Torah—and, on the other hand, he ruled that men would be defiled by eating blood and flesh of strangled animals.[116] Though he ultimately decided that some foods *do* defile, he contradicted his own assertion that he did not come to abolish the law.[117] Moreover, by annulling some of the dietary laws (and other laws as well), he left himself open to his own warning in Matthew 5:19 that "whoever then annuls one of the least of these commandments, and so teaches others, shall be called least in the kingdom of heaven." Furthermore, if man is not defiled by what goes into his mouth, then what was the "original sin" of Adam which Christian dogma has been advancing for two thousand years?

Ultimately, Christianity is not rooted in the Torah, and the efforts to conjure up roots therein have forced the entire theology into one bind after another. The whole dogma of "original sin" is itself indefensible (although necessary to give theological meaning to the death of Jesus, who—as a "Messiah"— was not really supposed to die); when considered on a deeper level, it contradicts not only the theme of the Torah but also Jesus himself. Similarly, Christianity runs into trouble with its "Trinity" concept. If there is more than one God, then the religion runs counter to the Torah's presentation of monotheism. If there is only one God, then is it the Father or the Son? Christianity necessarily declares that the Father *and* the Son (and the Holy Ghost, for that matter) are all God—but they are One and not Three. Of course.

To make matters more difficult, Jesus says in Matthew 12:32, "And whoever shall speak a word against the Son of Man, it shall be forgiven him; but whoever shall speak against the Holy Spirit, it shall not be forgiven him . . ." If Jesus and the Holy Spirit are one and the same, then this verse makes no sense. If they are different, then they are not the same . . . There are similar contradictions of the "Trinity" idea throughout the "New Testament," but—again—anything cited after Matthew 12:32[118] in criticism of this creation of Christian dogma would constitute redundancy.

What begins to materialize as we closely peruse the Christian Gospels and dogma is a pattern of contradiction and confusion. Only a Jew who has never really learned Torah can be pestered by Christian missionaries and "Jews for Jesus." Their Gospels are so flooded with errors of fact, misquotes, contradictions, and passages taken out of context that any Jew with a basic yeshiva education is safe from the missionaries. That success being experienced by Moishe Rosen and his fellow Baptists at the American Board of Missions to the Jews can be attributed to the breakdown in Jewish education, Jewish values, and Jewish traditions in the assimilated Jewish areas. Where Judaism is unknown, a void exists which can possibly be filled by a foreign religion. Where Judaism is firmly based, missionaries do not stand a chance—as is evidenced by two thousand years of unsuccessful crusades, inquisitions, and other efforts aimed at forcible conversion. When Jews know their Torah, they do not give it up for anything. Certainly not for the "New Testament."

How can a Jew take the Gospels seriously? Although the Isaiah 53 ploy is one of the favorite missionary arguments, it is reflective—in its misinterpretation and misrepresentation—of so many other Christian "proofs." As "evidence" that Jesus was predicted in the Torah, they cite Isaiah 7:14 as quoted in Matthew 1:23. Describing Jesus' birth, Matthew writes, "Now all this took place that what was spoken by the Lord through the prophet might be fulfilled, saying, 'Behold, the virgin shall be with child, and shall bear a son . . .' " Matthew's "proof" would deserve attention were that the prophecy of Isaiah. Unfortunately, it was not. Isaiah said, "Behold, the young woman is with child and shall bear a son . . ."

There are many virgins who are not young women; there are many young women who are not virgins. Isaiah prophesied that a *young woman* would give birth. He said nothing about virgins. He used the word *alma*, which means "young woman." He did not use the word for "virgin," "*betula*." It is that simple. For years and years, Christian theologians insisted on redefining the Isaiah version rather than on correcting Matthew's error. What they can't do is redefine the whole book of Isaiah, the entire context of which militates against the flagrant misquote. After all, the prophecy was presented to Achaz, King of Judah, at a time when the monarch was greatly troubled; Isaiah's prophecy was meant to cheer up Achaz by showing him that God would be with him. How would Achaz be encouraged by a prophecy whose fulfillment would not occur in his lifetime but some seven centuries thereafter? The whole idea of the prognostication was to give Achaz a tangible sign in his *own* lifetime. Hence, this "New Testament" error consists not only of misinterpretation and misquoting but also of reading an isolated verse out of its normal context.

A similar trick was tried by Paul in Galatians 3:16, where he says, "Now the promises were spoken to Abraham and to his seed. He [God] does not say, 'And to seeds,' as referring to many, but rather to one, 'And to your seed,' that is, Christ." This statement by Paul lacks true erudition. First of all, whenever the Bible desires to denote progeny, the word "seed" in the singular form is used, never plural. In Genesis 15:5, Abraham is told that his "seed" shall be numerous as the stars. (Or did Paul believe that Abraham looked up on a cloudy evening, when only one star was visible?) More to the point, God tells Abraham in Genesis 13:15-16, "For all the land which you see, to you will I give it, and to your progeny forever. And I will make your progeny as the dust of the earth so that if a man can number the dust of the earth, then shall your progeny also be numbered." Obviously, although the word for progeny (*zera*) is used in the singular form, it means progeny in the plural. (Or would Paul commit a sacrilege by comparing Jesus to dust?)

Everywhere one turns through the pages of the Gospels, similar errors, misquotations, misinterpretations, and contradictions occur. And there is no shortage of passages pulled out of context either. Perhaps the "New Testament's" most celebrated factual errors appear in Acts 7:14-16, where the simple task of copying data carefully is improficiently handled. We read:

> And Joseph sent word and invited Jacob his father and all his relatives to come to him, seventy-five persons in all.
>
> And Jacob went down to Egypt and there passed away, he and our fathers.
>
> And from there they were removed to Shechem and laid in the tomb which Abraham had purchased for a sum of money from the sons of Hamor in Shechem.

The mind is boggled by the multiplicity of the factual errors, so tightly knit together in this book which claims Divine inspiration. First of all, seventy persons went to Egypt, not seventy-five.[119] While the error may be insignificant numerically and ultimately of minor relevance historically, it is an error nonetheless. If the "Divinely inspired" Gospels could have made such a silly error in Acts, its authors could have done so in other places where they were recording matters on the basis of their own subjective impressions and not on the objective basis of inscribed history. More egregious is the clumsy effort to discuss Jacob's burial place. Jacob was not buried in Shechem; he was buried in Hebron.[120] The tomb which Abraham purchased was the Cave of Machpelah in Hebron—not in Shechem.[121] Abraham made the purchase from Ephron the Hittite—not from the sons of Hamor.[122] The land in Shechem was purchased not by Abraham but by Jacob.[123]

It is certainly not the desire of any Jew to demean the "faith system" of others. Having suffered from persecutors for so many centuries, we appreciate the need for all to have freedom of conscience. If there are those who were brought up in Christian homes, who were taught to attend church every Sunday, who were raised in the celebration of events like Christmas and Easter, they should not be denigrated. They are entitled to their beliefs, and they must never be ridiculed or scorned for such a creed. But it is time that such an approach were reciprocated. We have no desire to face hate, prejudice, and efforts aimed at our spiritual and physical extermination. If we have rejected Christianity, we have simply been true to our Torah and to our sense of logic. We have borne common witness to the effectiveness of Christianity as a system of "love," and we have suffered the sacrifice of millions of our holiest people on the altar of that "love." We have considered the many factual errors, distortions, misinterpretations, and misrepresentations evident in the Gospels, and we have not been impressed by its claim to Divinity. We have analyzed the theology based on faith in the "Son of Man,"[124] and we have calmly and humbly preferred to adhere to the wisdom of Psalms 146:3 of the "Old Testament" which warns: "Put not your trust in princes nor in the son of man, in whom there is no salvation."

The missionaries have nothing to offer our people; indeed, that is why—after two thousand years of failure in trying to get us to leave Judaism—they have finally fabricated the "Jews for Jesus" myth. Suddenly, our young people are offered the chance to convert to Christianity "without having to give up their Jewishness." Let the word go forth to every Jew that such a contrivance may work on Madison Avenue where they seek to sell "two breath mints in one," and "two anti-histaminic formulas in one." It does not work in Judaism. We believe in a true Oneness of God; Christians believe in a Triple-Godhead whose very essence is contradicted in their own Gospels, as we have shown. We believe that a man becomes holy and elevated through the performance of deeds (*mitzvot*), and we wear fringes on our garments (*tzitzit*) so that we may remember the commandments of God in order to perform them.[125] Christians do not perform the commandments of God as exemplified by the dietary laws, the wearing of *tzitzit*, the circumcising of all sons, the laws regarding family purity (*taharat hamishpacha*), and the laws of Rosh Hashana, Yom Kippur, Sukkot, Pesach, and Shavuot.

Madison Avenue can try the "Jews for Jesus" approach, but they will never succeed in obfuscating the differences between our two systems with glib phrases and slogans. We believe that every man can gain salvation directly from God on the basis of his own deeds; Christianity maintains that man is incapable of helping himself without accepting Jesus as "Messiah." We believe that, when one sins, he must sincerely repent by turning to God for forgiveness; such repentance (*teshuva*) is not achieved by confessing to an intermediary or by reciting fifteen "Hail Marys." A Jew achieves *teshuva* by coming to terms with himself and his misdeed, by recognizing that the sin was indeed wrong, and by earnestly regretting having committed such a transgression of the laws of God. In meditating over the essence of the deed, the Jew makes a personal commitment to himself and to God that he will summon up his inner strength the next time he faces temptation, and he will work to overcome the flaw in his character. He will pray to God, asking forgiveness and requesting strength. He will commit himself to performing loftier deeds in the future, deeds of charity, kindness, and love. That is how a Jew seeks atonement: by strengthening himself, by developing his talents, and by strengthening the inner potential to achieve greatness granted him by God. The Jew emerges from such an experience not only spiritually sanctified but a better person. How awesomely such a form of *teshuva* differs from a perfunctory confession to an intermediary who listens and forgives! How much more magnificent is the forgiveness *earned* by man-the-atoner than the proxy salvation supposedly granted man-the-by-stander! Is it any wonder that the history of the Jewish people speaks as it does and that the record of Christianity speaks as it does?

There is one last matter concerning salvation that must not be omitted. According to Christianity, every single Jewish man, woman, and child gassed, strangled, and cremated by the Nazis will forever burn in hell. If they lived perfect lives, died sacred deaths, breathed love till their last minute of existence on this earth—they still descended to hell and eternal damnation, according to Christianity. They bore the stigma of the supposed "original sin," and, not having accepted the Church and the Trinity, they had to descend from the crematoria of Auschwitz to the eternal fire of hell.

That is the ultimate meaning of Christianity. That is the religion of the "golden rule." Every one of our six million martyrs is relegated by Christianity to hell, incapable of ever attaining salvation. And, while they all burn for eternity, Archbishop Viorel "Valerian" Trifa traipses merrily from the national governing board of the National Council of Churches to freedom from the U.S. immigration service by crossing the border to Canada. While two-year-old children, who were gassed and cremated without baptism, are relegated to eternal perdition, the Crusaders who murdered Jewish communities "for the glory of Christ" revel in Paradise.

That is the creed and dogma of the "religion of love." It constitutes an unconscionable affront to the sensibilities of our people. And it represents the ultimate difference between Judaism and Christianity. Judaism never had to threaten other people of different faiths and backgrounds, for we love all men. According to our Talmud, whose authority is on a plane equal to that of the Torah, the righteous of all nations and creeds will share in the glories and happiness of the World to Come. That is the beautiful message of the Talmud. It is a pity that the Church fathers burned so many copies of this book over the past two millennia.

Despite all the persecutions unleashed against us by Christianity over the course of the past two thousand years, we do not condemn all of Christendom to eternal damnations and horrors. All men are created of God, and they all bear the common element of sanctity and holiness. If Christianity cannot accept us, we can yet live in a world of Christianity. But we cannot conceal our refusal to accept the soul-snatchers of the American Board of Missions to the Jews. For twenty centuries Jews died at the point of the sword, at the stake, on the rack, and in the gas chamber, rather than give up the Jewish faith and our eternal covenant with God. Perhaps the tactics may have changed from the *auto-da-fé* to the "Jews for Jesus Coffee House" and from the Grand Inquisition to the "B'nai Yeshua Retreat."

But our response to the Christian missionaries shall not change.

Notes

1) Moishe Rosen and William Proctor, *Jews for Jesus* (Old Tappan, N.J.: Fleming H. Revell, 1974), p. 45.

2) *Ibid.*, p. 28.

3) *Ibid.*, p. 51.

4) *Ibid.*, p. 54.

5) *Ibid.*

6) *Ibid.*, p. 57.

7) *Ibid.*

8) *Ibid.*, p. 58.

9) *Ibid.*, p. 59.

10) *Ibid.*

11) *Ibid.*, p. 60.

12) *Ibid.*, p. 62.

13) *Ibid.*, p. 63.

14) *Ibid.*, pp. 34, 122.

15) *Ibid.*, p. 52.

16) *Ibid.*, p. 114.

17) *Ibid.*, p. 89.

18) *Ibid.*, p. 72.

19) *Ibid.*, p. 89.

20) *Ibid.*, pp. 102-103.

21) *Ibid.*, p. 123.

22) *Ibid.*, p. 125.

23) *Ibid.*, p. 122.

24) The sons of Noah were forbidden to engage in idolatry, to commit blasphemy, to murder, to commit incest, to steal, and to eat the limb of a living animal. They were also required to establish courts and to appoint judges to enforce the laws.

25) Deuteronomy 8:1.

26) *Ibid.* 10:12-13.

27) Cf. *Ibid.* 24:16.

28) Numbers 23:10.

29) Other Biblical examples of atonement through prayer— without the use of blood sacrifices —can be found in Genesis 18 and in Numbers 11:1-2; 12:13-15; 14:11-12; 14:17-20.

30) Galatians 3:13.

31) Matthew 5:17-19; see also Matthew 19:16 ff.

32) A most compelling and thorough account of the history of bloodshed committed in the name of Christian faith can be found in Norman Cohn's scholarly study, *The Pursuit of the Millennium* (N.Y.: Oxford University Press Paperback, 1970).

33) Cf. Romans 8, Galatians 5:17 ff.

34) Cf. Matthew 5:32.

35) Zechariah 9:10.

36) Malachi 3:24.

37) Cf. Luke 14:26: "If anyone comes to me and does not hate his own father and mother . . . he cannot be my disciple."

38) Leviticus 19:18.

39) *Ibid.* 19:17. Cf. Exodus 23:4-5. See also Proverbs 25:21: "If your enemy is hungry, give him bread to eat; and if he is thirsty, give him water to drink."

40) Matthew 10:33. As an ultimate expression of hate, Jesus referred to those Jews who rejected his messianic claims as liars and as children of the Devil. (See John 8:44.) These slanders were later to be cited by Church fathers in defense of their barbaric persecutions of the Jews.

41) Matthew 15:26.

42) Dagobert D. Runes, *The Jew and the Cross* (N.Y.: Philosophical Library, 1966), p. 25.

43) The roots of Luther's diatribe can clearly be found in the words of Jesus, uttered in John 8:44. There, the "teacher of the golden rule" told the Jews, "You are of your father the Devil, and you want to do the desires of your father. He was a murderer from the beginning and does not stand in the truth . . . for he is a liar and the father of lies."

44) Runes, *op. cit.*, p. 39.

45) *Ibid.* (Eusebius was one of the key formers of Christian dogma.)

46) *Ibid.*, p. 40.

47) *Ibid.*

48) *Ibid.*

49) Edward H. Flannery, *The Anguish of the Jews* (N.Y.: Macmillan, 1965), p. 50.

50) Runes, *op. cit.*, p. 41. Malcolm Hay, *Thy Brother's Blood* (N.Y.: Hart Publishing, 1975), p. 25.

51) Hay, *Ibid.*, p. 27.

52) Runes, *op. cit.*, p. 61.

53) *Ibid.*, p. 62.

54) Hay, *op. cit.*, p. 28.

55) *Ibid.*

56) *Ibid.*, p. 29.

57) *Ibid.*, p. 26.

58) *Ibid.*, p. 56.

59) *Ibid.*

60) Norman Cohn, *op. cit.*, p. 77.

61) *Ibid.*, p. 78.

62) One cannot help but wonder how Christians could have secretly infiltrated such services if they did not have the horns which every Jew was said to have. One might also ask: "If Jesus suffered torture when pins were supposedly stuck into wafers, how did he feel while Christians throughout the world were, in fact, chewing up the same wafers? How did he feel being bit and chewed and swallowed?" Never was there a more absurd calumny than the "Desecration of the Host" slander.

63) Hay, *op. cit.*, p. 122.

64) *Ibid.*, p. 125. Runes, *op. cit.*, pp. 57-58.

65) *American Jewish Year Book* (Philadelphia: Jewish Publication Society of America), vol. 31, pp. 21-2.

66) Cohn, *op. cit.*, p. 131.

67) *Ibid.*, pp. 87, 138.

68) Runes, *op. cit.*, p. 63.

69) Cohn, *op. cit.*, p. 68. As the Jerusalem synagogue burned, the Crusaders danced and sang, "Christ We Adore Thee."

70) Hay, *op. cit.*, p. 37.

71) Cohn, *op. cit.*, p. 70.

72) *Ibid.*, p. 103.

73) Runes, *op. cit.*, pp. 56-57.

74) See Poul Borchsenius, *The Three Rings: The History of the Spanish Jews* (London: George Allen & Unwin, 1963), p. 223.

75) Abraham Leon Sachar, *A History of the Jews* (N.Y.: Alfred Knopf, 1973), p. 211.

76) Borchsenius, *op. cit.*, p. 225.

77) This holy day, literally "The Ninth Day of Av," saw the destruction of both Holy Temples the Jews had erected in Jerusalem. (One was destroyed by the Babylonians, and the other by the Romans.) Many other Jewish national tragedies have been recorded on this, the saddest of all days in the Jewish calendar.

78) The more conservative figure is cited in Cecil Roth, *History of the Jews* (N.Y.: Schocken, 1961), p. 227. Sachar notes the existence of the higher estimates as well.

79) There have been many attempts to define this unusual word, which has ultimately made its way into our modern vocabulary. See, e.g., Max I. Dimont, *Jews, God, and History* (N.Y.: Signet, 1964), p. 250.

80) Hay, *op. cit.*, p. 73.

81) *Ibid.*, p. 87.

82) *Ibid.*, p. 93.

83) *Ibid.*, pp. 164-165.

84) *Ibid.*, p. 166.

85) Adolf Hitler, *Mein Kampf* (Cambridge, Mass.: Sentry, 1943), p. 564.

86) An engrossing account of this sordid period in Church history can be found in Guenter Lewy, *The Catholic Church and Nazi Germany* (N.Y.: McGraw-Hill Paperback, 1965), Chapter 10.

87) Arthur Morse, *While Six Million Died* (N.Y.: Ace Publishing, 1968), p. 17.

88) *Ibid.*, p. 18.

89) *Ibid.*

90) *Ibid.*, p. 19. See also John F. Morley, *Vatican Diplomacy and the Jews During the Holocaust* (N.Y.: Ktav, 1979).

91) Eliezer Berkovits, *Faith After the Holocaust* (N.Y.: Ktav, 1973), p. 17.

92) Cited in Hay, *op. cit.*, p. 314.

93) See the full account in Howard Blum, *Wanted: The Search for Nazis in America* (N.Y.: Quadrangle, 1977), pp. 82-144.

94) *Ibid.*, p. 91.

95) *Ibid.*, p. 93.

96) *Ibid.*, p. 95.

97) *Ibid.*, p. 96. The national death toll after the three-day Iron Guard revolt was put at 10,000.

98) The National Council of Churches consists of the leaders of thirty major Protestant denominations in the United States.

99) *New York Times*, 10/20/76 and 10/22/76.

100) *Ibid.*, 10/20/76/.

101) Such a charge was made by the American Jewish Committee. See *Jewish Press*, 10/29/76.

102) *Jewish Week*, 11/7/76.

103) "Memorandum to Friends and Colleagues of the Office on Christian-Jewish Relations," (internal memorandum circulated by the National Council of Churches), 11/10/76.

104) *Jewish Press*, 5/13/77; *Jewish Journal*, 5/13/77; *Jewish Week*, 5/15/77.

105) See, e.g., *New York Times*, 11/9/79. In the *Jewish Week*, 1/27/80, the Anti-Defamation League charged that the NCC was trying "to undermine and reverse Christian support of Israel." (Cf. *Jewish Journal*, 2/1/80.)

106) *Jewish Journal*, 2/15/80; *Jewish Week*, 2/17/80. See also the memorandum distributed by the American Jewish Committee on 2/26/80 charging the NCC with "an anti-Israel bias."

107) See prepared statement by James A. Rudin, submitted to the NCC Middle East panel on 2/6/80. The charge is made on page 4.

108) *Jewish Journal*, 8/11/78.

109) Leviticus 19:2.

110) Isaiah 60:18, 21; 62:11-12.

111) Matthew 10:34-35.

112) Many points in the discussion of Isaiah 53 have been in print for hundreds of years in *Chizuk Emunah*, a Hebrew volume authored in the sixteenth century and recently issued in English translation under the title *Faith Strengthened* (N.Y.: Sepher-Hermon Press, 1970) by Isaac Troki. The book consists of a methodical verse-by-verse

analysis of the Christian scriptures. It is a worthwhile tool for use by any serious scholar of the "New Testament."

113) Matthew 21:12.

114) *Ibid.* 5:43.

115) *Ibid.* 15:11.

116) Acts 15:29.

117) Matthew 5:17-19.

118) Cf. Mark 3:28-29 and Luke 12:10. Consider, as well, problems caused by Mark 13:32.

119) Genesis 46:27; Deuteronomy 10:22.

120) Genesis 50:13.

121) *Ibid.* 23:16-19.

122) *Ibid.*

123) *Ibid.* 33:19.

124) Jesus referred to himself by this term on more than a score of occasions. See, for example, Matthew 8:20; 9:6; 10:23; 12:8, 40; 13:37, 41; 16:27-28; etc.

125) Numbers 15:39-40.

CHAPTER **2**

The Unification Church
Worshipping the Sun-moon

No longer call New Moons . . . holy
convocations . . . (ISAIAH 1:13)

Then the moon shall be confounded and
the sun ashamed when the Lord of Hosts
shall reign in Mount Zion and in
Jerusalem . . . (ISAIAH 24:23)

You're waiting for a bus. The pretty Korean girl walks over and asks, "Would you like to buy *News World*?"

Or three young men approach you, explaining that they are doing a study of American religious attitudes for the Ford Foundation or Brookings Institute. "We have three questions we would like to ask you," they say, "but, first, can you give us your name, address, and home phone number?"

Perhaps you are going to the grocery. You cross the street and see fifteen youthful men and women dressed in their "Sunday best" singing "God Bless America." As you stop to watch them, you note that they are all clean-cut and smiling. Half of them are Korean and the group's conductor is Korean, but some of the people singing in the back look like they might even be Jewish. You listen to their complete rendition, and you are about to leave. But, as you turn your back, you suddenly hear them start singing again. They are singing "God Bless America." Eventually, you go to the grocery, buy a bag of pretzels, and return home. Although you have been gone for ten minutes, upon your return you find the bright-faced chorus still there, still singing "God Bless America."

They are the Moonies, loyal followers of Korean evangelist Sun Myung Moon. They will sing for him, distribute literature for him, sell newspapers for him, lie for him, pry for him, try for him, and maybe even die for him. He is their leader and landlord. Some believe he may even be their Messiah. All of which is not inconceivable for a man who claims to have regularly conversed with Jesus and to have been worshipped by him.

Sun Myung Moon was born on January 6, 1920, in North Korea. From his earliest days, he was fascinated by the world of mysticism, and he dabbled in spiritualism. His hobby seems to have paid off, for in 1936 — at the tender age of sixteen — he was personally approached by Jesus Christ who told him that he must complete the work necessary to bring about the salvation of mankind. After 1936, Moon met with Jesus on many other occasions, usually in a remote mountain range in North Korea. By 1945, Sun Myung was on his way to glory. Or so it seemed.

Alas, two years of preaching in North Korea culminated in his imprisonment. Some say he was incarcerated because of opposition to Communism. Others say that his trip to the jailhouse was occasioned by gross sexual impropriety. In any event, Moon made the best of his stay by conversing with Jesus, Moses, and Buddha. It would seem that the North Koreans, despite their opposition to organized religion — or any religion for that matter — have, at least, the basic decency to grant visiting rights to theological figures with international reputations . . .

By 1950, Moon was set free. He moved to South Korea, relegating his Broad Sea Church to an untimely demise. But his ministry had not come to an end; in 1954, he was back in business. Founding the Holy Spirit Association for the Unification of World Christianity (better known as the "Unification Church"), Sun Myung revealed a new theology to mankind. It was based on his "Divine Principle." According to Moon, God is a composite of male and female forces—known as "yin" and "yang" in Eastern religions. The purpose of Creation was to have Adam mate with Eve and conceive perfect offspring who would reflect the "yin-yang" nature of God. Unfortunately, Satan sexually tempted Eve, and the pollution she absorbed was transmitted to all her children. God's plan, as Moon interpreted it, was foiled. There were no perfect children.

But all was not lost. According to the Korean evangelist, God tried again when He sent Jesus. Jesus was supposed to find the perfect mate—a Jewish Roman Princess, no doubt—and, yes, have perfect children. But John the Baptist messed things up, in Moon's version, and Jesus ended up getting crucified before he could have those perfect children. God's timetable was set back again, and the Jews—for not accepting Jesus—were to be held accountable. Therefore, in Moon's opinion, the Jews deserved the Nazi holocaust: "During the Second World War, six million people were slaughtered to cleanse all the sins of the Jewish people from the time of Jesus."[1]

In our generation, God decided to try again. According to Moon, a perfect Son of God was born in Korea some time between 1917 and the late 1920s. This man would go on to marry the perfect wife and finally have those perfect children. By 1981, the "Third Adam" was to reveal himself to the world as the new Messiah, ready to lead the forces of good in an apocalyptic battle against Satanic Communism. (As Moon was constructing his theology, he probably never even realized that he himself had been born in Korea between 1917 and the late 1920s . . .)

In 1954, Moon's future was still in a state of eclipse. His wife, who apparently lacked the realization that she had married the "perfect husband," asked for and received a divorce. A year later, the "perfect husband" was back in prison. Some say he was avoiding the draft. Others say that his return engagement with the clink was occasioned by gross sexual impro-

---

1. The numbered notes to chapter 2 begin on page 94.

priety. Indeed, Moon's sexual activities have been publicly discussed on more than one occasion. The charges stem from reported "sexual purification" teachings and actions attributed to him in Korea. According to one leading Presbyterian minister in Seoul, the Rev. Won Il Chei: "If we believe those who have gone into the group and come out, they say that one has to receive Sun Myung Moon's blood to receive salvation. That blood is ordinarily received by three periods of sexual intercourse."[2]

Arao Arai, author of *The Madness in Japan*, charged that Moon taught his flock that "in order to purify oneself of the Satanic blood we inherited and in order to go to heaven after death, humans must have intercourse with those who have God's blessings. This is what they call the ritual of blood sharing or ritual of holy spirit exchange."[3]

It was not long before the Korean Presbyterian Church excommunicated Moon. Nevertheless, self-ordained and firmly in charge of his Unification Church, Sun Myung was not to be stopped. Perhaps he had violated pure Christianity—whatever that may be—by introducing spiritualism into his church. Perhaps he had outraged his Presbyterian peers by asserting that Jesus did not rise from the grave after three days. He may even have thrown them off balance when he announced that God had chosen South Korea as the "New Israel." But, as long as Moses, Jesus, and Buddha came by to "rap" with him, Moon would stick to his guns.

And not only his guns. He would stick to his marble vases as well. And his machine parts. And his ginseng tea. And his pharmaceutical goods. And his titanium products. And his concrete. And all the other items his corporations produce, day-in and day-out, helping make him one of the wealthiest industrialists in South Korea. Moon's air rifle and weapons company is but the tip of an iceberg valued at over $15,000,000. As ministers go, Moon is most successful. He attributes his financial success—in all humility—to God. There is quite a bit of truth to this claim—more than meets the eye—as we shall soon see.

For eighteen years, Moon preached his "Divine Principle" throughout Korea. Seeking to "unify" Eastern and Western thought, he simply succeeded in unifying the different branches of Korean Christianity—all of whom joined together in opposing him. By 1972, it was time to move on. God told Moon to go to America. Humbly, Sun Myung complied. After all, if by 1969 Americans were already going to the moon, why couldn't Moon go to America?

He took America by storm. Or, at least, he took America. Converting his assets from air rifles to American real estate, Reverend Moon embarked on one of the most ambitious land-buying schemes to hit the United States since the days of the Louisiana Purchase. In less than five years, he succeeded in acquiring:

* the 42-story, 2000-room New Yorker Hotel (cost: over $5,000,000)
* the 8-story, block-wide Manhattan Center (cost: over $2,000,000)
* the Christian Brothers theological seminary in Barry-town, N.Y. (cost: $1,500,000)
* the former Columbia University Club (cost: $1,200,000) the 22-acre Belvedere Estate in Tarrytown, N.Y. (cost: $850,000)
* the Long Island City Loft's Candy Factory (cost: $700,000)
* the Irvington Estate in New York State (cost: $670,000)
* a mansion on Boston's Beacon Hill (cost: $500,000)
* a yacht (cost: $225,000)
* headquarters in each of the fifty states
* campus houses throughout the country like the $35,000 brownstone located near Columbia University in New York City.

In addition, Moon owns more than $8,000,000 worth of land in upstate New York and huge chunks of turf in other areas like Booneville, California.[4] His capital is especially well invested in light of the fact that his Unification Church claims tax-exemption rights on all real-estate holdings, citing its religious status. Thus, it really *can* be said that Rev. Moon's financial success is greatly "due to God."

Moon's ability to buy up so much land is due in no small measure to his Church's wealth. In one year, the Church reported an income of $12,000,000. Outside the United States it does nicely, too. In Japan alone, the Unification Church has assets of over $20,000,000.[5] While Moon's youthful followers, known as Moonies, explain to inquisitive reporters that all the money comes from their arduous efforts to sell candy, flowers, and peanuts, it is believed that there may be other sources of cash as well. It is true that Moon has one of the world's largest pools of cheap labor at his disposal. After all, his Moonies give up all their worldly possessions when they join the Unification Church, and thereafter they are expected to perform whatever duty the Church leaders demand. Such services to the cause may include working at the Church-owned printing press in San Francisco, the Moonie dry-cleaning business in Denver, or the Washington tea house. Whether they are sent to one of those establishments or to any of the other myriad concerns of the Unification Church, they will put in a hard day's work for the Reverend Moon. In return, they will get room and board.

Occasionally, they may get more than they bargain for. One twenty-nine-year-old woman, Christine Coste, was delivering newspapers to an East Harlem tenement when she was strangled, stabbed, stuffed into a box, and thrown off the building's roof. Two months later, another member of the Unification Church was mugged while selling candy in the Bedford-Stuyvesant section of Brooklyn, New York, and had to be hospitalized with a fractured skull. A third representative tragedy saw twenty-year-old Jean Billette shot dead after midnight one evening while peddling roses for Moon's church in the South Bronx section of New York City.[6] For Steve Hassan, the son of a Conservative Jewish family in Queens, tragedy struck on the road after he had gone for several months at a furious pace, raising money twenty hours a day, seven days a week.

While at the wheel of a Moonie van, he fell asleep and collided into oncoming traffic.[7]

Despite these incidents, there has been no evident change of heart in Unification Church leadership circles. Young Moonies are still dispatched to the streets to raise money. Some can be seen holding large buckets labeled "Fight Drug Abuse," pleading for donations. Others will tred gamely from door-to-door in some locations, raising money for any number of "worthy causes." And ardent salesmen continue to peddle Moon candies, flowers, and peanuts. But, still, questions remain to be answered regarding the source of the Church's enormous assets. For years the United States government has been probing ties between the Unification Church and the South Korean government. Allegations that individuals closely associated with Moon might be linked to such agencies as the Korean Central Intelligence Agency (KCIA) have been made in Washington. One individual under considerable scrutiny has been Col. Bo Hi Pak, Moon's frequent traveling companion and interpreter. The Unification Church has repeatedly denied the veracity of such charges, but a study published by a subcommittee of the House Committee on International Relations has pointed to clear connections between Moon and the South Korean government. Especially noteworthy were findings linking the Moon organization to the KCIA.[8] Another report, first published in the *Washington Post*, revealed that informed sources in the United States Department of Justice were looking into allegations that demonstrations organized by Moon in 1974 on behalf of the embattled presidency of Richard M. Nixon were inspired by the Korean CIA. According to Justice Department informants, the KCIA had asked the ubiquitous Bo Hi Pak to mobilize support for Richard Nixon, in the heat of the historic Watergate scandal, in order to establish a basis for future South Korean requests of support from the United States.[9]

By 1974 demonstrations were part of a religious crusade by Moon to uphold the Nixon presidency. As Moon saw it, the President of the United States is chosen by God. Therefore, any effort to hold Nixon accountable for possible wrong-doings would be an act of national rebellion against God. The Korean evangelist arrived in America in time to teach the nation that a president must be above the law; fortunately, the people of America did not agree with that interpretation. Nevertheless, Moon's heavily financed campaign — which included more than $70,000 worth of newspaper ads — did not fail completely. For his efforts he was invited to the White House by President Nixon, who also sent him a personal letter of appreciation. Moon humbly accepted the letter, which was subsequently circulated by the Unification Church to the national media, noting that he had only been performing the command of God. According to Moon, God had appeared before him in three separate visions urging him to prevent the impeachment of President Nixon.

The year 1974 was a very busy one for Moon. Having begun with a crusade in support of Nixon, he continued barnstorming his way through the country, even after the president resigned. Although he hit more than thirty cities on behalf of Nixon and the Unification Church, his big effort was aimed at New York in September. As the summer began, swarms of Moonies descended on the great metropolis, equipped with literature and smiles. By the hundreds they staked out every street corner, buttonholing tens of thousands of pedestrians. Anyone willing to listen would learn that the True Father, Rev. Sun Myung Moon of Korea, was on his way to Madison Square Garden, where he would speak the Word of God on September 18. Free tickets were handed out everywhere. Thousands of wall posters were pasted up throughout the city, all carrying a brief message about the September 18 affair and sporting a huge photograph of a smiling, waving Moon. At times, it seemed as though the city were experiencing a Peking-style Cultural Revolution. But, unlike the Maoist version, this happening was a capitalist venture through and through.

Moon spent more than $30,000 as he flew two hundred of his foreign-born supporters into the United States to help with leaflet distribution. He paid thousands of dollars for their hotel-room accommodations and meals. To rent Madison Square Garden, he laid out $40,000, and he disbursed thousands more to printers. In order to assure himself media coverage, he hosted a splendid roast-beef banquet in the grand ballroom of the Waldorf-Astoria hotel for sixteen hundred guests. The tab was in excess of $40,000. Just to be safe, he also doled out more than $300,000 for television, radio, and newspaper advertisements. By September 18, with half a million dollars having been pumped into the city's unsteady economy, Moon descended on New York.

Twenty thousand people filled the Garden, while hundreds of other ticket-holders were turned away, informed that tickets had been distributed to more people than the Garden could accommodate. While the deceived ticket-holders milled around outdoors, Moon spoke inside. And he spoke. And he spoke. The two-hour Korean address, translated into English, sentence-by-sentence, not only wore out Moon's interpreter but also bored his audience. More than 75 percent of the crowd walked out of the auditorium before the speech was over.[10] They had come to satisfy their curiosity; having seen the man whose face was plastered all over their city, they left. Those who stayed beheld one of the most unique exhibitions of loquacity to ever hit the town. During his two-hour performance, Moon sang, clapped his hands, and ran across the stage. His speaking style was further punctuated by an assortment of karate kicks and chops, as well as by his propensity to alternately jab and embrace his translator.[11] Describing his vociferation, the *New York Post* reported: "Moon's voice, like a clarinet, has three registers — a low guttural rumbling, a regular yell, and a high-pitched yell."[12] In the course of his lengthy screed, Moon ventured beyond his standard "Divine Principle" exposition by revealing that Billy Graham is the new John the Baptist, sent by God to "prepare the way of the Lord."[13] Noting that the Jews foolishly expect the Messiah to arrive in a fiery chariot — an observation derived after many years of intimate acquaintanceship with the Jewish community of North Korea, no doubt, inasmuch as such a notion is foreign to the other 99.99 percent of the world Jewish community—Reverend Moon revealed, "Billy Graham does not come in a chariot. He comes from North Carolina."[14] He also disclosed, perhaps to Graham's astonishment, that Korea will be the new Eden.

Although Graham did not join Moon's bandwagon, hundreds of young people did. Drawn in by a variety of factors ranging from deceptive invitations to join a "creative community project" which is "into some really deep relationships and feelings"[15] to desperate efforts to find something meaningful in the world, young Americans participated in Unification Church programs. Although many had come to the lectures, study groups, and rap sessions to simply "check things out," they found it difficult to leave. Indeed, many ex-Moonies have revealed that it is virtually impossible to leave.

A Unification weekend begins very pleasantly. All newcomers are made to feel "at home," and they are treated with great love and personal attention. As Paul Engel, a former Moonie, explained: "I had lost faith in myself. I had lost faith in other people and in the world as a potentially good place. I was a college graduate, traveling, with no definite direction, disillusioned about personal relationships, and alienated from the world."[16]

At this point, Paul was invited to a "lecture on educational principles . . . just a group of people looking for a better way of life, and they were called a 'Unification Center.' " Paul next found himself at a weekend seminar sponsored by the "Unification Center": "It felt wonderful to be served, to be given such attention, and made to feel important. Lectures started rather low-keyed . . ."[17]

But the tone and tempo of the program accelerated. In the highly emotional "Fall of Man" lecture, the young people were made to feel guilty over their imperfect natures and were told that they were being influenced by Satan. By this time, the program had become considerably more rigorous, and many of the students were having trouble staying awake during the classes. Nevertheless, "if you became sleepy or tired during a lecture," according to Engel, "you were kept awake by being told to stand or having your back rubbed or struck."

After the enormous load of lectures had mentally drained them, the new people were led on a mountain climb. When they had all reached the peak, they were told that Moon is the new Messiah and that all who rejected him would burn in hell. "By this time," Paul said, "we had been worked on so intensely and had been so psychologically swung from joy to fear and back again that it was hard not to believe it." Adding to the climate was the very nature of the group's isolation from society. "We were prevented from seeing newspapers or listening to radio or TV," according to Engel. "Everyday sights looked foreign to me, as though they were from another world. I had been reduced to a dependent being, unable to cope with the world, and I felt compelled to stay with them."[18]

Paul's version of the "Unification Center" experience mirrors those of many other ex-Moonies. First lured by lectures, study groups, and even offers of employment,[19] the young people soon find themselves on one of Moon's huge, out-of-the-way estates. Only intending to spend a weekend with the group, they find the initial warm experience of shared hopes and quiet flattery refreshingly different from the cold world to which they are accustomed.[20] Moon's name and the Church are not mentioned during the initial phase, and there is nothing to indicate what is in store, as experienced Moonies subtly exert social pressures on the new visitors to "stay just a little longer" or to come back for a week. The second phase, however, is more intense. The potential recruits are given little sleep and poor meals consisting of high-starch comestibles. They are subjected to a physically and emotionally draining program of singing, dodgeball, lectures, calisthenics, lectures, eating, lectures, and more lectures. As the lectures begin to consume up to fifteen hours of the day's activities, the young arrivals find themselves exhausted and pressed to remain awake during the intense and highly emotional classes given by trained Unification Church staffers.

Slowly, diagrams and charts are produced in rapid succession, all leading up to the implication that Moon—born in Korea between 1917 and the late 1920s—is the new Messiah. Psychological pressures are intensified as lecturers charge that all who oppose Moon are in the grasp of Satan. Parents opposing Moon are depicted as possessed of Satan, and they are portrayed as the ultimate weapon used by the Devil against Truth and God. The new people are assigned companions of the opposite sex, who spend every available spare moment reinforcing the day's lectures. The companions urge the potential Moonies not to leave, to "stay just a little longer." And, through it all, very little time is allowed for privacy. People are denied the opportunity to think things through; when lectures are not in session, they must participate in all scheduled sports or in long singing sessions. Frequently, the meals are preceded by a thirty-minute concentrated song period.

As the intense psychological pressures continue, day after day, young people find it hard to leave. For the first time in many of their lives, they are being told that they are loved. They are being begged to stay. "Please don't leave us now," a female Moonie told one young Jewish student. "We love you so much. You are such a beautiful person. How can you leave us?" Such a plea is reiterated by one Moonie after the other, and the young person—starving for the affection he was denied in the cold, harsh world of material pursuits and impersonal relationships—is impelled to stay. He has not heard a radio or seen a newspaper for a week or more. The only people he has seen are all these wonderful people asking him to stay "here, where you belong, where you are wanted." He looks at them, scanning from face to face, and there is not one who does not want him to remain. They are really concerned about him. He looks, even gropes for just one face in the crowd to assure him that his place is back home. He cannot find such a face. Not even one.

The temptation is great. It is especially hard for a young person without roots, without his own faith, without his own beliefs, without a conception of his own destiny to withstand. He is being offered a faith. He is being offered love in this world and salvation in the next world. The wonder is not that he stays but that so many of his peers have not come to join. As Reverend Moon explains: "Many American young people are neglected; they're thirsty for love. When they come into our movement, they're really inspired, they're really happy. For the first time, they see something and somebody they can trust and love."[21]

They trust Moon and his associates completely. They are taught that Moon and his wife are their "true parents" while those who brought them into this world are nothing but tools of Satan. They are assured that the Unification Church will provide for their needs, and, in return, they are expected to turn their worldly possessions over to the Church. They are frequently sent off to Unification branches far away from their parents' houses, thereby facilitating the break from the old life and the adjustment to the new. Quite often, they drop out of school in order to devote all their time to the Church. All their love and affection must be devoted to the Church as well.

If the new Moonies are married, they must agree to split up. Their children, if they have any, are taken away from them and are put into nurseries where they are later taught that Moon and his wife are their "True Parents."[22] Single Moonies are discouraged from becoming involved in personal relationships. The males and females are segregated from each other, except in cases where a Moonie of one sex is assigned to be a "companion" for a potential recruit of the opposite sex. Instead of developing close relationships with each other, Moonies are urged to devote their feelings to Moon by means of intensive work and worship. Some sing hymns of praise to Moon all day.

When marriages do take place, they are very strictly controlled by the Church. A prospective bride or groom must submit to the Church leadership a list of five choices from which the Unification staff agrees upon an appropriate spouse. Before the wedding, each individual must confess all previous sexual sins to "The Father," and they must beg Moon's forgiveness. Once Moon joins them together, the newlyweds are prohibited from living together or sleeping together for forty days. Afterwards, the husband and wife are generally assigned to different Unification Church outposts, thereby separating them.[23] Although married, their lives are still devoted forever to Moon. The incredible control Moon has over his followers, even to the extent of de-personalizing their marital relationships, is exemplified by the mass marriages he enjoys conducting. In a 1975 affair staged in South Korea, Moon joined together 1800 people at one time. The nine hundred brides and nine hundred grooms were required to vow that they would not sleep together or live together for a period of twenty-one months following the wedding ceremony.

Moon's grip is firm, and one who enters the realm of the Unification Church finds it virtually impossible to leave. If he tries to depart on his own accord, he may be physically restrained — or threatened accordingly. If he does abscond, he may expect to be visited at his original home repeatedly or to be targeted for an endless barrage of telephone calls from former colleagues, begging him to return "for just a little while."

There are other ways to leave the Unification Church. In April, 1975, a twenty-three-year-old convert to the group committed suicide at the seminary in Barrytown. On August 23, 1976, the *New York Post* reported the death of a twenty-four-year-old Moonie who jumped out of a window on the twenty-second floor of the New Yorker hotel. In addition, other deaths at the New Yorker have been reported since the Moon purchase of the building.

The most emotional of the ways to leave the Unification Church is to be kidnapped by a de-programmer. Parents of Moonies, in exasperated states of depression over their children's decisions to stay with Moon, have been turning to high-priced "de-programmers" who kidnap Moonies, lock them up in small motel rooms, harangue them, scream at them, and threaten them until they "snap out of it." In most states, this tactic has been declared illegal. While it is understandable that a parent will do anything to win back a child lost to the clutches of the Unification Church, the act of kidnapping is a most unfortunate response, though it is reflective of the intensity of the state of desperation. On January 19, 1976, Fay Goodman and her brother Milton Mosk were arrested with a group of four other men for having kidnapped her son, David, who had become a Moonie. David, who had spent more than six months in Tarrytown, pressed the charges against his mother and uncle.

More disquieting has been the response of those parents who have given up the battle to save their children. When Reverend Moon staged a million-dollar media event at New York's Yankee Stadium in June 1976, one of those in attendance was Hyman Stein, a former Pittsburgh cabbie who now resides in Florida with his wife, Ida. When asked why he came, he explained that he wanted to see his twenty-six-year-old son, Joe, who had joined the Moonies. He also wanted to meet the young Frenchwoman whom Moon had chosen for Joe to marry. When asked whether he wanted to see his son leave the Unification Church, Hyman Stein said, "Our son is happy, so we're happy."[24]

Differing in approach from both the Goodmans and the Steins, most parents of Moonies have organized themselves into groups seeking to bring legal action against the Church. In many cases, parents have succeeded in gaining custody of Moon-influenced children. There have, however, been failures too.

Moon is a very difficult man to fight. When he told *Newsweek*, "God has ordained or hand-picked me . . . Korea is the chosen nation of God. I was ordained by God . . . I am in daily communication with God,"[25] he was informing the world that he means business. He is financially established, and he is politically powerful. His young women have been known to stalk the halls of Congress, bringing elected representatives tea, cookies, and flowers. One of these girls, Susan Bergman, successfully wiggled her way into a friendship with former Speaker of the House Carl Albert. In New York State, Moon sent his lobbying teams to Albany, where attractive young women met with state senators, requesting letters of endorsement for a Unification Church project. Moon had suggested that "three pretty girls" be sent to talk to each state senator. The plan was enacted, with the young women bearing gifts of ginseng tea and vases of tulips for the elected legislators. Led by Susan Bergman, the group succeeded in obtaining the signatures of a number of influential state officials who later claimed they had been unaware of the girls' ties to Moon's church.[26]

To add to the efficacy of his lobbying efforts, Moon sends women of various ethnic or racial backgrounds to lobby legislators of the same background. Thus, Italian-born Moonies were sent to meet with an Italian state senator, while Olga Molina, a Latin woman in her twenties, was sent to influence Hispanic legislators.[27] As a further incentive to elected officials, Moonies offer to circulate petitions for candidates needing signatures to qualify to run for various offices. In another case, two thousand Moonies were sent into a representative's district to clean the streets. One state senator summed up his colleagues' attitudes towards the Moonies in Albany: "These were sweet girls. They put you at ease. They sent me flowers. They were the most terrific propagandists I've ever encountered."[28]

Moon's political clout is also maintained through the use of "front groups," of which more than sixty have been tied to his Church. Ranging from Project Unity, the One World Crusade, the International Culture Foundation, the International Federation for Victory over Communism, and the Collegiate Association for the Research of Principles (CARP) to the Freedom Leadership Foundation, the World Freedom Institute, American Youth for a Just Peace, Professors' Academy for a World Peace, and the Committee for Responsible Dialogue, these front groups win over unsuspecting professors, students, and people of all backgrounds. More significantly, many of them work to influence federal legislation. The Freedom Leadership Foundation, for example, spends nearly $60,000 a year in efforts to affect government policy. Sponsoring full-page ads in major American newspapers and conducting scholarly seminars, many of Moon's front groups subtly introduce his ideas to large numbers of trusting individuals. Thus, we find that Neil A. Salonen, who spoke at a Freedom Leadership Foundation rally on behalf of South Korea held at the New York Hilton, also spoke at a Unification Church meeting four weeks earlier in the same room in the Hilton. In fact, Salonen is the president of both the Freedom Leadership Foundation and of the Unification Church of America. He is also the president of the International Culture Foundation. Salonen, who was raised in New York, has traveled with Moon throughout the United States, Japan, and Korea.

Another Moon front-group is the Collegiate Association for the Research of Principles (CARP). Innocently named, this group has branches on college campuses throughout the United States. Its purpose, despite its impressive name, is to promote the "Divine Principle" and the Unification Church among college students; the only principles it researches are those conceived by the Reverend Sun Myung Moon. Whenever it applies for student recognition on a campus, it denies affiliation with the Unification Church. At Columbia University, a number of Jewish groups conducted an investigation into CARP's background; the resulting conclusions not only revealed its tie with Moon but also uncovered a systematic effort on its part to cover up the relationship. In response to the findings that CARP had lied to the Student Governing Board of Columbia University's Earl Hall Student Center, the Moonie group was expelled from the center which recognizes more than a score of other religious student groups. Defending the group's efforts to cover up the relationship with the Unification Church, Michael Urena, chairman of Columbia CARP, explained that there are times when mendacity should be considered permissible — when it seeks to achieve a greater good than the simple telling of the truth. As an example, he explained that CARP was justified in lying about its background in order to win recognition by the Earl Hall Student Governing Board.

This concept of lying for a greater good is not Urena's invention but an actual teaching of the Unification Church. Known as "celestial deception" or "heavenly deception" (depending on the particular translation of the Korean original), this notion permits acts of deceit performed in defense of the Church. Thus, it can be assumed that the Church will stop at nothing to expand its influence.[29]

If "celestial deception" has been the unofficial theme of the front-group effort, it has certainly been an effective one. Moon's cunning efforts to influence public opinion have even gone to the point that he has begun publishing a newspaper called *News World*, which represents itself to be just another daily journal.[30] Nevertheless, the "heavenly deception" which most concerns the Jewish community is that involving Dr. Mose Durst and his organization, "Judaism: In Service to the World." Durst, who sits on the board of directors of the Unification Church's theological seminary in New York and who has served as president of a number of Moon front-groups, has assumed the presidency of this one as well. His group sends out young female Moonies who claim to be Jewish for the purpose of attracting the support of Jewish communal leaders. Claiming that the group promotes Jewish religious, cultural, and spiritual values, the young women ask Jewish organizations to endorse programs they sponsor. While "Judaism: In Service to the World" has been uncovered in San Francisco for what it really is, its presence must serve as a chilling reminder to the Jewish community that the Reverend Sun Myung Moon has his eyes set on our young people.

Even more chilling was the report published by the National Council of Young Israel, a national coalition of synagogues committed to observant Judaism, which warned that the Moonies might be planning to infiltrate Jewish houses of worship. The community alert was issued by the body's national president, Nathaniel Saperstein, after a non-Jewish woman believed to be a missionary for the Unification Church sought membership in the Young Israel of Boro Park. "I call on all Jewish synagogues to be aware of this danger," said Young Israel official Irving Bunim. "These people will stop at nothing in their attempts to convert us to their beliefs."[31]

It is true that Moon has mocked Judaism. Aside from the 112 anti-Semitic references which appear on the pages of his *Divine Principle* textbook,[32] Moon has publicly deprecated Judaism in Madison Square Garden and elsewhere. Citing the heinous charge that the Jews killed Jesus and thereby incurred the eternal punishment of God, Moon has written and repeatedly said that the Nazi holocaust was the Jews' just deserts for the "sin of rejecting Jesus and crucifying him." Nevertheless, he has succeeded in attracting large numbers of our young people. According to Richard Greenwald, an ex-Moonie, 40 to 50 percent of the Church's members are Jewish.[33] The propensity of Jews, especially from middle- and upper-class homes, to join groups like Moon's led Maurice Davis, a columnist for the *Jewish Post and Opinion*, to organize one of the anti-Moon groups, "Citizens Engaged in Reuniting Families" (CERF). Davis, who conducts worship sevices at the Jewish Community Center of White Plains, a Reform temple, became interested in the Unification Church after two young people affiliated with his temple joined the Moonies. Noting that many Jewish parents are asking, "What is the need that we do not fulfill?" Davis cited the statement of one of the youths who joined Moon: "Now, at least, I believe in something. My parents believe in nothing."[34]

It is in that statement that the roots of the Moon problem are revealed, and it is from that statement that we can derive a path to recovery. Dr. Ernest Giovanoli, a psychiatrist at Northern Dutchess County Hospital who studied a number of individuals affiliated with the Unification Church, reported that the movement had done much good for some of the "lost souls wandering around . . . It gives them a purpose, structure, direction . . ."[35] While Dr. Giovanoli emphasized that he was not endorsing the group, his point was professionally honest. Reverend Moon *has* done a considerable amount of good for many of those young people who joined his Church. While he may have torn their souls away from the Jewish people, he at least taught them that they have souls.

Reverend Moon has succeeded where we have failed. In the words of Paul Engel, whose experience with the Moonies was discussed earlier in this chapter:

I think back, and I wonder how this could have happened to me. For a few years I went to a Reform

Sunday School and [I] had a perfunctory bar mitzva. At our home, Passover was about the only Jewish thing we did, and that usually was a social dinner and nothing else . . . Maybe I was thirsting for a religious faith with strong emotional ties.

If I have learned anything, it is that Jewish students should be taught everything there is to know about Judaism but in a warm, family-oriented atmosphere.[36]

Engel's statement should be memorized by every Jewish parent in America, for it constitutes the key to cracking Moon's stranglehold on so many young Jews. If the Unification Church offers a religion, a belief in a Messiah, a faith with strong emotional ties—what does it offer that Judaism lacks?

Nothing.

The reason that so many young Jews are susceptible to Moon's appeal—and it is not unlike the reason that other young Jews find themselves snared by the Christian missionaries discussed earlier—is that they have been denied an *authentic* Jewish upbringing. Raised in a society which stresses material success and social climbing—while ignoring, if not forthrightly denigrating, spiritual growth and religious observance—these young Jews find themselves starved. Spiritually starved. They are seeking meaning. They are groping for an understanding of the world around them. They are trying to find their place in that world.

When they are denied a chance to have a Jewish heritage, they will turn elsewhere. When they are served a Judaism of bagels, borscht, and bar mitzvas, they will vomit materialism out of their systems, even if they have to undertake a program of austerity to do so. If they cannot find roots, spirituality, meaning, and God in their homes and schools, they will seek out roots, spirituality, meaning, and God in others' homes and schools. And if their search leads them to a multi-millionaire charlatan from South Korea, then so shall it be. For, in comparison to the sterile "Judaism" of suburban America—a "Judaism" bereft of spiritual meaning and reduced to valuing every deed in the brutally cold, harshly pragmatic terms of dollars and cents—the Unification Church offers warmth, community, and spirituality. In contrast to the impersonal "Conservative" and "Reform" movements—which castrated Judaism of its life and meaning by discarding from its warm body the beautiful rituals and the eternal significance of Divine Revelation at Sinai—the Unification Church offers a touch of mystery, a confession that every last nook and cranny of the universe has not been scientifically reasoned away.

How ironic it is that so many of my generation have rejected all the values foisted on us! We were taught to pursue "success" and "riches." We were taught to be "rational" and to reject the "superstitious beliefs" of our grandparents. It was explained to us that prayer and Orthodox observance and parochialism were things of the past. We were assured by "rabbis" dressed in black robes, encircled by mixed choirs, and reinforced by Church-like organs, that the Jews were not really a "Chosen People"—and that we could therefore relate to our non-Jewish friends without any guilt feelings. We were told that Jews "don't really believe that God gave a Torah to Moses" and that "many of the prophets may never have existed." We were fed Bible criticism, and our religious inclinations were nurtured with doubt. And that was to make of us better Jews!

Of course my generation is revolting against "Jewish" values! Of course my generation has joined the search for meaning and purpose! Of course members of my generation have found their ways into the Unification Church! Now they work for Moon at slave wages. Now they have an outlet for their innate knowledge that there exist mysteries in this world which the greatest scientist shall never be able to explain. Now they can worship in an "Orthodox" form, giving full vent to their need to express devotion to that Being who created the world. Now they have a reverend who needs no black robes, no choirs, and no organs to create an atmosphere of sanctity. Now they have a Korean "Chosen Nation" through whom they can vicariously experience the awesome meaning of bearing God's witness to all mankind. Now they have a prophet—albeit a false one, but a prophet nonetheless—through whom they can receive the "Word of God."

Where else could they have heard the Word of God? In the suburban temples, where "rabbis" are paid enormous salaries to sound impressive, speak sonorously, and stay out of the caterer's way? Could they have heard the Word of God in Maurice Davis's Jewish Community Center of White Plains? On February 25, 1977, the *Jewish Post and Opinion* published these words by columnist Davis: "The festival of Purim, with all its lovely nonsense, remains as one of our most entertaining of holidays. Nothing about it is serious. Nothing about it is factual . . . The story is fiction. It is secular. And it gives every appearance of being straight out of Arabian Nights."

This was "Rabbi" Davis's description of the holiday which commemorates the salvation of the Jews who were under Persian rule, as recorded in the Book of Esther. If the Book of Esther—canonized by our ancestral Sages as an intrinsic component of the Bible—is "nonsense" and "fiction," then what makes the Book of Ruth, the Book of Samuel, or the very Pentateuch itself more authentic? If the "rabbi" doesn't believe in the Book of Esther, should his young congregants be expected to? What Judaism did "Rabbi" Davis bequeath to those two youths who left his flock to join Moon? Did *he* observe the Sabbath according to its laws? Did *he* teach belief in the Torah as the embodiment of God's spoken word to Moses and to all of Israel? Did *he* exemplify authentic Judaism?

Of course young Jews , searching for truth, left the confines of a temple which was devoid of authenticity. Of course they could not accept a "Judaism" built on a cynical rejection of the very pillars which maintain the faith. Of course they were attracted to a Moon who, at least, believed in *something*! So what if Sun Myung Moon claimed to speak with Moses? At least he maintained that Moses was real, that Moses really existed. If Sun Myung Moon is a multi-millionaire charlatan, then he differs from those who "rabbify" in all the sterile temples of suburbia only by virtue of his greater financial wealth.

If Sun Myung Moon has taken young Jews away from their homes and away from their families, he has not taken them away from their faith. For that infamous excision of a four-thousand-year heritage had been successfully performed long before Sun Myung Moon ever came on the scene.

Notes

1) Cited in "Reverend Moon and the Jews," a paper presented by Earl Raab, executive-director of the San Francisco Jewish Community Relations Council, at the 1976 plenary session of the National Jewish Community Relations Advisory Council. The paper was subsequently published in *Congress Monthly*, December 1976. (The reference appears therein on p. 9.)

A number of similar references appear in Moon's *Divine Principle* (Washington, D.C.: Holy Spirit Association for the Unification of World Christianity, 1974). Consider these three examples:

"Jesus came as the Messiah, but due to the disbelief of and persecution by the people he was crucified. Since then, the Jews have lost their qualification as the chosen people and have been scattered, suffering persecution through the present day." (p. 147)

"The chosen nation of Israel has been punished for the sin of rejecting Jesus and crucifying him." (p. 226)

"Satan confronted Jesus, working through the Jewish people . . ." (p. 357)

2) Cited in William J. Petersen, *Those Curious New Cults* (New Canaan, Conn.: Pivot, 1975), p. 250.

3) *Ibid.*

4) In some U.S. cities, residents have begun to fear for their jobs, as Moon has established industries which directly compete with local businesses. (See, e.g., *Wall Street Journal*, 6/30/80.)

5) Many of the above figures have appeared repeatedly in the general press. See, e.g., *Newsweek*, 6/14/76.

6) *New York Post*, 6/2/80.

7) *Newsday*, 2/6/80. After a long convalescent period, Steve visited home, where he was successfully "deprogrammed."

8) *Investigation of Korean-American Relations* (Report of the Subcommittee on International Organizations of the Committee on International Relations, 10/31/78), pp. 351 ff; 370-2.

9) *Washington Post*, 11/8/76.

10) *New York Post*, 9/19/74.

11) *Ibid.*

12) *Ibid.*

13) *Ibid.*

14) *Ibid.*

15) *Newsweek*, 6/14/76.

16) *Jewish Week*, 6/20/76.

17) *Ibid.*

18) *Ibid.*

19) *Newsweek*, 6/14/76.

20) *Ibid.* See also *Newsday*, 2/6/80; *Miami News*, 1/26/78.

21) *Ibid.*

22) *Ibid.*

23) *Ibid.*

24) *New York Post*, 6/1/76.

25) *Newsweek*, 6/14/76.

26) *New York Post*, 6/25/76.

27) *Ibid.*

28) *Ibid.*

29) One Moon gimmick saw the Church offer college students a five-day winter vacation in Florida (including transportation, food, and lodging) for only twenty dollars. Debbie Block, a nineteen-year-old co-ed, put it well: "I didn't know what I was getting myself into." She expected "fun, sun, and surf." Instead, she ended up at a Moon indoctrination center. (*Jewish Journal*, 1/11/80)

30) In fact, its first president and publisher, Dennis Orme, has deep Moonie roots, having established the Unification Church in England together with his wife (*Columbia Daily Spectator*, 10/5/77). See also *Our Town* (a New York City publication), 9/10/78, which revealed that the paper had received six million dollars in Moon funds during the prior two years.

31) *Jewish Press*, 1/11/80; *Jewish Week*, 1/13/80.

32) See "Jews and Judaism in Reverend Moon's *Divine Principle*," a report by James Rudin, published by the American Jewish Committee (December, 1976), p. 6.

33) See *Jewish Observer*, March 1976. Marc Tanenbaum, in an introduction to the Rudin report (*ibid.*), estimated the figure at 30 percent. The *American Journal of Psychiatry*, 2/79, put the figure near 50 percent.

34) *New York Post*, 9/16/74.

35) *New York Times*, 10/1/75.

36) *Jewish Week*, 6/20/76. Cf. *Jewish Post and Opinion*, 3/3/78,

which tells the story of a Jewish co-ed who joined Moon's church despite eight years of attendance at a Reform temple's Hebrew school.

CHAPTER 3

Gurus, Buddhists, and other east winds

And Solomon's wisdom excelled the wisdom of all the children of the east . . . (I KINGS 5:10)

. . . and the east wind brought the locusts. (EXODUS 10:13)

When Sun Myung Moon brought his multi-million-dollar religion to the United States, he was certainly not the first. Many New Yorkers actually sneered in 1974 when they learned that Moon had rented Madison Square Garden for his first major appearance in the Big Apple. After all, they recalled, Guru Maharaj Ji had begun in Shea Stadium.

Guru Maharaj Ji had come to America to bring peace to the country and the world. Born on December 10, 1957, in Hardwar, India, and named Prem Pal Singh Rawat, the precocious youngster quickly grew into the spiritual shoes left behind by his holy father in 1965. Renamed "Guru Maharaj Ji" alias "Lord of the Universe" alias "The Perfect Master" alias "The Creator of the World," the young boy assumed the leading position in his family's "Divine Lights Mission." Although the youngest of four brothers, Maharaj Ji was chosen by his parents to inherit the mantle of responsibility and the family fortune because he evinced a certain ethereal quality most uncommon in children his age.

By the time Maharaj Ji was twelve years old, he was winning new adherents to the Mission. Although based in India, where gurus are a dime a dozen, the kid had a special flare. In 1970, for example, he celebrated his thirteenth birthday by riding through Delhi in a golden chariot, followed by more than a million supporters. When the procession concluded, he announced that he would bring peace to the world. Before his fifteenth birthday, he would bring his vow one step closer to fruition. He would come to America.

By the summer of 1972, Maharaj Ji was hard at work in the United States, building a base of operations in Colorado, where a festival sponsored by his group attracted six thousand young people—two thousand of whom decided to join the Divine Light Mission. Expanding his influence to other states, Maharaj Ji succeeded in establishing more than forty Divine Light centers representing some fifteen thousand devotees in the country by year's end. (In less than six more months, those figures would double.) While Maharaj Ji's dutiful deifiers were falling under his trance, the guru's thoughts were shifting to finance. He grew from a teenage guru into a teenage corporate executive, supervising a religious empire consisting of stores, restaurants, painters, plumbers, carpenters, automobile repairmen, a record company, a movie firm, and a publishing house. It was not long before "The Creator of the World" was reported to be suffering from ulcers.

But he suffered in style. Chauffered around town in either one of his two Mercedes-Benz limousines or in his $30,000 Rolls-Royce,[1] Maharaj Ji managed the Divine Light Missions's pursuit. At the end of a hard day of religious expansion, he would come home to his $80,000 residence in Denver. Surrounded by riches everywhere, the Indian-born "Lord of the Universe"

1. The numbered notes to chapter 3 begin on page 131.

decided to splurge on a Houston Astrodome crusade. Scheduled for late 1973, the three-day affair was to usher in the "New Age." Unfortunately, despite the massive give-away of tickets to "Millennium 73," attendance was sparse, and the program proved uninspiring.

This setback to world peace notwithstanding, Maharaj Ji persisted in promoting his Divine Mission. He continued crusading, imparting wisdom to young people in search of something meaningful, and collecting the tithes assessed his loyal followers. His magazine grew impressively, reaching six-figure-circulation status. His group's membership rolls surged beyond the fifty-thousand mark.[2] He even attracted a nationally respected hero of the youth counter-culture, Rennie Davis (an alumnus of the 1968 Chicago riots), who barnstormed through the college campuses of America seeking to attract converts. By 1974, things had developed so nicely for "The Perfect Master" that he decided to take a bride. Rejecting traditional Hindu austerity, the sixteen-year-old "Creator of the World" chose as his mate a former airline stewardess, Marilyn Johnson, whom he declared to be the reincarnation of the Indian goddess Durga.

All this did not exactly sit well with the guru's mother, Mataji. Adding to Mataji's woes was her concern over the lifestyle of her filial "Lord of the Universe." She had never complained in the past, as her son shuttled between mansions in Los Angeles, New York, London, and other major world centers. But now things were getting out of hand. For one thing, Indian officials of the Divine Light Mission were beginning to charge that Maharaj Ji was "haunting night clubs, drinking, dancing . . ."[3] For another, Maharaj Ji and Marilyn barred Mataji from their $400,000 California estate.[4] Disappointed that her Divine scion had traded the celestial spirits for the liquid version, she regretfully announced that Maharaj Ji was no longer "The Creator of the World." Replacing him with her oldest son, twenty-four-year-old Bal Bhagwan Ji, the Holy Mother of the Divine Light Mission explained: "Whatever a mother does, she does for the good of the child . . . He has broken the discipline and ideals that behoove a guru, but I will accept him as a son anytime."[5]

When asked whether her decision was prompted not only by the "despicable, nonspiritual way of life"[6] of the former "Lord of the Universe" but also by a desire to share in the massive funds collected by the Mission in the United States, Mataji humbly replied, "There is no jealousy about this."[7]

The ex-"Creator of the World" did not allow this excoriation to go unanswered. Admitting that "I am not God," he nevertheless maintained, according to the *New York Times*, "I cannot be thrown away for any reason whatsoever." Such a contention would have to be taken seriously as long as he could hold on to followers like the devotee who told a reporter: "We must unquestioningly do whatever Maharaj Ji tells us. If he told us to slit your throat, I would do so in an instant."[8]

On at least one occasion his venerators very nearly did just that. During a lecture on "Divine Knowledge," a prankster walked up to Maharaj Ji and threw a pie in his face. Swarms of devotees responded by mauling the practical joker, whose skull was crushed by a blackjack in the ensuing melee. Defending the assault, Rennie Davis warned, "This is not the age to turn the other cheek. This Savior will not be crucified.[9]

The problem is that "this Savior" will not "save" either. Although the $650,000 debt run up by his Mission has, in recent years, been reduced to a mere $80,000—thanks to the steady influx of members' tithes[10]—Maharaj Ji has not brought peace to America, to India, or even to his own family. He and Mataji are battling each other in the courts of India,[11] and fewer Americans are joining his Denver-based Mission. Even the birth of his first daughter, Premlata, has not boosted the membership rolls. Nevertheless, he still has a following, as was evidenced when three thousand of the faithful waited at Atlantic City's Convention Hall for hours, expecting him to speak.[12] Although he never showed up to address the group—he was busy meeting with the board of his Divine Light Mission — his devotees accepted the explanation of his spokesman: "He comes when he wants. If he does not come, he does not come."[13]

What did Maharaj Ji offer young people? He offered them "a path to God." He offered them a chance to taste the mysteries of the universe by acknowledging that they exist. He offered them a road to salvation. His Divine Light Mission provided a sense of community, a feeling of "belonging," for so many of those alienated youths who joined. Ultimately, Maharaj Ji—who attracted a great many young Jews to his ranks[14]—provided the same things to young people that Sun Myung Moon and the "Jews for Jesus" offer.

And, because these sacred qualities, so richly abundant in authentic Judaism, were never presented to young Jewish men and women during their maturation periods in suburbia, they looked elsewhere for the spiritual treasures they could not find in the temple gymnasium or in the bar mitzva cake.

SRI CHINMOY

A far more subdued and respectable Hindu guru, Sri Chinmoy, has been attracting followers in the United States as well. Chinmoy, who conducts meditation sessions for United Nations delegates and staffers, is representative of the more mainstream brand of Hinduism being introduced in America. As such, his theology and presentation deserve our consideration.

Chinmoy is a peaceful fellow. He wouldn't hurt a fly—especially one which he believes might be a reincarnated friend. Deeply religious, he sincerely believes the many teachings of the Hindu faith. Thus, while the vast majority of the world population view with disfavor India's rigid "caste system," Chinmoy necessarily defends it. He explains that each caste is like a limb of the body, and it is therefore perfectly natural to keep them separate from each other.[15]

To Chinmoy, the ultimate guide to existence is the *Bhagavad-Gita*, frequently known as the "Bible of Hinduism." This work, which is part of the *Mahabharata*—a huge collection of material often compared to the writings of Homer—consists of a poetic dialogue between "Sri Krishna, the incarnate of God" and Arjuna, a warrior about to participate in a major battle. Arjuna is consumed with misgivings about entering the conflict; Krishna's advice to him constitutes the essence of the *Gita*'s teachings. Although unknown to most Westerners, the *Bhagavad-Gita* directs the lives of millions of people in the East.

It is in the *Gita* that we find notions like reincarnation — a concept alien to Americans but widely accepted in India. This holy work of Hinduism presents both the dietary regulations which bar the consumption of beef and the special laws aimed at protecting cows. It also outlines the need for India to forever preserve her caste system. Since the teachings are attributed to Sri Krishna (i.e., Lord Krishna), who was a physical embodiment of God according to Hinduism, they are treated with utmost reverence. After all, a person who violates the commandments of a holy man who is the actual incarnation of God Himself is rebelling against God, too.

The Hindu scriptures explain that, whenever men forget the lessons disseminated by an "Avatar" (i.e., a master who is, in fact, the physical incarnation of God), He must return to earth in yet another body to revive His teachings. Accordingly, Lord Krishna's figure was the eighth Avatar form taken by Vishnu, a Hindu god. The Avatar concept has, not surprisingly, created quite a bit of chaos in India. As Chinmoy notes, "In India, practically every disciple claims his Guru to be an Avatar, the direct descent of God. A flood-tide of enthusiasm sweeps over them when they speak about their Guru. The spiritual giant Swami Vivekananda could not help saying that in East Bengal, India, the Avatars grow like mushrooms."[16] We have just seen a manifestation of this confusion during our consideration of the Divine Light Mission.

"When wickedness reaches the maximum height, God has to don the human cloak in the form of an Avatar," Chinmoy explains. And, although "Sri Krishna is the beloved Boatman who untiringly plies his Boat of consciousness between India's unparalleled history and her unrivaled spirituality,"[17] sometimes an Avatar may appear outside peerless India. For example, Chinmoy maintains that Jesus was an Avatar who came to earth to counter the wickedness of Herod.[18] In fact,

Chinmoy is most complimentary when referring to Jesus: "Jesus came. The world heard . . . Jesus smiles. The world becomes."[19]

Nevertheless, if Jesus was "The Son" in Chinmoy's paradigm, Buddha was "The Prince" and Krishna was "The King."[20] Eventually, Chinmoy's Avatar concept becomes quite confusing. If Jesus is to be portrayed as God incarnate, there arise many problems which transcend the contradictory statements regarding the Trinity attributed to Jesus in the Gospels. Shouldn't Hindus respect the teachings of Avatar Jesus, baptize themselves and their children, celebrate Easter Sunday, or—at the very least—consider themselves a Christian denomination? Even more puzzling is the Avatar role assigned to Buddha. Buddha denied the existence of God, and he refused to be looked upon as anything more than an enlightened teacher. How can Chinmoy, then, ascribe Avatar status to Buddha? Indeed, Chinmoy himself sees the problem; rather than backtrack, however, he utilizes the time-honored device of esoteric poetry: "The buddha had no God. But he had Divinity in its fullest measure."[21]

Judaism maintains that *every* person is created in the "image of God." The very conception of a human being is a manifestation of "Divinity in its fullest measure." But Judaism rejects all claims that God incarnates Himself. Although the Avatar doctrine is consistent with classical Greco-Roman theology/mythology, it runs counter to fundamental Jewish thought. Consider the ramifications of the Avatar tenet: any man can come along, claim to be God, and demand total obeisance. How can it be discerned whether or not he *is* an Avatar? Chinmoy responds that one can recognize an Avatar if he possesses the gift of inner vision or if he is blessed by the Avatar Himself. This compounds the difficulty: How can it be ascertained whether or not a self-proclaimed Avatar, who assures his potential venerator that "He" has granted him a rare blessing by revealing to him "His Divine Essence," is telling the truth? There is no ultimate barometer with which to measure some "Avatar Veracity Index"—and nothing corroborates this criticism more potently than Chinmoy's own confession that "in East Bengal, India, the Avatars grow like mushrooms."

When one considers the centrality of the Avatar belief in Hindu theology, the ultimate question becomes clear: Isn't something a bit shaky?

Further complicating Hinduism is its doctrine of reincarnation. Many Hindu gurus try to portray their religion as a way-of-life which stresses quiet meditation and inner peace over all else. Such a presentation is simply not true. The concept of reincarnation is an intrinsic part of the Hindu faith. According to the *Bhagavad-Gita*, the body is finite while the soul is everlasting; the eternity of the soul, however, is not defined in terms of a life-after-death but in terms of an endless series of rebirths. In Chinmoy's words: "Each human incarnation is but a brief span and it can never determine the end of the soul's eternal journey. None can achieve perfection in one life. Everyone must needs go through hundreds of thousands of incarnations until he attains Spiritual Perfection."[22]

And how does one, during the course of his "hundreds of thousands of incarnations," finally reach "spiritual perfection"? Chinmoy's answer is predictable enough. One should "come into contact with an Avatar and remain under his guidance. To have an Avatar as one's guru is to find a safe harbor for one's life boat."[23] Ultimately, if one is to succeed in finding Truth, if one is to reach perfection, he must seek out and learn from an Avatar.

Fortunately, for those individuals who are seeking bliss, there is an Avatar alive in this very generation. According to his disciples, he has scaled such extraordinary heights that it could not be otherwise. In one day, he composed 843 poems, they say. On another day, he produced 16,000 paintings. This Avatar, according to those of his disciples with whom we have spoken, is none other than Sri Chinmoy! He "embodies the realization of God and unity with God," they exult. Indeed, one might almost note that "a flood-tide of enthusiasm sweeps over them when they speak about their Guru."

And what does Sri Chinmoy teach? For one thing, he

preaches the eternal importance of India's "caste system." There are four castes: Brahmin (Priest), Kshatriya (Warrior), Vaishya (Agriculturist), and Sudra (Laborer). Having tailored his Hinduism to the American scene—recall, for example, his readiness to ascribe Avatar status to Jesus, albeit on a plane lower than that of Buddha—Chinmoy does not speak of "the untouchables." It seems as though mainstream American society is not yet ready for the notion that an entire class of human beings, from the moment of birth, pollute all people they touch. As an example of the awesome power of the sacred caste system—which originates in the Vedic writings, where "the Brahmin is the mouth of Purusha, the Supreme personified; Kshatriya is Purusha's two arms; Vaishya his two thighs; Sudra, his two feet"[24]—Chinmoy notes the Hindu legend that Karna (a member of the Sudra caste) was killed in the Kurukshetra War because he sought to learn archery, a subject taught only to those born as Kshatriyas.

On the other hand, Chinmoy notes that it is praiseworthy for an authentic Kshatriya to do battle. In fact, the act of war is a Kshatriya's ultimate "duty." In the *Bhagavad-Gita*, Lord Krishna tells Arjuna the Kshatriya that he must fight, even if it means killing members of his family. There is nothing more holy that Arjuna can be expected to do in light of the caste into which he was born. Arjuna takes Krishna's advice and enters the conflict. Krishna joins Arjuna as his charioteer but vows that he will not participate in the bloodshed itself. Nevertheless, Krishna "had to break his promise"[25] on two occasions during the conflict. "Here we learn," says Chinmoy, "that the Guru, the Master, can at any moment break his own promise in order to help, to save, in order to win a victory for the disciple."[26] (By espousing such a moral structure, Chinmoy has undoubtedly endeared himself to the many United Nations delegates and staffers who attend his meditation sessions.)

On another occasion, Krishna out-muscled Indra, the God of Rain. According to the legend cited by Chinmoy, Krishna became upset during his childhood years by his parents' regular practice of worshipping the Rain God. The Boy Avatar felt it would be more appropriate for them to pray to the hill on which their cattle grazed. They concurred and changed gods, a matter which angered Indra quite a bit. Furious that he had been rejected, Indra unleashed a seven-day rain torrent. Unfazed by all this, eleven-year-old Krishna simply raised the hill with one of his fingers and utilized it as a massive umbrella, protecting his family from the week-long flood. Lord Indra, aware that he had been outsmarted, conceded defeat to Krishna.

Chinmoy tells other Krishna myths as well, all of which he sincerely believes. When he finally begins discussing the importance of meditation, he has already presented a full-scale theology. According to Hindu thought, meditation—sitting for long hours, contemplating a one-syllable sound known as a "mantra"—is the ultimate path one must follow if he hopes to actually achieve true unity with God. Chinmoy is ostensibly one of the more learned meditators, having attained "complete and inseparable oneness with God" according to the jacket description of one of his books. What is his secret? How did he do it? According to the guru: "AUM is the mystical symbol supreme. AUM is the real name of God. In the cosmic manifestation is AUM. Beyond the manifestation, furthest beyond is AUM . . . We have to chant AUM . . ."[27]

There is one final aspect regarding Sri Chinmoy's Hinduism worth noting. "They say in the West, food has very little to do with faith. In India, the link between food and faith is almost inseparable. Our Upanishadic Seers cried out . . .'Food is the Brahman,' " Chinmoy explains. The best class of Hindus eat fresh, pure, soothing foods, while the lowest of individuals consume stale, tasteless, impure filthy comestibles. Such dietary concerns are not simply a matter of "common sense"; they constitute nothing less than purposeful compliance with the dictates of "Holy Writ."

Sri Chinmoy's theology, then, is doubly instructive: it tells us not only how far the young Jew opting for Hinduism has gone in the course of his desperate search for spirituality, but also how far his community has strayed by never sharing with him the knowledge that he could have satisfied his yearnings by digging for roots in his own socio-theological backyard. His parents feared that "he would be too intelligent for all the Bible nonsense"; yet his intense intelligence—nurtured by an upbringing devoid of God, the bar-mitzva smörgasbord notwithstanding—led him to Chinmoy's Lord Krishna. The principal of his "Reform" Talmud Torah did not have the *chutzpa* to teach him that the entire nation of Israel, in the millions, stood at Mount Sinai and beheld Divine Revelation. So he looked elsewhere for a theology whose god, Lord Krishna, "revealed himself" to one man, Arjuna, according to the testimony of one man. His rabbi never expected him to live up to the laws of *kashrut*—surely no bright, young boy would see the sense in abstaining from pork in the post-trichinosis millennium—so he embraced a theology which virtually deifies cows. In the modern generation of "fun, fun, fun," no one was so foolish as to suggest that he sit, sit, sit for a few years in a yeshiva and meditate for hours on the precious words of the Torah. So, off he raced to Chinmoy, where he could meditate for the rest of his life on the word "AUM." In his youth, the "Reform Prayer Book" he saw on *Kol Nidrey* evening was expunged of references to Israel as the Chosen Nation of God and of expressions of the eternity of the soul. So he chose to ride the ferry conducted by the Boatman of "India's unparalleled history and her unrivaled spirituality," and to prepare himself for an improved existence in his "next incarnation."

No one ever expected him to study the Torah in Hebrew, but he now studies the *Bhagavad-Gita* in Sanskrit. His rabbi was always too busy to sit with him—after all, there were so many obligations to the community that the very act of delivering the three-minute invocation at Talmud Torah "confirmation exercises" was a powerful display of the rabbi's commitment to "our Jewish young people." Today, Sri Chinmoy literally sits with him—on the floor. His "rabbi" wrote in the congregational bulletin that the Book of Esther was a lovely tale, albeit apocryphal, so today he finds Divine realism in accounts of the face-off between eleven-year-old Lord Krishna and Lord Indra instead.

The point we must discern from an empirical study of young Jews who have joined Hindu gurus like Sri Chinmoy and Maharaj Ji is that God gave the Jewish nation His Torah not to entertain but to satisfy, not to restrict but to nourish. There is an innate passion which drives young Jews to "know themselves," to understand the meaning of the world, to find their roots in that world's development. Although Alex Haley sparked Italians, Poles, and countless other groups into seeking out their histories, as the subject matter of his study of "Roots" captivated an entire country, he did not stimulate a response in those who were raised in an environment imbued with the spirit of authentic Judaism. *Our* Book of Roots was compiled by God, and He presented an autographed copy to the Jewish nation when every man, woman, and child assembled before Him at Mount Sinai. We cannot find fault in the people of India who look to the *Bhagavad-Gita* for roots and meaning. What alternative choice have they? The nation of India did not receive the Torah. Indeed, the very basis of the *Bhagavad-Gita* is so structurally weak that we can only sympathize with a people whose "Bible" consists of a mythology attested to by only one man—the author—who is supposedly still alive today somewhere in the Himalayas (although no one is certain as to where he can be found meditating).

More significantly, we cannot find real fault in those young Jews who rejected their sacred and awe-inspiring heritage for the emptiness of a theology which breeds Avatars like mushrooms and which accords cows the sort of respect denied to humans born into the wrong caste. What choice did these young Jews have? What sort of Judaism were they presented with? What Jewish values did they ever learn? What Jewish text were they ever taught? What real Jewish pride were they ever given? No, the fault for leaving the Jewish fold is not theirs.

If culpability is to be determined, it must be traced back to its origin. Those who allowed young Jewish souls to starve and thirst for all the years from childhood through adolescence, those who denied young Jews the authentic education they deserved and who foisted on them instead Talmud Torah systems whose curricula were carefully structured to avoid the inculcation of either Talmud or Torah—those are the ones who must probe their consciences to divine the true source of that sense of alienation which underlies the defections from Judaism which have so stigmatized my generation.

MAHARISHI MAHESH YOGI AND TRANSCENDENTAL MEDITATION

Yet another influential Hindu guru—better known than Chinmoy though not nearly as outrageous as Maharaj Ji—is Maharishi Mahesh Yogi. Yogi became famous in the late 1960s when, after a period of initial failure, he finally attracted a bona fide representative of the youth counter-culture, George Harrison. Harrison brought along his fellow Beatles, who retreated to Wales where they learned Yogi's answers to the mysteries of life. Inasmuch as the Beatles determined what was "in" and what was "out," it was not long before Mia Farrow, Shirley MacLaine, and the Rolling Stones were sitting at Yogi's enlightened feet. In no time, the guru was claiming 300,000 followers world-wide, a figure which not only augured well for the future prospects of world peace but which also enabled him to establish a million-dollar center in India and to purchase a Mercedes limousine.

To Yogi, the essence of life is "Transcendental Meditation" (or "TM"), a practice which requires nothing more than fifteen minutes in the morning and fifteen minutes in the evening. In return for faithfully practicing TM every day, a person is promised not only "bliss-consciousness" but also a better reincarnation in his next life. According to the guru, Lord Krishna guarantees it. The basic starting point for the Maharishi is the *Bhagavad-Gita*, a book which he describes as "the encyclopedia of life." By following the *Gita*'s teachings, all mankind will experience peace and love, Yogi promises.

Of course, there are a few matters to be resolved before total peace envelops the entire universe. For example, what are we to do with all those Kshatriyas whose highest duty to Krishna is to go to war? The guru strongly defends the caste system: "Purity of blood is at the basis of long life for a family and a society . . . The intermixing of castes . . . has the direct result of upsetting the social equilibrium."[28]

And, if purity is to be maintained, it is for the purpose of preserving each caste for its Higher Province, for its "allotted duty":

> "Allotted duty" is that which it is natural for one to do, that for which one was born . . . An important aspect of natural duty is that it is imperative for a man; if he does not perform his allotted duty, he will be engaging in actions which lie outside the path of his own evolution . . .
>
> A man's duty is apparent by virtue of his birth in a particular family. Thus, Arjuna is born a Kshatriya and it is natural for him to fight.[29]

In the case of a Kshatriya, it is not only "natural" for him to fight but *essential* that he devote himself to war:

> The Lord's purpose is to convince Arjuna that, from the point of view of his duty, the only worthwhile course is to shake off his reluctance to fight and face up to the action for which he is born . . . He wants to bring home to Arjuna that to him, born a Kshatriya, fighting is natural; it is his normal duty in life . . .
>
> What will happen if Arjuna does not participate in the battle?
>
> . . . To abstain from fighting . . . would bring loss of fame and would plainly be sinful . . . The Lord says to Arjuna: You should realize that, whether you die on the battlefield or whether you survive, you stand to gain because fighting is in accordance with the natural course of your evolution.[30]

There is, of course, more to the Hindu thought of Maharishi Mahesh Yogi than the caste system and the obedient acceptance of the notion that the soul endlessly reincarnates itself from one form of being into another. Perhaps the most famous aspect of his theology is the practice of TM. As Yogi understands the *Gita*, a good Hindu should not overly deny himself the pleasures of the world. Total austerity—a theological imperative advanced by many Indian gurus—is inappropriate, in Yogi's opinion. Rather, a person should allow himself the inevitable participation in the "relative/experiential domain" while balancing that involvement with twice-daily transcendental meditation exercises. The purpose of TM is to "unite the heart (devotion) with the mind (knowledge) in order to achieve transcendental consciousness and other-worldly bliss." By performing this feat, one elevates the mind and establishes it in the Self; he leaves the sphere of relativity and enters the realm of Absolute Being. By departing from the duality of experiential existence, one can proceed on the path leading to Union with God through the Knowing of Self.

The value of all this is that the mind which has attained the state of Ultimate Bliss will remain content, even after it returns to the field of activity from that of transcendence. In this religious framework defined by Krishna as "Karma Yoga" according to the *Bhagavad-Gita*, one can function effectively in the society around him. Thus, Yogi lauds his approach by noting its advantages over the teachings of other Hindu gurus whose "wrong interpretations" of the *Gita* have led to an "increase in dullness and inefficiency, particularly in the lives of young people in India."[31] Moreover, by meditating as the Maharishi prescribes, one clears away all sins: "The Brahmabindu Upanishad declares that a huge mountain of sins extending for miles is destroyed by Union brought about through transcendental meditation, without which there is no way out."[32]

Because Yogi ascribes such *religious* significance to TM—indeed, he cites the instructions of "Lord Krishna" in defense of his espousal of such meditation—the act must be seen in its true light: part-and-parcel of a Hindu cult, a ritual which bears no less weight in Yogi's theology than does the act of baptism in Christianity. Transcendental meditation, when performed exactly as Yogi prescribes, is yet another step away from Judaism. The young Jew who seeks out Maharishi Mahesh Yogi for an understanding of the "True Path of God" is turning his back on the road offered by Judaism.

But does that young Jew know he is rejecting the Jewish avenue to God? Does that Jew know that there in fact does exist such a highway? Maharishi offers something sensible: a method which makes one aware that he has a Self (Soul) and a mind—and an understanding that both are of far greater spiritual significance than the physical cravings, desires, and lusts which seem to actuate so much of modern society's day-to-day undertakings. He does not advocate an extreme renunciation of the world, just a sensible limit on the leeway to be accorded the senses.

One can easily perceive why such a religious venture would attract enthusiastic converts, especially like those fleeing from the materialistic emptiness of the bastions of Jewish assimilation in America. Raised without religion, they will naturally evince curiosity about the strange cults of India which promise "union with God" and "personal knowledge of God." They have seen the separation of devotion and knowledge, of heart and mind in American Judaism. The parental mind teaches that God is a myth, that the Bible is old-fashioned ("even *zeydeh* changed when he came to America"), that the observant Jews are "hypocrites" and "fanatics" while the assimilated ones are "enlightened," that the dietary laws are archaic, and that the whole notion of a Jewish education is meaningless except for its use in transmitting a fifteen-verse *haftora* over the course of four years. That is the *mind* young Jews see in their parents' heads.

But the Jewish *heart* is different. For some reason, the same parent who does not believe in God insists on attending *Kol Nidrey* services on Yom Kippur. The same parent who ridicules the Bible expects the son to learn a *haftora*. The same parent who derides the parochialism of the Orthodox and who breathes liberalism and universalism for two decades suddenly goes crazy when the young Jewish woman raised with such values brings home a non-Jewish beau or when the son introduces the family to the girl-friend he got to know while munching on a batch of "Alice B. Toklas Brownies."

My generation was raised according to the dictates of the assimilated Jewish mind, while it was endlessly baffled by the irrational deviations of those who yet bore within their breast Jewish hearts. Was the mind right, or was the heart right? If the mind devoid of authentic Jewish values was right—why the bar mitzva, why the Catskills, why the bagels and the chicken soup and the Passover chopped liver, why the Talmud Torah education, why the Jan Peerce records? If the heart which was so much closer to tradition was right—why *such* a bar mitzva, why *such* hotels, why *such* a Passover (without even a *seder!*), why *such* an "education"? We beheld a parental generation whose hearts and minds were out of touch with each other; now we behold gurus from India who assure us that they have brought with them the key to uniting these two lifelines. Can we be blamed for seeking to "know ourselves" and to find out who we are?

Maharishi Mahesh Yogi says he knows the secret. It was transmitted to him by His Divinity Swami Brahmananda Saraswati Jagadguru Bhagwan Shankaracharya of Jyotir Math (also known as "Guru Deva"). This holy swami—to whose lotus feet Yogi dedicated one of his books—taught him that mind and heart could be united by transcendental meditation. To a youth alienated from Judaism, and unacquainted with those studies which have stripped Yogi bare, TM can seem reasonable.

Young Jews who have joined the Maharishi are not fleeing from reason; they are fleeing from a society which so sanctified science and knowledge and reason that it forgot that other aspects of life must exist alongside the dictates of the mind. Like the Beatles, young Jews will eventually find that Yogi cannot satisfy their needs either, because TM leads nowhere. In an aphorism presented to a group of students at Columbia University in 1975, Rabbi Meir Kahane commented, "Ultimately, those searching for the Creator of the Universe will find that the 'spirit which is within man' is not God but heartburn."

TM is one more manifestation of the desperate extent to

which young Jews will go in the hope of finding something "real" and "spiritually rewarding." The whole mystery which Yogi brought with him is really quite simple. The *Bhagavad-Gita* instructs the individual in search of God to sit down. He should be in a subdued state, surrounded by a clean environment, and should sit in a seat which is neither very high nor very low. The reason that he must sit—rather than recline or stand—is that, according to the *Gita*, Lord Krishna said he must sit. Expounding on this, the Maharishi adds: "The first point the Lord wants to make clear is that meditation should be performed in the sitting position and not lying down or standing."[33]

Moreover, Krishna requires that the neck and head be upright and that the eyes gaze on the front of the nose.[34] Yogi insists that there is no need to sit in the standard "lotus" position; all that is necessary is to sit in a quiet, comfortable posture. At this point, the potential convert—all set and ready to meditate—receives the special, hidden, mysterious key to success for which he is paying Maharishi Mahesh Yogi a week's salary. It is something he cannot find in any book in the entire world—no, not even in the *Bhagavad-Gita*.

It is his own, personally tailored *mantra*.

The Maharishi, or one of his specially trained assistants, looks over the newcomer very carefully in an effort to determine which mantra will lead him on the lane to eternal bliss. The mantra—a one-syllable sound, generally consisting of no more than two or three letters—is secretly presented to the new devotee who must *never ever* reveal his secret mantra to anyone else . . . or—egads!—it will never work for him again. While skeptics believe that Yogi has fewer than a dozen "secret mantras" which he doles out to his 300,000 followers, true adherents insist that the mantra must be specially tailored for them. Why else would he charge individuals like the Beatles and others a week's salary for his special services?

Once a new devotee receives his mantra, he need simply meditate on it twice every day, fifteen minutes in the morning and fifteen minutes in the early evening. That is all it takes to achieve inner harmony forever, transcendental consciousness, and bliss. Nothing else is expected because nothing else is necessary. According to the *Bhagavad-Gita's* account, Lord Krishna assured Arjuna that any individual who properly meditates will earn a better reincarnation in his next life; moreover, any true Hindu who meditates properly for many consecutive lives may one day merit the great honor of being reborn as a swami himself.

There is no ethical or moral structure to Yogi's theology. A person can commit the gravest of deeds but still attain the highest goals conceivable if he meditates nicely. Yogi is unconcerned with *karma* (deeds); the only karma which worries him is that regarding the appropriate form of meditation. If one learns the route to transcendental consciousness, he need not perform good deeds. Of course, he can better his lot if he performs *yagya* (rituals), but TM is the essence. In fact, TM even affects the success of the performance of yagya. One time-honored yagya form consists of worshipping the many Hindu gods. Yogi explains that the best way to worship a Hindu god is by "experiencing" his or her name in the subtlest states, until the mind transcends that subtlest state and reaches "bliss consciousness."[35] Such an action, not surprisingly, will earn the meditator that god's greatest blessing.[36] Other forms of yagya include: performing Vedic sacrificial rituals, subjecting the body to periods of heat, cold, and other "purifying" experiences; and doing certain special breathing exercises.

Maharishi Mahesh Yogi's religion of transcendental meditation, then, is but one more cult which provides values foreign to those of Judaism but which offers hope to those young Jews who were raised in homes bereft of authentic Jewish spirituality. For those who never saw a father put on *tefillin* in the morning—an action which constitutes the ultimate affirmation of the intrinsic bond between the heart and the mind—and who never learned the awe-inspiring *Shema Yisrael* which has served our people for thousands of years as an indescribably rich base for twice-daily (once in the morning, once in the evening) other-worldly meditation, it cannot be sur-

prising that Yogi's yoga presents an exciting alternative to
the perfunctory pursuit of "pleasure" which so typifies middle-
and upper-class Jewish life. Raised in an environment where
everyone was so busy achieving "success" that there was never
any time in the morning or evening to consider the deeper
meaning of existence, a young person is bound to emerge
alienated. Surely, he concurs, one should be able to take out at
least fifteen minutes twice a day in order to maintain a sensible
perspective of his role in the world. If one cannot find the time
for half an hour of introspection daily, then his existence
—successful though it be—cannot really be called "living."

Judaism has always recognized the need for a person to
come to daily terms with his innermost self. Through morning
prayer, he carefully examines himself before beginning his
physical day. He meditates on the world, on his role in that
world. He acknowledges his debt to his Creator and expresses
devotion. He binds his heart and mind together with *tefillin*,
and he scales the greatest spiritual heights as he intones:
"*Shema Yisrael . . .*" After his prayers, he enters the world that
much more steady in his own sense of being. Again he will take
time from his materialistic day—once in the afternoon and
later in the evening—to search himself, to express devotion, to
meditate. Time will be set aside to study a spiritually
rewarding authentic Jewish text—the Torah—and he will
luxuriate in its ethereal splendor, sublimely relaxing his mind
even as he develops its powers. The sacred commandments,
mitzvot, will also surround him during the day, reminding him
that he is a spiritual being. Authentic Judaism allows the
individual to enjoy this world's pleasures by providing for
all human needs: spiritual and physical. It provides an opportunity for the Jew to participate in the "relativistic,
experiential" world of action, and it allows him to revel in a
state of other-worldly bliss. It unites the heart with the mind,
and it focuses their unified powers on both planes of reality.
Without suppressing natural physical needs, it helps define the
supremacy of the states of reason and understanding over those
of craving and lust.

The laws God gave the Jewish people were meant to direct His nation towards conducting their lives in a manner which would be characterized neither as austere nor as hedonistic but as human. If Hindu gurus have succeeded in attracting to their ranks young refugees from America's assimilated Jewish communities, they have done so not because they have discovered a secret path to fulfillment which Judaism lacked but because they offer an artificial imitation to young Jews who have never tasted the product in its natural, organic form.

BUDDHISM

Although the Hindu gurus, by virtue of their respective charismatic appeals, pose an especially serious threat to young Jews seeking a meaningful alternative to that neo-Olympic competition — cynically termed the "rat race" — which so omnipotently drives everyone around them, there are other Eastern religions attracting alienated seekers as well. Of them all, Buddhism stands out as the most exotic.

Buddhism came into being approximately five centuries before the commencement of the common era. Siddhartha Gautama, a young man depressed over the prospect of old age, embarked on a search for the meaning of life. Near the Neranjara River, he found an ascetic order. He joined their ranks and, for the next six years, underwent mortifications, abstained from food, and practiced difficult breathing exercises. Despite all the self-inflicted pains and sorrows, he remained unsatisfied, so he decided to carry his search elsewhere.

Siddhartha began meditating in isolation. He considered the nature of birth, death, happiness, sorrow, health, sickness, pleasure, and pain. At the age of thirty-five, he suddenly realized that all of existence is sorrowful, that all of life is painful; for arriving at this conclusion, he became known as the "Buddha" or "Enlightened One." For the next forty-five years, he traveled everywhere his legs would take him to spread the knowledge he had conceived: All life is sorrowful; there is no such thing as happiness.

Somehow, Siddhartha also discovered that all beings undergo an endless series of reincarnations. Convinced that he himself had lived through many previous lives, he preached that not only is one's present life bereft of any pleasure and full of anguish but so, too, will all his future lives be (as, in fact, were all his previous existences). Lest one come to the hasty conclusion that this young fellow was a pessimist, it must be noted that he proposed to mankind the ultimate path to happiness: complete extermination. According to Gautama, since every moment of being is comprised of suffering, there can be no better moment than the one in which man extinguishes himself. As the Enlightened One perceived things, the absence of sorrow would be the ultimate experience of pleasure. Therefore, he proposed that all men spend the rest of their lives attempting to exterminate themselves. What greater happiness could anyone ever hope for?

Siddhartha denied the existence of God. He also denied the existence of a soul. What, then, could account for the reincarnation factor of which he was so firmly convinced? If his "previous existence" lacked a soul, what continued into his newer body form? Something like a soul, only different. When a being dies, according to Gautama, a spirit is sent to a newly born being. That spirit acts like a billiard ball hitting a second one: while it does not trade places, it does give it a determined push. Hence, one could be reincarnated without either body or soul being transferred from life to life.

The Enlightened One brought his new philosophy to his old group of ascetics. They joined him in proclaiming to all of humanity the sorrow of life. Bewailing their countless previous existences—all of which they now realized had been marked by nothing but pain, grief, and sorrow—they, too, sought self-extermination. Unfortunately, even suicide would not bring them the happiness they desired because such an action would only lead to a new incarnation and more pain.

As Siddhartha presented his philosophy, it became apparent that the only way a person could ever hope to exterminate himself would be through the rigid controlling of all his natural impulses. Desires would have to be suppressed. Every last physical and emotional need—thirst, hunger, warmth, love — would have to be destroyed. Only when a man would totally annul his very final ambition, want, and desideratum would he be assured of a chance to achieve complete annihilation of his spirit at the time of his death. Upon reaching *nirvana* — the total extermination of the spirit remaining after death—there would be nothing left. To Siddhartha, such a goal was to become the ultimate purpose of life. He had found the meaning he sought.

Eventually, Gautama's time for nirvana came. Surrounded by his assemblage of ascetics, he told them to remember his teachings. There would be no value in their venerating him, he explained, since he wouldn't be around to know the difference. Certain he had achieved his long-sought goal, Siddhartha expired. The monks he left behind redacted his many sermons during the course of three monastic councils convened after his death. Of special interest was the second of the councils which screened all utterances and doctrines which had been attributed to Gautama from the period of his "enlightenment" to the time of his passing. Insisting that the "Buddha's knowledge was conceived all at once—when he was thirty-five years old—and that the perfection of his intellect could not have been improved during his remaining forty-five years, this monastic group harmonized all the statements and thoughts he had uttered during his nearly five decades of "Buddhahood" so that future students of Gautama's words would assume that, even while he was in his early years, he was capable of reflecting on life with the knowledge-experience of an octogenarian. Thus even his most orthodox followers attributed a supernatural level of acumen to the deceased teacher who had spurned deification. Over the course of time, the orthodox Buddhists—known, generally, as Hinayanans—would be supplanted by even more imaginative adherents, the Mahayanans.

Hinayana Buddhism was established on the principle that all life is suffering. Everything is tormenting, and only complete self-decimation brings on liberation from the travails of continued, endless existence. True, a life conducted in a pious manner might pay off in terms of a better reincarnation next time around; nevertheless, the ultimate agony engendered by *samsara* (the perpetual cycle of rebirths) is not thereby abated. Even to be reincarnated in a sphere of gods would be but another miserable existence, still short of the goal of self-extinction. Building up "good karma" (a series of spiritual merits accrued through the regular performance of good deeds) would be the aim of a weak person, hoping to use his current life to launch himself onto a higher spiritual plane in his next incarnation. An individual capable of realizing nirvana in his present existence, however, would be foolish to waste his life trying to develop good karma—an act which in itself would indicate the presence of ambition and desire—when he could, instead, hope to permanently extinguish himself.

When one finally earns a high-level rebirth, he must make the most of his unique opportunity to self-destruct. He must obliterate all cravings and desires by developing the "Right View." Such a perspective entails cognition that all is impermanent, all is suffering, and all is ugly. Thus, Buddhism elevates the notion of self-discipline to its maximum implications. Not only are Hinayanans expected to control "immoral lusts" but they must even repress normal impulses; it, therefore, comes as little surprise to find so many Buddhist monks practicing a mode of austerity which truly appears to border on masochism.

Hinayana thought asserts that each person must achieve extinction on his own. Neither prayer nor belief in celestial beings will bring any assistance to the individual seeking nirvana. (Indeed, there is no one for the aspiring Buddhist to worship. Siddhartha succeeded, theoretically, in exterminating himself.)

Of course, once one achieves nirvana-after-death, he must give up all his knowledge and teachings, as his being disintegrates and self-destructs. "Perfect extinction" means just that—nothing survives. There is no soul to live on; there is no Paradise or World to Come. In short, Hinayana Buddhism defines nirvana as: ". . . the sphere where there is neither earth nor water nor fire nor air nor . . . non-perception or perception; neither this world nor a world yonder nor both . . . This is the end of suffering."[37]

The other, more fanciful branch of Buddhist thought is that of Mahayana. It differs sharply from Hinayana Buddhism in certain key ways. While Hinayana promotes a one-way path leading to the ultimate egress, Mahayana slows down the race to nirvana by injecting the alternative half-way goal of Bodhisattvahood. According to this fanciful addition to traditional Buddhist thought, it is maintained that a person about to achieve perfect extinction upon death may defer the moment of nirvana in order to continue in an other-worldly existence as a "Bodhisattva," who will use all the powers at his ethereal disposal to help other, less fortunate people reach the "liberation" as well. He will miraculously intervene in worldly affairs from his celestial abode on behalf of any Mahayana Buddhist who invokes his name. In fact, he will submerge his spirit into the pits of hell, if need be, to assist a loyal suppliant.

Clearly, Mahayana Buddhists were not satisfied with the final charge of Gautama, who pleaded that his followers live by his teachings and not by extra-worldly spirits. If he were to return to see Mahayana practice, he would not recognize the system as his own.

According to Mahayanans, for example, the task of achieving a better reincarnation through the accumulation of good karma need not devolve on the individual himself. Rather, the proper faith in the right Bodhisattvas can do the job equally effectively. A Bodhisattva will transfer all his personally achieved "good karma" to any worshipper in need.

Thus, while Hinayana maintains that good karma is non-transferable and that each person must attain his own nirvana, Mahayana differs totally. If the former requires immense amounts of faith, then what can be said of the latter? Gautama himself opposed the worship of deceased beings, as he maintained that they either dissolve or reincarnate.

But Mahayana Buddhism is too immersed in its richly

evocative scheme to be deterred. Physically deceased Buddhas—"as numerous as grains of sand on the banks of the Ganges"[38]—are busy answering prayers; although they cannot be perceived, they can be spiritually "experienced." One Bodhisattva, the legendary Avalokitesvara, is believed to be ready to enter the gates of perdition in order to help others. More picturesque are the depictions of Vajrapani who bears a thunderbolt scepter. Of course, these saints do not compare with the Transcendent Buddhas like Amitabha, who took upon himself forty-six vows to lead all his followers into a paradise which he would create upon his death. (It is supposed that he kept his word.) Other Transcendent Buddhas are believed to rule over a wide network of other paradises as well. All one need do is call on the Bodhisattva or Transcendent Buddha desired.

It is impossible to avoid comparing Mahayana Buddhism with many forms of modern-day Christianity. The notion of vicarious atonement is present in both. While a Christian looks to Jesus' death for purification from "original sin" and for salvation, the Mahayana Buddhist invokes the name of a Bodhisattva in order to receive karmic credit. Even the most wicked of people may turn to Amitabha for good karma; he will never refuse a request.[39] The salvation-through-faith motif marks both systems. Likewise, the patron-saint factor runs parallel in the two theologies. While a Mahayanan will turn to Avalokitesvara for assistance during a dangerous trip in a desert or at sea, a Catholic will look to Saint Christopher for similar protection. Yet another similarity is evident in these two religions' attitudes towards relic worship. Mahayanans believe they can earn deliverance by revering holy relics, by creating Buddha images, and by offering flowers or incense to the various Transcendent Buddhas. The adoration and virtual worship of relics in certain branches of Christianity (such as Catholicism) is not different.

Of course, all roads lead to nirvana in Mahayana Buddhism. The aspiration to be reincarnated in a Transcendent Buddha's paradise is but a partial goal. The ultimate target is to attain "Enlightenment" and learn the path to self-extinction.

Within Mahayana, there are denominations which differ from each other in application. One form, Yogacara, contends that everything is "Mind" only and that it is essential for the individual seeking liberation to come to this realization. A far more publicized branch of Mahayana—and one which attracted many alienated youths during the 1950s and 1960s—is that of Zen Buddhism. Zen is so mystical that it is irrational—and proudly so. Founded in China in the sixth century by an Indian monk, it utterly rejects "logic" and "rationality." Contending that there are hidden universal truths which the intellect can never comprehend, Zen Buddhism seeks to develop the inner faculties to their fullest in order to learn the answers to these mysteries which transcend the realm of established reason. The process of amplifying the intuitive resources is conducted through meditation. An aspiring Zen Buddhist considers one of the specially formulated *koans* (irrational riddles), and he meditates on it for years, if necessary. (The nature of one such koan—"What is the sound produced by one hand clapping?"—illustrates why the meditation period can extend for such a long span.)

The meditation process, however, is not the final goal; it merely serves as a link to the ultimate self realization, known as *satori*. Satori—an experience which Zen masters claim cannot be explained because of its intrinsically personal nature—is the moment of "enlightenment." It comes in a "flash," changes a person's entire understanding of the world, and can never be described. In the irrational world of Zen, satori is the illogical peak. It is the "revelation of truth," the "inner enlightenment," and the essence of Zen. Only after searching deeply into the true nature of one's inner being can satori be achieved. Satori cannot be reached through standard "book knowledge." Because Zen rejects all intellectualism and reason, it maintains that satori emanates from a wellspring of inner cognition. Zen opposes the performance of rituals; it is unconcerned with worldly awareness. To attain satori, one must call upon a faculty "higher than the intellect." One must look into his very being. If he does, and if he patiently meditates on an ap-

propriate koan, he will attain the "flash of enlightenment."
Consider this awe-inspiring example:

> A monk asked Joshu to be instructed in Zen. Said the
> master, "Have you had your breakfast or not?"
> "Yes, master, I have," answered the monk.
> "If so, have your dishes washed," was an immediate
> response which, it is said, at once opened the monk's
> mind to the truth of Zen.[40]

Imagine, if you will, the depth of illumination experienced by
this monk! A good thing it was for him that paper plates had
not yet been invented. . . .

Yet another moving moment in the annals of Zen was the
instant that Kyogen, one of Hyakujo's very best disciples, was
struck by the bolt of satori. Residing in a hut in Nan-Yang, he
was innocently doing his day's chores. While weeding and
sweeping the area outside his domicile, he mindlessly brushed
away a rock, and it struck a bamboo. The sound produced by
this historic collision raised Kyogen's mind to satori. He was
never the same again. (Neither was the bamboo.)

As many other such examples would indicate, Zen Buddhism is not a model of logic. It is, at best, irrational and
paradoxical. According to many other observers, it is either
foolish or an outright hoax. It proudly condemns reason and
postures itself on a plane above it. It praises the moment of
satori but makes no effort to describe it. Zen masters, when
requested to define this ultimate experience, will not do so. In
one recorded case, a master responded to such an inquiry by
kicking a ball. On another occasion, replying to a similar
question, a master slapped a monk in the face. (When the monk
later reached his own satori, he returned to the master and
slapped the venerable sage in *his* face!)

It is not surprising that Zen succeeded in attracting
beatnicks of the 1950s—among whom there were too many
Jews—and that it successfully took root in heteroclite San
Francisco. That most curious of poets, Allen Ginsberg, gave
Zen a big push, helping do for it what Rennie Davis did for

Maharaj Ji and what the Beatles did for Maharishi Mahesh Yogi. The local interest stimulated the construction of a $300,000 Zen monastery just south of the world of Haight-Ashbury, not a bad achievement for a cult which adheres to the basic tenet that "all life is suffering and pain."

In the end, then, Zen is a strange version of a strange way of life. Although expressing its rejection of rituals, Zen elevates the act of meditating on koans to a holy rite itself. It plays the game of esoterics—so effective an approach in attracting young Jews searching for the inner meaning to a life which is ostensibly without purpose. It says, "We can't explain what Zen is like, man. First, you gotta join up and give it a chance. You'll see. It'll blow your mind." It sounds like the mystical yellow-brick-road to inner truth. If that sounds ridiculous, it is not beyond the realm of possibility in the mind of the young Jew who was led by the people he trusted up a rainbow of suburban temples, Sunday schools, and *haftorot*. When he reached the Day of Reckoning—the bar mitzva—he found that the leprechaun (charitably described by his parents as a "rabbi") had left him with a pot-of-gold which was spiritually empty. If the Zen monastery will not offer him more than did the suburban temple, it will not offer him less.

We dare not overlook the ironies underlying the proclivity of certain young Jews to join Zen monasteries. For, if Bodhidharma—the Indian monk who founded Zen in the sixth century—was last seen meandering around China with a sandal on his head, at least he had something on his head! The young Jew, raised in the midst of a highly intellectual, perfectly rational, and technologically reasoned society, nevertheless was deprived of spirituality. He innately understood that there are mysteries in this universe which defy the impeccable scrutiny of the most professionally programmed computer. He realized that, despite all the logic he had been fed by his "enlightened" Jewish parents, he still lacked the deeper, hidden understanding. He wanted to probe for the mysteries which the Zen masters, at least, acknowledged were there.

Buddhism is so antithetical to authentic Judaism that it

holds no attraction for a person raised in the light of Jewish
tradition. We look upon the world as a beautiful, wondrous
creation of God. We marvel in the bright sun, in its glow and its
warmth. We feel the cool breeze. We smell the naturally fresh
and sweet fragrances of the country air. We look at flowers and
see grass and countless varieties of trees. We taste the refreshing fruits and mouth-watering vegetables produced by
God's earth. We participate in the world, and we find in it not
only harmony but true beauty. How different from the
Buddhist contention that all life is suffering and misery!

The roots of Buddhism are to be found in the nature of
Gautama's search. He spent six years tormenting himself with
a group of ascetics before seeking the ultimate "enlightenment." What kind of world view could he have been expected to
emerge with? How loathsome to Jewish thought is his contention that every moment is painful and that self-extinction is the
ultimate "liberation"! Siddhartha elevated the practice of
pessimism to a fine art, and his disciples followed suit. One of
the key exponents of Zen had this to say, in describing the
misery of life: "Teething is more or less a painful process.
Puberty is usually accompanied by a mental as well as a
physical disturbance . . ."[41]

We Jews call that "physical disturbance" the process of
"maturation." Is there truly not one positive aspect to be found
in the puberty "disturbance"? Is there nothing to be gained by
such growth? Does not puberty lead to the realization of some of
the most pleasurable aspects of life? And what of teething? Is
there nothing but sorrow, pain, and misery in having teeth? Do
not teeth help make food more enjoyable? Don't they enhance
facial beauty and assist in the speech process? Is there nothing
to be said for teething?

Judaism acknowledges the sorrow and pain of life. No
culture need explain to the Jewish people what misery this
earth can hold for its inhabitants. But we believe that, while
there is a Divine purpose in the tragedies men bear, there is also
Divinity in the joyful experiences — and they are many — of life.
If Siddhartha and his monks meditated on the woeful nature of

their every moment and bewailed their hundreds of previous miserable incarnations, they were conducting themselves in a manner not unlike countless other ascetic and flagellant movements which grew during other periods of world history. Judaism never shared such a view of God's bountiful creation. In the Torah we read that God looked down upon the earth after constructing each of His new creations, "and God saw that it was good." Our sages ordained that we recite appropriate blessings on any of a number of pleasant occasions. We praise God for all manner of foods: wine, bread, fruits, vegetables, and all other culinary delights. We thank Him for so many things that, over the course of any day, we generally recite about one hundred *berachot* (blessings). We recognize the good, and we thank God for it.

It is tragic that so many Jews, deprived of an upbringing based on authentic Jewish values, must veer away from the positive approach we espouse. But what can be expected? Did they ever hear *berachot* recited *in earnest*? Did they ever learn from their parents or "rabbis" to appreciate the gifts of God? Were they raised in happy, warm, loving families?

In so many cases, they did not and were not. Parents ran after material values and ignored spiritual wealth; they sought opulence, but they did nothing to enrich their souls. The parents did not observe the Torah laws. The "rabbi" did not observe the Torah laws. The Torah's description of the creation of man was denigrated; instead, it was maintained by the "scholars," all mankind evolved from monkeys. (How great a difference is there between believing that one *evolved* from an ape and that one was *reincarnated* from an ape?) Everywhere, authentic Jewish values were swept under the socio-theological rug. Some young Jews were able to adapt to such a lifestyle; many others fled.

The "Reform Prayer Book" deleted all references to an afterlife. How far would the trek be to Gautama's ethic of extinction? The reckless trend towards "Accommodation Judaism" expunged the calendar of happy occasions. *Shabbat* was converted into a Christian Sunday, inevitably divested of all its joy and spirit. Festivals like Sukkot, Pesach, and Shavuot were stripped of the spiritual treasures inherent in each. Young Jews did not participate in the building and decorating of *sukkot*. They never experienced the passionate dances with the scrolls on Simchat Torah, the mystifying and wondrous traditions of the authentic Pesach *seder*, and the all-night Torah-learning festivities on Shavuot. Purim was mocked as a barbaric observance, based on a fictitious account comparable to the legends of the "Arabian Nights." Lag b'Omer—a festive occasion for centuries—was erased from the suburban Jewish almanac altogether. Instead, the only times the young Jew was "shlepped" to the temple were on sad and bitterly woeful occasions. He went to recite *Kaddish* for a deceased parent. He went to attend a *Yizkor* service for the deceased. He went to the unbearably lengthy and solemn Yom Kippur services. And that was the extent of his acquaintance with Judaism. Of course he developed a pessimistic world view! Every time he went to the temple, he was there for the express purpose of either praying for the dead (*Kaddish/Yizkor*) or praying that he shouldn't die (Yom Kippur). Compared to such a "Judaism," Buddhism could even have appeared optimistic! He never knew authentic Judaism, and he was utterly "turned-off" by the half-baked, ruthlessly compromised versions presented to him.

How tragic that he never knew the joys of Jewish life! If only he had been in the midst of the frenzied Simchat Torah celebration, perhaps he could have understood what authentic Judaism can be. But even then, could he have comprehended—in the light of his meager "Talmud Torah education"—what ecstatic sentiments underlay the festive occasion?

The road from assimilated "Judaism" to Buddhism was short indeed. Deprived of a meaningful spiritual heritage, he left his community for richer fields. He would be willing to put up with Bodhisattvas and Transcendent Buddhas and patron saints and relic worship and endless periods of meditation. In search of spiritual meaning and inner truth, he would put up with anything.

He could have been satisfied within the realm of authentic Judaism. If Judaism insists that life is wonderful and that the world is beautiful, it nevertheless recognizes the need for discipline in partaking of its pleasures. Lusts, cravings, and desires are regulated—not to the point of near-masochistic austerity, as in Buddhism, but to a sensible degree. The Torah records God's laws concerning eating, sexual relations, and other physical aspects of human life. We are uplifted from the animal realm as all carnal needs are spiritually sanctified through the regulations governing their gratification. Non-kosher foods and improperly slaughtered kosher animals are off limits, but *kashrut* provides for a world of comestible delights to be savored. Adultery, incest, and homosexuality are forbidden, but marital relations are permitted, nay extolled. Judaism recognizes the need for control of the cravings, lusts, and desires which can drive a human being to the lowest depths of beastliness, but it simultaneously rejects as abhorrent any claim that normal physical needs must be denied. As such, it allows man to enjoy life, while it provides him with the spiritual fulfillment so concomitantly necessary. Undoubtedly, Judaism could have satisfied the young Jew who left the assimilated walls of suburbia for Buddhist disciplines. And it would have left him unashamed to slake a thirst, to feel warmth, to experience love.

It is ironic that the cold, rational surroundings of the temple could not provide for the spiritual needs of the young Jews who went off to the Buddhist fields. The proponents of the "Reform" movement "understood" that the bright, young Jew would never believe in the authentic Jewish eschatology, so they expunged the theology of belief in a World to Come. They redefined the soul out of existence. And, while some young people went off to the Christian missionaries and others joined the Moonies, yet other Jewish youths turned to the Bodhisattvas and Transcendent Buddhas of Mahayana Buddhism. Disillusioned with a millieu which attempted to reason God out of existence, they rebelled by joining a lifestyle which prided itself on its opposition to common sense and logic. How tragic that they never knew the middle path of authentic Judaism! They did not have to choose between reason without spirituality and spirituality without reason. If only they knew . . . Real Judaism acclaims the role of the mind, the intellect, sharp logic. But it also confesses that there exist inner mysteries beyond our cognizable grasp. There are texts—the Talmud, the Kabbala—which can help penetrate the most carefully hidden secrets in the universe, but the study of these works may take decades, indeed a whole lifetime. Would a person prepared to meditate on a koan for years and years in a Zen monastery not have been able to find fulfillment meditating on deeply complex Talmudic questions and dilemmas in a yeshiva?

Ultimately, we cannot avoid the conclusion that the study of Talmud *would* have been fulfilling to the person seeking out koans to consider for decades. Because of the other-worldly nature of many sections of its volumes and volumes, the Talmud could have provided the spiritual key to fulfillment lacking in the temple astrology classes and absent from the "rabbi's" sermons. It could have led to that search for truth in one's inner being, and it could have revealed the ultimate "enlightenment." If only yeshiva had been presented as a viable alternative to public school and the Talmud Torah, it could have made the Jewish difference. How unfortunate it is that the Sunday school could not at least engender the well-known expression of gratitude uttered by so many Zen Buddhists throughout the centuries, as they described their masters' lessons: "I owe everything to my teacher because he taught me nothing."[42]

A comprehensive examination of the various Eastern religions which have attracted alienated Jewish youths leads us to a recurring series of conclusions. Though the lessons may be painful, they must nevertheless be faced. For, despite the fact that Zen and some of the Hindu gurus are not the threats they were a few years ago, the Eastern-religion menace has not passed, as we shall regretfully see in our look at the bizarre group known as the "Hare Krishnas."

Notes

1) William J. Petersen, *Those Curious New Cults* (New Canaan, Conn.: Pivot, 1975), p. 233.

2) *Newsweek*, 3/8/76.

3) Petersen, *op. cit.*, p. 239.

4) *Ibid.*

5) Associated Press (news dispatch), 4/11/75.

6) *Ibid.*

7) *Ibid.*

8) Petersen, *op. cit.*, p. 238.

9) *Ibid.*

10) *Newsweek*, 3/8/76.

11) *Ibid.*

12) *New York Times*, 12/21/76.

13) *Ibid.*

14) An article in the *Jewish Post and Opinion* (2/24/78) cited figures which indicate the startling possibility that Jews may comprise as much as 70 percent of the cult's membership.

15) The implications of the Hindu caste system were evidenced in a bloody riot in 1980 which saw eleven "untouchables" murdered in northern India, after they ventured out of their segregated neighborhood. (*New York Times*, 5/12/80)

16) Sri Chinmoy, *Commentary on the Bhagavad-Gita* (Blauvelt, N.Y.: Steiner Books, 1973), pp. 36-37.

17) *Ibid.*, p. 123.

18) *Ibid.*, p. 37.

19) *Ibid.*, p. 130.

20) *Ibid.*, pp. 123, 127, 130.

21) *Ibid.*, p. 128.

22) *Ibid.*, p. 56.

23) *Ibid.*, p. 38.

24) *Ibid.*, p. 8.

25) *Ibid.*, p. 136.

26) *Ibid.*, p. 137.

27) *Ibid.*, p. 115.

28) Maharishi Mahesh Yogi, *On the Bhagavad-Gita* (Harmondsworth, Middlesex, England: Penguin Books, 1974), pp. 66-68.

29) *Ibid.*, pp. 191-192.

30) *Ibid.*, pp. 108-113.

31) *Ibid.*, p. 171.

32) *Ibid.*, p. 299.

33) *Ibid.*, p. 406.

34) *Ibid.*, p. 408.

35) *Ibid.*, p. 293.

36) *Ibid.*

37) *Udana*, Pali Text Society Edition, 8, I, p. 80. Cited in Hans Wolfgang Schumann, *Buddhism* (Wheaton, Ill.: Quest Books, 1974), p. 82.

38) Schumann, *ibid.*, p. 106.

39) *Ibid.*, p. 137.

40) D. T. Suzuki, "Zen Buddhism," in Allie M. Frazier (ed.), *Buddhism* (Philadelphia: Westminster Press, 1969), p. 280.

41) *Ibid.*, p. 267.

42) Petersen, *op. cit.*, p. 176.

CHAPTER 4

Hare Krishnas
Avatars, Mantras, and young Jews

*It is better to hear the rebuke of the wise
than for a man to hear the song of fools.*
(ECCLESIASTES 7:5)

*Hare Krishna
Hare Krishna
Krishna Krishna
Hare Hare
Hare Rama
Hare Rama
Rama Rama
Hare Hare*

They sing their mahamantra song indoors and outdoors, day and night, summer and winter. They sing it in cities, in towns, on college campuses. They sing it in the rain, and they sing it in the sun. They sing it when they awake. They sing it when they eat. They sing it before they go to sleep. Their married members sing it for six consecutive hours before engaging in their once-monthly intimate relations. And their leader sang it twenty-four hours daily—even while he slept . . .

Their mahamantra song is called "Hare Krishna," in honor of their God who is named "Hare Krishna." And, although they were incorporated in the United States in 1966 as the tax-exempt "International Society for Krishna Consciousness (ISKCON)," they too are "Hare Krishnas." Who brought these peculiar singers, replete with tinkling instruments and countless publications for distribution, to Western shores? Who convinced so many young people to trade in their pants for saffron robes and their dresses and skirts for saris? Who sold them on sneaker footwear? Who talked all those youths into shaving their heads, transforming so many Western scalps into veritable cue balls (save the remaining topknots)?

His Divine Grace Abhay Charan de Bhaktivedanta Swami Prabhupada. That's who.[1]

The story goes back to the days of the *Bhagavad-Gita*. When Lord Krishna came to India to teach Arjuna about the caste system and all those other Hindu beliefs, he had not come for the last time. True, his was the eighth human form taken by that Hindu god, Vishnu, who found it necessary to return to earth on a regular basis in light of the propensity of the Indian people to forget his lessons. Nevertheless, Lord Krishna was to reappear. We have already seen that, to this day, "Avatars grow like mushrooms" in India. Accordingly, it should come as no surprise that one such manifestation of this theologically agaricaceous phenomenon took India by storm five centuries ago. Born in Goudiya, a province of Bengal, he became known as Lord Sri Krishna Caitanya Mahaprabhu, after claiming to be the incarnated version of yet another Krishna comeback.

Caitanya's biography was recorded in the *Adi-Lila*, a holy book authored by Krishnadasa Kaviraja Gosvami in the sixteenth century. Inasmuch as the present-day "Hare Krishna" philosophy is based on the teachings of Lord Sri Caitanya,[2] it is worthwhile considering the story of this "incarnated God" (or *Avatar*) who came to earth in the guise of one of his own devotees, according to the *Adi-Lila*.

From the moment he was born, Caitanya stood out as a god. The first sign of his Divinity, according to the *Adi-Lila*, was the fact that he cried a great deal during the years of his infancy. From all parts of the province, women came to watch the baby cry. But that was not all. Miraculously, the Divine whelp's whimpering would cease whenever he would hear a lullaby consisting of the words "Krishna" and "Hari." From this, it

1. The numbered notes to chapter 4 begin on page 165.

became apparent to all his venerators that the as-yet-illiterate god was trying to convey to mankind his Divine desire that all people chant the "holy names Krishna and Hari" on a regular daily basis.[3] (These childhood incidents served to inspire the growth of Hindu cults which stress the importance of chanting the "Hare Krishna" mahamantra song over all other human actions and forms of devotion. One cannot avoid commenting that, had Caitanya been born in the United States, the group might have come to be known as the "Rock-a-Bye Baby" religious sect instead.)

In any event, it was not long before this sacred tot began to perform greater miracles. Indeed, "after some days the Lord began to crawl on His knees, and He caused various wonderful things to be seen."[4] (For some reason, however, modern-day Hare Krishna devotees have refrained from instituting the act of crawling on the knees as a sacred rite, Lord Caitanya's personal example notwithstanding.) The miracles did not end, for "after some days the Lord began to move on His legs and walk." Verily, "He mixed with other children and exhibited varieties of sports."[5]

As a young boy, Caitanya continued to amaze the world. On one occasion, his mother brought him a meal of rice and sweetmeats. The young god tossed his food aside and began eating dirt instead. His mother snatched the dirt from "God's" hand and asked him why he chose to munch on clumps of earth rather than eat the meal she had prepared. In tears, "God" replied that, since everything either comes from the ground or derives its nourishment from things which come from the ground, it seemed to him that he might as well eat dirt in its original form.[6] His compassionate mother took Lord Caitanya—the supposed incarnate of God—in hand and explained:

> My dear boy, if we eat earth transformed into grains,
> our body is nourished, and it becomes strong. But if
> we eat dirt in its crude state, the body becomes diseased
> instead of nourished, and thus it is destroyed.[7]

In the words of the *Adi-Lila*:

> The Lord replied to His mother: "Why did you conceal
> self-realization by not teaching Me this practical
> philosophy in the beginning? Now that I can understand
> this philosophy, no more shall I eat dirt. Whenever I
> am hungry I shall suck your breast and drink your breast's
> milk."
> After saying this, the Lord, smiling slightly, climbed on
> the lap of His mother and sucked her breast.[8]

Fortunate, indeed, was the young "God." According to the late
A.C. Bhaktivedanta Swami Prabhupada, founder of the Hare
Krishnas whose commentary on the *Adi-Lila* is studied by all
true devotees, the "philosophy" that all things—despite their
different forms—are, in fact, identical constitutes a deviation
from normative Hindu thought. If one accepts such a philosophy, warned Prabhupada, "his advancement is doomed
forever."[9] Thus, had the eternal Lord Caitanya—nothing less
than God Himself, according to the Hare Krishnas—not been
taught this lesson by his mother, this "Creator of the Universe"
would have been doomed forever! (It is a wonder that Caitanya
is worshipped rather than his mother.) Moreover, he would
have eaten dirt for the rest of his days, unaware that vegetables
and fruits differ in nutritional content from clumps of mud.
Such a "God" do the Hare Krishnas venerate.

Caitanya was not through. Consider these awe-inspiring
words, found in chapter 14 of the *Adi-Lila*, which describe the
Lord's continued impact on mankind:

> As usual for small children, He learned to play, and with
> His playmates He went to the houses of neighboring
> friends, stealing their eatables and eating them.
> Sometimes the children fought among themselves. All the
> children lodged complaints with Sacimata [Caitanya's
> mother] about the Lord's fighting with them and stealing
> from the neighbors' houses. Therefore, sometimes, she
> used to chastise or rebuke her son . . . Thus rebuked by

His mother, the Lord would go in anger to a room and break all the pots within it. Then Sacimata would take her son on her lap and pacify Him, and the Lord would be very much ashamed, admitting His own faults.[10]

It becomes apparent, slowly but surely, that Lord Sri Krishna Caitanya Mahaprabhu was a most extraordinary god. He would steal candy from babies. He would fight with other boys. When admonished, he would regress into furious juvenile tantrums, breaking his mother's kitchenware in the process. And, according to Prabhupada—the individual most responsible for bringing the worship of Caitanya to the West: "In some houses He would steal milk and drink it, and in others He would steal and eat prepared rice. Sometimes He would break cooking pots. If there were nothing to eat but there were small babies, the Lord would tease the babies and make them cry."[11]

When Lord Caitanya grew up into a young man, he continued to exhibit some of his more youthful divine traits. On one occasion, he ran through the streets of a city with a club in his hand, ready to kill all non-believers.[12] Eventually, when he calmed down, "the Lord came to His external senses . . . and threw away the club."[13] Another time, the Lord was chanting "Gopi, Gopi" instead of his usual "Hare Krishna" song. A student, surprised by the change of lyrics, asked the Lord why he wasn't invoking the standard words of deification. "Hearing the foolish student, the Lord, greatly angry, rebuked Lord Krishna in various ways. Taking up a stick, he rose to strike the student."[14] The student, without delay, made his exit.

Lord Caitanya's inability to outgrow his childhood temper was matched by his continued tendency to lapse philosophically. Despite his mother's teaching, he occasionally reverted to the days when he theorized that eating dirt is as nutritionally wise as is consuming fruits and vegetables. For example, he came to the conclusion that cows are no different from mothers and that bulls are no different from fathers: "The Lord said: "You drink cows' milk; therefore the cow is your mother. And the bull produces grains for your maintenance; therefore he is your father. Since the bull and cow are your father and mother, how can you kill and eat them?"[15]

This teaching — based on the same "philosophy" which led Caitanya to eat dirt instead of rice and sweetmeats — serves as one of the core teachings of the Hare Krishna cult. Hare Krishnas do not eat meat, and they are forbidden to wear leather shoes — lest they ingest or walk around on their mothers' skins.

Of course, many people would tend to disagree with Lord Caitanya's "Divine" lesson. Even in an era which has been marked by a major "generation gap," few rebellious youths would actually assert that cows are their mothers and that bulls are their fathers. Nevertheless, His Divine Grace Abhay Charan de Bhaktivedanta Swami Prabhupada stood behind this teaching of Caitanya, as is evident from these words written in his commentary of the *Adi-Lila*:

> . . . In any civilized human society, no one would dare kill his father and mother for the purpose of eating them . . . We especially stress the prohibition against cows' flesh because . . . the cow is our mother . . .
>
> She is a mother for all time; it is not, as some rascals say, that in the Vedic age she was a mother but she is not in this age . . . The cow is a mother always; she was a mother in the Vedic age, and she is a mother in this age also. . . .[16]

Because Prabhupada insisted that the statement equating cows with mothers is a manifestation of Caitanya's "eternal wisdom," all Hare Krishna members must abide by this fanciful declaration. Adding to their motivation is a warning appearing in chapter 17 of the *Adi-Lila*:

> Cow killers are condemned to rot in hellish life for as many thousands of years as there are hairs on the body of the cow.[17]

Moreover, one can never atone for the killing of such a "mother." Lord Caitanya told one of his "cow-killing" contemporaries: "You are going to hell; there is no way for your deliverance."[18] Indeed, the fearsome threat of burning in hell is repeated throughout the *Adi-Lila*, and it appears regularly in Prabhupada's own writings as well. In its twelfth chapter, the *Adi-Lila* warns: "A person without Krishna-consciousness is no better than dry wood or a dead body . . . After death, he is punishable by Yamaraja."[19] Yamaraja, according to Prabhupada, is the Superintendent of Death who has said, "[He] whose heart never throbs as he remembers Krishna and His lotus feet . . . must be brought before me for punishment."[20]

Not even all the heart-throbbers get by. Hindus who do not belong to the Hare Krishna sect have to pay a price, too. "Anyone who is against the cult of Sri Caitanya Mahaprabhu should be considered an atheist subject to be punished by Yamaraja . . . Be one a learned scholar, a great ascetic, a successful householder . . . if one is against the cult of Sri Caitanya Mahaprabhu, he is destined to suffer the punishment meted out by Yamaraja."[21] Only members of Prabhupada's Hare Krishna cult, then, can hope to escape Yamaraja.[22]

The threats of hell—so effective a tactic in frightening young, confused people into joining cults, as many of the Christian missionary groups have shown—appear again and again in the *Adi-Lila*. When Caitanya lost his temper after being asked why he was chanting "Gopi, Gopi" rather than "Hare Krishna," he responded not only by picking up a stick with which to strike his questioner but also by "rebuking Lord Krishna."[23] Now, one need not be a dialectician in order to perceive that there is something puzzling in this account. If Caitanya was, in fact, an incarnated Lord Krishna, who had come to the earth in the guise of one of his own devotees in order to teach mankind how to praise him, how can it be that he "rebuked Lord Krishna"? Such a question the *Adi-Lila* cannot easily answer. Indeed, there are so many contradictions between the actions of "Lord Caitanya" and the supposed purpose of his "mission" that the *Adi-Lila* puts all the questions to rest with one major threat of hell-fire:

One cannot understand the contradictions in Lord Caitanya's character by putting forward mundane logic and arguments. Consequently, one should not maintain doubts in this connection . . . If one simply adheres to mundane arguments and therefore does not accept this, he will boil in the hell of Kumbhipaka. For him there is no deliverance.[24]

(For the benefit of the uninitiated, Prabhupada explained that, in the hell of Kumbhipaka, one is "put into boiling oil . . . from which there is no deliverance."[25])

The Hare Krishna religious cult came to the United States in the 1960s. As we have seen, Caitanya was said to be an incarnation of Vishnu, the Hindu god. In the course of his efforts to promote the regular chanting of the mahamantra, he succeeded in gaining a following. His followers (called "Vishnuites" or "Vaishnavas") continued to pass down his teachings from generation to generation. In 1922, a twenty-six-year-old man who had studied at the University of Calcutta met a Vishnuite guru, Sri Srimad Bhaktisiddhanta Sarasvati Gosvami Maharaja, a leading proponent of Caitanya's brand of Hindu thought. The young man, Abhay Charan De, was soon attracted into the Goudiya Vaishnava Society.

After more than a decade of tutelage, Abhay Charan De had advanced so significantly that his guru asked him to travel to the West in order to introduce Caitanya's philosophy of *sankirtan* (mahamantra-chanting) to the other half of the world. Although the request was made in 1936, some three decades would yet elapse before Abhay would pick up his boarding pass. In the meantime, the promising recruitee founded an English-language publication, "Back to Godhead," which he began producing regularly. For his efforts, he was bestowed the title "Bhaktivedanta" (i.e., "Devotion").

In 1954, at the age of fifty-eight, Bhaktivedanta renounced his wife and five children, a most noble Hindu act. Five years later, he cut off his ties with the rest of society. He was now worthy of the "Swami" designation. In 1965, Abhay Charan de

Bhaktivedanta Swami set sail for the United States. Although he arrived in Boston, he proceeded on to New York City where he set up shop in 1966. Searching for potential Hindu gurus, he made his way through the city's Bowery district. It was during this historic period that his last name, Prabhupada, was given him. The honorific, which means "at whose feet masters sit," was most appropriate; the perpetually inebriated "masters" who populate the Bowery do spend most of their lives in the sedentary position (albeit on the sidewalks of New York).

Prabhupada rented a small apartment in Manhattan's Lower East Side, where he began giving classes in the *Bhagavad-Gita*. Shortly thereafter, he staged his first public sankirtan singing/dancing sessions in nearby Greenwich Village. Large crowds gathered to behold the strange sight of the euphoric septuagenarian. It was not long before Allen Ginsberg, fresh from his Zen Buddhism experiences, came along to dedicate new examples of his "poetry" to Lord Krishna. Prabhupada was on his way. In 1968, he opened a printing press. Later, he established the Radha-Krishna temple in Brooklyn and some forty other centers throughout the United States.

The International Society for Krishna Consciousness experienced a major boost when Beatle George Harrison, fresh from a disappointing experience with Maharishi Mahesh Yogi decided to join the bandwagon. Harrison made a number of huge contributions to Prabhupada's movement, such as a $20,000 gift for the publication of a Hare Krishna book.[26] In addition, Harrison, who frequently visited the London Krishna temple, produced a major record, "My Sweet Lord," which included in its lyrics the mahamantra. The record succeeded in subtly moving many non-devotees into superficially chanting the "holy names." Although individuals in the West who softly hummed the words of "My Sweet Lord" to themselves during the period of its hit run did not intend to thereby perform an act of fealty to Lord Krishna, they unknowingly contributed to the great satisfaction of the many Hare Krishna leaders who reveled in the awareness that hundreds of thousands of people were, for the first time, chanting the mahamantra. Another

Harrison hit record, "Govinda" (number one on England's charts for a while), was comprised of prayer music from the London Radha-Krishna temple.[27]

The *Mahamantra* (loosely defined as the "great invocation") consists of the three names of the Hindu god Vishnu: Hari, Krishna, and Rama. According to the Hare Krishnas, when it is chanted in the appropriate manner, it serves as the key to eternal bliss. Caitanya came to earth primarily for the purpose of teaching mankind the overriding significance of the mahamantra; the song was his legacy:

> Sri Caitanya Mahaprabhu contributed the greatest benefit to the people of East Bengal by initiating them into harinama, the chanting of the Hare Krishna mahamantra. . . .
>
> In this age . . . there is no other means, no other means, no other means for self-realization than chanting the holy name, chanting the holy name, chanting the holy name of Lord Hari.
>
> In this age . . . the holy name of the Lord, the Hare Krishna mahamantra, is the incarnation of Lord Krishna. Simply by chanting the holy name, one associates with the Lord directly. Anyone who does this is certainly delivered.[28]

Because of this "divine" injunction, Prabhupada taught that all Hare Krishna members are expected to chant at least sixteen rounds of the mahamantra daily. This is the secret which sets the International Society for Krishna Consciousness above all other Hindu groups:

> Our Krishna consciousness movement stresses the chanting of the Hare Krishna mantra only, whereas those who do not know the secret of success for this age . . . unnecessarily indulge in the cultivation of knowledge, the practice of mystic yoga, or the performance of fruitive activities or useless austerities. They are simply wasting their time and misleading their

followers. When we point this out very plainly to an audience, members of opposing groups become angry at us . . . We cannot make compromises. . . . When they say they are as good as we are, we must say that only we are good and that they are not good. This is not our obstinacy; it is the injunction of the *sastras* (i.e., scriptures). We must not deviate from the injunction of the sastras.[29]

Moreover, Prabhupada taught his followers that there is more than one way to spread Lord Caitanya's message:

Anyone who chants the holy names . . . without offense is certainly extremely fortunate, and whether Indian or non-Indian, Hindu or non-Hindu, he immediately comes to the level of the most pious personality. We therefore do not care about the statements of *pasandis* who protest. . . . We have to follow in the footsteps of Lord Caitanya Mahaprabhu, executing our mission peacefully, or if necessary, kicking the heads of such protesters.[30]

The crucial elements in the Hare Krishna faith, then, are the acceptance of the *Adi-Lila* as a divine book of eternal truth and the belief that Caitanya was, in fact, the incarnation of the Hindu god Vishnu. Any questioning of the Divine perfection of Caitanya is an act punishable by eternal damnation, for such a breach constitutes a deathblow to the entire structure which houses Prabhupada's theology. One must accept the *Adi-Lila*'s description of Caitanya's childhood: the lullaby story, the dirt-eating incident, the food-stealing/pot-breaking/baby-teasing adventures, the subsequent temper tantrums. Simultaneously, one must believe that this deeply troubled individual was none other than the Creator of the Universe.

If such a fantastic and obviously fragile system is too shallow for most sensible people, with the support of figures like Ginsberg and Harrison, it nevertheless began to catch on in counter-culture circles. Prabhupada succeeded in attracting a number of bright young people, seriously confused by the materialistic world around them and searching for spiritual realism. By the 1970s, he had attracted some five thousand followers,[31] ranging in age from eighteen to thirty-five.[32] The new adherents have included students at some of the most respected Ivy League universities.[33]

When joining, a new Hare Krishna completely cuts off all ties with his old life. For starters, fresh recruits are required to change their names to Sanskrit alternatives. (One young Jew from Hewlett, Long Island went from Steve Hebel to Swarup das Adhikary.[34] A Jewish girl from Chicago entered the cult as "Wendy"; within a short amount of time, she learned to answer to "Rukmini" instead.[35] Paul Wax of Illinois became "Pundarika."[36]) Moreover, a change of appearance accompanies the name adjustment. Men give up their shirts and blue jeans for saffron robes while women shift into saris. Leather shoes are discarded—out of respect for "mother"—and sneakers take their places. Each man has his head shaved in a special way so that only a long topknot remains, allowing Lord Krishna to get a good grip on his scalp when the time comes for him to be yanked into heaven.

Not surprisingly, all these changes make it extremely difficult for frantic parents to successfully track down children who join the group. To compound the labyrinthian burden, many new devotees move to Prabhupada temples in distant states, thereby further cutting their past ties and leaving desperate relatives with little alternative but to hire private detectives. Unfortunately, even a Sherlock Holmes cannot overcome some of the other obstacles confronting those parents seeking to win back their lost sons and daughters. In one case, Bernard Zackheim of Sebastopol, San Francisco—a seventy-year-old Jewish sculptor who loudly complained after his two boys were sucked into the Hare Krishna movement—was targeted by Krishna devotees for revenge; his sons were sent on to India, and a group of Hare Krishnas severely damaged two precious works of art in his home.[37]

The group's ready use of violent tactics in order to maintain their ranks is not limited to the parents trying to intervene. Harassment and threats of physical force are also common forms of pressure applied against young members trying to leave. One highly publicized incident saw Steven Eisenberg, a former Krishna cultist, file suit in Philadelphia, asking damages from ISKCON for allegedly holding him at Krishna quarters against his will for five years. Eisenberg asserted that he had suffered severe mental setbacks and had sustained physical injuries which left him unable to work.[38] Like the Moonies, the Prabhupada cult does not give up its recruits easily. A young person who joins the Hare Krishnas learns, slowly but surely, that it is virtually impossible to get out. Eighteen-year-old Susan Murphy of Massachusetts was lucky to win a court order from judge Ellis F. Brown, barring Hare Krishna members from hounding her; the injunction, proscribing their "interfering with the personal liberties" of Ms. Murphy, came after the former cult member was subjected to an abusive harassment campaign for trying to leave the group.[39] While some strong individuals can withstand the enormous pressures and threats of physical violence, most cannot. Not everyone has the courage to seek a court order against a group which has, on many occasions, shown its alacrity to implement Prabhupada's command to "kick the heads" of opponents.[40] Even more intimidating is the fact that the cult leaders know the address and phone number of those individuals seeking to leave.

Nor is it to be inferred that Hare Krishnas are too exotic or devotionalist to be capable of committing acts of violence. Images of the Jonestown, Guyana massacre—a bloody drama indelibly sealed in the memories of all Americans who recall the mass suicide committed by devotees of the People's Temple cult under the command of their crazed leader, the Reverend Jim Jones—came to many observers' minds in March, 1980, when California police raided the gun shop of a Krishna member near Berkeley. The police search, which grew out of a complaint about stolen credit cards, turned up 300,000 military-type bullets, 50,000 copper-jacketed slugs, nine tons of gunpowder, and bullet-making equipment. Another search revealed more weapons at the New Mount Kailasa farm community, a Hare Krishna retreat in the same area. Among the items discovered were riot guns and a grenade launcher. Meanwhile, residents of Moundsville, West Virginia, have complained about Hare Krishnas stockpiling weapons and conducting target practice in the woods. As if that were not sufficient, Berkeley police later obtained a warrant to search an automobile near the ISKCON temple there and found inside the car two loaded pistols, a Walther P-38 and a 9-mm. Browning, two military-type assault rifles, two .22-caliber rifles, ammunition, and a locked briefcase containing an Ingram submachine gun.[41]

When questioned by reporters, Hare Krishna leaders defended their group's preoccupation with such weapons by saying that they were needed for "self-defense." One such spokesman, Tapanacarya Das, said:

> Well, yes, we do have some guns. But the armament isn't for ourselves. I want to protect the deity, Lord Krishna . . .
> You have never seen our deity? I will show him to you. Right now, he's sleeping . . .
> [Regarding the stolen credit card,] that's true, the credit card. There was a boy and he did have stolen credit cards. It was a person who was here. It was a person who had a bad habit.[42]

Eventually, Tapanacarya Das drew a curtain to reveal Lord Krishna for his interviewer. The reporter, Wayne King of the *New York Times*, noted that "to those without god-consciousness, Lord Krishna appears to be a blue-turbaned, saffron-cloaked mannequin . . ."

Commenting on the police findings, Lieut. Jeff Markham of the Lake County (California) Sheriff's Department said:

> They have pretended for years to be a peace-loving group that was only concerned about their religion, but events of the past six months have shown me personally that they are not what they pretend to be. . . . What

legitimate religious organization do you know that keeps an arsenal?

After the Jonestown tragedy, it's a matter of great concern to us.[43]

Indeed, for a "spiritual" society, the Hare Krishna sect maintains a most unique ethical-moral structure. To raise money, they go into the streets dressed in their ceremonial garb and try to sell Prabhupada's books for as much as $13 a volume. But they have other, less "spiritual" methods as well. "Sankirtan girls" (i.e., female cult members who are especially effective at collecting money on street corners) will go to their outdoor posts wearing civilian clothes. They will disguise themselves by donning regular slacks instead of saris and by not marking their foreheads with the ritual chalkmarks.[44] Stationed at museums, at shopping centers, and at busy corners, they will sell boxes of incense for a dollar, explaining that the money is being raised for "Bangla Desh."[45] Such fund-raising can net as much as $530 in an eighteen-hour period.[46] In one month, 120 Hare Krishna devotees gathered over $30,000 for the cult by simply averaging a daily intake of ten dollars per person.[47] One young woman raised more than ten dollars in less than two hours at a New York City subway station. "The slogan 'Bangla Desh' worked a lot of the magic," she subsequently noted.[48]

Though the "Sankirtan Girls" can wheedle thousands of dollars by appealing for "Bangla Desh," they have learned to change their slogans in accordance with the dictates of the times. Indeed, while they will explain their success in raising substantial sums by saying that "Krishna does it,"[49] there have been times when they might more appropriately have attributed their good fortune to the assistance of Christianity's "Santa Claus." In December, 1976, it was reported that Hare Krishna members were wangling funds for their cult by dressing as Santa Claus volunteers—replete with red suits, white beards, and cries of "Ho, Ho, Ho." Utilizing the winning formula established during the days when they passed cigar boxes for "Bangla Desh," the Santa Clauses never informed their contributors that all proceeds were going to the Hare Krishna chest. According to the "Volunteers of America," one of the country's philanthropic groups (and one which raises substantial sums of money every winter through Santa Claus volunteers), the Hare Krishna impostors cut into their earnings, drawing away as much as 33 percent of the annual contributions made to legitimate "Sidewalk Santas."[50] *Newsweek* magazine, commenting on this disturbing phenomenon, wrote, "Unnerved shoppers have found themselves pursued by the aggressive Krishna Kringles, who have even grabbed pedestrians in their search for donations."[51] Not surprisingly, these Hare Krishna fund-raisers were arrested in Denver for violating a city charity-fraud statute,[52] and in Charleston, West Virginia, three Hare Krishnas dressed in Santa Claus outfits were arrested for illegally soliciting funds.[53]

If the Hare Krishnas' proclivity for engaging in acts of cunning misrepresentation is reminiscent of the Moonies' policy of "celestial deception," we should not be surprised. For, like the members of Sun Myung Moon's Unification Church, those who have joined the International Society for Krishna Consciousness learn their ethics not from God but from a human being claiming Divine authority. Moon, as we have seen, insists that he has conversed with Moses, Jesus, and Buddha and that they have implied to him that he is the "Third Adam."[54] Prabhupada, on the other hand, traced his special "power" to Lord Krishna and Caitanya, both of whom he claimed to personally represent. In the words of a society publication: "Srila Prabhupada is in a line of disciplic succession going back directly 500 years to the time when Lord Caitanya appeared in India, and from there back still further—5000 years—to the time when Lord Sri Krishna first spoke *Bhagavada-Gita*."[55]

Hare Krishna devotees treat the late Prabhupada with so much reverence that they attempt to imitate his every "Divine" trait, including snacking on Bengali candy balls[56] and mispronouncing English words like "devotee."[57] He used the words "puffed up" instead of "conceited" and "take rest" instead of "go to sleep," so his followers do likewise.[58] Having been the founder and "ultimate standard of Krishna-consciousness,"[59] Prabhupada is revered absolutely. His English translations of the *Bhagavad-Gita*, the *Adi-Lila*, and other such Eastern texts are believed to have been perfect. His interpretations of Caitanya's teachings are assumed to have been without error.[60] Indeed, many Hare Krishnas assert that, if he was not an actual "incarnation of God," Prabhupada—at the very least—had direct contact with Lord Krishna.[61] Accordingly, his photograph appears in all ISKCON publications, and it is prominently displayed in every Hare Krishna temple.[62]

Because of the enormous amount of awe Prabhupada inspired—his venerators describe his extraordinary powers by noting that he chanted the mahamantra twenty-four hours a day, not only when awake and asleep but even on one occasion when he lay anesthetized on an operating table[63]—there have never been any challenges to his authority. His words are studied and cherished—even when imagined during the course of a nocturnal dream. (One New York woman who dreamed that Prabhupada had asked her whether she planned to travel to India by car was told that she should consider the imaginary conversation with all seriousness and that she should ponder the query as though it were a masterfully constructed Zen riddle designed to provoke satori. "Prabhupada knows you better than you know yourself," she was told, "because he knows God and you do not. He can give you your spiritual name instantaneously."[64])

And because of the awe which Prabhupada has inspired—and his authority extends, of course, to other leaders in the cult who were associated with him—the new recruit finds that he loses control over his life when he joins the International Society for Krishna Consciousness. All decisions are made for him by the ISKCON leadership. How he dresses, what he eats, when he awakes, where he will spend his day: all these matters are determined not by him but by the cult's top brass. Every member's daily schedule is carefully planned out in a fashion which permits minimal free time. Accordingly, a young person who wanders into the Hare Krishna group finds himself subjected to intensive pressures to stay in the sect, while he is allowed virtually no opportunity to seriously deliberate on the ramifications of such an awesome decision. There is no chance to speak with parents or close friends in the early phases; instead, one is led to believe that the young men and women of the cult are the only true friends in whom he can confide. From the moment a lost youth enters the Krishna temple, he is pressed to remain. And, while the community demands that he give his soul over to them, he is stripped of his freedom of solitude. Ultimately, then, the proselytizing tactics of the Hare Krishnas are virtually identical to those of the Moonies (and, to a slightly lesser degree, to those of the Christian missionaries). The social insecurity of a potential recruit is skillfully manipulated as he is made to feel that he has finally found not just one person but a community of individuals who love him and who truly care for him. He is subjected to enormous doses of peer pressure, and he is made to understand that he will "break the hearts" of all his "new friends" if he "deserts" them.

How can a young, sensitive individual withstand such pressure? How can he walk out on those who have shown him the love he never received from his parents? How can he leave the people who have offered him the spirituality he never learned from his "rabbis"? How can he look twenty, forty—perhaps as many as one hundred—young men and women who have befriended him in the eyes and say, "I cannot stay here." In theory, he can do it quite easily. In practice, such an utterance is not easier than "telling off the boss."

Compounding the young person's problem is the meticulously crafted daily schedule to which he is subjected while he is within the cult's perimeters. When spending a weekend at a Unification Church retreat, as we have seen, his every minute is absorbed; activities ranging from singing to attending lectures to playing dodgeball to attending lectures to climbing mountains to attending lectures sap him of his physical and mental vigor. So it is with the youthful individual whose idealistic quest for Truth takes him to a Krishna temple. The program is rigorous. Everyone must wake up at four o'clock in the morning. Quickly, they must wash themselves and apply white chalk-mud (specially imported from India) on their foreheads in accordance with cult ritual.[65] By 4:30, they must be prepared to "prostrate themselves before the deities." As they assemble for the morning service—exhausted from inadequate sleep—the statues of Krishna and the other Hindu gods are uncovered. Garlands of fresh flowers are placed around the idols' necks. Rapidly, the service begins.

How alert is the young, impressionable individual who has just been lured into ISKCON? How alert can he be at four-thirty in the morning? He has just awakened from a brief sleep on a rocky, hard floor because Krishna devotees are forbidden to sleep on beds in their dormitories. (They are permitted sleeping bags and blankets.[66]) In such a state of mind, it is not surprising that he participates in the recitation of special prayers on behalf of the small potted plant which is worshipped at the New York temple in the belief that it is the reincarnated form of a female Krishna devotee.[67]

During the afternoon, after a morning of *Bhagavad-Gita* indoctrination, a short nap is permitted. But that nap may not exceed one hour. Not surprisingly, the shortage of sleep leaves its mark. Hare Krishnas find themselves, in many instances, exhausted around-the-clock. Nevertheless, they must participate in the hectic routine of services, classes, and outdoor singing, dancing, and begging. Those who complain about the lack of sleep or who need to take additional naps are "excruciatingly embarrassed."[68] They must drive their bodies through each day's program, their physical/mental/emotional needs notwithstanding. If they are tired, then such is Krishna's will. If they are too tired to think, that too is Krishna's will. And, if they have just joined the society and are now being pressed to remain in ISKCON forever, then the fact that they are too tired to think clearly is undoubtedly Krishna's will. Or, at least, Prabhupada's.

Sleep is not the only physical necessity denied Hare

Krishnas. Their diet, based on the vegetarian principles of the *Bhagavad-Gita* and the *Adi-Lila*, is seriously inadequate. Although one can consume a wholesome and nourishing meal without eating meat, the Hare Krishnas do not. Their daily intake is frequently protein-deficient and, more important, sugar-congested. Meat, fish, and eggs are not eaten by devotees; therefore, the Hare Krishnas rely on milk for their protein needs. However, for some reason, some cult leaders mix two cups of sugar into every gallon of milk served.[69] The sugar intake is so high that it has been estimated that Hare Krishnas consume five times the amount of sugar ingested by average people.[70] The ramifications of such a diet are enormous.

Many laymen assume that sugar is a good substance to eat when some "instant energy" is desired. In fact, the consumption of sugar leads to a major reduction in body energy. Although the sweet substance may provide a momentary surge, it stimulates certain body secretions which work to directly counter the immediate effects. Accordingly, doctors have learned that hypoglycemia — a body affliction which causes serious fatigue — can result from the regular over-consumption of sugar. Because diets consisting of high quantities of sugar can lead to serious levels of fatigue, the Hare Krishnas face extraordinary exhaustion. When the nature of the diet is considered in light of the acute shortage of available sleep time, it becomes evident that Hare Krishna devotees are chronically tired. The fact that young people are subjected to intensive courses in ISKCON/Hindu philosophy while they are kept in such a state of fatigue leads to the inevitable question: To what extent does the nature of Hare Krishna indoctrination border on "brainwashing"?

The poor health of Hare Krishna members is appalling. According to one observer who spent a winter with the cult:

> I could not share their scorn for the body. I like to be healthy . . . I was annoyed that three of us had to live in a cold, empty, unlit room. . . .
> It was often said around the temple that [Jadurani] was a

frail girl, disposed to be sick. During the
last days of my stay, she languished in a cold, airless
upstairs room, coughing blood, with no one even telling
her to go out and get a little fresh air or sun, no one
demanding she follow the recommendation of the doctor
she had seen and have the TB test. . . .
During the Christmas-New Year's season, a good three-
fifths of the temple was obviously sick. Red eyes, badly
running noses, coughs, exhaustion were everywhere. A
large part of the class dozed off every morning and were
ignominiously expelled from the room or made to
stand up, heads still nodding. The customary treatment
was to stop drinking milk, believed to produce mucus, and
assiduously to chew ginger root.[71]

Although the Krishna life may seem to be a real "turn on" to
uninitiated students who get their information from the carefully prepared propaganda handouts distributed by devotees,
the reality is somewhat different. Aside from the fatigue
problem, there are other aspects of the ISKCON life which are
less than enticing. Women are mistreated and are barred from
all cult management decisions. In fact, women are even kept
out of the kitchens of many Krishna temples because of
"inefficiency and talking too much."[72] As the sect's leaders see
things, "To be born into a female body is a punishment for
mistakes or sins in previous lives."[73]

Even more unsettling is the Hare Krishna approach to
sexual relations. According to one of Prabhupada's more
alluring pamphlets, married couples find great happiness in
ISKCON: "Husband and wife live in mutual cooperation for
spiritual progress."[74] It is worthwhile exploring this assertion
because many young people who join the group would never
have set foot inside a Krishna temple if they had known what
was in store for them.

All sex outside of marriage is forbidden by the cult. This
ruling, in itself, is not unlike that of authentic Judaism, and it
undoubtedly represents a spiritually refreshing change from life

in the suburbs. Where ISKCON parts company from Judaism, however, is with regard to the regulations governing marital relations. A Hare Krishna couple may engage in sexual relations only once a month, on the fifth night after the wife's period. And, on that solitary occasion, the couple must chant the mahamantra for nearly six hours before beginning.[75]

It is not surprising that the Hare Krishna sex code is one of the last things explained to a new member of the cult, usually well after he has been indoctrinated in all other ways. Once again, then, we find a similarity between ISKCON and the Unification Church. Both offer the promise of a lifestyle which will be deeply fulfilling on an interpersonal level; yet both subsequently present extraordinarily restrictive sexual regulations which actually bar the opportunity to live a normal, married life. Moonie couples, as we have seen, are frequently expected to part from each other shortly after marriage and may never see each other again. Hare Krishna couples, on the other hand, are kept virtually celibate during their years together—which are also few. Male cult members are urged to do as Prabhupada did and renounce their wives and children. This leaves them unmarried for the rest of their lives, and it leaves the women divorced at young ages. Moreover, since divorced women may never remarry, many female Hare Krishnas are doomed during their twenties to remain alone for the rest of their lives.

As for the unmarried, they may not be alone with individuals of the opposite sex at any time. Men and women eat in different rooms and sleep in opposite sides of the Krishna temple. As such, the sexual rules which govern Hare Krishna members are infinitely more strict than those which applied to "Lord Krishna," who had 16,000 wives according to the *Mahabharata* scriptures.

Before a young Jew enters the International Society for Krishna Consciousness, he should be told what lies ahead for him. While on the surface the Prabhupada cult may appear to be spiritually rewarding, it will not provide what authentic Judaism can. In ISKCON, there are no ethics. One may raise money deceptively, threaten members who want to leave the group, and destroy priceless items owned by parents who refuse to give up the hope that they may one day win back their children. As Lord Caitanya beat up his friends, stole food from their homes, teased babies, and destroyed his mother's pots when he was scolded, so do the modern-day Hare Krishnas lack an ethical value system. Their "ethic" is the chanting of an eight-line ditty, day and night, which will supposedly win for them eternal bliss. All other ethical principles fall by the wayside.

In addition, their services consist of the worship of statues which represent the tens of gods venerated by Hindus. There is a god of rain, a god of lightning, a god of the ocean, and a god of morning. There are gods for everything under the sun. On the one hand, Hindus claim to be monotheists; on the other, every Hindu worships a different god. What binds so many of the Hindu groups together is their fealty to "Lord Krishna."

To the objective observer, the Hare Krishna option appears to be one of the least appealing of all the cults discussed in these pages. Yet, bright young people have been joining ISKCON. And, of those who have joined the Hare Krishna movement, an estimated 33 percent are Jewish.[76] Deprived of a Torah education, they have found something spiritual in the *Adi-Lila*. Never having learned about Moses, they have turned to Lord Caitanya. That bright young individuals could have turned to so vapid a theology as that offered by Prabhupada indicates just how desperate they were in their struggle to find a spiritual meaning to their lives.

Consider the nature of the Prabhupada appeal. He acknowledged that material life, in and of itself, is without meaning. There is a greater force in this world than man can conceive, he asserted. There has to be. It is Vishnu/Lord Krishna/Lord Caitanya. None can come to know Krishna by simply going through the boring, empty motions of mundane existence. Only by transcending, by chanting the other-worldly mahamantra (ordained by "God" himself), can one come to an awareness of the Supreme Being:

The transcendental vibration established by the
chanting . . . is the sublime method for reviving our
transcendental consciousness. . . . Our consciousness is
now adulterated by the material atmosphere . . . The
illusion is that we are all trying to be lords of material
nature . . . We are trying to exploit the resources of
material nature, but actually we are becoming more and
more entangled in her complexities. . . . This illusory
struggle against material nature can be stopped at once by
revival of our eternal Krishna consciousness.

[The mahamantra] is the transcendental process for
reviving this original pure consciousness . . . There is no
need therefore to understand the language of the mantra,
nor is there any need for mental speculation nor any
intellectual adjustment for chanting this mahamantra. It
is automatic from the spiritual platform. . . .[77]

Prabhupada (who died in late 1977) appealed not to "reason"
but to spirituality. His movement is a defiant rebellion against
the impersonal culture of materialism. It does not offer a
"sensible" alternative to "material nature" but an irrational,
mystical chant. One need not know the mahamantra's
meaning, nor need one even be acquainted with the Sanskrit
tongue. The mantra works for everyone. For the young Jew who
never learned from his parents or his Talmud Torah teachers or
his "rabbi" the Jewish mahamantra (and it is much, much
more than a simple, empty chant)—Shema Yisrael Hashem
Elokeiynu Hashem Echad—such an approach is not only
fascinating but ostensibly unique. And Prabhupada made the
most of it:

The earth is . . . the property of God, but we the
living entities, especially the so-called civilized human
beings, are claiming God's property as our own. . . . This
false claim of proprietorship by the human race on earth is
partly or wholly the cause of all disturbances of peace on
earth. . . .
Therefore, if you want peace at all, you will have to

change your consciousness into Krishna consciousness, both individually and collectively, by the simple process of chanting the holy name of God. This is a standard and recognized process for achieving peace in the world . . . This is practical, simple, and sublime . . . Peace and prosperity will be the immediate worldwide result.[78]

It is clear that the Prabhupada antidote to the poison of obsessive materialism will not be more effective than would cough drops be in treating cancer. Nevertheless, Prabhupada diagnosed the illness, something few upper-class suburban "rabbis" have been able to do. When Prabhupada asserted that chanting the mahamantra would be a "recognized process for achieving peace," he did not bother explaining who "recognized" it. But, to the young Jew searching for a way out of the repugnant race for riches which has seen the earth's ecology devastated by unscrupulous exploiters, no one had to grant "recognition" to Prabhupada's tonic. Prabhupada spoke of the earth as "God's property." How many suburban temples give the impression that Judaism recognizes that the earth ultimately belongs to God and not to the temple's board of trustees? Consider how thousands of dollars can be thrown out in a three-hour bar mitzva staged to impress everyone in the temple but God. At home, enormous amounts of money are expended on cars, furniture, stereos, and other such symbols of the "good life." Yet, expenses for spiritual nourishment are limited to bare necessities. The hypocrisy and double-standard is evident in all aspects of daily life, and the lessons are not lost on highly impressionable young Jews.

Naturally, there are some young Jews who "play along." They come to terms with materialistic society and accommodate themselves accordingly. But, if we are to understand what has driven so many Jewish youths into the hands of the foreign cults, let us not seek solace by avoiding the honest, though painful, soul-searching necessary in coming to grips with the problem at hand. Prabhupada did not offer luxuries;

he demanded sacrifices. He did not sit in a theological Pentagon—out of sight—telling others what to do. He went out with his charges and led them in every activity he expected them to perform. He danced in the streets. He sang the mahamantra in the snow on wintry days. How different he was from those well-paid "rabbis" who emerge from the Temple woodwork on but the most rare of occasions!

What rabbi demands spiritual sacrifice in suburbia? Prabhupada expected those who could write to contribute to the Hare Krishna magazine. Individuals with business backgrounds would be required to participate in the cult's business ventures. Everyone was to give of himself because "Krishna-consciousness is not an idler's philosophy."[79] Everyone was to study the *Bhagavad-Gita*, eventually in the original Sanskrit. And, of course, everyone was to participate in the outdoor chanting, dancing, leaflet-distributing, and begging (sankirtan). The Hare Krishna routine—which reflects Prabhupada's Spartan style to this day—is a hard and grueling experience, but it is one which ostensibly offers a sense of purpose to life. And it is certainly more spiritual than those deviant forms of dollar-Judaism which have expunged from authentic Judaism the words of Psalm 24: "The earth and its entire contents belong to the Lord."

Of course, many who join the Prabhupada faith make their decision in a desperate effort to find an avenue to self-discipline. Unaware that Judaism offers an opportunity to develop internal strength of character, they simply grasp at the first lifestyle they have known that offers an alternative to the drug-sex culture of the tragic 1960s.

An extraordinary proportion of Hare Krishnas are former drug users.[80] One typical devotee admits to having been in nine different mental hospitals.[81] Many others, like George Harrison and Allen Ginsberg, have spent long years haplessly wandering from one "religious master" to another in search of the authentic Truth they know exists somewhere; one girl, fresh from the Maharishi, joined Hare Krishna after becoming frustrated with the $50 mantras of the "bogey yogi."[82]Paul

Wax, a young Jew from Illinois, became a Hare Krishna after experimenting with drugs, seeing psychiatrists, and spending months in a hospital.[83] Having seen their lives break down during the course of their permissive/free/"anything-goes" years, they turn to Prabhupada's cult desperately seeking a spiritually disciplining lifestyle to set them straight. How tragic it is that so many hundreds of young Jews seek out ISKCON for the self-discipline they could have found in authentic Judaism!

Thus, it is not at all rare to find young people with backgrounds completely devoid of religious influence joining the Hare Krishnas and thrusting themselves into the performance of all the different cult rituals. Young Jews who never learned Hebrew engross themselves in special classes in Sanskrit and Bengali. Although their parents and "rabbis" were loathe to "shove religion down anyone's throat" and, therefore, never encouraged them to study Torah in yeshivot, they eagerly pore over the *Bhagavad-Gita* and the *Adi-Lila* at the Krishna temple. Denied the spiritually uplifting laws of *kashrut* during their childhood years, they turn with joyful enthusiasm to the special dietary laws of their cult. Told that "enlightened Jews" do not accept the Torah's teaching that the soul is eternal and that there will be a World to Come, these idealistic young men and women — who instinctively know, as authentic Judaism teaches, that there is an eternal component in every human being — reject the "Judaism" of the suburbs for a Hare Krishna theology which preaches reincarnation. Their act of joining Prabhupada's sect is no less a boldly defiant statement rejecting the compromised "Judaism" of the modern period than it is an act of fealty to "Lord Krishna." Everything they find in the Hare Krishna society could have been located in authentic Judaism . . . if only they had looked. If only they had been led to look!

Instead, a young Jewish girl like Wendy of Chicago joins ISKCON, changes her name to "Rukmini," and wakes up at four o'clock every morning to wash, dress, and care for Hindu statues. As the head *pujari*, in charge of all deity work at the New York Krishna temple, this assimilated twenty-three-year-old Jewish woman learned to sing fluently in Bengali and Sanskrit.[84] A magazine report described her role in ministering to the metal and stone statues of Krishna and other Hindu gods in the temple: "Rukmini thought of Krishna as her son, and she tried hard to please Him throughout the day: dressing Him in richly bejeweled gowns . . . , making sure the curtains were closed when He rested, singing and talking to Him while she bathed Him in rose water. . . ."[85]

How spiritually starved young Wendy had been is clearly evinced by her part in the Krishna cult. She was raised without the authentic Jewish values which carried our people through thousands of years, including many centuries spent under the burden of the most oppressive of persecutions, and the "Jewish spark" in her soul sent her on a desperate road in search of God. That she left her assimilated Jewish milieu is tragic. It is not surprising.

Wendy is not alone. Young Paul Wax, whose childhood included visits to Santa Claus and other such "Jewish" phenomena, joined the Hare Krishna temple of Evanston, Illinois. His mother, who sold a glib account of Paul's spiritual destruction to the *New York Times*, quite naturally wondered why her son had rejected the "nice, middle-class college/career, laurel-acquiring fantasies we were nurturing for this first-born."[86] After all, the witty Ms. Wax noted, "[Being a Hare Krishna] isn't, as they say, work for a Jewish boy."[87] Together with her husband, Sheldon, she saw her troubled boy float from drugs to psychiatrists to hospitals. When he dropped out of school at the age of eighteen in order to become a Hare Krishna, she experienced "a sort of relief . . . If the sect sounded strange, at least it held out hope of safety, structure, companionship."[88] These essential emotional needs were apparently unavailable in the Wax home, as his mother noted in one of her few serious moments: "What's hard to confront is that many of our children have found something they couldn't get elsewhere."[89]

One of the things Paul could not get elsewhere was a religious upbringing. His mother, who proudly described herself as "permissive," matter-of-factly asserted that she did not believe in the Torah. Hers was a home without faith in God, and Paul's *pintele Yid* (Jewish spark) hungered for Divine nourishment. Never imagining that God could be found in the spiritually barren temples of assimilated Jewry, he sought out the Prabhupada temple instead. Indeed, his Mother the Writer noted the cruel irony: "When Paul first joined, I suggested to our parents that they could field unwelcome inquiries with: 'Paul? He spends so much time in the temple, we hardly see him.' If it implied that out there in Illinois a rabbi was in the making, maybe it wasn't so misleading. The time that I heard him lecture the 'congregation' in English, then Sanskrit, he sounded like the quintessential Talmudist."[90]

Only he was not a Talmudist. Having been denied an education in such authentically Jewish texts as the Talmud, Paul turned to Prabhupada's *Bhagavad-Gita* and *Adi-Lila* instead. He changed his name to "Pundarika" and began to learn Sanskrit. In no time, he looked and sounded "as if he'd grown up along the Ganges," according to his mother. (The shocking change did not unsettle the Wax line: "My father says he doesn't care for Paul's tailor," commented Pundarika's merry mom.)[91]

Of course, his parents took everything in stride; indeed, Sheldon and Judith Wax could not have reacted otherwise. Proudly permissive, these two quintessential Jewish "good sports" responded to their son's spiritual suicide by joking about it. When Paul told his father about the Hare Krishna magazine, "Back to Godhead," Sheldon quipped, "Catchy title."[92] Later, Judith asked her husband what he would do if Paul decided to marry a female cult member and to send his children to a *gurukula* (a Hare Krishna boarding school). Sheldon replied, "I'll pretend they told me 'Boola Boola.' "[93] On another occasion, Judith the Writer (whose spouse was a *Playboy* editor) contemplated the ramifications of Paul's decision to begin writing for Hare Krishna publications: "Thank God (and Lord Krishna), he sounded happy with the new development. So were we. But I guess we shouldn't take it to mean that our son has gone into the family business."[94]

No, Paul did not enter "the family business." On the contrary, he rejected all the materialistic values cherished by his parents and sought spirituality instead. He studied diligently and rose to the highest ranks of the society, lecturing in Sanskrit to groups of young people like himself. Eventually, he desired to travel to the Holy Land—India.

As Paul's Krishna-consciousness "expanded," his attitude to his own family began to change. Whenever visiting his parents, he would harangue. Once, his sister cried to him, "You never ask about *my* life." In response, he explained that "it was her eternal soul that concerned him."[95]

His mother, in turn, visited the Krishna temple on Sundays when an "open house" festival was conducted. When Paul's friends tried to explain why they rejected the "folly of sense gratification and material pursuits," they did not realize the futility of their efforts. After all, Judith later wrote, "Who could concentrate on fine points of theology?"[96] Nevertheless, she did not hesitate to join in the Krishna fun: "In time we came to like those occasional Sunday visits . . . I'd risk transcendental take-off with a sort of midlife jigalong of my own."[97]

She even tried chanting the mahamantra, but her unctuous underpinnings got the best of her. Naturally, she did not mind the holy lyrics. In fact, she later wrote that "the tune is so grabby I find myself humming it around the house when I'm not working on hits from the 40s."[98] Nonetheless, she joked, "Though I tried to chant the mantra, the part that goes 'Hare Rama, Hare Rama' churned in my head as 'Hare Rama, I'm the Mama.' "[99] Despite everything, Judith Wax—who was not able to determine where she went wrong with Paul—felt that her Hare Krishna connections were not without purpose: "Ultimate Truth hasn't been given even to me, so if—as the Krishna fold tell me—the fact that I am the mother of a "true devotee of the Lord" automatically puts me in a state of spiritual advancement . . . I accept! Whatever gods may be, I can use all the points I've got coming."[100]

(It seems as though the tendency to respond to spiritual tragedy with glib humor transcends the Wax household. One "gorgeous young woman" whom Judith met at the Krishna temple told her that her Ohio family had sent a rabbi after her, in the hope that he would successfully persuade her to leave the cult and return to her Jewish home. The "rabbi" undoubtedly won for himself a special place in modern Jewish history when, after tasting some of the culinary delights prepared by the Hare Krishna gourmets, he confided to the young Jewish woman he was sent to bring back, "Listen, if I didn't have so many commitments, I'd join up myself."[101] For some inexplicable reason, the Ohio family did not find their daughter accompanying their "spiritual leader" on his return trip. . . .)

The spiritual death of Paul Wax alias Pundarika (Hebrew name unknown) culminated with his journey to India, the Holy Land of Krishna. There, he found "his people." Sitting on the floor of a Krishna temple, he recites the mahamantra all day, breaking away from the routine only for the purpose of studying advanced Sanskrit or lecturing on the *Bhagavad-Gita*. He is "dirt poor," suffers from dysentery, and must walk miles in the hot sun because he cannot afford the few cents necessary to pay for a rickshaw ride.[102] Nevertheless, he has found the spiritual fulfillment for which he starved and thirsted during his younger years. Unaware that he could have found a Holy Tongue (Hebrew), a Holy Scripture (Torah), a Holy Land (Israel), and a lifestyle worthy of a Holy People in Judaism, Paul Wax assumes that he has found the only meaningful alternative to the "permissiveness" and "materialism" of his youth. A reporter for the *New York Times* wrote to Judith Wax: "Pundarika is totally devoted, expects to do this the rest of his life, seems to have made peace with himself. I am impressed that he reads the *Bhagavad-Gita* in the original Sanskrit, has learned large chunks of it in Sanskrit, and continually quotes from it in ordinary conversation . . ."[103]

As for his mother, who converted his tragedy into a pleasant, almost impersonal family-magazine article, she was content to play the role of the permissive Jewish liberal to the very end: ". . . My husband and I do the work we chose, so we ought to be able to allow the same to our progeny—as long as what they do is legal, fulfilling to them, nondamaging to others."[104]

A different response to the tragedy of Paul Wax appeared in the letters column of the *New York Times Sunday Magazine* a month after his mother's article appeared:

> Paul was raised on "nice, middle-class, college-career, laurel-acquiring fantasies"—a diet which does not satisfy the soul of a Jewish boy searching for meaning and purpose, searching for God.
>
> For a young Jew, it is but a short trip from Santa Claus to Hare Krishna. I know; I also traveled that road. When I saw the emptiness, I returned to the Jewish way. I pray that Paul and all my other brothers and sisters who have strayed from the Torah path will also return. They will find a warm welcome.[105]

Ultimately, then, the Hare Krishnas are but the most bizarre of the many Hindu groups which have set up offices in the West in recent years. The ability to attract young Jews is inversely proportional to the quality of Jewish education provided them. Those raised in homes where love is shown, where authentic Jewish values are taught, and where spirituality is imbued will not go off to ISKCON.

Only those Jewish youths who were raised like Paul Wax and the hundreds of thousands of Paul Waxes—denied a real Jewish upbringing, starved of Jewish knowledge, refused a truly Jewish education—are prey for the Prabhupada cult. They who were taught to believe in the gods of "success," "materialism," and "honor" have learned that their parents' deities were as statues of brass. They who were taught that "Science" has all the answers have found that there remain mysteries beyond the grasp of science and that these inexplicable phenomena point to the inevitable conclusion that there is, indeed, a greater power and intelligence than science can ever hope to discover.

Seymour Cain, a respected student of religion, has written: "Men are still men, and they still face in an age of technological and social revolution the age-old problem of human existence, its origin and goal, and the search for the ultimate core of reality and value, which may give human life its meaning and direction. And they do not find the answers to these eternal, perennial questions in the concepts and methods of modern sciences or ordinary pursuits as such. . . ."[106]

Cain's insight helps us better understand the words of the president of the Hare Krishna temple in Freeport, Long Island, who articulated the reason that his cult had chosen to establish a base in that suburb of New York City: "People here are educated and have had an opportunity to experience what materialistic civilization has had to offer. They are generally frustrated and experience a spiritual vacuum that they are acutely aware of, and they are receptive to spiritual ideas."[107]

For those who were denied the teachings and way of life offered by authentic Judaism, the Hare Krishna cult presents an alternative to the meaningless groping and competing so inherent in the "rat race." Unaware of the spiritual bounty known as "Judaism," they have given their souls to Abhay Charan de Bhaktivedanta Swami Prabhupada and his disciples for nourishment.

The tragedy is theirs.

And it is ours.

Notes

1) Prabhupada, about whom more will be written later in the chapter, autocratically led the Hare Krishna movement until his death on November 14, 1977. He died of heart failure at age eighty-two in Vridaban, India. (See *New York Times*, 11/16/77, p. B-2.)

2) Cf. "On Chanting Hare Krishna" (a pamphlet distributed by ISKCON), p. 15: "We need only accept what is coming down to us in the line of disciplic succession from Krishna and from Lord Caitanya."

3) *Ibid.*, p. 13. See also A. C. Bhaktivedanta Swami Prabhupada, *Sri Caitanya-Caritamrta: Adi Lila* (Tokyo: Bhaktivedanta Book Trust, 1974), vol. 3, pp. 65-66.

4) Prabhupada, *ibid.*, p. 141.
5) *Ibid.*, p. 142.
6) *Ibid.*, pp. 142-144.
7) *Ibid.*, p. 146.
8) *Ibid.*, pp. 147-149.
9) *Ibid.*, p. 145.
10) *Ibid.*, pp. 152-154.
11) *Ibid.*, p. 154 (Prabhupada's commentary on the text of chapter fourteen).
12) *Ibid.*, p. 307.
13) *Ibid.*, p. 308.
14) *Ibid.*, pp. 384-386.
15) *Ibid.*, p. 339.
16) *Ibid.*, pp. 340-342.
17) *Ibid.*, p. 346.
18) *Ibid.*, p. 345.
19) *Ibid.*, p. 39.
20) *Ibid.*
21) *Ibid.*, pp. 39-40.
22) *Ibid.*, p. 39.
23) *Ibid.*, p. 386.
24) *Ibid.*, pp. 415-416.
25) *Ibid.*, p. 416.
26) Faye Levine, *The Strange World of the Hare Krishnas* (Greenwich, Conn.: Fawcett Gold Medal, 1974), p. 36.
27) *Ibid.*
28) Prabhupada, *op. cit.*, pp. 210, 269.
29) *Ibid.*, p. 271.
30) *Ibid.*, p. 371.
31) *Newsweek*, 4/5/76.
32) Levine, *op. cit.*, p. 20.
33) *Ibid.*
34) *Ibid.*, p. 23.
35) *Ibid.*, p. 24.
36) Judith Wax, "Sharing a Son with Hare Krishna," *New York Times Sunday Magazine*, 5/1/77, p. 41.
37) *Jewish Post and Opinion*, 5/20/77.
38) *Ibid.*, 5/30/80.
39) *New York Times*, 4/24/77.
40) Prabhupada on the *Adi-Lila, op. cit.*, p. 371.
41) See *New York Times*, 3/28/80; 4/13/80; 6/9/80; 6/12/80; 6/17/80.
42) *Ibid.*, 4/13/80.
43) *Ibid.*, 6/9/80.

44) Levine, *op. cit.*, p. 50. See also *Newsweek*, 4/5/76.

45) Levine, *ibid.*, p. 51.

46) *Ibid.*, p. 50.

47) *Ibid.*, p. 35.

48) *Ibid.*, p. 56.

49) *Ibid.*, p. 50.

50) *Newsweek*, 12/27/76.

51) *Ibid.*

52) *Ibid.*

53) *New York Times*, 12/16/76. In a federal court decision handed down in 1980 by U.S. District Court Judge Howard G. Munson, the Krishnas were condemned for "a widespread and systematic scheme of accosting, deceit, misrepresentation, and fraud" which included using "experienced thieves" to teach new members. (*Newsweek*, 9/29/80)

54) For a thorough treatment of Moon's theology, see chapter two.

55) "On Chanting Hare Krishna," p. 3.

56) Levine, *op. cit.*, p. 19.

57) *Ibid.*, p. 9.

58) *Ibid.*

59) "On Chanting Hare Krishna," p. 7.

60) Levine, *op. cit.* pp. 37-38.

61) *Ibid.*, p. 40.

62) In a magnificently opulent Hare Krishna palace built in Limestone, West Virginia, statues of Prabhupada abound. Devotees kneel and prostrate themselves before the gold idols to this day. (*New York Times*, 8/6/80)

63) Levine, *op. cit.*, p. 41.

64) *Ibid.*, p. 66.

65) *Ibid.*, p. 72.

66) *Ibid.*, p. 110.

67) *Ibid.*, p. 75.

68) *Ibid.*, p. 160.

69) *Ibid.*, p. 103.

70) *Ibid.*, p. 104.

71) *Ibid.*, pp. 158-159.

72) *Ibid.*, p. 147.

73) *Ibid.*, p. 145.

74) "On Chanting Hare Krishna," p. 3.

75) Levine, *op. cit.*, p. 150.

76) *Ibid.*, p. 20.

77) "On Chanting Hare Krishna," p. 10.

78) *Ibid.*, p. 8.

79) *Ibid.*, p. 4.

80) Levine, *op. cit.*, p. 20.

81) *Ibid.*, p. 84.

82) *Ibid.*, p. 23.

83) Judith Wax, *op. cit.*, p. 40.

84) Levine, *op. cit.*, p. 24.

85) Richard M. Levine, "Who Is Hare Krishna . . ." *New York*, 9/6/71, p. 30. (Cited in Faye Levine, *ibid.*, p. 74.)

86) Judith Wax, *op. cit.*, p. 40.

87) *Ibid.*

88) *Ibid.*

89) *Ibid.*, p. 42.

90) *Ibid.*, p. 46.

91) *Ibid.*

92) *Ibid.*, p. 42.

93) *Ibid.*

94) *Ibid.*, p. 46.

95) *Ibid.*, p. 41.

96) *Ibid.*

97) *Ibid.*

98) *Ibid.*, p. 40.

99) *Ibid.*, p. 41.

100) *Ibid.*, p. 46. Judith and Sheldon Wax died in May, 1979, when American Airlines Flight 191 crashed shortly after take-off in Chicago.

101) *Ibid.*, p. 40.

102) *Ibid.*, p. 46.

103) *Ibid.*

104) *Ibid.*

105) *New York Times Sunday Magazine*, 6/5/77. The letter was written by Yisroel Neuberger of North Woodmere, New York.

106) Seymour Cain, "The Study of Religion," *Midstream*, vol. 25, no. 5 (May, 1979), p. 33.

107) *Long Island Jewish World*, 3/7/80.

CHAPTER **5**

Marxism, a political cult
The Utopia without Jews

*The labor of the righteous leads to life;
the fruit of the wicked, to sin.*
(PROVERBS 10:14)

*There is a way which seems right to a
man, but the end thereof are the ways of
death.* (PROVERBS 14:12)

In the course of any thorough consideration of those cults
threatening young Jews today, it is vital to reflect on the
Marxist phenomenon as well. Clearly, Marxism does not fall
within the classical bounds of theology; indeed, to the casual
observer, it would appear to be an essentially political-eco-
nomic ideology. Nevertheless, as it is taught and practiced on
the campuses of America, Marxism transcends the secular
sphere and encroaches upon the religious. And, to the Jewish
community, the dangers posed by this "religion" are awesome.

Karl Marx, the movement's quintessential prophet and
bearer of Truth, was the dominant architect of the philosophy
which bears his name. As his position within the Marxist cult
parallels those of Reverend Moon, Maharishi Mahesh Yogi, and
Prabhupada within their respective groups, so do his writings
occupy a place equivalent to those accorded the *Divine Prin-*

ciple, the *Bhagavad-Gita,* and the *Adi-Lila* by their respective adherents. Thus, to understand the cult, we must first focus our attention on its founder and prophet. For, despite all the many latter-day "saints" who have reinterpreted and redefined the meaning of Marx's communism, it is from his own words that the essential values of the movement can best be ascertained.

Marx believed that, more than any other human factor, the role of economics had been the key determinant in the development of human history. Superseding man's religious affiliations, ethnic ties, political sympathies, and personal psychological quirks, it had been his economic status which affected him the most. His decisions—whether mundane or historic—were the inevitable results of his economic lot. Accordingly, Marx believed that an historic opportunity for world peace would be presented the day man would act to restructure the international economic order for the better. To achieve this, Marx called on workers throughout the world to unite in an international effort to seize the means of production from the upper classes. With a successful workers' revolution, the millions of laborers oppressed by merciless capitalist bosses would be able to establish themselves as the rulers of the new social order. A "dictatorship of the proletariat" would ensue, with *all* people being expected to work equally hard (in accordance with each individual's capabilities) and with everyone receiving an equitable portion of the final profits (in accordance with each individual's actual needs).

Because Marx classified all people on the basis of their positions in the economic order, he necessarily disregarded all other factors, including nationality, religion, and individual personality. If German workers, Spanish workers, American workers, and Russian workers were to unite into one large mass, they would have to overcome ethnic differences. If Christian, Jewish, and Moslem workers were to join together against Christian, Jewish, and Moslem bosses, their religious identities would have to fall by the wayside. If all members of the international proletariat were to merge together as one, then individual personalities would have to be remolded so as to conform with one basic class model.

Accordingly, Marx proclaimed war against the notions of national consciousness and religious commitment. Claiming that both were artificially contrived by the upper classes in order to keep workers perpetually divided, Marx declared their elimination essential to the ultimate success of communism. It is in this context that Marx's famous description of religion as "the opiate of the masses" takes on special significance.

On the surface, much of Marx's thought would appear to be extremely humane. His opposition to the brutal working conditions facing people laboring in sweatshops during the nineteenth century could strike a chord of agreement in most hearts. Workers were forced by greedy, unrelenting bosses to put in long and hard hours at shockingly low wages. Conditions were hazardous: factories were unsanitary and bred disease, and many buildings were virtual death traps, ready to ignite at the touch of a spark. During these early days of the Industrial Revolution, workers had no voice, were totally disorganized, and had to struggle desperately to please their employers if they hoped to avoid the poorhouse. In such an atmosphere, Marx's approach to "employer-employee relations" could indeed be seen, at least superficially, as a positive step.

Unfortunately, a deeper consideration of Marx's thought bears less fruit. On the practical, economic level, Marx misjudged emerging tendencies. He predicted that the first countries in which workers' revolutions would erupt would be those possessing the most advanced industrial economies. Ironically, the developed nations of the West by-passed his program entirely, while backward societies like those of Russia and China adopted communism. His ideas made no headway in the West because he neglected to anticipate the development of labor unions which would gain legal recognition and would be authorized to engage in collective bargaining with management. He failed to predict that, one day, workers would be paid handsome salaries, would be guaranteed minimum wages, would be protected by laws regulating working conditions, would be assured that they need not work more than forty hours weekly, and would be accorded countless other social benefits. Because Marx saw the brutal bosses of the nineteenth century as being hopelessly evil, he never considered the possibility that they might be tamed by the very "system" which had spawned them. His colossal error stands as a permanent reminder that even the brightest of thinkers can make mistakes. Marx, after all, was human.

Unfortunately, the Marxist cults of our present day have elevated Marx to the level of a god. Despite self-evident miscalculations, his writings are quoted as veritable gospel. True, Marxism developed in the wrong countries, at the wrong times, and under the wrong conditions. True, no workers' paradise has yet emerged—even in those lands where the "Proletariat Revolution" erupted. True, Communist countries are beleaguered with terrible amounts of misery and suffering. Despite all the failures, devotees of Marx continue to advance his theories and to call for revolutions in his name. Despite all the failures, they know that they will be vindicated. And how do they know?

Because Marx said it would be so, and anyone who disagrees is either a tool of the capitalists, a lackey of the imperialists, or a reactionary fascist.

To members of the Marxist cults, their prophet is above criticism. While different wings may argue over the sanctity of some of the later saints of the "religion"—Lenin, Trotsky, Stalin, Mao—all stand firmly behind the promulgator of the "faith." And woe unto anyone who turns elsewhere for salvation.

Jews turn elsewhere for salvation: "I lift my eyes to the hills; whence will my help come? My help comes from the Lord who made heaven and earth."[1]

To Marx the atheist, religious commitment is the result of an elaborate scheme concocted by the bourgeoisie of an earlier day who sought to create divisions within the international

1. The numbered notes to chapter 5 begin on page 204.

working class. To a Jew, religious commitment is a sincere and unshakable belief that this world was called into being by a Creator who gave His Torah to the nation of Israel at Mount Sinai, before the eyes of millions. Marxism requires the dissolution of all religions and national groupings as an essential prelude to the ultimate workers' revolution. Judaism, as a *religion* maintained by a uniquely constituted *nation*, stands before Marxism as a major obstacle. Something has to give way.

Because the Marxist cults are, of necessity, committed to the termination of all faith systems, they seek the ultimate disappearance of the Jewish faith. Inasmuch as they are dedicated to the obliteration of ethnic differences, they inexorably advocate the disintegration of the Jewish people, the nation of Israel. Thus, it comes as no surprise that Karl Marx himself wrote passionately against the continued existence of the Jews: "The political emancipation of the Jew or the Christian—of the religious man in general—is the emancipation of the state from Judaism, Christianity, and religion in general."[2]

Marx believed that the sensible way to put an end to Jew-hatred would be to put an end to Judaism. As an atheist, such a concept made perfectly clear sense to him—as it does to his devotees in our present period. But to Jews whose belief in God is not just a matter of "ethnic pride" or "national chauvinism" but a most sensible and realistic affirmation of a self-evident truth, such an idea is not only outrageous; it is a virtual call for a people's extermination.

Marx's opposition to Judaism transcended the philosophical sphere and bordered on the pathological:

Let us consider the real Jew: not the *Sabbath Jew* . . . but the *everyday Jew*.

Let us not seek the secret of the Jew in his religion, but let us seek the secret of the religion in the real Jew.

What is the profane basis of Judaism? *Practical* need, *self-interest*. What is the worldly cult of the Jew?

Huckstering. What is his worldly god? *Money.*

Very well: then in emancipating itself from *huckstering* and *money*, and thus from real and practical Judaism, our age would emancipate itself. . . .

We discern in Judaism, therefore, a universal *antisocial* element of the present time, whose historical development, zealously aided in its harmful aspects by the Jews, has now attained its culminating point, a point at which it must necessarily begin to disintegrate.

In the final analysis, the *emancipation of* the Jews is the emancipation of mankind from *Judaism.* . . .

Mammon is his idol which he adores not only with his lips but with the whole force of his body and mind. In his view the whole world is no more than a Stock Exchange, and he is convinced that he has no other destiny here below than to become richer than his neighbour. . . .

Money is the jealous god of Israel, beside which no other god may exist . . . The bill of exchange is the real god of the Jew. . . .

The *social* emancipation of the Jew is the *emancipation of society from Judaism.* [3]

Selah. The words of the prophet.

In writing of Jews and in discussing Judaism, Marx sounded more like a forerunner of Nazism than like the founder of its political antipode. He called the Jewish faith "repugnant," and he grieved that Polish Jewry had a high birthrate, noting that "they multiplied like lice." In an 1856 article published in the *New York Tribune*, Marx wrote: "We find every tyrant backed by a Jew, as is every Pope by a Jesuit. In truth, the cravings of oppressors would be hopeless and the practicability of war out of the question, if there were not an army of Jesuits to smother thought and a handful of Jews to ransack pockets . . . It is only because the Jews are so strong that it is timely and expedient to expose and stigmatize their organization."

Marx authored the infamous quote, describing Ramsgate as full of "Jews and fleas," and he wrote that the Jewish exodus from Egypt was prompted by Egypt's desire to expel "the people of lepers."

It is no wonder that the renowned economic historian, Dr. Edmund Silberner, once wrote: "Marx not only can but *must* be regarded as an outspoken anti-Semite."[4]

Faced with the unequivocally anti-Jewish rhetoric of their prophet, subsequent Marxist leaders continued the struggle against Judaism. In the Soviet Union, Lenin enacted stern measures against the Jews. Moreover, he empowered the infamous *Yevesekzia*—the Jewish section of the Communist Party—to forcibly disrupt the practice of Judaism. Comprised of individuals no less intolerant of the Jewish faith than had been the prophet, Marx, this committee embarked on a furious campaign against Judaism in the Soviet Union. Synagogues were seized and converted into Communist Youth Clubs. Rabbis and Jewish religious teachers were imprisoned. Yeshiva schools were closed down. Jewish children were forbidden to receive any instruction in Torah-related subjects. Jewish newspapers were barred. The Hebrew language was outlawed.

After Lenin came Stalin, and the situation—incredible as it may seem—deteriorated. Jewish poets were murdered. Zionists were rounded up and shot. And a horrifying plan to murder hundreds, even thousands, of Jews was to have been put into motion in late 1953, but Stalin's death stopped the momentum behind the project.[5] To this day, the tragic plight of Soviet Jewry is internationally known; indeed, the question constitutes one of the leading challenges facing human-rights organizations in our time.

Communist anti-Semitism has not been restricted to the borders of the Soviet Union. Just south of the USSR, Communist China has opposed all forms of religion since the first day that Mao Tse-tung took power. While it is fortunate that there are no Jews in the Chinese mainland, the nation of Israel has nevertheless been unable to avoid the Communist Chinese hate. During a state visit to Peking in the mid-1960s, Ahmed Shukairy—then a leader of Arab terrorist forces bent on destroying Israel—announced at a press conference that

Chairman Mao had asked him: "You Arabs are forty million, and the Jews are only two million. What are you waiting for?" And, in an historically significant gesture, Maoist China became the first non-Arab country to officially recognize the PLO. In 1975, a delegation representing the terrorist Al-Fatah met with Chinese leaders and were promised military assistance in their efforts to drive the Israelis out of the Middle East.[6] Later that year, it was reported that Arab terrorist units were being given military training at Chinese air force bases.[7] When Israeli troops staged their historic raid on Entebbe airport in Uganda and freed 103 hostages being held by Arab terrorists, the official Chinese press agency, *Hsinhua*, condemned the heroic operation as "Israeli aggression" and did not mention that hostages had been rescued. Indeed, it did not even mention that Arabs had hijacked an Air France plane, prompting the Israeli rescue mission.[8]

Despite China's unrelenting hostility against the Jewish State, the Israeli government cabled its sorrow and regret to Chinese Premier Hua Kuofeng when a series of earthquakes devastated parts of China in the summer of 1976. Hua replied by returning the cable to Israel together with a note explaining that since Peking does not recognize Israel it would refuse to accept the message.[9]

The *Jewish Week* aptly summed up the attitudes of Communist China towards Israel and the Jews in an editorial published on the occasion of Mao Tse-tung's death, under the lead "Mao Was Implacable Enemy":

. . . Apologists may seek to excuse Mao's savage attitude toward Jewish liberation as emplified in Israel by rationalizing that the emperor of 800 million people could not be expected to understand and preoccupy himself with a tiny nation of only several million people. Yet he was sufficiently aware of small nations to relish little Albania . . . The fact is that Mao understood the need of the Jewish people for self-government very well. He simply did not take kindly to people who valued human rights above beneficent regimentation.[10]

Although the Soviets and Maoist Chinese are the two largest Communist nations, they have not been alone in pursuing a policy of unremitting hostility against Israel and the Jewish people. Even the smallest of the Marxist entities have sought to contribute to the destruction of the Jewish State. During the 1973 Yom Kippur War, North Korean pilots flew Soviet MIGs for Egypt.[11] When eleven Israeli athletes were gunned down in cold blood by Arab terrorists during the 1972 Munich Olympic Games, the government of North Vietnam was the only non-Arab regime in the world to applaud the murders. In early 1976, press reports emanating from Syria indicated that nearly 1,500 military personnel from North Vietnam, North Korea, and Cuba had been sent to support the Syrian army.[12] According to *Time* magazine, 7,000 Cubans alone were in the Middle East.[13]

At an international conference on terrorism, it was reported that Cubans had been sent to PLO camps in Sidon and Tyre, Lebanon, to assist George Habash, an Arab terrorist, and his "Popular Front for the Liberation of Palestine," a Marxist gang which advocates the murder of Israeli men, women, and children. Subsequently, Habash arranged to have several hundred of his killers trained in Cuba.[14]

Yugoslavia, meanwhile, has offered heavy support for Arab terrorist groups on a number of occasions.[15] And terrorists affiliated with Yasser Arafat have been provided training under KGB supervision in Hungary and Bulgaria.[16] No less pernicious has been the aid and succor offered Israel's enemies by the government of East Germany. The East Germans have provided advanced weapons to the PLO for use in terrorist attacks against Israeli citizens.[17]

Communist support for Arab terrorism has been so broad-based that the very special role played by the Soviet Union in promoting the efforts of the PLO is often underestimated. The Soviets have helped Arab terrorists with organization, training, equipping, planning, and logistic support. In addition to providing clandestine training for aspiring killers, the Soviets have conducted classes in infantry, engineering, and artillery for PLO officers and officials. In one highly publicized effort, the USSR assembled more than fifty leaders of Arab terrorist groups for a special course. After checking into their respective Moscow hotel rooms, courtesy of the government, the Arabs were lectured on such subjects as Soviet history and culture. Next, they were flown to the Soviet military academy at Sanprobal where, for six months, they studied basic military field exercises, communications techniques, and terrorist tactics. Their classes included lectures in the use of detonators, chemical and biological warfare, incendiary devices, explosives, and anti-personnel mines.[18]

One of the more prominent alumni of these special Soviet training programs was Muhammad Abu Kassem, a young member of Fatah who studied under the KGB before participating in a PLO raid outside Tel Aviv. In the ensuing massacre, Kassem and his cohorts murdered Gail Rubin, a young American photographer, and fifty-seven Israelis. Eighty people were wounded.

Nor has the USSR merely limited itself to providing basic combat courses. Arab terrorists have received scores of T-34 tanks equipped with 85-millimeter guns, armored personnel carriers, and mobile artillery pieces from the Soviets.[19] Other Russian weapons, like the AK-47 Kalashnikov rifle and certain rockets, have also been incorporated into the PLO arsenal. With Moscow financing and arming the forces of Arab terror, virtually using the PLO as a cutting edge for Soviet penetration into the Middle East, it is not surprising that Yasser Arafat has traveled to Russia more than a dozen times to coordinate strategy with his benefactors.[20]

The world-wide communist campaign against the Jewish people extends to the shores of the United States as well. Marxist cults in America have fought unstintingly against Zionism and against the Jewish religion. One typical organization is the Communist Party of the United States of America (CPUSA). This group, which rigidly adheres to the Moscow political line, is relatively weak on campuses, despite the efforts of their youth movement, the Young Workers' Liberation League. Nevertheless, their opposition to Judaism is manifested regularly, especially through their own mini-*Yevesekzia* and its organ, *Jewish Affairs.*

Until his death in 1976, Hyman Lumer, a former national educational secretary of the Party, was the editor of *Jewish Affairs*. Every other month, he would publish articles on issues like detente ("There is no Soviet Jewish problem"), the Middle East ("The state of Israel is a gangster state, created by American imperialism and serving the interests of neo-colonialism as well as the oil cartels"), and Israeli politics ("Rakah, the Israeli Communist Party, is gaining new followers every day"). Savor this choice morsel from Lumer's editorial kitchen, first appearing on the CPUSA shelves in the November 8, 1975, *Daily World* and later reprinted in the September-October 1975 issue of *Jewish Affairs*:[21]

> On October 17, the Social, Humanitarian, and Cultural Committee of the U.N. General Assembly adopted a resolution stating that "Zionism is a form of racism and racial discrimination."
>
> . . . Is such a characterization correct? In our opinion it is unquestionably valid. Zionism is essentially racist in character and the State of Israel, built on its principles, is a racist state . . .
>
> Not least, there is the racist influence of Zionism in this country. The support of leading Jewish organizations to Shankerism . . . their labeling of anti-Zionism as identical with anti-Semitism and the resulting attacks against so-called "Black anti-Semitism"—these and other actions have served to drive a wedge between Jews and Blacks and to intensify hostilities, in the interests of monopolist reaction, which is the fountainhead of racism. . . ."

Although Lumer is dead, the anti-Jewish, anti-Zionist policies of the CPUSA continue. In one notorious case, the Party issued a two-thousand-word attack against the left-wing Yiddish daily, *Morning Freiheit*, after the journal called for an end to Soviet anti-Semitism. Although the *Freiheit*'s position on most issues is relatively comparable to that of the CPUSA, the fact that the small Yiddish paper dared to challenge Moscow on its persecution of Jews led to a furious response by CPUSA, in which the group charged that the daily had performed an "open service in the interests of United States imperialism."[22]

Perhaps the CPUSA enjoyed its finest moment when, in 1980, Zehdi Terzi—the official UN representative of the Arab terror gangs led by Yasser Arafat—spoke on their platform. Addressing the eighth anniversary dinner of *Jewish Affairs*, the spokesman for terror greeted the CPUSA *Yevesekzia* as "comrades." Terzi warmed up his audience by hailing the Soviet Union as the "inspiration of the PLO." Responding to Terzi, Herbert Aptheker (who succeeded Hyman Lumer as the chairman of the Jewish division of the American communists) was simply overwhelmed. Praising Terzi as "our comrade," Aptheker gushed that it "is a great honor to be addressed by the PLO."[23]

The Moscow-line CPUSA is not the only Marxist cult group in the United States; indeed, its YWLL is the smallest of those operating on campuses in America. Of far greater concern to the Jewish community is the Socialist Workers' Party (SWP), whose campus division, the Young Socialists' Alliance (YSA), is one of the most active among American students. Part of the "New Left," the SWP brands itself as "Trotskyite," in contradistinction to the "Marxist-Leninist-Stalinist" CPUSA. No less opposed to the Jewish religion and the Jewish State than the CPUSA, the Socialist Workers' Party advocates violent revolution throughout the world and the forcible extermination of Zionism, the national liberation movement of the Jewish people. In 1973, for example, the *International Socialist Review* published the SWP's call for the support of Arab terrorists in their "struggle to destroy the state of Israel."[24]

There are other Marxist cult groups active on campuses in the United States. Some, like Youth Against War and Fascism (YAWF) and Students for a Democratic Society (SDS), are supported by nationwide parent groups (Workers' World Party and Progressive Labor Party, respectively). Others, like the

Revolutionary Students' Brigade (RSB), are run solely by students. Despite minor theoretical differences in outlook, they all share a common antipathy toward the Jewish religion and the Jewish nation. As loyal Marxists, their position "on the Jewish question" is inexorable.

In a sense, it might seem surprising that so anti-Jewish a movement as Marxism would have so many Jewish recruits within its ranks. But, when considered in the light of the overall cult phenomenon, the paradox becomes less perplexing. Each of the religious cults we have considered differs sharply from authentic Judaism; yet, among each group's rosters are to be found a disproportionately high number of Jewish names. Why?

Again and again, we have seen that the exotic philosophies of these social-theological aberrations provide opportunities for spiritual expression not available to young Jews raised in assimilated Jewish environments where authentic Jewish texts are not studied, authentic Jewish values are not taught, and authentic Jewish practices are not respected. In a society which extols hedonistic gratification over religious commitment and which assigns greater value to material worth than to spiritual depth, the tendency among young people to rebelliously explore alternatives to the "rat race" must be seen as inevitable.

Consider the forces which combine to turn a young Jew away from his people and his heritage—and towards the Marxist cults. Born in suburbia to well-to-do Jewish parents, he learns the meaning of "success" at a young age. Success is a large home, replete with the "best" furniture, the "best" household appliances and luxuries, and the "best" domestic help "money can buy." Success is a spacious backyard located in the "best" of residential areas and a garage with room for, at least, two of the "best" cars "money can buy." Success is a lucrative medical practice or a partnership in a major corporate-law firm. Success is an education obtained at a carefully restricted private school. Success is a season's pass to all home-town football games. ("Ultimate" success is that same season's pass when it assures its bearer a seat at the fifty-yard-line.)

Naturally, such a value structure must lead to a breakdown in authentic Jewish concepts. The best Jew is no longer the one who anonymously contributes to small charities for needy widows, orphans, and paupers; rather, he is the one who writes out his check (after ascertaining that his contribution will be tax-deductible) to a well-known fund which will award him a plaque for his efforts.[25] The best Jew is not the one who sits in a house of study (*bet midrash*) for years, poring through such priceless texts as the Talmud, the Torah, and the great works of Jewish thought; rather, he is the one who prepares for medical school in the hopes of becoming a doctor—even though his weak grades may force him to enroll in a program in Italy, Poland, or Guatemala. The best Jew is no longer the pious individual who attends daily services, nor is he even the once-a-year Yom Kippur visitor; rather, he is the generous contributor to the UJA.

For some young people, this strange brand of "Judaism" may be palatable, but for tens of thousands it is not. Many of the best young people bear a formidable sense of guilt, knowing that they were raised in riches while other human beings were starving and freezing in inner-city ghettoes or in underdeveloped countries. They carry within their breasts a determination not to repeat the hypocrisies of their parents and not to repeat the mistakes when they raise *their* children. Judaism? It was a fraud, a cruel hoax. It was bagels on Sunday morning, the Catskills in the summer, and Miami Beach in the winter. It was chopped liver on Passover, incredibly expensive tickets to back-row seats on the High Holidays, and a "Chanuka Bush" in December. And, as every young Jewish male can never forget, it was that contemptuous farce called a "bar mitzva party," at which all his old and long-forgotten relatives were gathered from the dusty closets of the four corners of the earth in order to see how rich his parents were, to give him presents, and to stuff themselves like turkeys.

Of course sensitive young people will revolt against such a "Judaism"! During their pre-college years, while in their parents' homes, they have no choice but to co-exist with the

strange theology of "dollar-Judaism." Once free from their familial confines, however, they will naturally rebel against their
past.

One of America's premier social critics put it best. Writing
about the causes of the "youth rebellion of the 60s," Irving
Kristol noted:

> The important thing to remember is that this rebellion
> was not primarily directed against conservative, old-
> fashioned, capitalist America, though it sometimes talked
> that way. The original cadres of this rebellion were
> recruited from the sons and daughters of liberal parents.
> They had been born into "enlightened" upper-middle-
> class homes, raised in chic upper-middle-class
> suburbs, educated in "progressive" upper-middle-class
> schools. It was this world and its values that they found so
> suffocating, so empty of meaning . . . As one student put
> it, when asked to explain the reasons for his radicalism:
> "You don't know what hell is like unless you were raised in
> Scarsdale." These young people had seen the future
> promised by their liberal parents and were repelled by it.[26]

Because Marxist cults operate on campuses throughout the
United States, the possibility that one such group might
ensnare any particular student cannot be discounted. Indeed,
at some of the more sophisticated universities, there is an
element of counter-culture status which accrues to all who
choose the Marx option. When these natural factors are
combined with those special psychological elements shared by
so many of the young refugees from the suburban Jewish
milieu, the dangers posed by active Marxist cults loom as
formidable, if not overtly threatening.

Marxists call for a "redivision of the wealth" and the
"soaking of exploitative capitalist fat-cats." Who knows better
the evils of hedonistic materialism than the sensitive youth who
was raised in just such a milieu? Marxists call for an end to the
"profit-reaping bourgeoisie" and for a new order in which each
individual will be expected to contribute to the best of his

ability and will be paid in accordance with his need. For the young person who saw his lazy mother live in regal splendor—leaving her palace only for the purpose of an occasional peregrination to the beauty parlor or for an afternoon fashion show—while the maid who did all the work had to struggle to make ends meet, such an economic philosophy can indeed appear sensible and eminently fair. The fact that Marxism is opposed to Judaism—indeed bent on its destruction—is tragically disregarded. (Worse, in some cases it is perceived as an added bonus.)

Just as the Moonies and Hare Krishnas do not inform potential recruits at introductory stages that their theologies require devotees to severely regulate their sexual behavior to the point of near-celibacy, so do Marxist groups avoid discussing the totalitarian aspects of their "theology" when they sponsor lectures for newcomers. Instead, Marxists speak of the unfair economic order and the need to restructure it humanely. They call for an end to repression in all countries where human rights are gravely violated (by *right-wing* governments). They speak of injustice and frequently sound like the most humane of student activists. Indeed, much of their program is so moderated that they easily attract many non-Marxist students to their early-season lectures. When campus employees are denied legitimate wage increases or ostensibly bona fide social-benefits improvements, the Marxists rally on their behalf. (For many of those who never said a word during all the years that maids tidied their rooms, prepared their meals, and cleaned their homes, the opportunity to finally demand equity for the proletariat is most alluring.) To a great extent, it can be seen that new members of communist student groups are motivated by essentially wholesome and humane principles.

As these youths develop as Marxists, however, they begin to learn new aspects of the cult's ideology. The AFL-CIO is an enemy of the working man because it is willing to recognize the capitalist structure; it must be destroyed or by-passed. Workers must unite and violently overthrow the capitalist structure; accordingly, all factors dividing the working class—especially ethnicity and religion — must be wiped out. While human-rights violations in right wing or capitalist societies must be protested, those occurring in Communist countries must be seen as necessary preludes to the establishment of workers' utopias.

The deeper one's involvement in the movement gets, the less he is permitted to question the Prophet's vision. If Marx did not foresee the emergence of labor unions, then they can serve no positive purpose for the working man — unless they organize for a revolution of the proletariat. If Marx prophesied that a "dictatorship of the proletariat" would usher in a new age of equity and tranquility, then so it must be. Marx never said it would happen overnight; he simply said it would happen. Therefore, a faithful devotee of Marx must look upon the grave human-rights violations rampant within the Communist world as a sort of "test of faith." The misery and suffering in Marxist societies will pass. Marx said so.

Ultimately, Marxism requires more faith than do most other theological systems. It has never worked successfully, the Prophet's assurances notwithstanding. Indeed, most Communist countries suffer more severely than do free-market nations. Capitalism, to be sure, leaves wide room for abuse. Many individuals do become wealthy by immorally oppressing workers, by exploiting the resources of foreign nations, and by constructing ruses which defy all rules of interpersonal conduct. Many capitalist countries tolerate inhumanity and allow a society to develop in which a small few grow extremely wealthy while masses of people remain in the grips of poverty and despair. Surely, many of the Arab oil sheikdoms are models of this latter social structure. Nevertheless, a century of Marxism has shown that *it* is *not* the alternative to oppression, inhumanity, and hateful discrimination. Ironically, it has often aggravated the diseases it had been sent to cure. It does not work because it cannot work. The refusal by Marx's devotees to recognize this reality — after so many decades of objective laboratory-testing in the world arena — indicates the amount of blind faith required by this cult.

Philosophically, Judaism can recognize Marx's central error with considerable ease. While Marx believed in the inherent goodness—indeed virtual perfection—of the working class, Judaism regretfully differs. Marx contended that it was the capitalist's lust for profits which brought so much sorrow and tragedy to human history; if only the bourgeoisie could be overthrown and power could be vested in the hands of the working class, justice and equity would ensue. The workers would seize the means of production and would share the wealth fairly. What he neglected to consider was the possibility that workers, too, can be greedy and can seek power.

The Torah teaches that all men have within them psychological components which can lead them to perform good deeds or to commit heinous crimes. The *yetzer ha-tov* (good inclination) and the *yetzer ha-ra* (evil inclination) are in constant tension. From the moment a person is born, the two inclinations tug at each other, seeking to gain the figurative "upper hand." This tension is an essential component in man, for it is the basis of his freedom. Without the capacity to do evil, man would be little better than a robot; denied the ability to do good, he would be a veritable animal. That which makes man a special figure in the universe is his innate freedom of choice. In the words of the Talmud: "Everything is in the hands of Heaven except for the fear of Heaven."[27]Judaism maintains that, despite the fact that God directs the course of world events, He does not predetermine whether an individual will choose the path of good or the path of evil. That sacred decision is left for each person to decide.

Clearly, the Jewish conception of man differs sharply from that of Marxism. In the Jewish framework, there is as great a chance that a boss will choose to do good as that a worker will; conversely, a worker is just as prone to lust after evil as is a boss. Innately, both carry the two inclinations, the *yetzer tov* and the *yetzer ra*. Thus, a given member of the bourgeoisie can be more authentically virtuous in thought and deed than a corresponding figure in the proletariat.

To Marxism, the very suggestion that the cravings and

aspirations of the two economic classes can be compared is anathema. *All* bosses are wicked exploiters, devoid of compassion and mercy, bent on squeezing every last profit from the marrow of their employees. How can the bourgeoisie be mentioned in the same breath as the oppressed workers of the world, who will surely aspire to do all that is right and just the moment they achieve control of the international economic apparatus?

Judaism responds: "But is it so?" If every factory in the world were to post on its front door a huge sign, bearing the motto "From Each According to His Ability; To Each According to His Need," would every worker actually perform according to the best of his ability? Surely, Karl Marx — understanding the benefits which would accrue to the exploited — would give his best. And many, many other dedicated, ideologically motivated individuals would do likewise. But would *all* workers perform according to their ability, knowing full well that they would be guaranteed adequate compensation regardless of their output? Wouldn't large numbers of individuals attempt to cheat the new system — as, in fact, they do in most Communist countries today? Moreover, it can be asked whether it is absolutely just to deny extraordinarily motivated individuals those rewards which would be their due for outstanding achievement (or output). And, even if it is just to strictly enforce the principle that each individual be compensated only according to his established need, there remains a problem: many who would be physically capable of transcending the limits of duty will inevitably find their enthusiasm tempered when they realize that they have nothing to gain by exerting themselves.

Although there are major "kinks" in the Marxist system, a devotee of the cult might reply that *all* economic structures have "kinks." That is true, and that is the reason that Judaism would not inherently oppose the Marxist dogma were it not for Marx's call for the abolition of nations, religions, and many basic human rights. When Marx wrote to the "workers of the world" that, by uniting, they would have "nothing to lose but . . . chains," he neglected to inform them that they would also have to lose their right to worship God. The opposition of Marxism to religion has already been considered as its practice has affected the Jewish faith. Inasmuch as many Communist societies do not have large Jewish populations within their borders, a more thorough discussion of Marxist religious intolerance would include tragic volumes on the repression of devout Christians throughout Eastern Europe and Buddhists and Taoists in countries like China, Cambodia, and Vietnam. Such intolerance is not only theoretical but brutally real.

Indeed, there is no more potent confirmation that Judaism's conception of the nature of man is accurate than the results of Communist take-overs throughout the world. Interestingly, no workers' paradise has even been erected within a Marxist country; yet, Communist regimes have had no difficulty instituting severely repressive measures against all people who oppose them. The list of human-rights violations perpetrated by Marxist powers in recent years alone stretches as long as the "Gulag Archipelago" itself. The Polish government, for example, has repeatedly arrested and abused members of the Workers' Defense Committee, a dissident group organized to assist proletarians who were fired after striking or rioting over food-price increases in 1976.

Nothing illustrates more clearly the insecurity of the Polish government than its law forbidding citizens from owning mimeograph machines. Violation of the law carries with it a possible five-year sentence.[28] But despite such attempts to censor the thoughts of the Polish people, Communist regimes in Warsaw have been unable to win over the hearts and minds of their conquered citizens. A visit to Poland by Pope John Paul II sparked a massive, nationwide show of support for the religion so deprecated by Marxist leaders in Warsaw. And, in 1980, rises in the price of meat set off a strike by 17,000 workers at the Ursus tractor plant near the nation's capital. Within weeks, laborers in the tens of thousands walked off their jobs throughout Poland, striking for an end to the misery in their land.

In Czechoslovakia, "Charter 77"—which demanded an end to the denial of freedom in that country—sparked a frantic wave of repression. In one case, playwright Vaclav Havel was forced to resign his position as "Charter 77 spokesman" after serving a debilitating five-month prison term. And, in a fitting anti-Jewish effort, the Czech regime described those who signed the manifesto as "paid by Zionists to continue their subversive role inside the country."[29] In all, dozens of the signers of Charter 77 have been imprisoned for affixing their names to the call for freedom of conscience, and more than three score have been exiled from their native soil. Other signators have been subjected to denunciation and other forms of official harassment, including actions taken against their children. In some cases, pets belonging to charter signers have been found dead or nailed to house doors, and plainclothes goons have openly pummeled human-rights activists in the streets of Prague.[30]

Rumania's crackdown on human rights in recent years has centered around its brutal mistreatment of novelist Paul Goma. Goma was blacklisted, arrested (after co-signing an appeal for freedom that was transmitted to the West), and subsequently assaulted on three occasions by a professional boxer.[31] Dissident painter Sergiu Manoliu was sent out of the country after making contact with Radio Free Europe. As for the Jewish community, it has been reliably reported that nearly 20,000 individuals are trying to emigrate from the country, although fewer than 1,500 are permitted to leave in any year.[32]

Yugoslavian jails, meanwhile, hold hundreds of political prisoners, most of them Croatians seeking to establish an independent, non-Communist Croatia. Other prisoners include Slovenian intellectuals advocating political freedom in Slovenia and individuals charged with smuggling forbidden literature into the country. In addition, in one internationally publicized case, Srdja Popovic, a Belgrade attorney, was put on trial for expressing personal agreement with the dissenting political views of a client he was defending.[33]

The human misery and repression that is Communism has

appeared in the Western hemisphere, too, in Castro's Cuba. The failure to create a workers' paradise in Havana was dramatically underscored when, in 1980, the Castro government entered into a feud with the nation of Peru. Angered over a Peruvian decision to grant political asylum to twenty-five Cubans who had assembled on the grounds of Peru's embassy in Havana, Castro resolved to punish his South American neighbor. Accordingly, he withdrew the special Cuban security force whose assignment had always been to protect the territory occupied by the Lima embassy. Defiantly, he challenged Peru's government to provide its own security force and announced that anyone unhappy with the "struggle for socialism" was more than welcome to join the twenty-five political dissidents. He never dreamed that his words would be taken so seriously.

Within days, more than 10,000 Cubans—men, women, and children—crushed their way into the Peruvian embassy area. Desperately, they raced for the once-in-a-lifetime sanctuary. The image of a swarm of humanity seeking refuge from Cuba reached newspapers and television screens throughout the world, deeply embarrassing Castro and his Soviet benefactors. Fidel sought to save face by describing the refugees as "delinquents, antisocial elements, bums, trash, parasites, homosexuals, gamblers, and drug addicts."[34] But reporters from nations throughout the world wired back the simple facts, harsh though they be in judgment of a failed system of government: the group comprised of simple Cubans from all walks of life (including 2,700 children), who could no longer bear the tragedy, misery, and suffering encountered daily in Cuba.

Fidel, too, did some confessing. Despite the largesse of the Soviets, amounting to eight million dollars a *day* in handouts to Castro's paralyzed economy, Cuba was unable to control its deep economic crisis. Fidel spoke of a blight that had wiped out the country's tobacco crop for two consecutive years, forcing most Havana cigar factories to close. Compounding the aggravation were cases of sugar cane rot and swine fever. In all, the nation was mired in poverty, and it could not be surprising to the seasoned observer that ten thousand Cubans would willingly endure heat, filth, and hunger—not to mention meager sanitary facilities, water scarcity, and inadequate sewage—in the desperate hope that they might be allowed to leave the Havana hell. By crushing into the Peruvian compound, they hoped merely to join their 800,000 compatriots who had already fled from Castro since 1959.[35]

For those remaining behind, the Marxist experiment continues to be a living nightmare. The country suffers from inefficiency and mismanagement. For example, two years were lost in constructing a nuclear-power plant; only too late did experts realize that the site chosen for its construction was located in an earthquake zone. Bureaucratic corruption, likewise, is rampant, even to the point of provoking a steady stream of complaints in the letters column of *Granma*, the Cuban Communist Party newspaper. Black markets flourish, and public workers sneak off their jobs at midday to work on their own private farms.[36]

The Marxist effort in Cuba has been a dismal failure, succeeding in but one area; the Havana government has developed an all-encompassing state-security system, effectively policing the entire nation and wiping out all sources of dissent. As Cuba continues to receive its daily grants of eight million dollars from Moscow, and as the Soviets continue to provide Castro with his oil needs at one-third the world price (while buying his sugar at three times the going rate), it is to be expected that Fidel will continue conducting his dictatorship in the Western hemisphere along Soviet lines. The Marxist utopian dream has failed; the misery and repression continue.

Of all the nations who have enacted repressive measures, the Soviets have repeatedly stood out. They have jammed radio broadcasts, obstructed the efforts of journalists, denied legitimate requests for exist visas, suppressed attempts by local minorities to promote cultural expression, persecuted religious leaders, incarcerated human-rights activists, and sent leading dissident intellectuals to insane asylums.

Consider the chilling report on Soviet psychiatric abuse of

political prisoners presented to a congressional subcommittee in Washington by Leonid Plyushch, a Ukrainian scientist. Plyushch, who had been brutally confined for over two years in an asylum with mentally deranged hooligans, rapists, and murderers, described the effects of one common punishment technique, the forced injection of heavy doses of sulphur: "This patient groaned loudly for twenty-four hours. Mad with pain, he tried to hide himself under the bed. In despair, he broke the window and tried to cut his throat with the glass. Then he was punished again and beaten up . . ."[37]

Persecution of Soviet Christians was documented before the same subcommittee three months later, with special attention being drawn to the case of Reverend Georgi Vins, sentenced to five years of hard labor. A leader of the Council for Evangelical Christians and Baptists, Vins defied government-imposed restrictions on religion and was therefore sentenced to a Siberian labor camp, where he was forced to haul logs ten hours daily in temperatures as bitter as sixty degrees below zero.[38] In another internationally famous incident, Soviet dissident Andrei Sakharov appealed to President Carter to intervene on behalf of Vasily Romanyuk, a Ukranian Orthodox priest, who had been on a prolonged hunger strike in a Soviet prison camp, demanding a Bible.

Political dissidents have not fared much better than their religious counterparts. Pyotr Ruban was sentenced to eight years in prison for carving a wooden model of the Statue of Liberty on the occasion of the American Bicentennial. Yuri Orlov, the chairman of a committee formed to monitor human-rights violations in the USSR, was given the opportunity to do some on-the-spot investigating; shortly after the group was established, Soviet police arrested him.

Soviet Jews continue to suffer their own special fate, as exit visas are denied, as anti-Semitic television programs are aired nationally during prime viewing hours, and as virulently anti-Jewish writings appear regularly in the country's press. In many ways, the tragic case of Colonel Yefim Davidovich, a Soviet war hero who was decorated fifteen times during a distinguished career which ended with his retirement in 1969, typifies the situation facing Jews in the USSR. After Davidovich applied for a visa to emigrate to Israel, the government turned on him and began a campaign of abuse and harassment against him. He suffered five heart attacks and was actually denied admittance to a hospital on the fifth occasion. When Davidovich again recovered, his home telephone — an essential commodity in the event of a sudden medical crisis — was disconnected by the KGB secret police force. Shortly thereafter, Davidovich suffered his sixth heart attack — his last.

One of the most revealing commentaries on the state of affairs in Marxist Russia was the letter signed by seventy-two Soviet workers from forty-two cities in the USSR protesting the fact that they had been fired from their respective jobs for having complained about bad working conditions and managerial corruption in Soviet industries. Insisting that they were not "dissidents" but simple working people, they wrote:

> We are a vast army of Soviet unemployed, thrown
> out of the gates of Soviet enterprises for attempting to
> exercise the right to complain, the right to criticize, the
> right to freedom of speech.
>
> We undertook to offer publicly critical remarks against
> the plundering of socialist property, bad conditions of
> work, low pay, high injury rates, the raising of production
> norms leading to waste and low quality production.[39]

The letter's co-signers explained that they had met each other while seeking hearings for their individual complaints in the reception hall of the Soviet State Prosecutor's Office. Unfortunately, they noted, the hall is a scene of great tension because "it is difficult to foresee in advance who among those waiting will be seized" and taken to the militia station or to the admitting doctor at a mental hospital for a "conversation."[40] Stunned that so many workers had faced similar problems and noted identical forms of abuse and corruption, they decided to join together and speak out on behalf "of thousands of persons in the Soviet Union who openly challenge industrial abuses."

If the entire justification of the totalitarian system in the Soviet Union is that such repression is necessary to assure a "workers' paradise," then what can be said after it becomes clear that the country is a workers' hell? Food shortages are legion in the USSR. In Arkhangelsk, in northern Russia, milk is so scarce that it can be obtained only by doctor's prescription.[42] Distress slaughtering becomes inevitable, as fruit and vegetable crops emerge damaged year after year, as dairy production wanes, as grain harvests prove catastrophically inadequate.[43] Even as the Soviet Union has developed world-class weapons and armaments, their citizenry continue to subsist on a diet of starchy staples like potatoes.

If drastic food shortages lead to worker misery, the Soviet government has nonetheless constructed safeguards to prevent workers from taking their grievances to the streets. Independent trade unions are illegal in the USSR. All workers must belong to special unions, organized by the Communist Party and headed by paid party personnel.[44] Such trade unions do not challenge the Soviet system of which they are a leading part. Fired workers are not defended by union bosses.[45] Unions do not protest violations of labor safety regulations; nor do they defend the need to protect workers' hygiene.[46] Most significantly, strikes are illegal in this workers' paradise.

When factory workers walked off their jobs for eight days in the Ukraine, the strike coordinators were fired and their leader was put in jail for one year.[47] A one-day strike at the Kamenets-Podolski Agricultural Machinery Factory was stopped when thirty workers were fired for being "strike leaders." Two were sentenced to three-year prison terms.[48]

The litany is endless. In Uzbekistan and southern Kazakhstan, fifth-grade children are required to work at thinning cotton in school. While out in the fields, the students are still registered as though they are in class. They are expected to produce their daily output even in heavy rains. It is not surprising that medical check-ups of these children have revealed that some forty percent of them suffer from rheumatism.[49]

In the Usugly Fluorite Mines, workers struggle in weather that falls below freezing for most of the year. In most cases, both husband and wife must labor in the mines for eight hours daily, then return home for six hours' work, feeding and milking cows, caring for chickens, pigs, a vegetable garden, and other food sources. If they do not do the work at home, their family does not eat.[50] Local stores never have eggs or milk; once a year, flour is available in limited supply (in bags labeled "Made in Canada").[51] The few regularly available food items include: vodka, poor-quality bread (in limited supply), and old, canned fish.[52]

There is misery, real misery, in the Soviet Union. Workers are hungry. Long hours and nineteenth-century conditions sap them of the vigor so essential to a free human spirit. Totalitarian laws and police-state measures repress whatever remains of that human spirit yearning to breathe free. In the USSR, a nation where three million people—some two percent of the entire population—are (or have been) compelled to do forced labor, the miracle is not that so few have risen to dissent against the institutionalization of misery. The miracle is that any at all have dared to rise up in protest, that any have found the physical strength, internal fortitude, and raw courage to speak out. The Gulag Archipelago—the Soviet prison system— and the network of Soviet mental hospitals holding political dissidents bear witness to the presence of men and women yearning to be free. They also bear compelling witness to the failure of Marxism. Despite the asseverations of the Prophet, despite the assurances of the Saints, despite the continued assertions of the cult devotees, Marxism has not worked. Every time it is tried, it fails miserably—without exception—leaving its victims worse off than they were previously.

Ultimately, a detailed study of the effects of Marxist doctrine, as it has been implemented throughout the world, reminds one of the perspicuous aphorism: "In a capitalist society, Man exploits Man. In a communist society, it's the other way around."

Ostensibly, the Jewish approach is the more difficult. Yet,

as the Talmud explains, "there is a road which is short but long and a road which is long but short."[53] We have seen how easy it is to overthrow a weak capitalist structure and to replace it with a Marxist regime. In Russia, China, Vietnam, and Cambodia — among other places — such revolutions have succeeded in this century. But did they *really* improve the lot of man? Did they *really* usher in a worker's paradise?

Consider Vietnam. For more than a decade, the United States of America was embroiled in an undeclared war against North Vietnam. Eventually, a large-scale movement emerged in the United States calling for an end to the conflict — or, at the very least, for a termination of the American involvement in the battle. What possible sense did it make for the government of the United States to send its best young people to die for a mendacious and corrupt right-wing dictatorship? It is essential to note that, although many of the leading participants in the anti-war movement were of pronounced left-wing sentiment, the vast majority of those who called for an end to the conflict were of comparatively centrist political bent.

The anti-war cause was, by all measures, a good cause — and the war was, by all comparative standards, an unfortunate (if not totally immoral) one. After years of political pressuring and lobbying, the movement succeeded in achieving its long-sought dream: America extricated herself from the bloodshed in Southeast Asia. The armed forces of the United States first departed from Vietnam and, later, from neighboring Cambodia. Peace would finally come to the region.

But, the humane intents of the anti-war movement notwithstanding, did peace really descend on Vietnam and Cambodia? To be sure, *Americans* were finally at peace. But what ever happened to the people of Vietnam and Cambodia? Not long after the US pull-out, both nations were "liberated" by Marxist forces, the Vietcong and the Khmer Rouge respectively. Finally, the right-wing fascists were ousted, and workers' paradises could be established under the enlightened guidelines of Marxism. But were they?

Since 1975, when the Vietcong overthrew the Thieu regime

and annexed South Vietnam, the reports of suffering and human-rights violations emanating from the newly reconstituted "Vietnam" have been staggering. If the situation has not become appreciably worse than it had been under Thieu and Ky, it has certainly not become better. Unemployment has become more severe since the Marxists took power, and wages leave workers with "barely enough to feed one person, let alone a family."[54]

More egregious have been the blatant human-rights violations. Literally hundreds of thousands of people—estimates range as high as half a million[55]—have been incarcerated in "re-education camps." One who lived to tell of their plight was Nguyen Cong Hoan, a radical Buddhist peace advocate who testified before the House International Relations Subcommittee on International Organizations in 1977.[56] In a special column he wrote for *Newsweek* magazine shortly after his testimony on Capitol Hill, he elaborated:

> To a Vietnamese like myself, who detested the corrupt and repressive Thieu regime and considered the Communist victory a liberation, [the admission of the government of Vietnam into the United Nations] should bring joy. But after living for nearly two years in Communist Vietnam, I feel precisely the opposite emotion.
>
> I escaped from Vietnam to tell the world the truth about what is happening in my country. Within days after Hanoi's troops came to my town, such widely proclaimed policies of the Viet Cong's National Liberation Front as religious freedom, democratic liberties, peace and neutralism went out the window. . . .
>
> The new authorities rule by force and terror. What little freedom existed under Thieu, is gone. The An Ninh secret police are dreaded—worse than any previous Vietnamese regime. There is no freedom of movement or association; no freedom of the press, or of religion, or of economic enterprise, or even of private personal opinion.

Rights of habeas corpus, or of property, are either unknown or flouted even as the government redefines these rights. Fear is everywhere. . . .[57]

Even more shocking than the tragedy in Vienam has been the repression in neighboring Cambodia. In a *Time* magazine report published one year after the Khmer Rouge Marxists overthrew the American-backed government of Lon Nol, the gruesome tale of terror revealed that over 500,000 Cambodians had died under the brief Communist reign. "Whole families — and sometimes entire villages — have been massacred . . . [Refugees] tell tales of people being clubbed to death to save ammunition. Others have been bound together and buried alive by bulldozers, or suffocated by having plastic bags tied over their heads."[58]

Thus, in but one year of Marxist rule, ten times more Cambodians died than did American soldiers in the preceding ten years of conflict in Southeast Asia. In all, one-tenth of the entire Cambodian population had succumbed during this first twelve months. Despite the terror, however, the economy did not straighten out as Marxist theoreticians had predicted. In fact, a subsequent *New York Times* report revealed that two years after the Communist "liberation" of Phnom Penh the country was "desolate . . . beset by crop failures and disintegrating irrigation systems."[59] Indeed, the economy had taken a severe turn for the worse, with hunger and disease having sharply increased since the Khmer Rouge take-over. One reason for the economic decline was described by Tap Krean, a thirty-five-year-old refugee from the country, who found that Marxist theory did not work in actual practice:

> We still worked very hard the first year. But, then, the Communists took away half our harvest, and we found that no matter how hard we worked, we still got only our two bowls of rice gruel each day.
> So, while usually we paid attention when we plowed, not to skip any space, to plow neat rows close together, last year no one paid any attention. We plowed

like that, this space, that space. And there was nothing to kill the weeds, and the dikes broke.[60]

Another aspect of the Marxist ideals which did not work out was the principle of sharing the wealth equally. Repeatedly, it was reported that local Communist leaders lived better than everyone else. They, unlike regular Cambodians, were permitted to own their own pigs and chickens, and they were allowed to grow small vegetable gardens for their personal use.

Despite the economic problems, however, the aspect of Marxist rule in Cambodia which most concerns Judaism is that of the repeated cases of gross inhumanity and opposition to basic freedoms. Describing the social upheaval which has turned Cambodia into "one of the most eerie and most savage nations of modern times," *Newsweek* magazine presented this picture of 1978 Cambodian life:

> The workday seldom varies. Men, women, and children are roused at dawn and sent out into the fields. After a mid-day rest break, they toil on until dark. There are no holidays, no days off. The sick must rely on untrained medics who treat cholera with Pepsi-Cola and typhoid with coconut milk . . .
>
> Anyone who breaks the rules faces immediate execution. The transgressor is usually clubbed to death with a pick handle. But in special cases, like those of starving workers who are caught cannibalizing dead bodies, there are special tortures. They are buried in the ground up to their shoulders and beaten to death — or their heads are chopped off and jammed onto pointed stakes.[61]

Clearly, Cambodia has not evolved into a worker's paradise. Rather, it has become a veritable "country of walking dead."[62] Eighty percent of Cambodia's children are starving; yet, less than 5 percent of the country's rice lands are being cultivated. There are ten deaths in Cambodia for every birth. Only 20 to 30 percent of the surviving adult population is male; the overwhelming majority of the women are widows.[63]

Considering these statistics and the most chilling of all—the fact that, in the first five years since the Communist "liberation" of Cambodia, the national population had decreased by nearly three million (constituting more than 30 percent of the Cambodian people)—Peter J. Donaldson wrote in the *New York Times* that "the only modern parallel to the events in Cambodia, from a demographic point of view, is the Holocaust."[64]

Ultimately, then, the outrages perpetrated by the Thieu-Ky dictatorship in South Vietnam and the Lon Nol dictatorship in Cambodia have not been halted since Marxist forces "liberated" the two regions. In fact, the few meager rights that existed have been abrogated as well, and shocking human-rights violations have become commonplace. And, through it all, the lot of the worker has not improved. Marxism has proven to be that road which is "short but long."

Judaism does not oppose the economics of sharing. Nor does Judaism look lightly upon the plight of the working man. On the contrary, it was the Torah which powerfully presented to humanity the notions of economic justice:

> And when you sell something to your neighbor, or when you buy something from your neighbor's hand, you shall not defraud one another . . .
>
> You shall not oppress a hired worker who is poor and needy . . . On his day you shall give him his wages, and let the sun not descend on it [before he is paid], for he is poor and he sets his heart on it . . .[65]

The Torah is replete with laws regulating business dealings and economic transactions. These laws ensure honesty and justice. Consider these verses in Leviticus 19:

> And when you reap the harvest of your land, you shall not wholly reap the edges of your field; neither shall you gather the gleanings of your harvest. And you shall not glean your vineyard; neither shall you gather the single grapes of your vineyard. You shall leave them for the poor and the stranger . . .

You shall not defraud your neighbor, neither shall you
rob him. And do not retain with you overnight the wages
of a hired worker until the morning [after his payday].
You shall do no unrighteousness in judgment. You
shall not unfairly favor the poor; nor shall you overly
honor the mighty. Rather, in righteousness shall you judge
your neighbor.
You shall commit no unrighteousness in judgment in
measures of length, of weight, or of quantity. Just
balances, just weights . . . shall you have.

The Talmud reasserts the Torah's theme in the most emphatic
tones. Whole Talmudic tractates are set aside for the sole
consideration of economic justice. Jewish law, moreover, does
not simply satisfy itself with the prohibition of such dishonest
practices as deceptive advertising.[66] Rather, it transcends
standard "morality" by preaching the sanctity of conducting
one's business *lifnim mi-shurat ha-din*—in accordance with
principles which extend beyond the bare letter of law and which
conform more perfectly with the absolute spirit of the law.[67] So
deeply concerned is Judaism with economic justice—and so
awesome is the Jew's responsibility to conduct his financial
affairs with the utmost integrity—that the Talmud teaches
that the first question asked of a deceased man's soul when it
comes before the throne of the Almighty for judgment is: "Did
you transact business honestly [during your days on earth]?"[68]
To help man better himself, God gave the Jewish people His
Torah and obligated the Jews to live by its laws. While all of
mankind is expected to obey seven basic laws,[69] the ultimate
perfection of humanity will be realized on the day of which
Isaiah spoke so beautifully:

And it shall come to pass in the latter days that the
mountain of the Lord's house shall be established on the
top of the mountains, and shall be exalted above the
hills; and all nations shall flow to it. And many
peoples shall go and say, "Come and let us go up to the
mountain of the Lord, to the house of the God of Jacob;

and He will teach us of His ways, and we will walk in His paths; for out of Zion shall go forth the Teaching, and the word of the Lord from Jerusalem."[70]

That is what the Jews were chosen for. Not for racial superiority. Not for national chauvinism. But for the awesome responsibility and obligation to bear witness to all of mankind that there *is* a "long road which is short." Man *can* strengthen himself and overcome his inclination to do wrong. Man *can* lift himself up to uncharted human heights of generosity and kindness. For that reason alone—to teach all of mankind that lesson—was the Jewish people called to Mount Sinai by God and obligated to live by the Torah laws and thereby bear witness to all of humanity.

The Torah, then, is the Jewish response to such holy scriptures of the Marxist cults as *Das Kapital*. It speaks of a God in Heaven as embodying the absolute Good—in contradistinction to Marxism, which assigns that role to the international proletariat. And it longs for the day of Messianic redemption for all mankind—unlike Marxism, which aspires for the utopia to be ushered in by the ultimate dictatorship of the proletariat.

Although Judaism offers the more optimistic and intellectually satisfying approach to the problems of mankind, it also presents to man the formidable challenge—the challenge of morality. In Marxist terms, the "soul" of the bourgeoisie is lost and can never attain salvation; antithetically, the collective "soul" of the proletariat is so wholesomely pure that it can be forgiven the worst of sins on the simple grounds that capitalist society leaves it with no alternative. Mass horrors and tortures perpetrated by Marxist nations are simply "necessary preludes" to the establishment of workers' utopias, ultimately inconsequential moral mishaps occasioned by generations of capitalist abuses. In such a redefined conceptualization of morality, the Gulag Archipelago becomes a remodeled vacation resort while Southeast Asian "re-education camps" become government-sponsored universities. Succinctly put, morality becomes devoid of actual meaning, a subjective yardstick which condemns a Mussolini but pardons a Stalin, incriminates a Lon Nol but expiates a Khmer Rouge.

There is no authentic morality in Marxism. Any action—no matter how heinous—is permissible if it will hasten the demise of the bourgeoisie and will advance the cause of the proletariat. In Lenin's words—subsequently quoted by Stalin in defense of his infamous persecutions—morality can be reduced to these terms: "Whoever weakens in the least the iron discipline of the party of the proletariat (especially during the time of its dictatorship) actually aids the bourgeoisie against the proletariat."[71]

Judaism proudly differs. Morality is not reducible to the subjective fancies of man but is defined and laid down by the objective consciousness of God. Moreover, morality transcends economics on the register of factors which have determined the evolution of history, and it towers above economic considerations on the list of societal components which must be positively restructured and refined prior to the dawning of a better age.

If Marx—whose father was descended from a long line of rabbis—missed the entire message of authentic Judaism, we should not be surprised. Unable to cope with the brutal Jew-hatred prevalent in early nineteenth-century Germany, his parents deserted the Jewish faith and embraced Christianity, succumbing to the missionaries of their period. Accordingly, they baptized Karl at the age of six. To perceive why Karl Marx grew to disdain *all* religions is not hard. Clearly, his parents had little use for Judaism, and their conversion to Christianity was motivated more by a desire to raise their social and economic position than by a sudden urge to worship Jesus. What, indeed, could religion have meant to young Karl Marx? It is not difficult to understand why he came to look upon religion as a meaningless contrivance, a purposeless label which had nothing to offer but division.

What Marx never considered was that there were other Jews as well. Deeply sincere, devoted, and committed Jews. Jews who thought of their Torah and faith not as mere adjectives to their lives but as their raison d'être. There were such Jews, and there are still such Jews.

In many ways, it can be said that today's young Jewish Marxists have made the same decisions as did their prophet because they faced the same familial tensions as did he. Where parents live by the pseudo-theology of "dollar-Judaism," a social system which not only negates but abases authentic Judaism, the temptation to turn away from the covenant God made with Abraham and reaffirmed at Mount Sinai (before the eyes of a nation) is great. Judaism becomes a "game," with the high-salaried "rabbi" serving as little more than a first-base coach. It loses its ultimate meaning and purpose: the charge to bear God's witness to mankind by living a holy and sanctified life in accordance with the dictates of the Torah, the quintessence of morality and ethical responsibility.

Not for nothing did the Talmud warn: "It is an obligation to publicly expose religious hypocrites, in order to prevent the desecration of God's Name."[72] For the ultimate victim of "dollar-Judaism" is neither the parent who faces bankruptcy trying to pay off a $15,000 bar mitzva nor the relative who invades the local pharmacy in a desperate effort to stock up on antacids for the ride home therefrom — but the young, deeply sensitive thirteen-year-old boy who will never forget that spiritually barren rite into which he was cast.

He will not forget. And, to the later despair of his community, he may not forgive.

Notes

1) *Psalms* 121:1-2.
2) Karl Marx, "On the Jewish Question," in Robert C. Tucker (ed.), *The Marx-Engels Reader* (N.Y.: W.W. Norton and Company, 1972), p. 30.
3) *Ibid.*, pp. 46-51.

4) These shockingly bigoted quotes were assembled by Dr. Silberner in substantiation of his charge. See: Dr. Edmund Silberner, "Was Marx an Anti-Semite?" *Historia Judaica*, vol. 11, no. 1 (April, 1949), pp. 3-52.

5) There are a number of detailed works on the situation of Soviet Jewry, past and present.

6) *Jewish Journal*, 2/11/75.

7) *Jewish Telegraphic Agency*, 6/23/75.

8) *New York Times*, 7/8/76.

9) *Jewish Press*, 8/13/76; *Jewish Week*, 8/22/76.

10) *Jewish Week*, 9/19/76.

11) *Jewish Press*, 10/31/75; *Jewish Week*, 11/9/75.

12) *Jewish Week*, 2/8/76.

13) *Jewish Journal*, 2/27/76.

14) *Jerusalem Post*, 7/5/79. See also the transcript of the speech delivered by Representative Jack Kemp.

15) *New York Times*, 12/6/76.

16) *Jerusalem Post*, 7/5/79.

17) *Jewish Journal*, 6/23/78; *Jewish Week* 1/20/80.

18) See Herbert Krosney, "The PLO's Moscow Connection," *New York Magazine*, 9/24/79.

19) *New York Times*, 2/13/80.

20) See "The Soviet-PLO Axis," a report published in 1980 by the Anti-Defamation League.

21) Don't bother yourself too much over the fact that an article which *first* appeared in *November* was *later reprinted* in October. The CPUSA does not adhere carefully to the capitalist, neo-colonialist, imperialist calendar.

22) *New York Times*, 5/15/77.

23) *Jewish Journal*, 2/29/80; *Jewish Week*, 3/2/80.

24) *Human Events*, 8/24/74.

25) This modern version of "Jewish philanthropy" is evident, for example, every week in the *Jewish Week*, a newspaper published in New York with the financial backing of the Federation of Jewish Philanthropies of Greater New York. Every issue includes pages of photographs of donors to the Federation, each of whom sports a plaque awarded him for his check.

26) Irving Kristol, "Looking Back on Neo-Conservatism," *American Spectator*, 11/77.

27) Tractate Berachot 33b.

28) *New York Times*, 6/13/80.

29) *Jewish Journal*, 5/13/77.

30) *Newsweek*, 11/5/79.

31) *New York Times*, 3/30/77; 4/14/77.

32) *Ibid.*, 2/17/77.

33) *Ibid.*, 3/2/76; 3/11/76; 3/24/76.

34) *Ibid.*, 4/13/80 (Week in Review); cf. *Newsweek*, 4/21/80.

35) *Ibid.*

36) *Newsweek*, 5/26/80.

37) *Psychiatric Abuse of Political Prisoners in the Soviet Union—Testimony by Leonid Plyushch*, 3/30/76 (Washington, D.C.: U.S. Government Printing Office, 1976).

38) *Religious Persecution in the Soviet Union.* 6/24/76 & 6/30/76 (Washington, D.C.: U.S. Government Printing Office, 1976).

39) *Washington Post*, 12/20/77.

40) *Ibid.*

41) *Ibid.*

42) *Newsweek*, 7/7/80.

43) *Ibid.*

44) *AFL-CIO FTUN*, 9/79.

45) *Ibid.*, p. 8.

46) *Ibid.*

47) *Ibid.*, p. 13.

48) *Ibid.*

49) *Ibid.*, 11/79, p. 9.

50) *Ibid.*, p. 10.

51) *Ibid.*

52) *Ibid.*

53) Tractate *Eruvin* 53b.

54) *Newsweek*, 10/31/77. In 1980, *monthly* wages in Vietnam were averaging thirty-two dollars, while goods were in such scarce supply that prices were out of control. Government stores were empty, their shelves bare. A can of Coca-Cola was selling for $6.40, and a pair of blue jeans went for $275. These figures are especially noteworthy, coming *five full years* after the Communists conquered South Vietnam. (*Wall Street Journal*, 6/5/80)

55) *Ibid.*

56) *Washington Post*, 7/27/77.

57) *Newsweek*, 10/31/77.

58) Patrick J. Buchanan, "Year One of Cambodia's Liberation," *Boston Herald-American*, 4/20/76.

59) *New York Times*, 5/2/77.

60) *Ibid.*

61) *Newsweek*, 1/23/78.

62) *Ibid.*

63) Statistics published by Oxfam-America, 11/79, in *Moment* magazine.

64) *New York Times*, 4/22/80.

65) Leviticus 25:14; Deuteronomy 24:14-15.

66) See, for example, *Choshen Mishpat* 228:9, which forbids the deceptive packaging of meats, whereby they are made to appear beefier than they really are, and the deceptive packaging of old utensils, whereby they are re-painted and sold as "brand new."

67) In Tractate *Yoma* 86a, for example, Abbaye—a leading Talmudic sage—taught that one must go to the greatest trouble in order to assure that he conduct his business honestly and that none be misled to erroneously suspect the slightest impropriety. Accordingly, whenever Abbaye purchased meat from two partners, he paid the full bill to each of them. Only afterwards would he bring them together and square his accounts with each.

68) Tractate *Shabbath* 31a.

69) The seven laws given to Noah, for transmission to all mankind, appear in chapter one, footnote 24.

70) Isaiah 2:2-3.

71) Arthur P. Mendel (ed.), *Essential Works of Marxism* (N.Y.: Bantam, 1971), p. 291.

72) Tractate *Yoma* 86b. See also Rashi commentary *ad loc.*

2

AMERICAN JUDAISM
IN TURMOIL

And Aaron said, "Let not the anger of my
lord burn hot. You know the people, that
they are set on mischief."

(EXODUS 32:22)

A circumspect consideration of the cult phenomenon — especially as it has affected American Jews — should not be limited to an exploration of the theological counter-culture. While much is to be learned from the inner philosophies of the "Jews for Jesus," the Moonies, the Buddhists, the Hindu gurus, the Hare Krishnas, and the pseudo-theistic Marxists, there remains, nevertheless, one more religious community whose actions have contributed to the turmoil presently gripping American Jewish life.

The community in question is American Jewry itself.

If bizarre religious cults have made headway in their efforts to recruit young Jewish devotees, it has become clear that their successes have not evolved *ex nihilo*. On the contrary, it is they who have come to offer meaningful alternatives to the spiritual void presently plaguing so much of American Jewish society. Again and again it has become apparent that the most wholesome and inspiring values of the respective cults are abundantly present in authentic Judaism. Yet, to the consternation of the American Jewish community, tens of thousands of young people are deserting the very Judaism which nurtured them, in order to embrace foreign theologies. Why?

Can it be that these young Jews never learned what authentic Judaism asserts? Can it be that they were never taught the rich spiritual values of Jewish life, the historic potency of Jewish faith, the awesome challenge of Jewish commitment? Can it be that — despite the fact that they were treated to the best private education America could offer — they remained ignominiously ignorant of Jewish knowledge? Can it be?

To be sure, the American Jewish community has constructed an elaborate "educational network." Temples offer Sunday School curricula for children of dues-paying members. Adult education programs are promoted by many Jewish institutions. Some synagogues even provide expanded "Talmud Torah" classes, which offer instruction as frequently as three or four days weekly.

And, yet, a void ostensibly remains. Christian missionaries

misquote the Torah, and thousands of young Jews do not realize the deception. Consider, by the way of contrast, how long it would take the same youths to discern the difference between political fascism and the American constitutions's Bill of Rights. Indeed, these young people do not even know their very history! The mention of "Crusades" conjures up no memories of Jewish martyrdom at the hands of Christian swineherds; at most, it evokes a picture of a televised spiritual rally conducted by Billy Graham or the Reverend Ike. (The mention of "inquisition" or "pogrom" does not even elicit that much imagery.) While young Jews anxiously submerge themselves into the study of Alex Haley's roots, they remain tragically unconscious of their own.

The cults do not—indeed, cannot—offer a sensitive young Jewish soul anything warmer in spirit than authentic Judaism; on the contrary, the spiritual riches of Torah laws and concepts tower above those of the theological counter-culture. (Indeed, the few saving graces of most cults are those concepts they preach which are emulative of the Jewish faith.) And, yet, young Jews by the thousands leave their spiritual homes. There has to be a reason. If the external society is not offering something better than Judaism, then it is hard to avoid the corollary: the American Jewish experience is providing young people with something less than real Judaism. Once more, the words of Paul Engel—the young man who left Judaism to the Unification Church—echo ominously:

> I think back, and I wonder how this could have happened to me. For a few years I went to a Reform Sunday school and had a perfunctory bar mitzva. At our home, Passover was about the only Jewish thing we did, and that usually was a social dinner and nothing else. . . . Maybe I was thirsting for a religious faith with strong emotional ties.
>
> If I have learned anything, it is that Jewish students should be taught everything there is to know about Judaism but in a warm, family-oriented atmosphere.

Yet, there remains a paradox. Paul did study at a Reform Sunday school, and his parents did provide him with a bar mitzva (albeit "perfunctory"). If Paul was given an apparent Jewish education and was welcomed into the Jewish fold upon his thirteenth birthday—the day when a Jewish boy becomes a Jewish man—then how did he emerge from his childhood so Jewishly troglodytic? Did *Paul* fail—or did the institutions of Sunday school and bar mitzva let him down?

The search for the answer to this latter question is a critical undertaking, for the truths it may reveal can provide the American Jewish community with a new formula, a new foundation on which to build. If the Sunday school has not met up to its expectations, why has it not? If the bar mitzva celebration—which, in many cases, serves to motivate a young man to learn a small portion of the Torah in the original Hebrew—has not succeeded in its ultimate task, where has it failed? Why have these institutions not stemmed the tide of Jewish assimilation, intermarriage, and even apostasy?

The investigation demanded by these questions is a vital one. Not so that people might find fault and wave accusing fingers at those who have uplifted baseless cows and sanctified them. During a period of turmoil—and, if American Jewry is enmeshed in anything, it is turmoil—there is little time for the trading of mutual recriminations. Rather, the investigation is vital so that we might discern where our communal structure is decaying—nay, rotting—in order that we might understand where American Jewish rebuilding must begin.

CHAPTER 6

Bar Mitzvas and Dollar Theology:

Wrong rites

> ... Everyone is a friend to a man who gives gifts. (PROVERBS 19:6)
>
> We remember the fish that we would eat in Egypt for nothing, the cucumbers and the melons and the leeks and the onions and the garlic. (NUMBERS 11:5)

What exactly is a "bar mitzva"? Of the millions of American Jews who have spent, collectively, billions of dollars to make them happen, it can safely be surmised that few really can answer the question.

The phrase *bar mitzva* stems partly from Aramaic, the language of the Talmud. *Bar* literally means "son of," and *mitzva* means "commandment." So, a "Bar Mitzva" is a "son of the commandment."

It does not mean "gala affair." It does not even mean "caterer."

When the Jewish nation gathered before God at Mount Sinai to receive His Torah, they assumed a massive challenge. And responsibility. They undertook, as a nation, to accept the very yoke of the kingdom of Heaven. Had the Jewish people turned away from Sinai, they would have been expected to live their lives as all others — in accordance with seven basic moral laws handed down by God to Noah and his descendants. By agreeing to receive the Torah, the Jews advanced an historically awesome step closer to the Divine — not simply because they agreed to receive it but because they promised to live by it. A unique relationship of reciprocity was established between God and the nation. God chose the Jews — because the Jews chose God.[1]

But for what did God choose the Jews? Ultimately, He did not choose them for riches. He did not choose them to live an easy life. He did not choose them to be a superior race or people, as if intrinsically better by birth. No, He chose the Jews for none of these things. Rather, God chose the Jewish people to bear witness to mankind that there is but one road to human perfection — the road of the Torah.

> Behold, I have taught you statutes and judgments, even as the Lord my God commanded me . . .
> Keep, therefore, and do them; for *this* is your wisdom and your understanding in the sight of the nations, who shall hear all these statutes and say, "Surely this great nation is a wise and understanding people."
> For what nation is there so great, that has God so near to it, as the Lord our God is in all things for which we call upon Him?
> And what nation is there so great, that has statutes and judgments so righteous as all this Law, which I set before you this day?[2]

What sets the Jewish people apart from others is their national *obligation* to live their lives in accordance with the 613 laws enumerated in the Written Law (the Bible) and elaborated in the Oral Law (the Talmud). When the Jewish nation conducts its affairs in a manner consonant with Torah guidelines, it is a "wise and understanding people," beloved of God and worthy

1. The numbered notes to chapter 6 begin on page 231.

of the admiration of mankind. When, however, it strays, the consequences are severe.

Because the Jews alone bear the burden of the yoke of Heaven, their responsibility is immense. If they do not observe the Torah, then no one will. Thus, the concept of "chosenness" is not a one-sided affair. That very same "Chosen People" status which can bring glory to the Jews can bring them tragedy—if they neglect their part of the covenant with God. "We shall do, and we shall obey," the Jews promised God at Sinai.[3] For better—and for worse—God has (anthropomorphically speaking) maintained the transcript of the famous day's conversation on file.

Because the unique relationship between God and the Jews centers around the obligation of the Jewish people to faithfully observe all the commandments of the Torah, the greatest moment in a Jew's life comes when he grows old enough to fall within the covenant of responsibility. Naturally, a child—still incapable of grasping complex concepts—cannot be expected to abide by an all-encompassing life-system. The laws are not just conceived as blanket rituals but are designed for a distinct purpose: to bring one closer to Divinity. Accordingly, a child too young to perceive the purpose behind the Torah laws is also too young to fall within the covenant of responsibility.

At what point does one mature sufficiently to enter the active sector of Jewish peoplehood and national obligation? Naturally, rates of maturation differ from person to person. In an effort to create a standardized system, Jewish law arbitrated that males of thirteen years are to be considered mature enough to enter the covenant of responsibility. (Females, judged by the rabbis to develop more quickly, were considered mature at age twelve.[4]) Therefore, when a boy reaches the age of thirteen-and-a-day, he is no longer considered a boy, excused from the awesome burden of fulfilling the laws of the Torah. Rather, he is looked upon as a mature young man, henceforth obligated to perform all the Torah commandments assigned by God. At this point in his life, he is no longer a child in his parents' care, answerable to them alone. He is now a veritable "son of the commandment"—bar mitzva—answerable to the Torah itself.

Because of the awesome holiness surrounding a young boy's thirteenth birthday, the rabbis ordained that a *seudat mitzva*—a special repast, replete with all the appropriate, religiously festive trimmings—be arranged in honor of the occasion, by his father.[5] The bar mitzva begins the meal by ritually washing his hands and reciting the prayer: "You are blessed, Lord our God, King of the Universe, who has sanctified us with Your commandments, and commanded us to lave our hands" and breaks bread, first reciting the prayer: "You are blessed, Lord our God, King of the Universe, who brings forth bread from the earth," as he does whenever he eats bread. Then, during the meal, he delivers a *devar Torah* (a brief but insightful commentary on some aspect of the Torah). Finally, at the dinner's conclusion, the young man is the one honored with the opportunity to lead the recitation of the Grace. This was the style and manner in which the rabbis welcomed a new "son of the commandment" into his new role.

It would be erroneous to assume that the young "bar mitzva" was being introduced, at this meal, to these prayers for the first time in his life. Quite the contrary; he has been training in the performance of *mitzvot* all his life. By this time, he has been intensively schooled in Judaism, becoming familiar with the Hebrew language and occupied with the study of Torah. Indeed, as a religious "graduation exercise," this very repast was quite a bit anticlimactic. For—usually on the Sabbath preceding the festive dinner—he had already demonstrated his Jewish knowledge by reading a portion of the Torah scroll before the entire congregation of his family synagogue. The "bar mitzva repast," then, was meant primarily to allow the young man to enjoy—and to sanctify—himself. Upon its conclusion, he would be an *acknowledged* Jewish man. And the following day, he would be on his way back to the yeshiva to continue his never-ending pursuit of Jewish knowledge.

These are the roots of the "bar mitzva" ceremony. These are the authentic Jewish values from which they emanated, and these are the sacred intentions the rabbis had in mind when they declared the great importance of arranging such a holy, yet festive, feast. One wonders what the rabbis would have said had they foreseen where it all would lead. Consider, for example, the "bat mitzva" (a celebration equivalent to the bar mitzva, in which a girl is welcomed into the covenant of responsibility upon her twelfth birthday) described in this 1977 news report:

> For the bat mitzvah of their daughter, Jolie,
> Mr. and Mrs. Stanley Cohen of Hartsdale, N.Y. thought
> of the idea of a different kind of banquet for the 70 guests,
> and the outcome after a long search was a menu of
> Japanese steaks cooked on a hibachi table on their own
> grounds. Mary Cohen, according to the Yonkers, N.Y.
> *Herald Statesman*, combed the countryside for a
> Japanese restauranteur who would prepare the meal on
> their patio. She finally reached *Tanaka*, of Eastchester,
> who liked the challenge. So the hibachi table was
> carted into a moving van to the Cohen domicile and then
> lugged to the patio. In addition to steaks, the menu
> included sushi (marinated raw fish), lamb brochettes,
> stuffed cheese, eggs with red caviar, tiny fishcakes, and
> marinated stuffed seaweed. No one calculated the cost of
> the affair, and the write-up in the *Herald Statesman* by
> Joan Undercoffler devoted not one word to the bat
> mitzvah service, nor was the name of the house of worship
> where the bat mitzvah took place or the rabbi mentioned.[6]

One wonders what the rabbis would have said . . .

Today, the bar mitzva ceremony has lost all touch with its very roots. A Jewish couple will spend five-figure sums, frequently bankrupting themselves, for the sole purpose of "putting on a show none of our neighbors will ever forget." Hyperbole? Consider this: "Entertainer Neil Sedaka, who is performing at Miami Beach's Fountainbleau, found a check for $100,000 in his suite with a note saying the money was his if he'd perform at the Bar Mitzvah of the check-signer's son . . ."[7]

Yes, even six figures.

While some Jewish parents can barely keep-up-with-the-Goldbergs, others literally incur debts beyond their means in the race to stage the most lavish bar mitzva in town. The "best" hall is rented. The "best" caterer is engaged to offer the "best" meat available—and, Torah commandments notwithstanding, it need not necessarily be kosher. (In one case, a San Antonio rabbi complained that 80 percent of the bar and bat mitzvas being held in his region were non-kosher.[8]) The "best" band is engaged. Other added attractions can include: a master of ceremonies, a comedian specializing in after-dinner humor, and even scantily clad go-go girls. In short, anything goes.

And anyone goes. While most guests go wild and most waiters go crazy, many parents go broke—and one celebrated bar mitzva parent came close to going to jail.

> NEW YORK —What could have been the most expensive bar mitzvah in years in more than one way has led only to grief for [name deleted], father of the boy, who has been found guilty of defrauding the Monticello Raceway, of which he is president, of $4,856.
>
> The affair was at Grossinger's, and the bill was so devised by Grossinger's as to appear as a charge against the raceway. . . . Grossinger testified that the affair had been billed at cost and otherwise would have totaled charges of between $12-15,000.[9]

The defendant was fined $9,000 by Federal District Judge Milton Pollack, was ordered to pay the prosecution costs, and was sentenced to two years' probation. Moreover, as a result of his ill-fated horseplay, he resigned from his position at the raceway.[10]

One wonders what the rabbis would have said . . . [11]

And one wonders what all this does to the young, sensitive bar mitzva boy. Having been raised in an assimilated community, bereft of authentic Jewish values, he cannot be expected—even under the best of prevailing circumstances—to emerge from his parents' home with an overwhelming sense of Jewish commitment. There is, nevertheless, some hope that bits of Jewish consciousness may have inadvertently been imparted to him over the years. The bar mitzva pageant negates that hope.

Consider the bar mitzva experience from the boy's point of view. He is twelve years of age, and his parents have never expressed any real Jewish sentiments to him. Suddenly, they tell him that he will be expected to learn a *haftora*. A what?

Because American Jewish boys do not have the Judaic erudition they should have, there is not even the remotest possibility that they would be called on to read from the Torah scroll. They might just as well read from the *Bhagavad-Gita* in the original Sanskrit. But, with the *haftora*, they have a fighting chance. The *haftora* is a short excerpt from the post-Pentateuchal writings in the Bible; it is recited in the synagogue on the Sabbath, immediately after the much longer reading from the Torah scroll (i.e., the Five Books of Moses inscribed in the format established by Talmudic tradition). Since most parents agree that a bar-mitzva boy should be able to show *some* Jewish literacy, they decide—at the eleventh hour—to enroll their sons in special Sunday school programs or Talmud Torahs where, at the very least, the *haftora* (the equivalent of one typewritten page of Hebrew) is transmitted over a year's time.

The boy dutifully trudges to the Hebrew school, week-in and week-out, hopelessly attempting to learn a foreign language which has no meaning to him. All his life, he has heard his parents mock authentic Jewish values and denigrate sacred Jewish texts. What possible significance can the *haftora* have to him?

The parents realize that their son is not making too much progress at the Sunday school, so they begin enticing him by telling him that all his friends and relatives will be coming to his bar mitzva to hear him. He had better learn his *haftora* well, or the parents will never be able to look his grandfather in the eye again. Besides, if he does well, he will undoubtedly be given any number of gifts. And not just fountain pens. Nowadays, people give US Savings Bonds. And electric trains. And cash.

The young boy is now presented with the profit motive. What better reason can an American Jewish youth have to prepare adequately for his bar mitzva? Business, after all, is business. The boy girds his intellectual loins and starts making headway. Rather than waste his time trying to decipher the Hebrew letters, he draws on his innate "Yankee ingenuity" and purchases a tape-recording of his *haftora*. Is there money to be made on the bar mitzva day? Fine. The cost of the *haftora* recording can be deducted as a business expense. Besides, why should he waste his time learning how to *read* the *haftora* when, in less than half the time, he can simply commit it to memory?

The bar mitzva day approaches. His parents begin renting the banquet hall (the one with the chandeliers in the bathroom), hiring the caterer (the one who offers two smorgasbords, one kosher and one non-kosher), selecting the band (the one which knows "*Hava Nagila*" and all the tunes from "Fiddler on the Roof"), choosing the master of ceremonies (the one who knows two Myron Cohen routines and who, for good measure, never misses Henny Youngman when the telephone company contracts him for "Dial-A-Joke"), and deciding on a photographer (the one who does "such a beautiful job" at the Hadassah conventions).

The day of reckoning draws nigh. His parents take him to get a tuxedo. The hard questions demand immediate answers: The dais will hold only twelve people—who gets bumped?— What flavor should the bar mitzva cake be? Will the Goldsteins sit at the same table as the Berkowitzes, or are they still arguing over the damage little Meredith Jennifer did to the Goldsteins' prize petunia collection?

The big Saturday comes. It passes. Not too bad. True, the *haftora* rendition did not compare with Robert Merril's. But since no one in the family reads Hebrew, at least it sounded scholarly. And best of all, it's over. One more day to go.

The big Sunday comes. It passes. It could have been worse. Where did all of those great-aunts and second-cousins come from? Gee, was it hectic! Like a Radio City Music Hall with Torahs! But it's over. It's finally over.

Yes, it is finally over. For the young Jewish boy who has been subjected to a year of hypocrisy, it is *all* over. He still cannot read Hebrew—nor does he want to. He still does not know why it was called a "bar mitzva"—nor does he care. (It was never hard to figure out what the "bar" referred to—that was where everyone lined up for drinks. But what does "mitzva" mean?) He still has not learned any authentic Jewish concepts or practices—and, now that the day of reckoning has passed, he will never have to spend another day in Hebrew school. After all, as Uncle Jerry said when he forked over those fifty bucks, "My boy, today you are a man."

In many ways, the bar mitzva experience was best summarized by Rabbi Jacob Chinitz of Philadelphia in this "Bar Mitzvah Glossary" he compiled:

A   *Acharon*—the extra *aliyah* added on Sabbath when more of the relatives than the minimum of seven have to be honored by being called to the Torah.

B   Bar—precedes the party.

C   Caterer—the supreme authority on procedure.

D   Dietary laws—sometimes observed at the party, accompanied by Sabbath smoking, photography, and music.

E   Entrance—when all the guests are seated, the parents and the boy enter with a flourish, as at a coronation.

F   Faith—represented by one of the candles on the cake.

G   *Gelilah*—an honor given to one of the uncles who cannot recite the blessings.

H   *Havdalah*—usually omitted at the Saturday night party.

I   Illiterate—some of the relatives called to the Torah.

J   Joy—fills the hearts of the parents when their darling starts the *Haftorah* in peace and finishes in peace.

K   *Kiddush*—the first stage in the culinary celebrations.

L   Lights—lit by aunts and uncles on the cake, symbolizing the highest ideals, and then extinguished by the Bar-Mitzvah boy.

M   Man—what the boy becomes today.

N   Name—Bar mitzvah is the first occasion for the use of the Hebrew name since the Bris.

O   Ostentation—hallmark for all the above.

P   Pictures—next to the caterer, the photographer is the highest authority. He poses the boy, the rabbi, the cantor, and the scroll.

Q   Questionable—the above practices.

R   Record—What the boy learns his *Haftorah* . . . from.

S   Sunday—when it coincides with Rosh Chodesh, Chanukah, or Chol Hamoed, is popular for the Bar-Mitzvah day.

T   Thursday—also popular as the chosen day when it is Thanksgiving.

U   Ushers—they ask at the door, "Are you Jewish?" If the answer is yes, they give you a tallis.

V   Vestibule—where the guests leave the gifts for the boy, unless they take them inside the sanctuary.

W   Wedding—the next time the Bar Mitzvah will see the rabbi.

X   Xerxes—his wealth is needed for the above.

Y   *Yekum Purkan*—comes right after the *Haftorah*, while the boy is being kissed by his aunts.

Z   Zevulun—one of the names a Bar Mitzvah almost never has.[12]

Tragically, the bar mitzva syndrome has become the symbol of so much of what is wrong with American Jewish life today. The one-upmanship knows no bounds. In one case in Long Island, New York, parents hired a motorcycle racer to drive their son to the front door of the temple at which the affair was scheduled to take place. The splendid grand entrance of the "son of the commandment" was somewhat marred, unfortunately, by the lad's imprudent decision to faint upon arrival. In Scottsdale, Arizona, on the other hand, guests at the bar mitzva of Greg Hoffman were greeted by a fiddler on the Hoffman roof, courtesy of the doting hosts.[13] Not satisfied with the traditional forms of sacrilege, one Jewish couple won nomination as top contenders for the "Bad Taste in the Jewish Community Award" after spending $2,000 for a "Car Mitzva," commemorating the thirteenth year of their Rolls Royce.[14]

And then there was the infamous Harvey Cohen bar mitzva, held at Miami's Orange Bowl, an open-air football stadium. The parents shamelessly invited two hundred guests to the spectacle, featuring a sixty-four-piece band, bartenders dressed as referees, waitresses dressed as cheerleaders, and pom-pom girls wearing sweaters emblazoned with the letter "H" for "Harvey." (The rabbi was presumably in the broadcasters' booth, dressed like Howard Cosell. . . .) Prior to the game—er, bar mitzva—guests had received invitations in the mail printed in the shape of football tickets. They were not to be disappointed. After being wisked onto the field by golf carts, they packed away a six-course dinner, while cheering as the Orange Bowl electric scoreboard lit up with the words: "Happy Birthday Harvey."[15]

The one-upmanship knows no bounds.

One sensitive and deeply gifted young Jew who was a victim of the bar mitzva pageantry was Michael Medved, best known as the co-author of *What Really Happened to the Class of '65?*, the best selling novel which was subsequently made into a television series. In a moving article he wrote for a California Jewish students' magazine, Michael told the story of "What Really Happened to the Bar Mitzvah Class of 5722?" Discussing the "Hebrew school experience," Michael remembered:

> . . . My mother promised me that once I learned to read Hebrew the services would instantly become meaningful and interesting—but not so interesting that we would have to attend them more than five or six times a year. By the age of ten, I could read enough Hebrew to follow the cantor on most of his operatic flights, but I still didn't understand a word of it . . . In Hebrew school, they made no effort to teach us about these prayers. Instead, we memorized a few inane conversations about two Israeli

friends who meet on the street and ask each other what their names are. . . .

At first, I was genuinely excited by the prospect [of attending Hebrew school]. . . My father built up my expectations by telling me stories about honey cakes baked in the shape of Hebrew letters and wise, gentle rabbis with long grey beards. Instead of the rabbis he promised, I found only neurotic young Israeli women who could barely speak English, let alone control a class. Several of them proved unable to get through an hour of "teaching" without excusing themselves into the hall for cigarette breaks. . . .

I often arrived late for Hebrew school . . . I will always remember the feeling of walking down that hallway about ten minutes after class had started, and listening to the noise behind the closed classroom doors. An outsider taking the same stroll would have thought he was visiting an insane asylum, not a school. From each room came shouting, banging, weeping, stamping, singing, and hysterical laughter.[16]

Soon, it was time to prepare for the bar mitzva, "a solemn responsibility . . . It certainly was a solemn responsibility—I had six months to learn two pages of Hebrew, and if I didn't learn it I was in big trouble. No one bothered to explain to me what I was studying. I was given a tape recording of something called a Haftorah . . . My job was to memorize the tape recording and to be able to repeat it, with no questions asked."[17]

Michael made it through his *haftora* with ease on his bar mitzva day. Moreover, he delivered "a little speech about the danger of nuclear war and my job, as a Bar Mitzvah boy, to help bring peace to the world." For all this, he remembers being awarded such beautiful gifts as wallets, ties, savings bonds, and "one deluxe, over-sized volume that told the history of General Dynamics Corporation, the parent company of my father's aerospace firm." Looking back on the entire experience, Michael had these moving thoughts:

From my present perspective, it is hard to see my Hebrew school experience in anything but negative terms. The fact that I learned everything which my San Diego synagogue attempted to teach me led me to believe that my understanding of Judaism was complete. As I grew up and judged that training as empty and meaningless, I began to view all of Judaism in the same terms. I remember too well the arguments I had with my parents when, at age 20, I wanted to marry a Gentile.

"Look ," I used to tell them, "you may say I'm giving up something. But what am I sacrificing? I know all about the Jewish religion. Wasn't I Bar Mitzvahed? Wasn't I one of the best students they ever had? So don't try to tell me about it—I know it's hollow. I know it's a fraud. I know it's a joke."[18]

What became of Michael Medved? Something happened at age twenty-two, and he began putting on *tefillin* for the first time. At twenty-three, he assumed the sacred *mitzva* of *kashrut*. At twenty-five, he participated in an Orthodox service for the first time. Although he was somewhat taken aback by the proceedings, he was deeply moved. "The services may have seemed alien and difficult," he recalled, "but they were unmistakably authentic. The air of fraud and phoniness which I associated with all Jewish congregations seemed to be missing entirely. I began to think that my difficulties in accommodating myself to Jewish tradition might reflect my own shortcomings, and not a defect in the religion."[19]

What an immense honor it is for the Torah of Israel that so sensitive a soul as Michael Medved's is willing to give Judaism a second chance! He was spiritually betrayed by a Jewish community which had so compromised itself as to render its collective "soul" all but obsolete. He was taught a "Judaism" that was not authentically Jewish. He was treated to a bar mitzva celebration which was devoid of its most essential component: that of *mitzvot*—commandments. He was presented with a "Judaism of accommodation" which was so far removed from the authentic version that he could not help but express his own sense of rancor towards the "fraud" and the "hollow . . . joke" it had all become.

Michael Medved returned to his people. But so many of his peers did not. What really happened to the bar mitzva classes of the 5720s and the 5730s? Unfortunately, a crisis of alienation and assimilation overtook most of the graduates. And, as we have seen, a bumper crop of foreign cults emerged in America, attracting some of the finest of them. One young man who understood what was happening to his colleagues was Jonathan Braun, a talented writer, who penned this analysis of the crisis:

> The children of the Establishment Assimilationist have left Miami and Queens Boulevard to build communes in the American wilderness, publish nihilist newspapers in the East Village, cut sugar cane in Cuba, and in some extreme cases, run obstacle courses in Arab terrorist training camps.
>
> And the parents, the well-meaning, middle-class parents who so terribly wanted their Cathy and Eric to be 100% Americans, are puzzled. Why, they ask, are their children dressing like Gypsies, wearing Afros, and smoking dope?
>
> "Where did I go wrong?"
>
> The Assimilationists went "wrong" when they ceased being Jews and became, instead, Americans of the Jewish faith. They went "wrong" when they replaced the Sabbath meal with the TV dinner, the *challah* with the package of cheese doodles, the synagogue with the bowling alley—in short, when they deserted a rich and beautiful culture of four-thousand years for a cult of plastic pizza-eaters who retain their Judaism by peppering their conversation with a few Yiddish expressions and frequent comments on the superiority of Jewish rye bread.[20]

As Braun perceived, the problem transcended the bar mitzva syndrome and was traceable to a far more complex tragedy: the breakdown of genuinely Jewish values in American Jewish life.

After Judaism has been stripped of the Torah commandments, of its eschatology and teleology, of its very core — what is left for a young person to grasp? The ostentation of the bar mitzva? The materialism of the suburbs? The indulgence of the Catskills?

A society which denies its children spiritual depth must be prepared to pay a price. If absolute "reason" — bereft of Divinity — were the young Jew's only need, he would not be running off to mystical cults like Zen to find Truth. If atheistically absolute "ethical humanism" were sufficient to nourish his soul, he would not be in hot pursuit of Sun Myung Moon, "Jews for Jesus," Guru Maharaj Ji, Lord Krishna, and every other bizarre theology on the American scene. If absolute "comfort" were his innermost desire, he would neither be experimenting with the physical asceticism of the many strange cults, nor would he be participating in Marxist protests against capitalist exploitation.

A young Jew needs more than science, computers, technology, and all the other gods of reason. Never has Judaism denied the awesome value of reason and science. Never did Judaism commit the shameful crime of the Catholic Church which fought gains in scientific knowledge with all the ferocity that its medieval paranoia and hysteria could muster. Judaism, throughout its history, has treated science and objective knowledge as two of man's greatest tools. Maimonides, the sublime luminary whose writings on Jewish philosophy and Jewish law stand as intellectually profound today as they did when he first compiled them eight centuries ago, gained international acclaim in his time as a preeminent physician; furthermore, he achieved great scholarship in the fields of mathematics and astronomy.[21] No, Judaism never disowned knowledge and technology.

But, in the assimilated regions of American Jewry, the attempt has been made to have Knowledge and Technology — yes, gods with capital letters — disown Judaism. The hopelessness of the effort has been reflected by the successes of the foreign cults. Although Reason reigns supreme and computer printouts can produce every conceivable fact, young Jews still seem to be yearning for something more. Not necessarily something *else* or something *instead of*. Just something *more*.

The race to the cults and the flight from reason are rebellious actions. But they are also desperate cries emanating from the very souls of our young people, who embrace Buddhism and Hare Krishna in a reaction to the hedonism at home, and turn to Moon, Maharaj Ji, and Jesus in response to an upbringing bereft of religious commitment. But theirs is not only a revolution. It is a tearful pleading as well. "Someone, please, tell me who I am," they are begging. What is the purpose of my life? Where can I find the deeper truths which might reveal to me some of the greatest mysteries of existence? And please, please, lead me to my roots."

If young Jews are not raised to see that the answers to their questions can be warmly and completely offered by Judaism, then they will inevitably come to the realization that they have before them two remaining alternatives from which to choose: either to stop asking the questions, though they desperately thirst for answers, or to start drinking from foreign waters. The chances that they will select the former option are not growing stronger. Nor is there any virtue in choosing such a course. One should be free to ask questions; if there were no more questions remaining for man to ask, then even scientists—the high priests of atheistic society—would be obsolete. And if the former option is undesirable, the latter alternative is disastrous.

For every question there is an answer. And, for thousands of years, the Jew has been able to satiate his soul by turning to the Torah with his query. Perhaps the practice of Judaism in assimilated American suburbia has changed over time. But the Torah has not.

If young Jews are to remain genuinely Jewish, then one of the first steps their parents will have to take is to turn to the Torah with their question-of-questions: "Where are we going wrong, and what can we do now?"

And they will find the answer: Put the *mitzva* back into the bar mitzva.

Notes

1) Cf. Tractate *Berachot* 6a: The Holy One, blessed be He, said to Jewry, "You have made Me a unique subject of praise in the world, and I shall make you a unique subject of praise in the world."

See also Deuteronomy 26:17-18 (per Rashi): "You have set apart the Lord this day to be your God, and to walk in His ways, and to keep His statutes and His commandments and His judgments, and to hearken to His voice. And the Lord has set you apart this day to be His treasured people, as He has promised you, and that you should keep all His commandments."

2) Deuteronomy 4:5-8.

3) Exodus 24:7.

4) See Tractate *Niddah* 45b-46a. Cf. *Pirkey Avoth* 5:21 and commentaries of *Bartenura* and *Tos'fot Yom Tov, ad loc.* See also *Rema* on *Orach Chayim* 55:5.

5) *Orach Chayim* 225:2. See also *Magen Avraham ad loc.*

6) *Jewish Post and Opinion*, 7/22/77.

7) *Jewish Week*, 1/23/77.

8) *Jewish Post and Opinion*, 1/28/77.

9) *Ibid.*, 12/12/75.

10) *Jewish Week*, 2/1/76.

11) Rabbi Moshe Feinstein, one of the greatest twentieth-century Torah scholars, has written: "If I had the power, I would annul the bar-mitzvah ceremony as it is observed in our country because it is known that this ceremony has not brought anyone closer to the Torah and mitzvot—not even the boy himself, not even for one hour. On the contrary, in many places it actually brings [participants] to desecrate the Sabbath and to commit other transgressions . . ." See R. Moshe Feinstein, *Igg'rot Moshe* (N.Y.: Moriah, 1959), *Orach Chayim*, Section One, chapter 104.

12) *Jewish Post and Opinion*, 2/4/77.

13) *Jewish Week*, 1/16/77.

14) *Ibid.*, 1/2/77.

15) *Jewish Post and Opinion*, 5/26/78 and 6/9/78.

16) *Davka* (magazine), no. 18 (Spring, 1977), p. 37.

17) *Ibid.*, p. 38.

18) *Ibid.*, p. 39.

19) *Ibid.*

20) Jonathan Braun, "Neglecting the Jewish National Experience," *The Flame* (a publication of Jewish students at the City College of New York), February 1970.

21) Maimonides, whose greatest works include *A Guide to the Perplexed* and the *Mishneh Torah*, towers above all comparable examples. Nevertheless, he is but one of thousands of such examples. It might be noted in this context that Yeshiva University — a major educational institution run under the auspices of Orthodox Judaism — has as its motto and purpose the goal to synthesize Torah and Science.

CHAPTER 7

Assimilation:
The race to the melting pot

*In those days there was no king in Israel;
every man did what was right in his own
eyes.* (JUDGES 21:25)

*The way of a fool is right in his own
eyes . . .* (PROVERBS 12:15)

It was early evening on Monday, October 4, 1976, and throughout the United States millions of televisions were tuned to the ABC network. An historic moment was in the making as the highest paid newscaster in world history was about to begin her new career. Barbara Walters, a Jewish woman who had "made good," looked at her viewing audience, smiled, and said: "Good Evening." For Barbara Walters, it was truly a great moment.

It was also Yom Kippur.[1]

Founded at the turn of the century, the *Jewish Daily Forward* had compiled an impressive record in advancing the cause of organized labor over the years. As a sign of gratitude, three

1. The numbered notes to chapter 7 begin on page 263.

powerful unions—the International Ladies' Garment Workers' Union, the Amalgamated Clothing Workers, and the Seafarers' International Union—arranged a cocktail party in honor of the Yiddish paper.

On the tables of hors d'oeuvres were ham, bacon, large and small shrimps, and Alaska king crabs.

One of the epicureans present put it well: "There's nothing here that a Jew could eat."[2]

With inflation eating away at pocketbooks at home and abroad, the Dallas chapter of Hadassah decided on a novel project to help raise money for medical care in Israel. Seeking to bolster the sagging funds of Hadassah Mount Scopus Hospital in Jerusalem, the women's Zionist organization distributed circulars announcing to interested souls how they could advance this worthy Jewish enterprise. "Sunday, November 7, is HADASSAH FUND-RAISING DAY," the leaflet innocuously began, "AT BURGER KING."[3]

The race to the melting pot has become the great national sport of American Jewry. Not unlike Olympic athletes—so fulfilled by the competition itself that no financial remuneration need be offered them—American Jews have invested long, hard years of training and practice in pursuit of the great event's gold medal: Acceptance. To be accepted by the non-Jewish world as equals is the prize American Jewish society desperately seeks, and to win that recognition they will leave no stone unturned—even if the stones in question are the two which Moses carried down from Mount Sinai. One wonders whether Cecil B. De Mille himself could have predicted what would one day become of the Decalogue. Consider, for example, the current status of some of its precepts.

The first of the Ten Commandments was basically a charge to the Jews to believe in the God of Abraham, Isaac and Jacob Who took the nation of Hebrew slaves out of Egypt. While it is true that modern society has greatly disregarded this call, one would assume that, at the very least, its faithful observance would be an uncomplicated task for *rabbis*. After all, rabbis are *paid* to believe in God. Yet, a major 400-page study of the "Rabbi and Synagogue in Reform Judaism" revealed that only one in ten American Reform pulpiteers believes in God "in the more or less traditional Jewish sense."[4] Thirteen percent of those questioned defined themselves as outright agnostics, while one percent considered themselves atheists. Perhaps it was "Rabbi" Martin Siegel of Temple Sinai, a wealthy Reform congregation in Lawrence, New York, who put it best in this diary entry:

> A young man in the confirmation class told me today he doubts whether he wants to be Jewish because he doesn't believe in God.
> "I don't believe in God, either," I told him. "But that has nothing to do with being Jewish."[5]

Presumably, "Rabbi" Siegel would be one of the main beneficiaries of the Reform movement's own "Balfour Declaration," pronounced in 1978 by Balfour Brickner, a national leader of the Union of American Hebrew Congregations (the body representing American "Reform" laity). In his nationally publicized comment, Brickner—whose impressive rabbinical credentials include membership on the Clergyman's Committee of the Association for Voluntary Sterilization—confronted the question of faith head-on. Opposing the expulsion of "Reform rabbis" who become involved in the "Jews for Jesus" movement, Brickner said that the Reform Jewish movement has "rabbis" who are atheists, agnostics, and even homosexuals. "Should we throw them out?" he asked. "Where would we stop?"[6]

If the very first commandment of the Decalogue has suffered at the hands of the "Reform rabbinate," we shall not find greater comfort by considering the state of the subsequent Divine charge. As we have seen, the Second Commandment—which prohibits Jews from worshipping strange gods—has not fared well. The Third Commandment, on the other hand, has survived handsomely: "Thou shalt not utter the

Name of the Lord thy God in vain." Those who believe in Him do not violate this law, and those who drop out at the first of the ten holy directives have no reason to invoke His name anyway. Of course, the possibility remains that the following "holy" ceremony may have been an exception:

> TORONTO—Rabbi Garo Zimmerman plans to marry two myna birds some time in March because he believes the world is badly in need of a good laugh. He did not say whether the birds are Jewish or whether he intended to use a "bird chupah" [canopy].
>
> The rabbi said that the publicity that followed his announcement has brought him many protests but also a number of speaking engagements as well as many bookings for weddings into July.
>
> Rabbi Zimmerman did not say whether the pair of myna birds he intends to join in wedlock will receive a ketubah [Jewish marriage certificate].

Likewise, the Decalogue commands the Jews to remember and observe "the Sabbath day to keep it holy." The Talmud clearly delineates how a Jew is expected to "keep it holy," but it does not consider such theological dilemmas as the one which perplexed one American temple at the end of 1976: How can a Jew celebrate the Sabbath when it coincides with New Year's Eve? After much thought, the temple's administration decided on a suitable course of action. Members were informed in the temple bulletin that, after the Friday night services, they would be able to participate in a gala New Year's Eve party on the premises:

> 10:30 P.M.—2:30 A.M. Live music, entertainment, dancing, games, midnight supper, champagne toast. Stake out your table for your family and friends.[7]

As a fitting spiritual gesture, it was announced that, while tickets to the party would cost $12.50 per person, admission to the services would be free of charge.[8]

Other "Reform temples" have performed with equal aplomb

in confronting the Sabbath laws. Not unrepresentative of this readiness to abrogate basic Sabbath-day prohibitions when necessary is the California temple whose religious leaders distribute coloring books during Shabbat services so that worshippers can color in their emotions as the service progresses.[9]

Nor should the discerning observer overlook the role played by New York City's B'nai B'rith Women in the Sabbath free-for-all. In January, 1980, the Murray Hill chapter mailed to its members an invitation to come down to the "Roundabout Stage One" for a Saturday afternoon theatrical performance, starring such talent as Tammy Grimes, Jerome Kilty, and Philip Bosco. The following month, the fair ladies of B'nai B'rith sponsored "One Great Big Party" at "Neri's" restaurant. Members sending in $12 reservations were assured a scrumptious menu from which to choose. Among the delectable delights offered by BBW: mussels with cocktail sauce, spaghettini with clams marechiare, linguini with shrimp sauce, frog's legs alla provençale, shrimps and mussels Fra Diavolo, and shrimps and scallops with sauteed mushrooms.

Keeping their streak alive at three, the Murray Hill ladies chose the following month to be the date of their "Third Annual Spring Luncheon." For those wishing to spend their Shabbat afternoon in the manner designed by the leadership of these B'nai B'rith Women, a mere $6.50 would assure entry at the site of the luncheon, the Empire Chinese Restaurant, an institution no more kosher than the aforementioned "Neri's."

If such is the Sabbath observance of B'nai B'rith Women (an organization whose name literally means "sons-of-the-covenant women"), can we expect more from agencies of the local Jewish philanthropic federations operating in America from coast-to-coast? In New York, for example, the Lexington School for the Deaf conducts most of its weekend activities for children on Saturday. Virtually nothing is held on Sunday. Thus, deaf Jewish youngsters must make the choice between synagogue and swimming, courtesy of the Federation of Jewish Philanthropies. The same is true for adults who want tennis lessons, which are on Saturday morning.[10]

Such is the sad state of the fourth commandment.

One Jew who has successfully melted is the famous science-fiction writer, Isaac Asimov. "Well, since I engage in all of the American activities and virtually none of the Jewish ones," he told a reporter, "I suppose I've got to consider myself primarily an American and only secondarily a Jew . . . What I am advocating is assimilation . . ."[11] Rona Barrett, the TV gossip star who went on to achieve the pinnacle of Americanization—a nose job and a husband named Trowbridge—began life as Rona Burstein, daughter of Ida Lefkowitz Burstein.[12] The Queen of Quidnuncs is not alone in changing her name to mask her Jewish roots. Consider this excerpt from Hollywood's honor role:

> Rodney Dangerfield (Jacob Cohen)
> Tony Curtis (Bernie Shwartz)
> Steve Lawrence (Sidney Liebowitz)
> Kirk Douglas (Issur Danielovitch)
> Edward G. Robinson (Emanuel Goldenberg)
> Lee J. Cobb (Lee Jacobs)
> Beverly Sills ("Bubbles" Silverman)
> Harry Houdini (Erich Weiss)

While it has become difficult to identify entertainers who are Jewish, it should presumably be easier to identify *clergy* "of the Jewish persuasion." But, as black-robed clerics exchange pulpits—if not robes—there are no longer any guarantees. In one case, New York City's Temple Emanu-El announced that its spiritual leader, Ronald Sobel, would be exchanging pulpits for a Sabbath with Monsignor James F. Rigney of St. Patrick's Cathedral. Nevertheless, ecumenically speaking, the noble Sobel lagged four decades behind the congregants of Akron, Ohio's Temple Israel, whose Saturday services have been accompanied by Mr. Clarence Lightfritz's organ since 1937. During a speech he delivered to the worshippers at a ceremony honoring him for forty years of service, Mr. Lightfritz thanked the Jews for giving Christianity "two basic precepts on which our religion is built, the belief in one God and the Ten

Commandments."[13] Lightfritz may have been at fault for neglecting to thank the Jews for giving part of Arizona Christmas as well. Could it be that he missed the publicity accorded Temple Emanuel of Tempe, Arizona, when the congregation lent its *sukka* to the nearby Church of the Epiphany for their use as the manger in their annual Christmas display?[14] Few New Yorkers missed the half-page spread given by the mass-circulating *Daily News* to Marc Tanenbaum of the American Jewish Committee so that the famed ecumenist might issue his clarion call for a revival of "Christmas spirit." Rising to the occasion, Tanenbaum wrote: "Christmas, to me, means smiles and children and helping the poor and families being together again . . ."[15]

While many Christians' hearts have been melted by Tanenbaum's words, many Jewish souls have been melted by *tannenbaums* (cedar trees). Traditionally, those Jews en route to the melting pot must, at some time in their lives, come to grips with the most staggering of theological quandaries: To buy a Christmas tree or not to buy a Christmas tree? One who believes she has found the answer to the great "December dilemma" is Gail Levenstein, a mother of three: "We observe Christmas with a tree and presents, and we light the Hanukkah menorah and give gifts each night. My children feel no confusion whatsoever. There is simply no Christ in our Christmas."[16]

Similar to the Levenstein outlook, though more poetic in articulation, is this comment by James Kaufman, whose son sent a change-of-address letter to Santa Claus one December: "I don't think you have to wear your religion on your sleeve."[17] Julie Bober takes the same approach. As she sees it, "We live in this country, not in Israel." In addition to the potent geographical argument, she considers the feelings of her children: "It would be a shame to deprive my children and say, 'You can't have a Christmas tree because you're Jewish.'"[18] Accordingly, every December Julie and her husband, Franklin, display a Christmas tree (topped by a Star of David) and place both Christmas and Chanuka gifts under it.

Some American Jews even find it difficult to "deprive" their *rabbis* of Christmas. In one publicized case, a Rochester, New York, clergyman was so inundated that he chose to use his pulpit for a sermon in which he pleaded with the members of his Reform temple to stop sending him Christmas cards.[19] A 1980 survey of Los Angeles Jews, meanwhile, indicated that Christmas trees stand in 18 percent of their homes.[20]

Lost in all this disconcerting parroting of Christian ways is the realization that many American Christians are not flattered by this Jewish love affair with the *tannenbaum*. On the contrary, many are deeply offended and resentful that this symbol of their sacred holiday is arrogated by Jews, shorn of its meaning, and displayed jokingly as a "Chanuka bush."[21]

So warm has the "Christmas spirit" become in the regions where Accommodation Judaism is practiced that it infects the assimilationists year-round. Tisha b'Av, for example, is a Jewish day of mourning, a day of fasting and of remembrance. The Holy Temple in Jerusalem was destroyed on that day in 586 BCE by the Babylonians, and the Second Temple (which was built on the site of its predecessor's ruins) was destroyed on that selfsame day in 70 CE. The fortress of Betar, the last stronghold of Jewish independence before the revival of the Jewish State in 1948, fell to the Romans on that day in 135. The expulsion of the once-flourishing Jews of Spain was decreed on that day in 1492. In terms of sorrow and mourning, no day in the Jewish calendar approaches the bitter Tisha b'Av. Before the sun sets, ushering in the day on the Jewish calendar, Jews begin their mourning by fasting. They take off their shoes and wear no leather or fancy clothing for the duration of the fast. They go to the synagogue, where the Book of Lamentations is chanted in a somber tone, and they unabashedly weep. Grown men, young girls, rabbis, and laymen weep bitter tears as they remember the tragedy of the desolation of Zion. That is Tisha b'Av.

The Norwalk Jewish Center—presumably inundated with an extraordinarily potent dosage of "Christian spirit" the previous December—attempted to introduce a ritualistic innovation on the occasion of Tisha b'Av 5731. On August 1, 1971, the "Jewish Center" sponsored its first annual "Tisha b'Av Carnival."[22] Perhaps taking the lead from this Connecticut community, the Jewish Community Center of Houston, Texas, subsequently promoted a Tisha b'Av "Day at the Beach," while the YMHA of Brighton Beach, New York, chose this occasion to organize a "Boardwalk Party" which included drinks, food, and a band.[23] Adding a new culinary dimension to the festivities surrounding this time of tragedy and grief was a newspaper advertisement sponsored by a Queens, New York, kosher butcher store:

FOR A SALE LIKE THIS,
YOU HAVE TO WAIT TILL TISHA B'AV
TISHA B'AV IS HERE!
TISHA B'AV SALE!

Among the foods listed in this eye-catching announcement were various "glatt kosher" meats, fish products, puddings, and borscht.[24] All in all, it was a mouth-watering assortment of delicacies, well worth including in any melting-pot recipe. Kosher comestibles found their way into another favorite institution as well:

WESTBURY, N.Y. — Roosevelt Raceway, which started its 1977 season, will serve kosher dinners to groups making advance arrangements through the Raceway's Party Department.
The "kosher problem" had existed for many years, and numerous requests had been received from Orthodox Jewish groups for kosher cuisine. Despite a continuing search by Harry M. Stevens, Inc., the track's caterer, an accommodating supplier had been unavailing . . .[25]

Kosher harness racing opens the door to assimilation and acceptance for some, but others find it difficult to harness their *own* appetites; for them, there are alternative cauldrons in which to melt. In Indianapolis, the Jewish "Federation" holds its annual meeting at a local non-kosher Jewish country club.[26] One Jewish weekly in America's Deep South published recipes for marinated shrimp and quiche Lorraine, the latter spiced with bacon.[27] And, of course, there was this tempting offer printed in the bulletin of Temple Emanuel of St. Louis: "After a hard, hard, exhausting day, wouldn't it be great to have some pitstickers at Yen Ching or a lobster at Henrici's and then go to a movie at the Creve Coeur Cinema or an exciting Blues' game?"[28]

Tragically, the abandonment of authentic Jewish values has led not only to a breakdown in the scupulous observance of laws governing eating but also to a major crisis in the sphere of imbibing. While Jewish communities throughout the world gained great fame for centuries as disciplined and temperate drinkers, allowing themselves but one "indulgence" all week—for the sole purpose of reciting the hallowed *kiddush* over a glass of wine on the Sabbath—the race to be absorbed into American society has brought an end to this hallmark of Jewish honor in many assimilated strongholds. "Rabbis should attend open Alcoholics Anonymous meetings to learn about alcoholism and to prepare for counseling alcoholics," Dr. Stanley E. Gitlow, clinical professor of medicine at Mount Sinai School of Medicine, told a stunned audience of Jewish clergymen at Manhattan's Central Synagogue.[29] "Despite previous statistics to the contrary," he continued, "Jews have a drinking problem which requires immediate attention . . . The issue at hand is not whether there are Jewish alcoholics, but rather why we in the Jewish community refuse to recognize them . . ."

Dr. Sheldon Zimberg, director of psychiatry at the Hospital for Joint Diseases in New York, reiterated the point a year later at a symposium held at the Federation of Jewish Philanthropies. After reminding his audience of the days when hotels "hated to handle conventions of Jewish organizations"— not because of anti-Semitism but because Jews did not drink enough liquor to give the hotels a decent profit"—he somberly said, "That's all changed. Now they like the Jewish groups."[30]

In many ways, the alarming rise in American Jewish alcoholism symbolizes what the race to the melting pot really has to offer. That gold medal — acceptance by the non-Jewish world — is not cost-free for the American Jew. The sacrifices demanded are great.

Perhaps an even greater sacrifice has been the awesome collapse of the once-invulnerable Jewish family structure. For years, the Jewish family stood as an inviolate fortress, the envy of those on the other side of the moat. But, as the American institution of family has deteriorated, so has the legendary institution of the *Jewish* family.

In 1980 it was reported that twelve million children under the age of eighteen live with a single divorced parent.[31] As divorce has grown in America, it has become "big business." Movies (like the award-winning "Kramer vs. Kramer"), books, and television programs have used the motif of divorce successfully, playing on a contemporary theme which is very close to the American heart. The statistics are shocking: it is estimated that 45 percent of all children born in any given year will live with only one of their parents at some time before reaching age eighteen.[32] The number of children involved in divorce has tripled in the last twenty years.[33] And there is no end in sight.

For some time, American Jewry avoided being drawn into the social morass which has come to define contemporary Western civilization. An early priestess of this decadent culture, Jaqueline Susann, commented on the perception that Jewish men were the most reliable husbands and included such a depiction in one of her most forgettable works of non-literary value, *The Valley of the Dolls*. Were she alive today, she would find that the cherished stereotype has passed.

The Jewish divorce rate has begun to skyrocket. Estimates put the figures as high as 40 percent of all first marriages in the Jewish community. The gravity of this crisis was underscored in a 1979 report published by B'nai B'rith which concluded that a major erosion was taking place in American Jewish life. Key crises cited included: an increased intermarriage rate, a declining birthrate, falling attendance figures at religious schools, and a general breakdown in family cohesiveness.[34]

These problems, the fruit of a generation of "melting," bear with them long-term implications no less disturbing than their immediate crushing impact. As more Jewish marriages break up in divorce, as those who get married choose to emulate their non-Jewish neighbors by marrying later in life than Jewish tradition deems proper, as Jewish couples opt to have fewer and fewer children . . . a deadly demographic trend is evident. Jews have stopped "melting." They are now dissolving. The American Jewish birthrate has fallen below the replacement level; in 1980 it was 1.7 and falling. An additional corrosive agent in the Jewish societal fabric — the cancerous rise of intermarriage — is deserving of separate consideration, grave as it is. In this grand context, the words of Balfour Brickner are chilling, as he explains his position as an advocate of voluntary sterilization by Jews. He is responding to a resolution urging Jews to have more children: "It's stupid, and I would oppose it. You can't say that the world suffers from overpopulation and at the same time say Jews should ignore this."[35]

So as Arabs, Indians, Chinese, and Africans contribute to "overpopulation," Reform clergyman Brickner—a leader in American "Reform Judaism"—seeks to obviate the impending doom by urging Jews to voluntarily sterilize themselves.

Clearly, childbirth alone will not serve as a panacea for American Jewish survival. The crisis is too deep and complex for any simple cure-alls to be propounded. But advocacy of Jewish sterilization is, at best, a reflection of the dangers of troglodytic pulpiteering. At its worst, it can contribute to a posthumous victory for those of prior generations who would have seen the Jews disappear had their prayers been answered.

Like alcoholism, then, the breakdown of the Jewish family as a powerful institution serves as a sobering reminder that the race to the "melting pot" is not without cost.

Perhaps the reminder is sufficiently sobering to merit a consideration of a not insignificant Biblical incident, rarely given much attention by teachers in Hebrew School.

When Balak the King of Moab saw the approaching Jewish armies under the direction of Moses heading his way, he sought out the greatest prophet in all the world to invoke a Divine curse. His search brought him to Balaam the son of Beor, a man who could communicate with God. The Torah tells the story of Balaam and the fearful king, both conspiring to eradicate the Jewish nation. Special acts of "devotion to God" were performed, as a prelude to the great invocation on hand. Finally, the historic moment came, and Balaam (who had been warned aforetime by God that the words emanating from his mouth would be of Divine origin and not of his own volition) spoke:

> Balak, the king of Moab, has brought me from Aram, out of the mountains of the east, saying, "Come, curse for me Jacob, and come, execrate Israel."
> How shall I curse whom God has not cursed? And how shall I execrate whom the Lord has not execrated?
> For from the top of the rocks I see him, and from the hills I behold him. Behold, it is a people which shall dwell alone and which shall not be reckoned among the nations.[36]

Balaam could not curse the Jews, his own intentions notwithstanding. How could he curse this nation upon whom God had placed His everlasting blessing? No, this nation which would dwell alone was beyond curse. It was the very aspect of Jewish separateness which marked the Jews as a holy people. Balaam looked upon them and could only say, "*hen am levadad yishkon* — Behold, it is a people which shall dwell alone." And, when the terrified king heard the testimony of the prophet, he turned and screamed: "What have you done to me? I took you to curse my enemies, and here you have blessed them altogether."[37] Balaam had not simply offered a one-minute news commentary — open to rebuttal in accordance with FCC regulations. He had actually invoked a blessing for the Jews: a people which shall dwell alone.

Being alone is difficult and requires great internal fortitude; conversely, the status of separateness serves as a potent stimulant for the development of internal fortitude. Being different sometimes means surviving the hardships of passing through childhood without ever having a Christmas tree or passing through adulthood without ever experiencing the apparent joys of eating non-kosher food. God set His terms before the Jews in brutally honest fashion: "Now, therefore, if you will obey My voice and keep My covenant, then you shall be to Me a special people among the nations . . . And you shall be unto Me a kingdom of priests and a holy nation . . ."[38]

Unfortunately, the notion of Jewish separateness is antithetical to the values of those who seek acceptance. Driven by religious recreancy, they are willing to risk losing their children to cults and themselves to spiritual dissolution. And if it becomes necessary to breed the first cases of mass Jewish alcoholism in the modern period, then such is the price to be paid.

Nor is the breakdown of genuine Judaism limited to the world of gastronomy. In some cases, it extends to the sphere of astronomy as well. The Torah clearly condemns those who turn to fortune-telling, soothsaying, and other sorts of "divining," and it ascribes the term "abomination" to each of those practices.[39] Where that leaves the Jewish Ys and Centers (JYC) of Northeast Philadelphia is uncertain. In one memorable case, the JYC announced the scheduling of this class for children:

> *ASTROLOGY* — *Club 56* meets again from 7 to 8:30 p.m., this time to find out about horoscopes and other psychic phenomena. 5th and 6th grade members will learn how to read palms.[40]

One hesitates to ask whether the same "5th and 6th grade members" have as yet learned how to read Hebrew.

The ways in which American Jewish assimilationists train their children are strange indeed. One organization which has undoubtedly affected a number of young Jews is the American Jewish Society for Service (AJSS). In this historic advertisement which appeared in the prestigious *New York Times*, the AJSS called on Jewish youths to assume the task of "serving for seven rewarding weeks this summer":

Probably, you've never heard of us. But the Navajo
Indians in Crownpoint, New Mexico have. The migrant
workers in the Missouri Bootheel have. So have the
blacks of Lackawanna, New York . .

    For twenty-six years, we have organized and sent
summer work camps to help the disadvantaged. For seven
weeks every summer, our unskilled (at the beginning)
boys and girls have helped to build homes, schools,
community centers . . .

    Join us in our twenty-seventh year . . . This summer,
our planned projects will undertake home rehabilitation
in Massachusetts, Louisiana, and New Mexico . . .[41]

Regrettably, the soaring cost of space in the *Times* made it
impossible for the group to elaborate on its record. Fortunately,
though, a brochure forwarded to all who replied to the ad
expands on the annals of this admirable "Jewish Society for
Service." Founded in 1950, it seeks to "give Jews *and those of
other faiths* an opportunity to perform humanitarian service in
fulfillment of the highest teachings of Judaism" (emphasis
added). The work camps which are sent out by the AJSS
perform various construction services. "The campers are
predominantly Jewish, sixteen to nineteen years of age"
(emphasis added).

    Not only does the AJSS bring together Jewish and non-
Jewish teenagers, but it enables them to spend seven weeks
together in a socially relaxed atmosphere. They get to know
each other and, perhaps, to like each other. Is there not a
problem posed by a program which helps Jewish boys to meet
non-Jewish girls and Jewish girls to meet non-Jewish boys?
Apparently not, for there is no mention in the AJSS brochure of
any intermarriage concerns. In fact, one AJSS group, which
spent its summer working in Michigan, was housed in the St.
Francis Xavier Catholic School of Grand Rapids. Carl and
Audrey Brenner, the directors of that project, reported proudly
that "the CYO (Catholic Youth Organization) participated in
many of our activities, joining us on a few of our trips." The

AJSS won the Melters' Gold Medal of Acceptance in 1976, when Deacon Bernard Hall of St. Francis Xavier Church wrote, "The parish community of St. Francis Xavier Church deeply appreciated the experience of hosting the AJSS work camp during the summer. It was a very enriching experience for us and especially for our parish youth group who were in frequent and close contact with the AJSS work-campers."

Another work group spent its time in Rochester, New York, and was based in the Downtown United Presbyterian Church. Inevitably, one wonders what it is that makes the "American Jewish Society for Service" *Jewish*? Its campers are not all Jewish. The notion of bringing young adults of Jewish and non-Jewish backgrounds together in a social setting is not Jewish. The people who join the AJSS are neither eight-year-old boys who derive pleasure from pulling girls' braids, nor are they 128-year-old Soviet Georgians who find no greater joy than eating yogurt. They are between the ages of sixteen and nineteen, and they are at the stage in their lives when they are looking for companions of the opposite sex. In the words of one sixteen-year-old AJSS alumna: "The people we worked for loved us, and we loved them. And we loved each other, after we'd learned to live together like one huge family."[42]

What makes the AJSS Jewish? One work group, stationed in North Carolina, was treated to a dinner by the local Rotary Club and to a luncheon by the local Baptist Church. Is that what lends justification to such an organization? Or perhaps we can find the meaning to this riddle in the work done by an AJSS crew sent to Orkend, Maine, where the campers spent their summer helping a group of Carmelite nuns to carry on a local handicrafts project by building a two-story cooperative shop.[43]

What makes the AJSS Jewish? Perhaps it derives its ethnic tag from the three rabbis who helped found it: the late Ferdinand M. Isserman of St. Louis, Isidore B. Hoffman of New York, and Arthur J. Lelyveld of Cleveland.[44] Perhaps it is Jewish because Mr. Sanford Solender, executive vice-president of the Federation of Jewish Philanthropies of Greater New York, is one of its directors. Perhaps.

One might as easily ask: What makes a hospital sponsored by the Federation of Jewish Philanthropies *Jewish*—and worthy of receiving millions of dollars annually solicited in the name of Jewish philanthropy? "Jewish" hospitals sponsored by Federations of Jewish Philanthropies do not provide medical jobs exclusively for Jewish physicians. They do not serve the needs of Jewish patients only. In the vast majority of cases, they are not equipped with kosher kitchen facilities. The National Jewish Hospital of Denver, for example, was blasted by a Detroit attorney who recalled his humiliation when he sought kosher food in the hospital cafeteria, only to learn that none was available. Available instead were: ham, pork sausage, bacon, and other pork dishes.[45] The hospital's head dietitian compounded the outrage by noting that the hospital could prepare some special foods for kosher patients making a special request—but the meals would be rendered non-kosher since they would be prepared in non-kosher utensils.

In Boston, Beth Israel Hospital was accused of discriminating against an orthodox Jewish social worker who was denied a job after the institution's staff learned that the applicant could not work on Jewish religious holidays.[46] In New York, the Jewish Hospital and Medical Center of Brooklyn was sharply condemned after announcing its refusal to accept future circumcision patients referred by a group specializing in attending to the religious needs of Jewish immigrants from the Soviet Union.[47]

In contradistinction to Catholic charities' hospitals, moreover, Jewish ones rarely display identifying religious symbols.

Although "Jewish" hospitals are, in fact, non-sectarian (as they *should* be in a country whose constitution would consider it abhorrent for a medical center to deny assistance and professional care to a person on the grounds of religious or ethnic background), they nevertheless receive substantially greater financial allocations from Jewish Federations than do Jewish parochial schools. The preference of institutions like the Federation of Jewish Philanthropies of Greater New York to fund Mount Sinai medical centers rather than educational programs aimed at teaching young Jews about the original Mount Sinai has provoked a storm of protest in many segments of the American Jewish community. In 1970, Dr. Trude Weiss-Rosmarin, editor of a major American Jewish magazine, denounced the nature of Federation allocation priorities. Speaking at the biennial convention of the National Jewish Welfare Board, she praised the Torah Umesorah organization for its efforts to assist more than four hundred American yeshivot, and she criticized the considerably more powerful Federations for not pursuing a similar course of action. Dr. Weiss-Rosmarin expressed her support for those who have "served notice that they are set and prepared to restructure the Jewish establishment in keeping with those values to which the leaders of the Establishment pay lip service."[48] She cited the frequently repeated charge that Jewish education is "the stepson of organized Jewish philanthropy."

In 1977, seven lean years after Dr. Weiss-Rosmarin's speech, Rabbi Moshe Sherer, executive-director of Agudath Israel of America, reiterated the charge that the New York Federation "displays glaring insensitivity to the root cause of Jewish assimilation."[49] Elaborating on his strongly worded accusation, Rabbi Sherer said:

> An analysis of Federation's financial reports shows that out of a total of $24,841,197 in grants during fiscal year 1975-76 (ending June 30, 1976) only 5.9% went for Jewish education. The Federation budget for fiscal year 1976-77, which should reflect an appreciable increase in educational support, allocates an additional paltry sum of $80,950 to education—increasing the educational share of the total to a mere 6.1%.
>
> The cumulative increase over these past seven years—a period when the Federation has been professing greater concern over Jewish education—is only 0.6% . . . hardly a serious expression of an increased desire to meaningfully alter its priority system regarding education.

With Jewish assimilation on the increase, it is incredible that those who hold the purse strings of the Jewish charity dollar in New York City continue to display such glaring insensitivity to the root cause of the tragic phenomenon of Jewish assimilation. The Jew is dropping out of the fold not because he lacks hospitals or community centers but because he lacks the type of Jewish education necessary to enable him to withstand the ravages of a secular society. . . .

The Federation must now show that it has the courage to radically accelerate its snail-like pace of . . . funding for Jewish education. Otherwise, its topsy-turvy sense of priorities will be responsible for the loss of thousands of Jews from the Jewish faith. . . .

By all indications, the Federation is locked into a priorities system that is operating from inertia, without considering the changing needs of changing times. There can be no other explanation, for example, for allocating 27.4% of the 1976-77 budget for community centers and only 6.1% for education . . .[50]

Rabbi Sherer's powerful statement was not the only such criticism leveled against the New York Federation in 1977. During the Federation's "Sixtieth Anniversary Institute," a workshop on the subject of "Federation's Developing Role in Jewish Education" heard from Dr. Albert Hornblass, a member of the executive board of New York's Board of Jewish Education. Citing statistics pointing to increases in the levels of Jewish intermarriage and assimilation, Dr. Hornblass called on the Federation to make the funding of Jewish education its "number-one priority."[51] While 80 percent of the money allocated by the Atlanta Federation goes to Jewish education, Hornblass lamented, the level of the New York organization's support is "so low that any increase seems significant."[52]

Ironically, shortly after the Sherer and Hornblass appeals, a report was issued by the American Association for Jewish Education which revealed that the average salaries paid teachers working in Jewish day and supplementary schools were "too low to afford a head of a family a decent, comfortable standard of living as the sole wage earner."[53] Reacting with "shock and dismay" to the disclosure, Jerome Becker, president of the Metropolitan New York Coordinating Council on Jewish Poverty, called for "an immediate restructuring of Jewish communal priorities" to provide adequate wages and to upgrade the level of American Jewish education.[54] Rabbi Jack Simcha Cohen, executive-director of the Coordinating Council, noted that a closer analysis of the report indicated that the minimum annual salary for teachers in Jewish day schools was below the federal poverty level for a family of four and would qualify them for welfare programs, food stamps, and other such assistance programs. Thus, Cohen explained, most teachers in Jewish schools would be included in a listing of poor Americans. Summarizing, Cohen said, "the harsh facts are that a family head must virtually take a vow of poverty before entering the Jewish teaching profession."[55]

All these demands for a re-ordering of communal funding priorities, however, were overshadowed by an historic, even stunning policy statement issued by the national executive council of the American Jewish Committee. Meeting in Atlanta, Georgia, the Committee went on record for the first time in favor of a major effort to stimulate Jewish education. Specifically, this most prestigious and most secular of American Jewish organizations urged that "top priority" be given "to Jewish education in the allocation of communal resources for domestic needs."[56] Explaining why the statement was passed, E. Robert Goodkind, chairman of the body's Jewish Communal Affairs Commission, said:

> . . . Many of the prime movers in the American Jewish community have come to recognize in recent years their own feelings of inadequacy in the area of Jewish scholarship. They want to fill this gap for themselves, and to preclude similar feelings in future generations.
>
> We are recommending, therefore, that intensive efforts

be made to promote and intensify Jewish education
on several levels—for children and youth through
increased schooling and informal experiences as well as
Jewish Day Schools . . .[57]

The Committee clearly indicated that its call for increased
Jewish education was to be interpreted as a forceful call for a
total educational experience as typified by day schools; it was
not to be regarded as a perfunctory endorsement of the Sunday
school/Talmud Torah phenomenon. Accordingly, they urged "a
broad effort to increase the hours of formal and informal
schooling towards a goal of at least 3000 hours."[58] Goodkind
revealed that the figure was derived from a study by Prof.
Geoffrey Bock of the Harvard School of Education which
concluded that "unless you have 3000 hours of formal Jewish
studies, there is not much impact on the formation of a positive
sense of Jewish identity." The American Jewish Committee
also addressed its precedent-setting policy statement to Jewish
parents, urging them to give special consideration to the
possibility of providing their children with a Jewish day school
education, on the grounds that it offers students the maximum
amount of Jewish study and a suitable environment in which
Jewish education is effectively integrated with secular
schooling.

As the most responsible voices in the American Jewish
community begin to follow the lead of the Committee, the
pressure of enlightened Jewish opinion will force many of the
most influential assimilationists to reconsider their life-long
priorities. But such a conceptual overhaul will not be easily
effectuated. Long before the Federation/Jewish Education
imbroglio became a matter of intensive public consideration,
Kurt Lewin pondered the nature of minority-group leadership
and offered this incisive analysis:

> In a minority group, members who are economically
> successful, or who have distinguished themselves in
> their professions usually gain a higher degree of
> acceptance by the majority group. This places them

culturally on the periphery of the underprivileged group and makes them more likely to be "marginal" persons. They . . . are particularly eager to have their "good connections" not endangered by too close a contact with those sections of the underprivileged group which are not acceptable to the majority. Nevertheless, they are frequently called for leadership by the underprivileged group because of their status and power. They themselves are usually eager to accept the leading role . . . partly as a substitute for gaining status in the majority, partly because such leadership makes it possible for them to have and maintain additional contact with the majority. . . .

As a result, we find the rather paradoxical phenomenon of what one might call "the leader from the periphery." Instead of having a group led by people who are proud of the group, who wish to stay in it and to promote it, we see minority leaders who are lukewarm toward the group, who may, under a thin cover of loyalty, be fundamentally eager to leave the group, or who may try to use their power outright for acts of negative chauvinism. Having achieved a relatively satisfactory status among non-Jews, these individuals are chiefly concerned with maintaining the status quo and so try to soft-pedal any action which might arouse the attention of the non-Jew. . . . They are so accustomed to viewing Jewish events with eyes of the anti-Semite that they are afraid of the accusation of double loyalty in the case of any outspoken Jewish action.[59]

Lewin's penetrating thesis helps explain many of the more peculiar phenomena in American Jewish life. Why did the American Jewish Committee go to incredible lengths to fight for Barbra Streisand's right to purchase a $240,000 twenty-room luxury apartment in Manhattan's exclusive East Side (after her initial bid was turned down, allegedly for anti-Semitic reasons)[60] when it had not in recent memory engaged in similarly spirited battles on behalf of "the underprivileged" class of Jews? Why did the American Jewish Congress invest money and press releases in order to present Vidal Sassoon with its "First Annual American Jewish Congress Beauty Hall of Fame Award"?[61] Was there nothing of greater Jewish import at the time than for Arthur Hertzberg, the group's leader, to present Sassoon with a bronze plaque at New York's Pierre Hotel for his role in the "world of beauty and fashion"?[62] And why did the Anti-Defamation League of B'nai B'rith so fear the ramifications of the actions of the militant Jewish Defense League that its Philadelphia office felt compelled to present the FBI with a list of JDL activists in Pennsylvania?

This last incident provides an especially revealing look at the leadership of American Jewry. Kurt Lewin had written two decades earlier that the leaders "from the periphery . . . are chiefly concerned with maintaining the status quo . . . [and] are afraid of the accusation of double loyalty in the case of any outspoken action." But could even he have prognosticated that a major Jewish organization would betray members of its own community to an agency like the FBI? It is to the credit of many Jewish personalities, who strongly disagreed with the program of the Jewish Defense League, that they nevertheless excoriated the Anti-Defamation League in the strongest of terms, once news of the base deed spread. Eugene Borowitz, editor of *Sh'ma* magazine and an opponent of the JDL, termed the ADL act "intolerable."[63] Rabbi Bernard Berzon, president of the Rabbinical Council of America, termed the egregious incident a clear violation of Jewish law.[64] Henry Schwarzschild, speaking for the Synagogue Council of America, fumed:

> We have here from the FBI's own records proof that the Anti-Defamation League fingers to the Federal Bureau of Investigation fellow Jews of whose political activities they disapprove . . .
> A Jewish "intergroup-relations agency," funded by and acting within the American Jewish community, denounces other Jews to Mr. J. Edgar Hoover and his

minions! It is approximately as though a Roman Catholic archdiocese had fingered the Berrigan brothers to the FBI.

There is a long Jewish tradition of abhorrence for the *mosser*, the Jew who denounces fellow Jews to the state police.[65]

Although subjected to enormous community pressure to recant, the B'nai B'rith agency refused to back down. Both ADL national director Benjamin Epstein and the organization's special counsel, Arnold Forster, defended the action of their Philadelphia bureau chief, Samuel Lewis Gaber, whose name had been listed by the FBI as their "source of information" on the city's JDL chapter.[66] The Anti-Defamation League never wavered throughout the entire affair. Its national leadership genuinely believed it had committed no impropriety.

In critically reviewing the incident, it becomes readily apparent that this unfortunate matter was as much a symptom of the political melting process as is the rise in Jewish alcoholism a symptom of the social homologizing effort. For a group like the ADL, ostensibly committed to "Jewish values" and Jewish continuity, there exists a perpetual tension between Jewish and American priorities and obligations. To be sure, one's Jewish obligations need not conflict with one's duties as a citizen of the United States—when one understands the genuine value structure of Judaism. For the Jew who suffers from a severe ignorance of authentic Jewish values, however, unnecessary "dual loyalty" dilemmas emerge *ex nihilo*. By perceiving the Jewish Defense League as a potential stimulant of anti-Jewish feeling in the United States—a fear which has become somewhat obsolete, inasmuch as the group has existed for more than a decade without provoking any organized Jew-hatred in America—the ADL felt it to be the *Jewish* imperative to commit the universally condemned action. Although such a betrayal is contrary to both the letter and spirit of Jewish tradition, it is consonant with jingoistic Americanism.

Even more egregious—nay, disgusting—was the announcement in September, 1980, that the ADL would give its national award to Hugh Hefner, publisher of *Playboy* magazine. In the same year, the grand total for the top five ADL functionaries came to more than $300,000 in one single year's salaries. The indications were that the Jewish community of the United States was spending quite a bit of its charitable funds on the salaries of ADL leaders. In return for their investment in this time of inflation, American Jews were learning that their salaried guardians were dispensing with communal dignity to heap praise and legitimacy on the publisher of *Playboy* magazine. Quite a return on so substantial an investment!

The ADL, not surprisingly, was castigated by non-Jews as well as Jews for choosing Hefner to be so honored. Yet, the ADL stood firm, arguing that Hefner had advanced the cause of America's First Amendment by publishing whatever he wanted to publish, in complete disregard of societal morals. He had thereby advanced the cause of "freedom of press." Perhaps the ADL felt Hefner a more worthy choice than their own Sam Gaber who had advanced the First Amendment by giving the FBI names of fellow Jews with whom he disagreed politically. In any event, the paradox was especially evident to observers who remembered the directives sent to B'nai B'rith chapters throughout the country in the early 1970s by their national office forbidding them from allowing Rabbi Meir Kahane to speak at their meetings. Rabbi Kahane, a controversial figure, was thus denied the "freedom of speech" so respected by Mr. Hefner's adulators. Many B'nai B'rith members, interested in hearing Rabbi Kahane's ideas, found themselves following the course of action taken by the B'nai B'rith lodge in New York which, after much thought, secretly invited Rabbi Kahane to speak to the lodge's brothers. When the rabbi arrived, the lodge conducted its meeting in the following manner: (1) The meeting was called to order. (2) Two announcements were made. (3) The meeting was gaveled closed three minutes after it had begun. An announcement was made that everyone could go home. Those wishing to "hang around" could do so. (4) Everyone present chose to "hang around." (5) Rabbi Meir Kahane spoke for an hour, then fielded a half-hour of questions.

Perhaps Hugh Hefner would have been denied the ADL national award had its leadership remembered that *Playboy* had published a major interview with the selfsame Rabbi Meir Kahane a number of years earlier. Whether the ADL's bunny-watchers still maintained a copy of that interview on file — or whether it had already been mailed off to Mr. Hoover and the FBI — remains uncertain.

Then there is the case of one Allen B. Bennett, homosexual, ordained a Jewish clergyman by the Reform seminary, Hebrew Union College. In an interview with Philadelphia's *Jewish Exponent*, "Rabbi" Bennett discussed his ideas as a homosexual rabbi. Bennett discussed his homosexual temple in San Francisco and noted that he had no problem synthesizing his homosexuality with Reform Judaism. To underscore the point, Bennett pointed out that his speaking tour along the American east coast was being sponsored by the Reform movement.[67]

Happy — or gay — are those who assemble in Bennett's homosexual temple for he is prepared and ready to perform marriages between two men.[68] He seems undeterred by the four-thousand-year traditions of Judaism, nor does he have any problems with the laws of Leviticus 18:22 and the Talmudic commentaries thereon. Perhaps he was an advanced-placement student at HUC and was excused from having to learn Biblical law. Perhaps he takes solace in the declaration by Balfour Brickner cited earlier.[69] In any event, Reform Rabbi Bennett says to interviewers, "I don't recognize homosexuality as a sin." Can responsible members of the American rabbinate be blamed for refusing to recognize Bennett and his Reform boosters as rabbis?

At least all American Jews can recognize art. The American Jewish Congress, which supports the Martin Steinberg Center, an institution dedicated to the propagation of Jewish artistic forms, was undoubtedly filled with pride when the Steinberg Center included this announcement in its monthly "Jewish Arts Newsletter":

MERLE LADERMAN UKELES who creates what she

calls "performance art/mitzvah" has recently completed an eleven-month public art performance called "TOUCH SANITATION" in which she visited all 59 sanitation districts to meet and shake hands with most of the city's 8,500 sanitation men and officers. Merle considers this a Jewish Artwork and is currently working on a book, video and two exhibitions about "Touch Sanitation."[70]

It is ironic to note that the Steinberg Center was originally supposed to be a contribution by the American Jewish Congress to the generation of young Jews looking for Jewish meaning and guidance. How many young Jews have been touched by the American Jewish Congress is not easily verifiable, but it would not be unfair to suppose that the final tally would be less than the number of garbage men touched by artist Ukeles.

Nor is the B'nai B'rith Hillel Foundation doing appreciably better if this excerpt from its Spring 1975 newsletter is representative. The blurb was published under the heading "THIS IS WHAT IT'S ALL ABOUT":

> *From a Hillel Director:*
>> An 18-year-old freshman came up to me. I shook hands with him.
>> "I certainly liked seeing you, I mean, coming to the Hillel services this year."
>> "Thank you very much," I replied.
>> "Yes. I liked them. I'm going to come next year, too."
>> "Good," I said. "Thank you."[71]

That was the entire conversation! This is what it's *all* about? This is what B'nai B'rith Hillel Foundation is all about???

The dialogue would probably provide an evening's pleasure for existentialist Jewish theater-goers. It could be billed as a one-act play entitled: "Waiting for Godot or Next Yom Kippur, Whichever Comes First."

There are other ways to attract a crowd. Consider the 92nd Street YMHA, perhaps the most famous Federation-sponsored "Y" in America. In 1978, for example, this institution received a grant of $721,812 from New York's Federation of Jewish Philanthropies, a body which raises charity dollars from Jews and ostensibly allocates those dollars with wisdom for the Jewish community.[72] How did the "Y" use its $721,812? A look at its 1979-1980 season affords the interested citizen some insights.

The "Adult Interest Center" of the 92nd Street "Y" offered five different classes in photography, three classes in playing bridge, and a series of programs for singles. Lucky singles were offered classes in how to dance "the hustle," how to excel in bartending, and how to buy and drink wines. Classes on "the new sexuality" and "cooking with class" were also offered.[73]

In the spring of 1980, more classes for adults were offered. These included a complete repetition of all the many important Jewish classes cited above and some new programs, not least prominent being the special "Lecture Series at the 92nd Street Y." Among these vital offerings, easily justifying receipt of an annual Federation grant bordering on three-quarters of a million dollars:

* Josh White, Jr. and Oscar Brand: "Songs of Slavery: America's Hidden Anger"
* Bev White and the Josh White Singers: "Songs of Hope and Religion" (focusing on "Gospel music")
* "For the Love of Horses," a four-lecture series consisting of lectures on: "The New York City Horse," "The Show Horse," "The Racing Horse," and "The Pleasure Horse"[74]

With programming like that, it is easy to understand why the New York Federation chose to fund its community centers and "Ys" to the tune of $8,419,424 — a figure more than three times the allocation made by the same Federation to Jewish education.

Even more difficult to understand is why some Jewish community federations stand in the way of others who do try to promote Jewish education and other projects more beneficial than lectures on horses tend to be. For example, a few years ago the Lubavitcher movement, an outstanding group of totally dedicated Jews, constructed a gigantic Chanuka *menora* in Cleveland's Public Square (with prior municipal approval). Not only was much of the Cleveland Jewish community delighted with the idea but no less a personage than Mayor Ralph Perk himself beamed, "This is the first time one has been erected in such a public place in the city of Cleveland."[75] Mayor Perk, moreover, personally attended a candle-lighting ceremony held at the square during one of the nights of the Chanuka holiday, and the city fire department offered its help by providing a bucket-crane truck which raised the torch-kindling dignitaries to within reach of the huge *menora*.

While most of Cleveland marveled at the innovative idea of spreading the warmth of Chanuka in this creative fashion, the Jewish Community Federation of Cleveland denounced the action. His spirits not perked by the public ceremony, Howard M. Rieger of the Federation's community relations committee condemned this gross violation of "the separation of church and state principle."[76] Rabbi Leibel Alevsky of the Lubavitch movement could not understand the Federation's agitated state. Noting that his group was planning to conduct similar public lightings in Philadelphia and New York, the rabbi explained that the city government itself saw no harm in the event. What Rabbi Alevsky neglected to consider was that those Jews who are racing to the melting pot have no desire to melt under the warmth of a Chanuka candle.

Some prefer to practice their Judaism within the confines of their own homes. Mr. and Mrs. Seymour Lichtenstein of Great Neck, New York, for example, performed the most noble of Jewish acts by inviting Mr. Stokely Carmichael to their private residence for a fund-raising event sponsored by the Great Neck Committee for Human Rights.[77] The Lichtensteins personally contributed $5,000 to the cause, while their children — raised in the traditions of Jewish philanthropy — added another $25 to the coffers. More than $10,000 was raised, as the group heard from Mr. Carmichael and Mr. Moe Tandler, counsel to CORE (Congress of Racial Equality). So successful was the occasion that Mr. Carmichael's position on the question of Jewish survival was understandably lost in the euphoria. Perhaps under the warm influence of the Lichtensteins' largesse, he reiterated his stand two months later at a meeting sponsored by the Organization of Arab Students at the University of Michigan. After explaining the preparedness of Black militants for "armed revolution," he asserted that he and other socially committed members of his community were ready "to take up arms and die if necessary to help the Arabs . . . We intend to make it clear we will help the Arabs in any way we can, not only with materials, but with our lives."[78]

He did not, however, reveal whether the Lichtensteins — or their children — had as yet been approached for contributions to this newest of his ventures. Carmichael might have done well to call on the twenty-five Jewish students who participated in this rally a few years later:

> LONDON — Some 25 Jewish left-wing students . . . were among the crowd which participated in a . . . "Palestine Day" rally at Hyde Park. They and other demonstrators, most of them Asians, called for the liquidation of the State of Israel . . .[79]

Such are the ultimate fruits of the race to the melting pot. What could be worse than Jewish youth joining bizarre religious cults? What could be worse than Jewish youths marching for the liquidation of the State of Israel? Could there be anything worse? Yes:

NAZI'S FATHER IS JEWISH

SKOKIE, ILL. — The father of Frank Collin, the organizer of the July 4th Nazi parade in Skokie, is Jewish. He survived the Nazi death camp Dachau before arriving in Chicago shortly after World War II.

These revelations were reported by Mike Royko of the *Chicago Daily News*, a Pulitzer Prize winner, and Jack Mabley of the *Chicago Tribune* . . .

Frank Collin was arrested at a Nazi demonstration in 1969, and police records show his address at the time to have been the same as Max Simon Collin, his father . . .[80]

A Nazi. Born of a survivor of Dachau. When Max Simon Cohen came to the United States, he changed his name to Collin and, together with his non-Jewish wife, tried to raise Frank as a "good American." Frank grew up to found the Nazi Party of Illinois.

Yes, such *are* the fruits of melting. And of intermarriage.[81]

Notes

1) *Jewish Week,* 8/8/76.

2) *New York Times,* 10/9/75.

3) Apparently, non-kosher eating — though in violation of one of Judaism's most sacred traditions — makes for good fund-raising. A similar approach to filling Jewish communal coffers was tried in 1979 by the Jewish Community Centers of South Florida when their South Dade branch sponsored a "Purim Skating Carnival" — coordinated with Burger King, too. The fast-foods outfit assured the fund-raiser's success by distributing special "Burger King" coupons to each skater paying three dollars. The leaflet this time did not include the slogan "Have it your way." But it sported a logo replete with the hamburger.

4) *Jewish Post and Opinion,* 6/23/72.

5) Martin Siegel and Mel Ziegler (ed.), *Amen: The Diary of Rabbi Martin Siegel* (N.Y.: Maddick Manuscripts, World Publishing Co.; 1971), pp. 52-3.

6) *Jewish Week,* 4/9/78; *Jewish Post and Opinion,* 4/14/78.

7) *Jewish Post and Opinion,* 12/24/76.

8) *Ibid.*

9) *Jewish Week,* 1/22/78.

10) *Sh'ma,* 2/2/79.

11) *Jerusalem Post Overseas Weekly,* 10/3/77.

12) *Jewish Post and Opinion,* 7/74. See Rona Barrett, *Miss Rona* (L.A.: Nash, 1974).

13) *Ibid.,* 7/29/77.

14) *Jewish Week,* 1/2/77.

15) *New York Daily News,* 12/19/76. Christmas to the National Singles Council of Bnai Zion (the Jewish fraternal body), on the other hand, meant a "GALA X-MAS WEEKEND" at the Stevensville Country Club in 1975.

16) *Jewish Post and Opinion,* 11/28/75 (reprinted 12/9/77).

17) *Ibid.*

18) *Ibid.*

19) *Ibid.*, 12/7/79.

20) *Ibid.*, 1/4/80.

21) The Christmas tree is an object of religious meaning to observant Christians. The tree itself represents the wood of the cross. The star above symbolizes the stars in the sky which are said to have led the wise men to the manger. The tinsel on the tree symbolizes angels' hair. The wreath represents the crown of thorns that the Romans made the Nazarene wear. The red berries are for the blood on the crucifix. Even the exchanging of gifts has religious significance, recalling that the wise men bore gifts with them when they visited the manger.

22) After a series of strong protests against the event (including a widely publicized peaceful demonstration organized by the Fairfield, Connecticut chapter of the Jewish Defense League), the Jewish Center's administration announced that there would be no repetitions of the sacrilege.

23) *Jewish Post and Opinion*, 8/74.

24) *Jewish Press*, 7/23/76.

25) *Jewish Journal*, 3/4/77.

26) *Jewish Post and Opinion*, 2/11/77.

27) *Ibid.*

28) *Ibid.*, 11/19/76.

29) *Jewish Week*, 5/17/75.

30) *New York Post*, 3/4/76.

31) *Newsweek*, 2/11/80.

32) *Ibid.*

33) *Ibid.*

34) *Jerusalem Post International Edition*, 12/16/79; *Jewish Post and Opinion*, 2/24/78; *Jewish Telegraphic Agency Daily Bulletin*, 2/15/80.

35) *Lilith* (magazine), vol. 1, no. 4 (Fall/Winter, 1977/78), p. 17.

36) Numbers 23:7-9.

37) *Ibid.*, verse 11.

38) Exodus 19:5-6.

39) Deuteronomy, 18:9-13.

40) *Philadelphia Jewish Times*, 1/12/77.

41) *New York Times*, 4/29/77.

42) *Present Tense* (Winter, 1980), pp. 10-12.

43) *Ibid.*

44) The AJSS is not the first project on which Hoffman and Lelyveld have teamed. In 1942, they were among the founders of the "Jewish Peace Fellowship," an organization originally established to provide assistance and moral support to American men refusing to

serve in the free world's struggle against Hitler and the Nazis. (See, e.g., *American Jewish Year Book*, vol. 46, p. 442, which lists Lelyveld as the president of the organization and Max D. Ticktin as its secretary.) As for Ferdinand Isserman, his major claim to fame before co-founding the AJSS was his role in naïvely supporting Father Charles Coughlin, a 1940s Jew-baiter who provoked physical attacks against American Jews by broadcasting and publishing anti-Jewish material. Isserman defended Coughlin in the 1930s from charges of anti-Semitism, according to the *American Jewish Year Book*, vol. 37, p. 156.

45) *Jewish Post and Opinion*, 10/12/79.

46) *Jewish Press*, 6/27/75.

47) *Ibid.*, 4/9/76.

48) *New York Times*, 3/20/70.

49) *Jewish Press*, 2/18/77.

50) *Ibid.*

51) "Federation of Jewish Philanthropies Sixtieth Anniversary Institute, Summary of Workshop Seven: Federation's Developing Role in Jewish Education" (internal Federation memorandum), p. 1.

52) *Ibid.*

53) *Jewish Journal*, 11/18/77.

54) *Ibid.*

55) *Ibid.*

56) *Ibid.*, 11/4/77.

57) *Ibid.*

58) *Ibid.* This same call was reiterated the following year by Aryeh Dulzin, head of the World Zionist Organization. (*Israel Digest*, 2/24/78)

59) Kurt Lewin, *Resolving Social Conflict* (N.Y.: Harper, 1948), p. 45.

60) *New York Daily News*, 10/5/70.

61) *New York Times*, 12/15/75.

62) *Ibid.*

63) *Jewish Post and Opinion*, 5/28/71.

64) *Ibid.*

65) *Connecticut Jewish Ledger*, 5/20/71.

66) *Ibid.*

67) *Jewish Post and Opinion*, 12/14/79; *Jewish Week*, 12/9/79.

68) *Ibid.*

69) *Jewish Post and Opinion*, 7/22/77.

70) *Newsletter of American Jewish Congress Steinberg Center*, vol. 1, no. 16 (October, 1980).

71) *B'nai B'rith Hillel Foundation Newsletter*, Spring 1975, p. 17.

72) *Federation of Jewish Philanthropies, Annual Report—1978*, p. 16.

73) "The Adult Interest Center of the 92nd Street Y, 1979-80 Offerings" (booklet).

74) "Lecture Series at the 92nd Street Y, Spring 1980" (pamphlet).

75) *Jewish Post and Opinion*, 12/24/76.

76) *Ibid.*

77) *The Great Neck Record*, 5/25/67.

78) *New York Times*, 8/28/67.

79) *Jewish Journal*, 6/4/76.

80) *Jewish Press*, 7/1/77. See also *Newsweek*, 12/3/79, for account of Oscar Stohr, a former German Nazi, who was born to a Catholic mother and Jewish father.

81) Other famous intermarriage offspring include: Larry Layton— charged in the Guyana murder of Congressman Leo Ryan who had sought to investigate the People's Temple cult headed by Rev. Jim Jones; Mike Evans—founder of B'nai Yeshua, a Christian missionary outfit which seeks to convert young Jews; and William Najib Nasser—a PLO terrorist leader captured by Israel in a 1968 attack.

CHAPTER 8

Intermarriage:
"Where did we go wrong?"

And Ezra the kohen (priest) stood up and
said to them: "You have transgressed
and have taken to your homes foreign
wives, to increase the guilt of Israel. Now
therefore make confession to the Lord
God of your fathers, and do His will, and
separate yourselves from the people of the
land and from the foreign women."
Then all the assembly answered and said
with a loud voice, "Verily: As you have
said, so must we do."   (EZRA 10:10-12)

DAVID MANSHEL WEDS ELIZABETH WHITNEY

Elizabeth Burgess Whitney, daughter of Mr. and Mrs.
Joseph Cutler Whitney of Westwood and Edgartown,
Mass., was married yesterday to David Michael Manshel,
son of Mr. and Mrs. Ernest Manshel of New Rochelle,
N.Y.

The ceremony was performed at the Whitney home in
Edgartown by the Rev. John Greely, an Episcopal priest
of Peabody, Mass., and Rabbi William Seaman . . .[1]

MISS DI PAOLA WED TO RICHARD NATELSON

Jeri-Ann Di Paola, daughter of Mr. and Mrs. Victor Di
Paola of Rockville Center, L.I., was married yesterday
afternoon in Tuxedo, N.Y., to Richard M. Natelson.

1. The numbered notes to chapter 8 appear on page 284.

He is the son of Mr. and Mrs. Sydney Natelson of Stony
Point, N.Y., and Mount Laurel, N.J.

Rabbi Abraham Krantz performed the ceremony in the
rose garden at the Sterling Forest Gardens. He was
assisted by a Roman Catholic priest.[2]

In many American Jewish suburban regions today, the wed-
ding-announcements column has come to rival the obituary
page as the most feared section of the daily newspaper. Reports
of intermarriages proliferate at unprecedented rates, as young
Jews nonchalantly decide to sever their ties to a four-thousand-
year heritage while their parents scurry to their neighborhood
rabbis to ask THE questions: "Rabbi, why are they doing this
to us? What did we do to deserve this? *Where did we go
wrong?*" In the words of Jonathan Braun, the talented writer
who so powerfully captured this phenomenon, "If 'What is to be
done?' is the age-old question of the Russian people, then
'Where did I go wrong?' is the Jewish counterpart."[3]

In truth, The Question is no longer confined to the tragedy
of intermarriage. When Braun wrote his article, the Rev. Sun
Myung Moon had not yet arrived in America. The Christian
missionaries had not yet adopted the "Moishe Rosen" gambit
of portraying themselves as "Jews for Jesus." The Eastern
religions had not yet become a threat to Jewish continuity in
suburbia. Today, The Question is asked regularly, for any number of reasons. Nevertheless, of all the tragic by-products of the
American Jewish "race to the melting pot," it is an impending
intermarriage which is most prone to provoke The Question:

"Rabbi, where did we go wrong?"

The neighborhood rabbi, who has not seen the parents since
the previous year's Yom Kippur service and has not seen the
boy since he was "bar mitzvahed" ten years earlier,[4] would be
at a complete loss were it not for the frequency with which this
query has already been put to him. By now experienced in
handling the problem, the rabbi's eyes melt, his voice softens to
a near whisper, and his arms reach out, as he says:

Now, now. It isn't necessarily *your* fault. Believe me,

I'm a rabbi, and I have tens of parents coming in every week with the same problem. It's today's kids. They're a little bit crazy. We live in a new kind of society — free love, loose morals. It just isn't the same world that we were brought up in.

I assure you that your son is not rebelling against you. He loves you. I'm sure. You'll bring him in and we'll talk. The important thing is not to blame yourselves. He might be a bit confused. Besides, maybe the girl will convert, and they'll raise their kids as Jews.

What else should the rabbi say? What else *can* he say? Should he ask the parents whether they raised the child in an authentically Jewish home, in which genuine Jewish values were practiced and praised? Should he inquire whether or not the Sabbath was observed as a Jewish Sabbath should be kept? Should he interrogate the parents on the nature of the Jewish education with which they provided their child? The rabbi is not conducting a study commissioned by a research foundation; he is desperately attempting to comfort sorely grieved parents.

But, if he *were* conducting a study, he would arrive at the results reported by the Committee on Jewish Education of the Federation of Jewish Agencies of Greater Philadelphia which found that Jews raised in homes where authentic Judaism is practiced are least likely to intermarry.[5] The committee learned that Jewish secondary schooling has "a positive residual effect" on the way young Jews practice their Judaism in later years and that the effect manifests itself on every level of Jewish commitment: in personal observance, synagogue and organizational membership and activity, ties to Israel, and personal perceptions of the importance of Jewish values on family life and lifestyles.[6]

Tragically, young Jews do not receive meaningful Jewish educational opportunities in many assimilated regions. Raised by liberally oriented parents who decide that "religion should not be shoved down my child's throat; when he grows old enough, let him choose for himself whether or not he wants to be religious," these Jewish youths are, in effect, deprived of a free choice. How can they "choose" to live by a religion about which they are completely ignorant? Bereft of a Jewish education, they know nothing about the Sabbath, the dietary laws, or any of the other Torah commandments—save that which they have heard in the spiritual dark alleys of suburbia. How ironic it is that the same parent who determines that a child should be provided with sex education at a young age, in order to prevent later mis-conceptions (sic), is fiercely determined to prevent the youth from obtaining religious information at the same time! If a child cannot be expected to know intuitively how his own body functions, can he more readily be expected to understand the "mechanism" of his soul? How is a child to grow to make a truly free religious choice at a later moment in his life if, denied a Jewish background during his youth, his theological information derives only from the "spiritual alley"?

Myths regarding Jewish religious practice are not less prevalent than those concerning sexual reality. If an uneducated child can grow up believing that kissing causes pregnancy and that venereal disease is usually transmitted through contact with public toilets, is it not to be expected that he will grow up with religious misconceptions as well? An enlightened Jewish parent would never consider denying his child the most complete sexual education, but he would deny the child an opportunity to develop religious awareness.

Beyond the question of knowledge, there is a second aspect of intellectual disquietude occasioned by such an "enlightened" approach to Jewish youth-rearing. In the name of "freedom of choice"—a most noble value—a child is sent to a secular school rather than a Jewish parochial institution. In later years, he will choose for himself whether he seeks to be deeply religious, mildly committed, or thoroughly atheistic. And, whatever the choice, it will meet with parental acceptance because it will be his own "free choice." Would the same parent decide not to send the child to elementary school or, subsequently, to high school on the grounds that the child should be given the freedom to choose for himself whether or not he desires a secular education? Indeed, would the average Jewish parent—compelled by law to provide the child with a secular training—refrain from urging the child (in the most vociferous of tones when necessary) to do his homework? Perhaps the child, if given the freedom to choose, would prefer to watch television rather than to do his homework? Perhaps, at the age of seven, he would prefer to seek employment as a baseball announcer or as a fireman? Perhaps, inspired by a popular movie, he would prefer to become an illiterate gangster-boss? Would a Jewish parent permit the child absolute freedom of choice at the pre-teen level?

And when that child reaches his early teens, is he permitted to date any girl and to come home from the date at whatever time he pleases? Naturally, with maturity, he is given an ever-increasing range of personal freedoms—as well he should be. But absolute freedom of choice is not permitted him for quite some time. Only after he has been thoroughly educated in the style his parents have deemed most appropriate is he allowed the "freedom" to choose. By then, he has been subjectively trained, usually towards the goal of desiring a college ed-ucation. In college, he is trained to consider a professional career in medicine, law, accounting, or some other suitable area of "Jewish" employment. By the time the average Jewish youth's schooling has come to an end, it is highly unlikely that he will opt for the vocations he admired during his childhood. Certainly, he will be offered "freedom of choice." Will he choose to be a fireman? Will he choose to be a dog-catcher? Of course not. He has been subjectively trained. To be sure, he may pursue a field about which he knows absolutely nothing, but all odds are heavily weighted against the probability of such a "free choice."

Consider, as well, a child's cultural training. How many Jewish parents force their sons to study a musical instrument (usually a piano or violin) and force their daughters to attend ballet classes? The young boy may scream, holler, and curse that he wants to play ball with his friends rather than be confined in the house until he completes his daily musical exercises, but his "freedom of choice" is denied him on the grounds that "one day he will thank us for it." Perhaps he will never thank his parents for retarding his athletic development by imposing the daily rigors of homework and musical exercises on him? Such a possibility is discounted, for he is still "too young" to make such decisions on his own. How will he ever know whether he would like to be a musician if he is never given the chance to study the subject of music? How will the girl ever really know that she would not find ballet fulfilling if she is not given the opportunity to spend a few years practicing toe exercises? When it comes to so many fields of education, the enlightened Jewish ethic is: Expose the child. Give him a chance to learn the subject well enough so that he can make an educated decision regarding his future. If it is not his desire to perform in an orchestra, let him make that determination after he has, at least, learned how to read the musical scale. Before he rejects a career in medicine, ascertain that he has studied high-school biology.

How, then, can it be argued that a young Jew should be sent to a public (or private) secular school—and not to a yeshiva—in order to allow him the opportunity to "freely" decide, upon maturation, whether or not he wants to be Jewish? What freedom is he being given? Should he not first be exposed to Judaism? If he is expected to study high-school sciences before rejecting a career in medicine, should he not have a concomitant opportunity to study high-school-level Judaism before rejecting his four-thousand-year heritage? If he is required to do thirty-minute piano exercises and hours of homework every day, should he not be expected to put in a similar amount of time in doing his Jewish-studies assignments?

In short, if a Jewish child is to be given the freedom to reject Judaism, should he not be given the freedom to choose it, as well?

When a Jewish youth matures, he will meet Jewish and non-Jewish friends. And if he is sent to public school (or private secular school), the chances are greatly increased that he will develop warm friendships with non-Jews of his sex and of the opposite sex. If he has not been given a solid Jewish education—comparable to that offered him on a secular level—why should he not one day intermarry?

Because he has a religious duty? What religious duty? He does not even know as much about his religion as he knows about the violin or the composition of an amoeba. His religion is a meaningless label. If he had any religious duty, he fulfilled it when he read the *haftora* at his bar mitzva; that was all the Jewish literacy ever expected of him, and he was permitted to drop out of Hebrew school upon the completion of its recitation. So why should he not one day intermarry?

Because he has an obligation to "his people"? What people? He is an American. And he wants to marry an American. So what if she is not Jewish? She is pretty or smart or sensible or exotic—or whatever it is that he looks for in a young woman. Why should he not marry a non-Jew?

Because he has an obligation to the generations which survived four thousand years of Egyptian servitude, Amalekite wars, Philistinian attacks, Babylonian desolations, Roman desecrations, Christian crusades, inquisitions, blood libels, desecration-of-the-host slanders, pogroms, and holocausts? Yes, he has such an obligation. But does he know it? When did he ever learn the history of his people? He knows about Nathan Hale who proudly told the British hangman, "My only regret is that I have but one life to give for my country." Does he know that Jews went to the fiery stake of the Spanish Inquisition uttering words no less boldly defiant? Does he know that the Romans combed the skin of Rabbi Akiva off his body with steel prongs as a punishment for his defiant insistence on the right to teach young Jews the Torah—even though it conflicted with Roman law which banned all Jewish studies? And does he know this?—that as Rabbi Akiva was literally being torn to shreds, the words of this Jewish martyr were: "The Torah commands us to love the Lord with all our heart, with all our soul, and with all our might.[7] All my days I have been troubled by this commandment to love God with my soul. When, I wondered, would I have the opportunity to fulfill this commandment? Now I have that opportunity. Hearken, O Israel: The Lord is our God, the Lord is One."[8] Does he know of the Jewish heroes who were taken by British hangmen to the noose in the 1940s and who were put to death because of their efforts to establish a free Jewish state in Israel?

Of course he has "an obligation to the four-thousand-year link which made it possible for him to be born a Jew." But, without a Jewish education, how can he know of the obligation? All his life he was told that he would have "freedom of choice." His parents assumed that he would choose to be a non-religious Jew like them. How should he know he was not supposed to go the next step and to freely choose to totally alienate himself from even nominal Judaism? Is it his fault that he took his parents seriously?

A young Jew intermarries only after he has been totally convinced that the survival of Judaism and of the Jewish people is not more important than his achieving "happiness." Naturally, he could find a Jewish young woman who would make him no less happy than his non-Jewish friend. But why should he bother to wait for such a person to enter his life when he already has a wonderful companion?

Consider the question from his point of view. As a child, he went to public school and was encouraged to get a good secular education. His first brush with Judaism — and his last — came when he was sent to Hebrew School at the age of twelve to learn a *haftora*. It was made clear to him that he was being sent for that reason only — not for the purpose of becoming "religious." To encourage him, his parents promised him fine bar mitzva gifts and even told him that he would be permitted to learn the *haftora* from a tape recording without having to bother learning the Hebrew letters. Meanwhile, his success in secular studies was still of primary concern to them.

After his bar mitzva, he was permitted to stop attending Hebrew school. At home, his parents regularly mocked the "Orthodox fanatics," noting that they were equally "proud to be Jewish" but that they were "smart enough not to go overboard." As for him, he was free to be whatever he wanted to be. And, if he would want to be a doctor, then that would just be splendid.

He grew up and started dating girls, some Jewish and some not. His parents, not being the prejudiced type, never commented one way or the other. After all, he was doing so well in school that it seemed he was on his way to the Ivy League. His parents were proud of him, and he was happy to be achieving a modicum of success.

He made Harvard (or Berkeley), bringing even greater pride to his family. During his college years, he earned excellent grades. While dorming, he met a wonderful co-ed who was also studying to be a doctor. She was bright, pretty, and liked to ski. What else could he ask for? What else could his *parents* ask for? He never bothered to determine whether or not she came from a Jewish family because it never occurred to him that such a factor would be significant. Look, she could get a kosher cookbook and learn how to make chicken soup if that would make his parents happy. She might even be willing to read Martin Buber's *I and Thou.*

Why should he not intermarry? He earned good grades and studied to be a doctor. Those were the ideals his parents taught him to value, and he complied with their requests. He fulfilled their dreams. As for religion, he chose freely—just as they said he should.

Denied an authentic Jewish upbringing, deprived of a meaningful Jewish education, dispossessed of a four-thousand-year culture and heritage, Jews who intermarry have grown up without a spiritual foundation, without multi-generational roots. Unconcerned with religious or political ideas to any great extent but deeply interested in achieving "the good life," they turn to intermarriage.

But young Jews intermarry for the same reason that they join religious or Marxist cults. All reject Judaism as a viable avenue of self-expression because, having been denied an understanding of authentic Jewish values while being subjected to grotesque caricatures thereof, they regard Judaism as a vacuous system of empty faith, materialistic ritual, and endless self-mockery. They do not imagine that Judaism actually opposes materialistic splendor and endorses a lifestyle of financial moderation and personal humility. They do not consider the possibility that genuine Judaism outlines a lifestyle which includes spiritually uplifting rituals which control man's physical cravings without imposing on him ascetic abuses. They have virtually no idea that authentic Judaism asserts that there *is* a Creator who established the heavens and the earth, who guides the course of world development, and—most importantly—gathered the Jewish people to the foot of Mount Sinai to receive His Torah and to live by its commandments.

These young people are the victims of the "bar mitzva syndrome." They are the spiritually amorphous mass created by a childhood of bagels without *berachot* (blessings). They are a generation whose souls have been cooked away in their parents' melting pots. In the words of Michael Medved:

> . . . I remember too well the arguments I had with my parents when, at age 20, I wanted to marry a Gentile. . . . What could they do, my poor parents? They were good Zionists and committed Jews. . . . Having grown up in a secure Jewish environment with an Orthodox emphasis, they felt comfortable in rejecting major portions of their background. It never occurred to them that in order to make the same rejections and to arrive at the same enlightened point, their children would have to receive the same traditional background they did—not the bland inanity I tried to assimilate. When Torah is compromised, those compromises cannot be passed on intact from generation to generation. Once begun, the process of arbitrary alteration must continue, in one direction or another. How many families can you name that have been devoutly "Reform" for hundreds of years?[9]

Not the Schiff family, one of the pillars of "Reform Judaism" at the turn of the century. Jacob Schiff worshipped every Saturday at Temple Emanuel in New York City and gave substantial amounts of money to a number of Jewish institutions. In two generations' time, his family's Jewish roots have all but disappeared. When his grandson, John M. Schiff, was married by Father George B. Ford (a Catholic priest) to a non-Jewish woman, one Jewish clergyman wrote:

> Where are the children and grandchildren of this ardent Jew [i.e., Jacob Schiff]?
>
> They have intermarried, are totally assimilated, with no connection with Judaism, and no interest in the future of the Jewish people. While enjoying the enormous wealth their grandfather left, they have no regard for the religious faith and tradition which were so precious to him. . . .
>
> Monday, March 1st, the *New York Times* reported the marriage of John M. Schiff to a non-Jewish woman . . .
>
> Who performed the wedding ceremony? None other than Father George B. Ford, a Catholic priest, who came for the occasion to the groom's home in Old Westbury. As a gesture to his Jewish ancestry, a rabbi was present to offer a blessing.
>
> What kind of a blessing can a rabbi give to the union of a Jew and a Catholic which is solemnized by a Catholic priest? Can such an occasion bring joy to the heart of any Jew . . . ?
>
> Is it not demeaning for a rabbi to be a party to such arrangements? Would it not have been infinitely more dignified to have refused to participate in a ceremony which brings honor neither to Judaism nor the Jewish people?[10]

If it was demeaning for a "rabbi" to participate in the Schiff intermarriage, then another "Reform rabbi" has demeaned Judaism more than one thousand times. "Rabbi" Edwin Howard Friedman, commander of the pulpit at Bethesda, Maryland's Jewish Congregation, has exceeded the chiliad mark in intermarriage performances. Proclaiming himself the only "rabbi" in the Washington area who performs inter-marriages, Friedman explained to a reporter for the *Canadian Jewish News* that he does not necessarily advocate the practice. "I'm trying to deal with it in a creative, healthy way," he noted.[11] Unfortunately, the rest of the Washington-area Jewish community seems to have disapproved of his tactic, for he complains that "I've been treated like a pariah by the established Jewish community."

Friedman might find solace in this statement signed by three leading "Reform rabbis" in 1972:

> . . . The historic Jewish prohibition against inter-
> marriages was an expression of the ultimate importance of
> group identity. For Jews who believe
> that the preservation of Jewish identity is the most
> important Jewish enterprise, the ban on intermarriage is a
> rational restriction. However, for those Jews who do not
> accept this value system, the ban on intermarriage is both
> irrational and immoral.
>
> We do not accept this value system. We dissent from
> the belief that the primary moral obligation of every Jew
> is to promote and sustain Jewish identity . . .[12]

Where there is no longer any purpose in maintaining the distinct entity of the Jewish people as a separate nation chosen by God to bear witness to humanity, there is no longer any reason to ban intermarriage. Not surprisingly, moreover, all three of the letter's signers are in that category of "Reform rabbis" who have turned away from the charge of the First Commandment. By denying the existence of the God of Abraham, Isaac, and Jacob who revealed Himself at Mount Sinai before the eyes of an entire nation, they quite naturally see nothing significant in the eternal obligation of the Jewish people to observe the 613 commandments of the Torah. Having defined God, His Divine revelation, His Torah, and His commandments out of existence,[13] "rabbis" like these three need not travel much farther along their ideological paths in order to begin defining the Jewish people out of existence. It is not altogether surprising, in this light, that one of those who signed the letter, "Rabbi" Sherwin Wine of Michigan, subsequently issued a call to American Jewry to observe Christmas as an annual holiday.[14]

Raised under the spiritual tutelage of "rabbis" who themselves have deserted authentic Judaism, young Jews cannot be blamed for abandoning the God of their fathers. If all they know about Judaism is the little they hear during their year of Hebrew school (all of which is subsequently mocked at home), what weight can they be expected to attach to "the Jewish religion" and "the Jewish people"—the two sacred entities to which their loyalties are suddenly summoned? If a Jew "should" celebrate Christmas—or, at least, have a Christmas tree in his home every year—then what is so apostate about marrying a non-Jewish woman? Consider the confusion occasioned by "pastoral letters" like this one mailed by "Rabbi" Eugene J. Sack to the members of his Reform congregation in Brooklyn, New York, one December: "The message of Chanukah and Christmas, too, must be this: In a time of darkness, light a candle of hope. Surely this is why Jews, Christians, and the pagans before us made this time of the year, when the nights are longest, a time for lighting the festive candles."[15]

Were "Rabbi" Sack more efficiently trained in basic Judaism, he would have realized that the reason Jews light Chanuka *menorot* in December has nothing whatsoever to do with the length of winter nights.[16] The Chanuka festival commemorates the miracles of the Maccabean period, when the numerically small Jewish nation defeated the Syrian-Greek armies who sought to impose a ban on the observance of the Jewish religion. After their military victory, the Jews proceeded to the liberated Temple, where they hoped to rekindle the eternal lamp. Regrettably, they could find only enough ritually pure olive oil to maintain the lamp's glow for one day, and it would take a week before more could be prepared. Nevertheless, they lit the *menora*, expecting it to last for twenty-four hours. Miraculously, as they entered the Temple the following day, they found the lamp still aflame. For eight days the *menora* glowed; by then, a new supply of oil was ready to maintain the light for the future. It is in commemoration of that eight-day event that Jews light Chanuka candles every winter—for an eight-day period. The choice of time is occasioned not by the coincidental proximity to the winter solstice but by the actual date of the event. The miraculous period commenced on the twenty-fifth day of the Hebrew month of Kislev, which usually falls in the winter. The lighting of the Chanuka candles today is timed to coincide with that lunar calendar date. When it occurs in late December, that is when it is celebrated; when it falls in late autumn, then *that* is when it is commemorated.

While pagans treated the winter solstice with a sense of awe, Jews never lent any meaning of significance to the occasion. Antithetically, Judaism condemned in the strongest terms those who engaged in solar or lunar deification.[17] As for the period in which Christians have chosen to celebrate Christmas, there are undoubtedly many theologians who trace the holiday's timing to the pagan influences which affected early Christian practice. Sack may be erudite in the field of comparative theology, then. In terms of *Jewish* understanding, however, he stands naïve, if not ignorant. And that is a most charitable assessment.

But how many young Jews have ever studied *real* Judaism? How many have learned the *real* reasons that Jews celebrate Chanuka? If it is their parents' Jewish ignorance which keeps such "rabbis" as "Rabbi" Sack in the pulpit, it is the combination of both the parents' and the "rabbis' " naïveté which leads them to the threshold of intermarriage. A young Jew who is raised on a mythology which compares the rededication of the Holy Temple during the Maccabean period to the pagan worship of the winter solstice cannot be expected to attribute any meaning to Judaism once he matures enough to learn the absurdities of paganism.

What an overwhelming tragedy it is that parents who would

never allow their children to embark on adolescence believing that "babies come from storks" would permit them to grow up on such theological "back-alley tales" as that unraveled by "Rabbi" Sack on the occasion of Chanuka!

If intermarriage is to be curtailed, then young Jews must be provided with a Jewish educational base every bit as secure as is the secular-knowledge foundation with which they are endowed. They must study Judaism, just as they must study biology, mathematics, chemistry, physics, geography, economics, literature, foreign languages, music, and ballet. They must be taught their Jewish history as they are taught American history. They must be given a Jewish education which extends, at least, to the twelfth-grade high-school level — just as they are given a secular training for, at the "Jewish" minimum, a dozen years. And, of paramount importance, they must be offered a high *quality* of Jewish education not unlike the quality of their secular training. Would an enlightened Jewish parent send his child to a school which teaches English grammar from a collection of "Uncle Remus" stories? Would an enlightened Jewish parent have his child taught geography by an iconoclast who maintains that the earth is flat? Of course not. Accordingly, a Jewish parent should not have his child taught Judaism by those incapable of individuating Chanuka from the pagan observance of the winter solstice.

It is to be noted that an encouraging trend may be emerging. Although synagogue and temple congregants traditionally engage in the inevitable sequence of "political jockeying" against their local rabbis, they rarely challenge their clergymen on *religious* grounds. Despite their innate feelings that "rabbinical" assertions from the pulpit are not always consistent with normative Jewish thought, worshippers tend to shy away from theological confrontations because their very status as laymen leaves them open to spontaneous forms of "refutation without substantiation." The most courageous of challenges to the pulpit has generally been confined to comments of the sort penned by Bernard Marks, a Federation consultant:

If our spiritual leaders would stop giving us book reviews on Friday night, which I can read in the paper, if our spiritual leaders would stop being social workers, and be rabbis, and on Saturday morning give us the portion of the week, and teach us Judaism — as I learned it when I went to school, and as I am learning it now — I think that most of these problems [of intermarriage and assimilation] would be solved.[18]

But new confrontations of the sort which erupted at Jericho, Long Island's Reform Temple Or-Elokim may bode a hope for a day when deviating "rabbis" will be called to task by their own laity who, despite their ignorance of what is always Jewishly right, can at least perspicaciously discern what is Jewishly wrong:

RABBI IN ECUMENICAL FUNERAL CENSURED BY TEMPLE, 25-2

JERICHO — By a vote of 25 to 2, with two abstentions, the board of trustees of Temple Or-Elo[k]im, a Reform congregation, has censured its rabbi, Irwin C. Lowenheim, for having participated with a Catholic priest in an ecumenical funeral service in a Catholic church for the late George Morton Levy, president of Roosevelt Raceway.

Levy had requested such a service in a conversation shortly before his death with Msg. Thomas F. Cole, a long-time friend. At the service in St. Brigid's Church, Msg. Cole read from the New Testament from one altar, and Rabbi Lowenheim, standing at an opposite side altar, read from the Old Testament and recited the Kaddish at a graveside service in the non-sectarian Greenfield Cemetery.[19]

In a letter sent by the board of trustees to the congregation, the vote of censure was explained. "[It] was predicated upon the board's disapproval of the rabbi's participation in the funeral service . . . at St. Brigid's Roman Catholic Church. This action was in poor judgment and caused embarrassment to many of our congregants. Rabbi Lowenheim should have declined to participate in this service."[20]

Although such demands by temple laity for responsible Jewish conduct in the pulpit are encouraging, they will not stem the intermarriage tide if unaccompanied by a concomitant effort to provide qualitatively adequate Jewish education for young Jews. In the final analysis, it is clear that the cancer of intermarriage is curable. As one widely respected Jewish thinker has written:

> Parents, teachers, rabbis and other Jewish leaders must stop showing by their example that Jewish identity is meaningless. Persons and institutions with Jewish money and facilities must use them for things that are really Jewish. Hypocrisy and empty, non-spiritual value systems must be banished from our synagogues and Jewish organizations . . .
>
> If this is done, then and only then will our idealistic Jewish youth believe that the Judaism of their forefathers is worth preserving through the sanctification of Jewish marriage and the propagation of committed Jewish children.[21]

There *is* a path to recovery. The exodus of Jewish youths from their heritage and culture *can* be terminated. The allure of bizarre cults and the temptations of intermarriage *can* be successfully overcome. We come, once again, to a "long road which is short." It is the road of Jewish education and knowledge. It is the road of Jewish understanding and awareness.

It is the road which returns us to Jewish values.

Notes

1) *New York Times*, 9/11/77.

2) *Ibid.*, 7/12/76.

3) Jonathan Braun, "Neglecting the Jewish National Experience," *The Flame* (a publication of Jewish students at the City College of New York), February 1970.

4) If it is a Jewish girl who is intermarrying, the chances are substantial that the rabbi has *never* seen her before, since bat mitzvas are not celebrated as frequently as are bar mitzvas.

5) *Jewish Post and Opinion*, 8/12/77.

6) *Ibid.*

7) Deuteronomy 6:5.

8) Cf. Tractate *Berachot* 61b.

9) Michael Medved, "What Really Happened to the Bar Mitzvah Class of 5722?" *Davka* (magazine), no. 18 (Spring 1977), pp. 38-39.

10) Excerpts from bulletin of the Progressive Shaarei Zedek Synagogue, written by Theodore N. Lewis, and cited in *Jewish Post and Opinion*, 4/30/76.

11) *Jewish Post and Opinion*, 6/11/76.

12) *Ibid.*, 6/23/72. Letter signed by "Rabbis" Daniel Friedman, Philip Schechter, and Sherwin Wine.

13) *Ibid.*, 6/17/77. Sherwin Wine's Birmingham Temple has, in fact, deleted "God" from all liturgical services. See also *ibid.*, 3/24/78.

14) *Ibid.*, 3/27/77.

15) Eugene Sack, "A Pastoral Letter," *Congregation Beth Elokim Bulletin*, 12/20/74.

16) See Tractate *Shabbath* 21b.

17) Cf. Tractate *Avodah Zarah* 54b and 8a ff.

18) Cited in Rabbi Chaim Uri Lipschitz, "The Roots of Intermarriage," *Jewish Life* (Summer 1974), p. 33.

19) *Jewish Week*, 8/28/77.

20) *Ibid.* A report published in the *Jewish Week*, 12/11/77, revealed that Lowenheim had resigned from the congregation's pulpit.

21) Lipschitz, *op. cit.*, p. 36.

3

JEWISH VALUES

Now the Lord spoke to Moses, saying, "Speak to all the congregation of the children of Israel, and say to them: Holy shall you be, for I the Lord your God am holy." (LEVITICUS 19:1-2)

If there is one common link binding together the tragic phenomena plaguing American Jewry today, it is to be found in the breakdown of the community's commitment to those Jewish values which maintained the nation of Israel for four millennia. The exodus of sensitive young Jews from their homes to the foreign worlds of the bizarre religious cults, the alienation of Jewish youths from their parents' value structures and the alacrity with which those youths mock and denounce everything their parents hold dear, the readiness of thousands of Jewish adolescents to interdate and to subsequently inter-marry—all these spiritual and psychological crises can be traced back to a common source: the collapse of Jewish traditional values and their supplantation by concepts and notions derived from alien spheres.

In the "race to the melting pot," American Jewry has, of perceived necessity, shed its heavy cultural baggage. A heritage of four thousand years is not light; it burdens its bearer for every moment of his life. The Jewish legacy, as transmitted from generation to generation, is one not only rich with culture and warm with memorabilia but also weighty with responsibility. To be a Jew is not easy in the best of times; it is enormously difficult in the worst.

The American Jewish community has raised a generation bereft of cultural roots. God, Torah concepts, sacred commandments, and religious institutions have been consigned to the social furnace for rapid disposal. Even the comparatively "secular" Jewish limbs—those of history, geography, language, music, and art—have been virtually amputated from the American Jewish body. There is no link with the ancient past of Abraham, Isaac, Jacob, Moses, and David. There is no bond with the distant past of Judah Maccabee, Rabbi Akiva, Saadya Gaon, Judah Halevy, and Maimonides. There is no connection with the oppressive past of Roman desecrations, crusades, inquisitions, blood libels, and pogroms. There is even no tie to the recent past of Treblinka, Sobibor, and Babi Yar; there is but the most superficial of relationships to the concomitant past of Warsaw, Bergen-Belsen, Dachau and Auschwitz. And there is a tragic vacuum of knowledge regarding the State of Israel—both in terms of what it means to the Jewish people today and, far more tragically, in terms of what it meant to the Jewish people during the 1930s and 1940s when it was still absent from the world scene.

If there is a breakdown in Jewish communal cohesion, it is only the offspring of a collapse of genuine Jewish knowledge and values. Perhaps the important Jewish concepts were first shed in an earlier period in American history; today, the structure has deteriorated to the point that the very *names* for the values are unknown. The Sabbath—*Shabbat*—is a commonly known term, thanks to the Sunday Christian faithful. But how many Jews know what *tefillin* and *tzitziyot* are? How many have the vaguest notion of what *taharat hamishpacha*—family purity—entails, let alone why? *Tefilla, mezuza*, and *tzedaka* are barely cognizable; they might more appropriately appear in a Sanskrit Hindu text than in a discussion of Jewish values.

American Jews don't know the words which describe fundamental aspects of Jewish tradition. Can they be expected to understand the depths of the tradition itself? The English translations for many of the Hebrew words provide little clue. Of those who do not know what *tefillin* are, few are reminded by the English word "phylacteries." For those ignorant of the *mikveh* tradition, the term "ritualarium" does not help.

There are 613 commandments in the Torah, and their complexity absorbed the Tannaitic and Amoraic sages of the Talmud for centuries; their importance was great enough to merit the unending efforts of these rabbinic scholars, who sought tirelessly to understand and apply the laws of God. Since the time of Abraham and Sarah, Jewish parents have transmitted Jewish values to their children, Philip Roth notwithstanding, and that chain of Jewish commitment has continued to this day. Links have weakened in assimilated suburbia, but the chain continues intact. And rabbis continue to ponder the laws.

It would be substantially beyond the scope of this study to consider every concept, commandment, and Jewish value in depth. Just to peripherally review a modest sampling of these Jewish traditions is an awesome task. But, after a thorough consideration of the cults and a rigorous treatment of the phenomena of assimilation—the "Bar Mitzva Syndrome," the "race to the melting pot," and the crisis of intermarriage—it would be worthwhile to briefly explore the world of Jewish tradition and authentic values of the Jewish people.

And any such cogitation would have to begin with the source of Jewish purpose: the Torah.

CHAPTER **9**

Torah:
The book that out-sold Portnoy's Complaint

Only take heed and guard your soul diligently, lest you forget the things which your eyes have seen, and lest they depart from your heart all the days of your life; but teach them to your sons and to your sons' sons—the day that you stood before the Lord your God in Horeb, when the Lord said to me, "Gather together the people to Me, and I will make them hear My words, that they may learn to fear Me all the days that they shall live upon the earth, and that they may teach their children." (DEUTERONOMY 4:9-10)

It was to be an historic moment which would shape the future course of world history. A nation of slaves, freed from more than two centuries of bitter bondage in Egypt, now stood at the foot of Mount Sinai. For two days they had purified themselves in preparation for the advent of God. It was now the third day. As the morning began, thunder and lightning erupted, and a thick cloud descended on the mountain. A trumpet blast—the sound of the *shofar*—was heard softly in the distance. The sound grew louder and sharper, increasing in intensity rather than weakening.

The people were taken to the foot of the mountain by their leader, Moses. There they saw the entire Mount Sinai aflame, quaking thunderously. The trumpet continued to sound, louder, louder. It was a sight not to be forgotten, and it was witnessed by a nation of millions.

Shortly, an awesome sound was heard by the nation assembled below. It was the voice of God:

> I am the Lord your God, who brought you out of the Land of Egypt, out of the house of bondage.
>
> You shall have no other gods besides Me.
>
> You shall not make for yourself any graven image, or any likeness of anything that is in heaven above, or that is in the earth beneath, or that is in the water under the earth. You shall not bow down to them, nor serve them; for I the Lord your God am a jealous God, visiting the iniquity of the fathers upon the children to the third, and fourth generation of those who hate Me—but showing mercy unto the thousands of generations of those who love Me and keep My commandments.

The people were consumed with a deep and reverent awe. In panic, they shouted to Moses, who had descended from the mountain before God began to speak, "*You* speak with us, Moses, and we shall listen. But let not God continue, or we shall surely perish." The people were emotionally incapable of absorbing the voice of God.

Moses had been the trusted servant of the Lord; the masses of the Jews, however, were incapable of dealing with the awesome responsibility and fearful challenge of communicating vocally and aurally with God. The obvious concession was made to the nation of Israel. The remaining eight commandments of the Decalogue were related to the Jewish people by Moses. God spoke the first two charges only.[1]

If it was sufficient that Moses convey the remainder of the Ten Commandments and that he ultimately pronounce 611 of the Lord's 613 laws to the Jew,[2] then why did God bother to utter directly the first two of His commandments? The decision triggered panic and terror. For what possible reason could

1. The numbered notes to chapter 9 begin on page 316.

God—Who clearly could have perceived the nature of the response His personal charge would provoke—have wanted to directly issue the first two commandments Himself?

> Then the Lord said to Moses, "So shall you say to the children of Israel: You have seen that I have spoken with you from heaven . . ."[3]

It was God's intention not only to convey His laws but to directly reveal Himself to the nation of Israel, before their very eyes. It was His intention to spread the fear, the awe, that His presence would provoke:

> Only take heed and guard your soul diligently, lest you forget the things which your eyes have seen, and lest they depart from your heart all the days of your life . . . the day that you stood before the Lord your God in Horeb . . .
>
> And you came near and stood under the mountain; and the mountain burned with fire to the heart of heaven, with darkness, clouds, and thick darkness.
>
> Then the Lord spoke to you out of the midst of the fire. You heard the voice of the words but saw no image . . . And He declared to you His covenant, which He commanded you to observe in practice—the Ten Commandments. And He wrote them upon two tablets of stone. . . .[4]

Although the nation of Israel had witnessed the Divine revelation in the third month of their exodus from Egypt, the sight remained with them throughout their forty-year journey to the Promised Land. As they reached the threshold of the Land of Israel, Moses reminded them one last time of the day they had stood before God at Mount Sinai. For Moses, the repetition of the chronology of events which had occurred four decades earlier was not merely an exercise in historical narrative. It was a purposeful charge to the Jewish people:

> "Remember the days of yore; understand the years of generation after generation. Ask your father, and he will tell you; your sages, and they will relate it to you."[5]

The decision by God to reveal Himself was more than a conscious act for a single purpose; it was a lesson intended to serve as an everlasting instruction to the Jewish people. How do the Jewish people know there is a God? Because they saw Him, they heard Him, and they were stricken into so fearsome a sense of terror that they had to plead with Moses to intercede and ask God to allow a human to convey the final eight laws of the Decalogue. How do Jews know that it happened? Because they were there. If the Jews cannot scientifically *prove* that God created the world, they can nevertheless assert without any hesitation that they *know* God exists and gave them the Torah. Because they were there.

The *Bhagavad-Gita*, Hindu theology's holy book which relates the conversation between "Lord Krishna" and Arjuna the warrior, was not revealed before the eyes of the entire Indian nation. One man supposedly spoke to an "incarnated god," and his story is accepted as gospel truth by many nations.

The Unification Church's "Divine Principle" is predicated on the claim that Sun Myung Moon conversed with Moses, Jesus, and Buddha in a remote mountain range in Korea. The claim is advanced by Moon himself. No other Korean ever witnessed the conversations attested to by Moon; yet he has attracted a corps of believers.

The Buddhist concepts of *samsara*/reincarnation are derived from the teachings of Gautama who not only claimed no divine inspiration but claimed that there was no Divinity. On what did he base his asseverations? On his own meditations. And, just as people followed him to the world of asceticism in his earlier years, they proceeded along with his new ideas during his period of maturation.

How is it "known" that Jesus was the incarnation of God? Although his claim was backed by a small group of essentially uneducated men, it was rejected outright by the Jewish nation. Never did God reveal to the nation that Jesus was to be deified.

One of the great tragedies occasioned by the proliferation of alien religious orders and cults is that, aside from attracting thousands of Jewish youths away from their families and luring them to places unknown, they weaken the Jewish people by cheapening the concept of religious devotion. An intelligent person, considering the wide variety of faith-systems existing in the world, loses respect for the very notion that there is a God who created the world and who directs the course of its development. If many mock Hinduism for its multiple-god structure which maintains that there is but one all-powerful god but that every division of Hinduism is free to determine which of the many gods is the "one," then the never-ending chain of emerging "religions" brings degradation to all who live by *any* religion. Many atheists point to the windfall profits reaped by Sun Myung Moon's Unification Church and note that such "racketeering" is the essence of all theology. Karl Marx declared war on religion after seeing how it was used by charlatans to determine people's social and economic standing. Not surprisingly, Judaism has been classified with other "religions" and has, accordingly, been forced to pay a price.

Authentic Judaism begins with the Torah-presentation at Mount Sinai (though, of course, it dates back to the period of Abraham and Sarah in terms of its historical development). It is the Torah presentation which most significantly sets Judaism apart from any other "faith-system" in the history of mankind. Judaism is authentic; it is real. And it is real because a nation of millions witnessed its greatest moment. The Divine Revelation, then, is the key to Judaism. God knew better than anyone how "stiff-necked" and obstinate a nation the Jews could be. He knew that they would not accept any faith for long if they were not given first-hand proof of its authenticity. The Jews had seen the miracles of God: ten individual plagues meted out to the Egyptian people, each transpiring in exactly the fashion prognosticated by Moses. They had seen the miraculous splitting of the waters through which they had to traverse in order to save themselves from the oncoming Egyptian armies. Moreover, they beheld with their very eyes the waters' return to their natural state upon the completion of their trek—even though the soldiers and chariots of Pharaoh were yet in the midst of the sea. Was this not enough to instill

in the Jews a fear of God and an everlasting belief in Him?
No.

God knew what sort of nation the Jews were. They had to see God, to hear God, to virtually "feel" God. Otherwise, they would never stand steadfastly behind the Torah He wanted to give them. Moreover, the Jews were a rebellious people. They had finally been freed from the chains of 210 years of servitude; it would not be easy to bring them under a new burden—the yoke of heaven—without first providing them with an opportunity to glimpse Divinity. The Jews were called to Mount Sinai through Moses. When Moses took them from Egypt, he quite naturally commanded a deep sense of loyalty from the people; he had, after all, liberated them from two centuries of bondage. But, without the Divine Revelation at Sinai, it would have been no surprise if the Jews had rebelled against their very liberator. In fact, almost immediately after the Sinai encounter with the voice of God, the people constructed the Golden Calf, occasioning the wrath of God.[6]

The Golden Calf incident, moreover, was not an isolated example of Jewish rebelliousness against the authority of Moses and the word of God. The Torah relates many separate events which brought tragedy to the Jews because of their regrettably obstinate insistence on challenging the authority of Moses. The Korach rebellion saw a man demand the right to participate in the service which had been specifically designated for the children of Aaron.[7] During Korach's revolt, he questioned the very nature of Moses' right to continue ruling. When the Jews ran out of water during their march through the desert, they spoke bitterly against Moses and wished they had been left in Egypt rather than led to an unknown land.[8] When there was no food, they complained against Moses, not retreating until God assured them they would receive manna from heaven every day for the duration of their journey.[9] After being told to take a certain amount of manna daily—and not to stockpile it—individuals still attempted to gather more than their share.[10] Eventually, once the people learned to live with the system of daily manna collection, they complained to Moses that they did not like God's manna anymore because it lacked the taste and texture of the meat and fish they remembered during their wonderful days of Egyptian bondage.[11]

The Jews rebelled on so many occasions that they were eventually punished by God as an entire nation and as individuals: they were not permitted to enter the Holy Land during their lifetimes; rather, their children were assigned to inherit the land. As for them, their entire generation would die in the desert — every single one of those who had committed the terrible crime of supporting the ten spies who had arrived from the land with a hostile report.[12]

A people like the nation of Israel could never have accepted the false messiahs who so enthralled other peoples. The Jews could never have accepted a *Bhagavad-Gita* on the basis of Arjuna's word. They would have mocked anyone seeking to foist such a "theology" on them. Where was the proof that "Lord Krishna" had spoken to Arjuna? Indeed, where was the proof that there existed a "Lord Krishna"?

The Jews who traveled through the desert from Egypt could never have accepted a Sun Myung Moon, even if they had heard of Buddha and Jesus and knew what they represented to certain cultures. They could have told Moon, "We are not impressed. We deal directly with the Boss."

The Jews would never have accepted Prabhupada or his "Lord Caitanya" or Maharaj Ji or Sri Chinmoy or Maharishi Mahesh Yogi or Buddha. They would have stubbornly refused to be brought under such alien yokes, for they had communicated directly with God Almighty Himself. Such a people would not be easily swayed by mere attestations of Divinity by men. When Mohammed went to the Jews and sought to convince them to accept him as their Divine prophet, they rejected him. He never had a chance. He was up against a people who had stood before the Lord God at Mount Sinai and heard the Divine revelation. Mohammed, unable to win them over, turned his attentions elsewhere, finally establishing Islam for his followers and uttering the most vile of curses against the Jews for having rejected him.

Even Jesus was unable to gain a real following among the Jews. He claimed the right to a Divinity accorded no man. He claimed the authority to abolish certain Torah laws (although, on other occasions, he claimed that he had not come to alter "one tittle" of the law). How could the Jews have followed him or accepted him as a prophet? His own startling lack of Torah erudition, amply reflected in the misquotations from Torah attributed to him by his apostles,[13] immediately alienated the Jews. They had stood before God at Mount Sinai and had heard that He alone was their God. Jesus was to them just one more "Lord Krishna," "Lord Caitanya," Buddha, Maharaj Ji, or Sun Myung Moon.

The Jews *had* to be called to Mount Sinai if they were to fulfill their mission of bearing God's witness to man. Realistically, they could not have proclaimed a truth to humanity if they, themselves, had not been personally briefed by God.

That historic moment at Mount Sinai is what has bound together all the Jewish generations that have passed through the pages of history. Millions of people witnessed the event. They related the story to their children, and their children conveyed the message to their children. To this day, the Jews have transmitted the message of Mount Sinai from parent to child. That most significantly serves as the distinction between Judaism and all other "religions" in human history.

How do we know there is a God? Because we were there. And we saw Him—as we had to. The Jews subsequently challenged Moses' political authority. They murmered against God. They challenged the wisdom of their leaders. They violated commandments, sometimes breaking the very laws they had heard at Mount Sinai. But they never questioned God's existence— because they had seen and heard Him.

How do Americans know that Christopher Columbus existed? How do they know that Simon Boliver existed? How do they know Hammurabi existed?

Documents and artifacts help confirm the existence of previous generations. Word-of-mouth accounts add significant details. As history develops, it is confirmed for future generations by its live witnesses.

Judaism was confirmed by millions of live witnesses who stood at the foot of Mount Sinai. They were stubborn, "stiff-necked" ex-slaves who were not about to voluntarily subjugate themselves without cause. They could later challenge Moses on political or military grounds. They could later criticize the substance of God's manna. But how could they challenge or deny that which they had seen with their very own eyes?

It is no wonder that, although the Torah critically records every single rebellion against Moses and every murmuring against God, there is no case in which anyone denies God's very existence. A man breaks the Sabbath[14] in defiance of the fourth commandment, but at no time is there a denial that Ten Commandments were given at Mount Sinai. If Moses had ever demanded to be worshipped himself as a god, he would have been ridiculed out of the Jewish community; indeed, despite the continued evidences of his special relationship with the Lord, he faced resistance from Korach and other dissident elements. The Jews were not the sort of nation which could be easily maneuvered. Although they had been told by God, through Moses, that the Land of Israel would be theirs and that it was a wonderful place, they almost erupted into revolution when they heard the reports of the ten spies who had asserted that the land was one which could "consume her inhabitants."[15] They had not yet seen the land, so they were not only skeptical but bitterly cynical. But they did not challenge the existence of God. Because they *had* seen *Him*.

This aspect of Jewish history cannot be adequately stressed in a generation which has been beset by an onslaught of Jewish ignorance. To appreciate the magnitude of the Divine revelation's effect, one must return to the Jewish Book of Roots: the Torah. One must read about this strangely defiant nation. If Moses alone had sworn to the existence of God, he would not have been believed—despite the ten plagues, the splitting of the Red Sea, the falling of the manna, and the other signs and wonders which accompanied the Jews throughout their wilderness trek. Had fifty thousand Jews seen God at Sinai while the rest were absent, they would have been jeered. After all, the majority would not have seen Him! If half the nation had been at Sinai, the other half would have defiantly demanded, "Prove it!" If all but one of the Jews had been at Mount Sinai to hear the voice of the Lord, and one solitary soul had been left behind to make coffee, that individual would have remained an iconoclast to the end, and he would have raised his children to question the "so-called Mount Sinai affair."

Such a people were the Jews of the wilderness. And, to this day, such an obdurate people are the Jews. They will own Christmas trees. Their rabbis will assert that Christmas is rooted in the winter solstice, and that Chanuka is too! They will hold carnivals on Tisha b'Av. They will hold New Year's Eve parties on the Sabbath. They will intermarry and even inter-bury. The only way that the Jewish people could ever have maintained the Jewish religion for as long as they have is if they had—each and every single one of them—seen God.

They did.

God gave his Torah in two parts: one written, one oral. The Pentateuch represents the word of God as it was written down by Moses during the forty-year journey through the wilderness of Sinai. It constitutes the Written Law. The Oral Law was transmitted by word-of-mouth and was for centuries forbidden to be committed to paper. When the Talmud was finally compiled during the common era, these laws were written down.

The Written Law—i.e., the Pentateuch—is virtually meaningless to the Jewish people without the concomitant oral tradition. As a source of history, as a source of biography, and as a source of Jewish law, it stands incomplete. Only with the assistance of the Oral Law can the Five Books of Moses come to life. (In many ways, the two legal compendia are comparable to the two keys to a safe-deposit box. Without either one, the box cannot be opened.) Endless examples of the two systems' interdependence can be marshaled forth. For our purposes in this study, one significant case is worth consideration.

The Written Law, on three separate occasions, appears to proclaim the justice of the arbitrary administration of the infamous *lex talionis*—the law of revenge.[16] In all three cases, it speaks of enacting the barbaric "justice" of taking "an eye for an eye" and "a tooth for tooth." Yet, the Oral Law strictly warns the Jewish people against interpreting those passages literally. Rather, it sets forth an elaborate system providing for a monetary compensation to be awarded the injured party.[17] Jewish Law, throughout all the millennia of Jewish history, has been administered accordingly. Judaism, then, has never advocated the taking of "an eye for an eye," Jesus' erroneous assertions notwithstanding.[18]

Why was the Torah not given in a single unity? The *lex talionis* case also serves as a useful illustration of the significance of the Oral Law. Having committed the Pentateuch to writing, Moses and the Jews were open to spiritual larceny. If a people could translate the Hebrew words into their own vernacular, they could arrogate for themselves the Torah which was given specifically to the Jewish people. They could claim themselves as God's "chosen"—without being willing to fulfill the obligations incumbent on such a nation. They could call themselves the "real Jews" and, if powerful enough, torture the nation of Israel and claim that the physical weakness of the Jewish people was proof positive that no longer was God's covenant with Abraham, Isaac, Jacob, and Moses binding.

The course of history shows that that is exactly what the Catholic Church did. All of modern Christianity is predicated on the arrogation of the Torah. The Bible was translated and seized from the Jewish people. While the Church insisted that the Jews were no longer God's "chosen" and that *they* had been picked to supplant the nation of Israel, they lacked one vital instrument which could have helped them conceal their act of theological larceny. They lacked the key to the translated Bible. They lacked the Oral Law—for, at the time of Jesus, the Mishna and Gemara had not yet been redacted—and they purloined only the written word.

Without the Oral Law, they were poor impostors as "Jews." They never understood that it is incumbent on Jewish males to don *tefillin* every weekday morning. They could not comprehend what was entailed in the celebration of such festivals as the Sukkot holiday. Their women were ignorant of the laws of *taharat hamishpacha*. What did they know about the Oral Law? They thought they had the Bible!

To this day, Christian missionaries attempt to convert young Jews by pointing to the Bible's *lex talionis* references, unaware that they are holding but one of the two keys necessary to open the theological safe-deposit box of Judaism. (The tragedy, of course, is that one of the by-products of American Jewry's "race to the melting pot" has been the complete breakdown in Jewish religious erudition among the young, thus leaving them open to such ludicrous presentations.)

The Oral Law was given to protect the Jewish people from ever being victimized by theological larceny. It was the original defense against spiritual copyright infringement. What people live by the laws of Shabbat as defined by the Torah's Oral Code? The Jews rest on the *seventh* day, not the first. And they rest as the Torah instructed them to. Not by watching televised ball games. Not by going shopping or by traveling long distances vehicularly. Not by working at home. But by resting in accordance with the Torah's injunction: *"Lo ta'aseh chol melacha*—You shall do no means of creative work."[19]

In four different places, the Torah commands that God's words be bound "as a sign upon your hand and as frontlets between your eyes."[20] What does this mean? How are the words to be bound? Which words? What are frontlets? Where between the eyes—above the bridge of the nose, or elsewhere?

On Rosh Hashanah, the Jews are to observe "a day of blowing," according to the Bible.[21] What are they to blow? How are they to blow it? And for how many hours should they do so on this "day of blowing"?

God's command, says the Pentateuch, is that Jews should observe the solemn day of Yom Kippur by "afflicting your souls."[22] What does this mean? Is it an invitation to flagellants to run amok? Should Jews pull their hair out on Yom Kippur? Should they do as Iranian ascetics and beat each other with whips and chains? What "afflictions" does God have in mind?

The joyous festival of Sukkot is no less cryptically defined. In Leviticus, the Jews are commanded: "And you shall take for yourselves on the first day the boughs of goodly trees, branches of palm trees, and the boughs of thick trees, and willows of the brook; and you shall rejoice before the Lord your God seven days."[23] Which goodly trees does the commandment imply? Which thick trees? How are these different species to be "taken"? What are we to do with them after taking them?

Such questions abound as the Written Law is contemplated without subsequent Talmudic elucidation.

It is the Oral Law which fulfills the Pentateuch, and it is only in the codes' synthesis that Judaism can be understood — and can be *worth* understanding. In this generation which has been subjected to the most threatening theological challenges in Jewish history — threatening because, despite the inherent weaknesses of the foreign cults, they appear coherent to young Jews ignorant of their own religion, history, and heritage — it would be more than valuable to seek out the lessons of the Oral Law. Only a Jewish education — a meaningful Jewish education — can provide the key to opening the gates of the Talmud which, in turn, will provide the key to opening the door of the Bible.

Nevertheless, there is something encouraging to be seen in the proliferation of religious cults and alien theologies. They symbolize man's yearning for God, a never-ending desire to know his roots, both ancestral and spiritual. Man seeks out God because man intuitively senses His reality.

Jews, chosen of all the nations to merit beholding the Divine revelation at Mount Sinai, need no intuitive drive to recognize the existence of God. They have empirical proof. Yet, there are challenges to Judaism and to all theologies.

There are excellent dating processes which would appear to establish the earth's age in the billions of years, in contradistinction to Judaism which puts the earth's present life at less than six thousand years. Is Judaism in error?

Not at all. There are so many reasons that Judaism is not shaken by these dating processes that to list them all would fill a volume. First of all, Judaism claims the earth is less than six thousand years old. It makes no assertion that the earth's physical nature accurately reflects its age. When the Nazi concentration camps were liberated by the Allies after World War II, thirty-year-old men and women emerged looking like octogenarians. Their physical appearances in no way corresponded to their natural ages. The earth, too, has been subjected to severe physical pressures during its history. One notable example recorded in the Torah is the flood which occurred at the time of Noah. For forty days and forty nights, the face of the earth was subjected to torrents of steaming hot water.[24] At the flood's peak, the waters rose to a height of fifteen cubits, approximately twenty-five feet.[25] For 150 days—nearly half a year—the steaming hot waters "prevailed upon the earth."[26] Surely, one need not have a doctorate in geology to perceive that the flood could have radically altered the face of the earth, its layers, and its appearance. Subject anything to half a year of twenty-five-foot-high steaming waters, and it will age drastically.

Besides, while Judaism maintains that the earth is less than six millennia of age, it does not contend that the earth came into being at a developmental stage comparable to that of one day's existence. The first man, Adam, was created as a full-grown man, not as a one-day-old infant. From the moment of his creation, he had to fend for himself. He could speak and think. He could relate to a woman, Eve. Although he was one day old in reality, he was fully developed physically. The earth on which he was put was also fully grown. The fact that he was offered a wide range of trees' fruits from which to eat indicates that the land, on the sixth day of Creation, had already fully matured. Accordingly, Judaism is not baffled by dating procedures which set the earth's physical appearance in the billions of years. The earth, having been created in a fully matured state, was perhaps "billions of years old" at Day One. During the flood, it aged extraordinarily. It is only natural that the earth shows more years than her fifty-seven centuries would superficially indicate.

Nor is "evolution" a problem for Judaism. It is a scientific theory. Judaism, unlike medieval Christianity, welcomes scientific advances and discoveries—as long as they are "scientific." Regrettably, the good name of "science" is often cast into disrepute by unscrupulous individuals who seek to arrogate for themselves its cloak of objectivity. The Nazis, in the name of "science," sought to ludicrously redefine the very nature of man. "Scientists" worked to "prove" Aryans superior to all other races. Likewise, they "proved" Jews to be the most "inferior" of races. Nazi scientists experimented on living human beings and, in the name of science, performed some of the most egregious horrors and tortures perpetrated since the days of the Spanish Inquisition.

Today, too, "science" is often kidnapped from the laboratory and taken as a hostage to defend an untenable notion. Studies published by a Nobel laureate in the mid-1970s purporting to "prove" Blacks an inferior race appalled all men of good will. Is such an assertion "scientific"? Is it worthy of the protection of the cloak of "scientific objectivity"?

There are men who despised Jews and performed "scientific studies" for Nazi Germany. There are those who despise Blacks and who will perform "scientific studies" to "prove" them to be "sub-human." And there are those, like the Karl Marxes of social science, who despise theology and seek to utilize all the protection afforded by the institution of "scientific inquiry" for their purposes. Just as the racist "sciences" were cast into disrepute, so has much of the "Theory of Evolution."[27] Rather than seek to impose blackouts on such studies, Judaism has analyzed the empirical data produced and has remained as firm as it has always been.

Five thousand years ago, the land of North America was not developed for modern urban needs. Had someone photographed the American continent, he would have found the land barren of the landmarks of twentieth-century industrial society. Five millennia later, he would find large edifices, super highways, and all the other surroundings of "civilization." Were he photographing the earth's surface from outer space, it might not dawn on him that thinking beings called "Americans" had paved the streets, painted the white lines along the highways, and built the structures. He would be entitled to theorize. Perhaps the land, after five millennia, had been baked and hardened by alternating rain storms and periods of intense heat. Perhaps some white lava flow emanating from an unknown source had produced the white lines running across the center of the respective highways.

It would be a theory. Not a very good one. Perhaps it is an acceptable *theory* of science that all existence evolved from algae. It is not necessarily a very good one. Throughout the galaxy, one word stands out firmly: Purpose. The world is imbued with purpose and reason. The rain cycle. The orbits of planets. The construction of the human eye, nose, lung. The animal kingdom. Plant life.[28]

The world is imbued not only with reason but with immense order. Science does not interfere with faith—it strengthens faith. There is no greater testimony to the existence of God than the heavens and earth. It is no small matter that in prophesying to the Jewish people both Moses and Isaiah called forth the "heavens" and "earth" as their eternal witnesses.[29] The heavens and earth testify to God's existence. They are His star witnesses. There is, in every aspect of existence, proof of the existence of God the Creator.

As for the ostensible relationship between the physical structures of apes and humans, why should Judaism be troubled? Of course there exist animals comparable in anatomy to humans! Nothing attests more clearly to the sense of reason and order prevailing in natural society than this phenomenon. Man was told from his earliest time that the creatures of the earth had been given to him for dominion: "And God blessed them, and God said unto them: 'Be fruitful and multiply, and replenish the earth, and subdue it. And have dominion over the fish of the sea and over the fowl of the air and over every living thing that moveth upon the earth.' "[30]

Before the advent of the automobile, animals provided man with transportation. To this day, horses, mules, camels, and elephants are among the animals which haul men and inanimate objects from one place to another. Animals provide man with clothing (e.g., wool products) and with food; even the vegetarian who allows himself a glass of milk or an egg derives culinary pleasures from animals. Transportation, clothing, and food are only three areas of service to man provided by animals.

For some, animals provide companionship. For some, they provide a sense of security and effective protection. For some, they almost provide the sense of sight. The possibilities afforded man in maintaining dominion over the animal kingdom are endless and ever "evolving."

One way in which animals have been put to effective use for the benefit of man in the modern period has been through humane scientific observation and experimentation. New diseases require new forms of treatment and new cures. On what (or on whom) shall scientists experiment? Nazis experimented on Jews. Their choice was eminently practical. Having already determined that Jews were to be exterminated, they decided to use—and abuse—Jewish bodies, partly for scientific purposes, partly for sadistic pleasures. Regrettably, there are "civilized" scientists who today conduct experiments on animals which transcend the legitimate needs of man and which clearly constitute immoral torture of animal life, a grave violation of Jewish law. But there are humane forms of experimentation and scientific observation as well. Naturally, the best subjects on which to conduct such research are animals whose anatomies closely resemble that of man. The closer the correspondence between the respective neurological, circulatory, respiratory, digestive, and excretory systems, the more effective the research can be. It is eminently reasonable that God, having given man the intellectual capacity to devise medical cures for those diseases afflicting him, would have created animals anatomically similar to humans. The existence of the ape and monkey—animals so similar to human beings in certain physical senses—is powerful proof that the world was called into being by a conscious, purposeful, and omnipotent Creator.

A cynic might retort, "But, surely, God should have fore-seen the theological challenges which would be posed by such creatures. Why did He not avoid creating them? He would have spared man much confusion." Such a strain of argumentation closely parallels the exchange between the citizens of Rome and the Tannaitic rabbis in this famous *mishna*:

> The rabbinic elders in Rome were asked, "If your God has no desire for idolatry, why does He not abolish its various forms?"
>
> They replied, "If the objects of deification were unnecessary to the world, He would surely abolish them. But people worship the sun, moon, stars, and planets. Should He destroy His universe on account of fools?"
>
> The Romans retorted, "If so, He should destroy what is unnecessary for the world, and He should leave in existence those objects which are of necessity."
>
> The rabbis replied, "If He did that, it would merely strengthen the resolve of those worshipping the spared objects of deification because they would then say, 'It is certain that we worship deities for, behold, they have not been destroyed as were the false gods.' "[31]

It is reasonable that God created animals similar in physical function to man, and it would have been absurd for Him to have withheld them from us because of the propensity for some men to seek out "refutations" of the Torah's account of Creation. If there were no apes, "scientists" seeking to contradict the Torah would have to invent different theories — and they would. (As it is, the "science" world has been deeply shamed on more than one occasion as great "missing-link finds" have been exposed as hoaxes consciously and elaborately perpetrated by unscrupulous individuals.) This phenomenon can be reduced to the simple terms of the brief dialogue between Antoninus and Rabbi Judah the Prince:

> Antoninus said to Rabbi [Judah the Prince], "Why does the sun rise in the east and set in the west?"

He replied, "Were it reversed, you would ask the same question."[32]

There will always be men — whether they be called "scientists," "theologians," or "philosophers" — who will inquire about the nature of the universe. That inquiry can take one of two forms: healthy objectivity or cynical subjectivity. Judaism has always welcomed the former with open arms; few were as intensely inquisitive as were the rabbis of the Talmud. The world is filled with mysteries, and every new bona fide discovery can only strengthen the faith of the Jewish people. Rabbi Avigdor Miller's engaging work on questions of evolution and Jewish faith, *Rejoice O Youth*, is a masterful example of how scientific discoveries and analyses can potently serve to bolster — rather than retard — the intensity of Jewish faith.[33]

As for the cynically subjective "scholars," they too can strengthen Judaism. For, as their doctrines collapse under the weight of empirical data, Judaism emerges stronger, having weathered their "challenges." The medieval Church, because of its inherent insecurity, dreaded what Galileo or Copernicus might discover. The Jewish people — having stood before the Lord God at the foot of Mount Sinai, in the millions[34] — do not fear what objective inquiry will reveal. The discovery that the earth moves around the sun was a valuable contribution to our understanding of the way in which the universe functions. We look forward to future discoveries of such a caliber. As for "challenges" to the Torah, we will bear them, too. And, as always, we shall survive them.

It is unfortunate that Judaism has been arbitrarily classified with all the "religions" of the earth. Their weaknesses have redounded to the detriment of Judaism.

The Torah alone was Divinely revealed to an entire nation. The Torah has withstood the tests of time, having survived the efforts of "cynical science" and having been substantially buttressed by objective, empirically based science. Judaism never threatened those of other faiths with hell-fire and eternal damnation. Of all the world's "great religions," Judaism stands alone. Rabbi Avigdor Miller has written:

> Anyone who calls the Torah a "religion" is thereby falling into the fatal error of putting it into a category. The Torah is unique; *it has no analogy among the religions*. Those who commit this error do enormous injury to the reputation of the Torah, for the sins and faults of the religions are thereby imputed to the Torah.
>
> *All religions are the result of development.* The Torah did not evolve: in Abraham's lifetime the entire philosophy of Judaism appeared, and at Sinai the entire Torah was given at once . . . The Torah is unique in its teachings as the word of God and not of men. . . .
>
> The unacceptable claims and practices of the spurious religions damage the reputation of the Torah. Their priests earned an unpleasant name for the true *Kohanim*; their temples imparted an aura of hypocrisy to our places of worship; their numberless miracles put our true miracles into disfavor. Their so-called saints gave an unsavory taste to the true saints . . . All the inherent faults of the religions have no relation to the Torah. The Torah is not a religion; it is unique . . .[35]

The classification of Judaism as but another "religion" has served as the basis for many of the phenomena encountered during the "race to the melting pot." Since Christianity evolved from the Written Law without its Oral counterpart, "wings" of Judaism have emerged which seek to parallel America's majority "religion." Accordingly, assimilated temples have adapted their houses of worship to conform to the American church. "Rabbis" in flowing black robes, accompanied by organs, lead congregants in English-language responsive readings — just as in neighboring churches. Young Jews are organized into Hebrew equivalents of the Mormon Tabernacle Choir. "Ecumenical" conferences are organized to "share" Easter and Passover, Christmas and Chanuka, and other such occasions. The sanctity of the synagogue is compromised as the *mechitza* partitioning the sexes is taken down, and the seating is consciously arranged to resemble that of the local church. "Rabbis" shy away from sounding "too Jewish" during their sermons, so they revert to book reviews and vacuous ethical-humanitarian "musings." Significantly revealing is the trend by such Jewish clergymen as Eugene Sack of Brooklyn's Temple Beth Elokim to title their bulletin messages "pastoral letters" rather than "rabbinical" ones.

Raised in such an environment of compromise and confusion, young Jews naturally develop contempt for the "Jewish religion." They see in it a caricature of twentieth-century liberal Protestantism, and they know it is spiritually empty. They attend "Talmud Torah" schools which teach Israeli dancing, "ethical-humanist" short stories, Hebrew art, Jewish folk music—everything but Talmud and Torah. They are raised in non-observant homes which are indistinguishable from neighboring Christian ones. They see in the family rabbis all the charisma of plastic pulpiteers. It is not surprising that, before they ever open an authentic Jewish text like the Talmud, they have already made their "free choice": "Gee, I'll tell you, I'm just not into organized religion."

Neither is Judaism.

The time has come for young Jews to reconsider what they are giving up. The time has come for Jewish youths to transcend the spiritual illiteracy to which they were subjected and to learn what Judaism *really* is. Judaism is not another "organized religion" with various "wings." There is but one Judaism, and it is the way of life which was presented to an entire nation at Mount Sinai. Those "wings" which have opted for the world of "pastoral letters," ham sandwiches, and ostentatiously opulent bar mitzvas are not Judaism; they have flown away, as all wings inevitably do.

In an age of enlightenment, the most prized ethic of man is that which proclaims the virtues of pursuing knowledge objectively. The time has come for young Jews to pursue Jewish knowledge from an objective, unprejudiced perspective. Why has Judaism been rejected? Because it was presented as a foolish mythology during the youth's childhood? Fine. What intelligent Jewish youth would refuse to learn about the body's reproductive system in order to show his anger over his parents' efforts to convince him during his childhood that "babies come from storks"?

Babies do not come from storks, and Chanuka does not come from the winter solstice. If Judaism was presented in an immature manner during a youth's earlier years, he has an obligation to himself and to four thousand years of stubbornly proud ancestors to boldly seek out his roots. No sensitive, enlightened youth should reject Judaism because of the way assimilated regions of American Jewry have corrupted it.

It is not intellectually honest to abandon the Jewish faith because it was presented foolishly during childhood years. It is an insult to every cherished principle of enlightened inquiry to dissociate oneself from Judaism because "other religions" are chaotic, devoid of reason, and frequently counter-productive in terms of the bloodshed they occasion. It was Christianity which perpetrated the crusades, inquisitions, and blood libels "in the name of God." It was not Judaism. What a tragedy it would be if, in addition to the millions who died martyrs' deaths at the hands of Christian zealots, future thousands of Jewish youths will forsake their heritage because those bloody massacres have tarnished the reputation of "religion"!

Some parents foolishly "explained" to their children that God was to be called on as a "crutch" at a time of need. That is not authentic Jewish thought. It is ludicrous. If Jews simply wanted a "crutch," they could have turned to any of the myriad false gods proliferating on the American scene. There is only one reason that Jews believe in God. Not because He is their "crutch at a time of need." But because millions of Jews saw Him and quaked at the sound of His voice as they stood at the foot of Mount Sinai. Does God, nonetheless, serve as a crutch? Of course He does. Knowing that God is watching over the world is reassuring. But the sense of security provided by His omnipresence does not mean He does not exist. It is comforting to go to sleep at night knowing that the armed forces of the United States are trained and ready to defend our country from attack; that doesn't mean that they do not really exist. It is comforting for Israelis to see the *Tzahal*, their defense forces, standing guard over the Holy Land; that does not mean they don't exist.

If parents serve as a psychological "crutch" for children, does that mean that they are fabrications of the human mind? Of course not. Clearly, many nations—never having had the opportunity to act as eyewitnesses to the existence of God—felt compelled to establish mythologies to assuage their psychological anxieties. The Greek and Roman "faith systems," as well as many of those "theologies" discussed in this study, are classic examples of this reaction to human frailty. There is no Zeus or Jupiter to turn to. Nor will salvation emanate from Moon, Prabhupada, Maharaj Ji, or any of the other "saviors" of the nations.

Judaism, once again, cannot be classified arbitrarily with every other "religion" on the face of the earth. Most politicians appear to be dishonest; does that mean that, in the last four millennia, there has not been one honest politician? The Jewish faith is not one more teleological system. Let no Jewish child be satisfied with an upbringing which sees God described as a "crutch" or as a little old man with a long white beard whose tears cause rain to fall and whose sneezes cause hurricanes.

There is only one authentic version of what Judaism is: the Torah. It is the antithesis of the ethic of inquiry to discard Judaism without first learning the Oral and Written Laws of the Jewish faith. The statement "I don't believe in Judaism" is nothing short of irrational when based on ignorance. What does the average Jewish youth know about Judaism? Abraham, Isaac, and Jacob might just as well be "the three jolly fishermen" about whom children sing in kindergarten. Moses is the subject of a revered nineteenth-century "spiritual." Joshua "fit the battle of Jericho, and the walls came a-tumblin' down." Davey and Goliath are the boy and dog who star in a nationally syndicated American cartoon program. Moses is the one who looked like Charlton Heston, and Samson looked like Steve Reeves.

What do young Jews really know about Judaism? Do they know that thousands of years before the birth of Leon Uris there existed a book named Exodus which was not tailor-made for Paul Newman? What do they really know about the Bible? A popular song has them singing, "Jeremiah was a bullfrog." Do they know that there was another Jeremiah who prophesied to the nation of Israel? Or that there was a prophet in the Bible named Amos—this one not accompanied by Andy?

How can an intelligent Jewish youth call himself an agnostic or atheist without first having studied his roots and heritage? Although some perceive the denial of God's existence as being a statement of "sophistication," such self-aggrandizement is not necessarily warranted. One who rejects Judaism because of a faulty upbringing is acting out of pure emotion. One who looks bitterly upon a hypocritical society, which mouths platitudes to "God" but doesn't mean a word of it, is acting highly irrationally if he rejects his heritage on the grounds that "it is all hypocrisy." The society is hypocritical. Their assimilated "religious values" are hypocritical. But in no way do their actions negate the authenticity of the Jewish faith—the *genuine* Jewish faith.

A recent president of the United States, whose questionable acts led to his premature departure from the White House, made it his regular business to have Billy Graham, the nationally known Christian evangelist, visit him. The president frequently spoke about his close relationship with Graham and often liked to be photographed alongside the preacher. When the scandal which was to drive him from Washington erupted, the President attempted to maintain his relationship with Graham. Backed by a symbol of "religious commitment," he was able to more effectively portray himself as an "honest man." Many sensitive young Jews—among other sensitive young Americans—were deeply offended by this abuse of "religion." To compound the problem, the Rev. Sun Myung Moon began advertising in major American newspapers that the president was above the law of the land, having been "chosen" by God. It is not difficult to see why the reputation of

Judaism—as one of the "religions"—was tarnished along with those of all theologies. "What a fraud!" people felt. "If God decided that the president is above the law, then I want no part of 'organized religion.' "

How foolish it would be to abandon four millennia of Judaism because of such a scandal! The president may well have been a hypocrite. But what objectively dispassionate individual would reject the Torah revealed to the Jewish people at Sinai because of the affair? Is that a rational reason to lose faith in God? Is it any more sensible to turn away from the Jewish heritage because of the hypocrites in the Jewish community? Is it sensible to divest oneself of the cultural legacy passed on from Jewish generation to Jewish generation for nearly forty centuries simply because one desires to rebel against the empty values of spiritually bankrupt parents? Would it not be eminently wiser to reject the materialism and the "rat race"— and to return to the roots of Jewish tradition and Jewish life?

When doctors are indicted on charges of embezzling the government by manipulating medicare bills, do enlightened Jewish youths declare that they will stop seeking medical aid? Do they announce that they will leave medical school—or that they will stop taking pre-med courses? On the contrary. They talk about the need to "clean out the medical profession" and to "restore it to the ideals embodied in the Hippocratic oath." They are not alienated by the hypocrites; rather, they are drawn closer to Hippocrates. In a similar vein, many political observers noted the irony that the overwhelming number of individuals involved in the Watergate scandal were lawyers by profession. Did that drive intelligent Jewish students out of the law schools of America? It did not. Rather, it motivated idealistic Jewish law students to assert that they would seek to bring respect to the profession by volunteering their services for the needy and by joining public-service legal-aid societies.

In every field, in every country, in every way, there will be individuals who are hypocritical. It is important to recognize that they exist, and it is a moral imperative to expose them. The Talmud, sharply aware of the danger Jewish hypocrites pose to the Torah and the sanctity of the Jewish people, commands: "It is an obligation to expose religious hypocrites to prevent the desecration of the Name of God."[36]

It is time to expose the hypocrites. Those who "rabbify" in suburbia—and get paid a premium price for their efforts—although they do not believe in Chanuka, in Purim, or in anything besides getting paid. The temples which hold New Year's Eve parties while desecrating the Sabbath. Those who raise money for "Jewish" philanthropy by taking clients to bacon breakfasts, lobster lunches, and swordfish suppers. Those who send their children to Hebrew school for a year to memorize two typewritten pages but "absolutely not to become religious." Those who use their high-priced pulpits to conduct intermarriages and interburials. Those who sponsor Tisha b'Av carnivals and those who simply advertise glatt-kosher meat sales commemorating the occasion.

It is time to call for an end to the hypocrisy and for a beginning to Jewish authenticity. As thousands of Jewishly illiterate youths leave their people and heritage for bizarre cults and alien theologies—or just intermarry or assimilate into spiritual oblivion—it is time to plead for a termination of the "race to the melting pot" and for a return to the Torah which God gave the Jewish people.

It is time for parents to return. It is time for children to return. And it is time for "rabbis" to return.

Notes

1) Cf. Exodus 19, 20. See also Tractate *Makkot* 23b-24a.
2) Tractate *Makkot, ibid.*
3) Exodus 20:19.
4) Deuteronomy 4:9-13.
5) *Ibid.* 32:7.
6) Exodus 32.
7) Numbers 16. It is noted by Rashi, *ad loc.*, that the very basis of

the rebellion was rooted in Korach's contention that *all* of Israel had been present at Mount Sinai and, therefore, should have equal access to positions of leadership. Thus, even the rebellion of Korach was rooted in acceptance of Divine Revelation.

8) See Exodus 15:22-24, 17:1-4; Numbers 20:1-5.

9) Exodus 16:1-18.

10) *Ibid.*, verses 19-20, 26-29.

11) Numbers 11:4-6.

12) *Ibid.* 13-14:39.

13) For a fuller discussion, see chapter one.

14) Numbers 15:32-36.

15) *Ibid.* 13:32.

16) Exodus 21:24; Leviticus 24:20; Deuteronomy 19:21.

17) Tractate *Baba Kamma* 83b f.

18) See chapter one. Cf. *Mishneh Torah, Hilchot Chovel u'Mazik* 1:1-6.

19) Exodus 20:10. The spirit of the word "*melacha*," though often defined as meaning "work," is not accurately captured by that translation. *Melacha* is to be understood more as a form of action which interrupts *spiritual* relaxation than as an act which disturbs *physical* "rest." The Hebrew word for physical work is "*avoda.*"

20) Exodus 13:9, 16; Deuteronomy 6:8, 11:18.

21) Leviticus 23:24; Numbers 29:1.

22) Leviticus 23:27; Numbers 29:7.

23) Leviticus 23:40.

24) Tractate *Sanhedrin* 108b; Tractate *Rosh Hashana* 12a.

25) Genesis 7:20.

26) *Ibid.*, verse 24.

27) See, e.g., Dr. Duane T. Gish, *Evolution: The Fossils Say No* (Public School Edition) (San Diego: Creation-Life Publishers, 1978).

28) For an in-depth and engaging analysis of this phenomenon, see Rabbi Avigdor Miller, *Rejoice, O Youth* (N.Y.: Balshon Printing, 1962). Rabbi Miller presents a genuinely Jewish "Ode to Life," as he considers the nature of human life, animal life, plant life, physical phenomena, and every other mode of existence. His consideration is bolstered by his rich knowledge of the natural sciences. His is a book which clearly illustrates the principle that "science does not interfere with faith—it strengthens it."

29) Deuteronomy 30:19; 32:1; Isaiah 1:2. Cf. Psalms 19:2.

30) Genesis 1:28.

31) Tractate *Avoda Zara* 54b.

32) Tractate *Sanhedrin* 91b.

33) See also Rabbi Miller's *Sing You Righteous* (N.Y.: Balshon Printing, 1973).

34) Throughout this chapter, reference has been made to the fact that "millions" of Jews stood before God at Mt. Sinai. The Torah recounts that a census taken in the second year of the exodus from Egypt revealed that there were 603,550 Jewish men eligible for the "draft" (i.e., men of ages 20 and over — but not including those in the Levite tribe). Such a census was taken for military defense reasons. (See Numbers 1:46. Cf. Exodus 12:37; 38:26.)

It is abundantly reasonable to assume that there were at least as many women of that age range as there were men. (Note, moreover, that the Pharaoh had ordered that male children born to Jewish parents in Egypt be drowned, while female children were to be spared.) Together with their children, an estimate putting the Jewish community of the wilderness at three million would be conservative.

35) Rabbi Avigdor Miller, *Sing You Righteous* (N.Y.: Balshon Printing, 1973), pp. 22-24.

36) Tractate *Yoma* 86b.

CHAPTER 10

Judaism:
A discipline of liberation

*And you shall keep all the command-
ments which I command you this day, so
that you may be strong . . .*
(DEUTERONOMY 11:8)

Any return to Jewish authenticity must begin with a renewed
commitment to the *modus vivendi* outlined in the Oral and
Written Laws of the Torah. Although the Torah, from an
historical point of view, may be seen as a Jewish Book of Roots,
it is far more. It is an explicit code setting forth the values of the
Jewish people.

The obligations of the Jewish people may be arbitrarily
classified in any of a number of ways. Historically, they have
frequently been spoken of in terms of those commandments
which regulate man's relationship to God (*mitzvot bein adam
la-Makom*) and those which govern his relationship to his
fellow man (*mitzvot bein adam la-chavero*). Another popular
distinction has often been drawn between the 248 positive
commandments which tell us what God expects us to do and
the 365 negative precepts which inform us of those things God

expects us *not* to do. Currently, the most popular form of arbitrary classification is that which individuates between "ritual" laws and "moral-ethical" laws.

This last division is perilous because it presumes to assert that such ritualistic aspects of Judaism as *kashrut, Shabbat*, and *taharat hamishpacha* are devoid of deep moral-ethical significance. Conversely, such a classification would asseverate that justice is not as much a Jewish "ritual" as is the lighting of Sabbath candles or the wearing of *tzitzit*. Neither of these two assertions has any sound basis in Jewish tradition; rather, they are outgrowths of Pauline Christianity, which sought to abrogate the essence of Torah law while retaining the "spirit of the law." We have seen how Paul advocated "faith" shorn of deeds. Judaism has always differed sharply from the Pauline construct—ever since the day when the nation of Israel told Moses the lawgiver, "We shall do, and we shall obey."[1]

The two-thousand-year history of Christianity has served as an ominous warning to mankind that a system which extols "faith" alone—without regular, practical accountability through deeds—will not significantly uplift man. On the contrary, more blood has been spilled in the last two millennia by the Christian world than would have been conceivable in the years before Jesus lived.[2] Nevertheless, despite the proud record charted by Judaism during the same period, modern American Jews, seeking to assimilate into the mainstream of American life, have molded their "religion" to carefully conform to that of the country's majority culture.

In such an assimilated milieu, it is not surprising to find the proliferation of "Jewish religious interpretations" which conflict sharply with the genuine Jewish values expressed so clearly and boldly by the Torah. The popular distinction between "ritual" laws and "moral-ethical" laws, then, is an understandable (though regrettable) outgrowth of the "race to the melting pot." It serves the purposes of those seeking to shed their distinctly Jewish socio-theological garb in the midst of a

1. The numbered notes to chapter 10 begin on page 359.

Christian nation. And it creates an atmosphere of confusion among a small segment of Torah-observant Jews, who react to this trend by over-emphasizing the "ritual" laws at the expense of the "moral-ethical" ones, believing that such a response is necessary to maintain the survival of Jewish authenticity. As the assimilated regions of American Jewry downplay the significance of *kashrut, Shabbat,* and *taharat hamishpacha*— while espousing the value of living the "moral-ethical Jewish life"—their counterparts in the "Orthodox" areas assume upon themselves a greater obligation to stress those very laws in order to offset the imbalance.

Alas, in their alacrity to preserve "Torah-true Judaism," individuals sometimes lose sight of the balance they are trying to strike. Although the overwhelming majority of those Jews advocating continued authenticity in Jewish practice succeed in living their lives on a moral-ethical level beyond reproach, there emerge brutal exceptions. In addition to butchers who advertise kosher-meat "Tisha b'Av sales" and misguided individuals who approbate eating kosher food at institutions like Roosevelt Raceway, there are the egregious deviants from Torah law who scheme to cheat the government out of tax dollars, welfare dollars, medicare/medicaid dollars, and other such dollars. They will support their "House of God" with "Las Vegas Nites." They will conduct their law practices, accounting firms, and medical clinics as though the Torah were not applicable between the hours of 9 to 5 on all days except for weekends and legal holidays.

Happily, they are the exceptions. In practical numerical terms, they are not significant. Nevertheless, in a consideration of the breakdown in genuinely Jewish values across the United States, this group must be scrutinized and condemned with the same vociferation as that applied to the suburban assimilationists who have betrayed the letter, spirit, and tone of Jewish law by suggesting that it can be divested of its "ritualistic aspects" without being degraded.[3] The 613 laws of Judaism were given in their *totality* to Moses during his forty-day period of communion with God atop Mount Sinai.

The laws were given in their totality because they constitute a carefully devised life system. Those who comport themselves as though the performance of "ritual" alone makes one a "good Jew" are dangerous religious hypocrites whose actions betray the Torah and desecrate the Name of God. Those who would amputate "ritual" from Judaism, similarly, would deal a death-blow to the genuine value structure of the Jewish people. Of both groups did the Talmud write: "It is an obligation to expose religious hypocrites to prevent the desecration of the Name of God."[4] A "religious man" who disregards the voluminous mass of "moral-ethical" Jewish laws is a religious hypocrite. The one who preaches morality and ethics from the temple pulpit—and who concomitantly declares that Jewish "ritual" is "no longer binding"—falls into the same class. The two men conduct themselves so differently that they paradoxically fall within the same category of Judaism.

Moreover, they both perpetrate a grave disservice to the Jewish faith. The "rituals" are highly principled, morally impeccable, ethically based laws. *Kashrut* is not simply an arcane prophylactic against trichinosis. It is a system which uplifts the soul of man from that of a beast, which eats whatever it is fed or whatever it sees, to that of a holy being. Is that immoral—or devoid of moral-ethical content? *Taharat hamishpacha* is not simply an exercise in personal hygiene. It is a Divinely prescribed discipline which sanctifies a male-female relationship. Without it, Jews might just as well be a nation of individuals worthy of depiction in a Philip Roth or Silvia Tennenbaum novel; with it, a Jewish couple is elevated to the spiritual heights of Abraham and Sarah. Such "rituals" are deeply based in morality and ethics. To cast them aside as "religious rituals"—comparable to chanting "Hare Krishna" all day—is Jewishly unconscionable.

Judaism is not just a "religious faith system." It is an all-encompassing, twenty-four-hour-a-day, seven-day-a-week, never-ending way of life. Does that make it more difficult than what it has become in assimilated suburbia? Yes. Judaism is terribly difficult; it is not a hobby. God did not choose the

Jewish people to be His Wednesday-evening bowling partners. He chose the Jews to be His witnesses to humanity, to be a "kingdom of priests."[5] He did not give the Jews the Torah as though it were a lottery ticket whose holder wins the grand prize if he guesses correctly the seventy-five most important commandments. He gave it with the express intent that every law be considered eternally binding, subject to temporary suspension only in the event of externally imposed exigencies. While the destruction of the Holy Temple by the Romans consigned the commandments regarding sacrificial offerings to a status of suspension, the cure of trichinosis did not empower anyone to declare the termination of the laws of *kashrut*.

It is crucial that we return to Jewish values! The "Jews for Jesus" missionaries have used the inconsistency in assimilated Jewish practice to their benefit. A "Moishe Rosen" goes to a young Jew who has been raised in an assimilated milieu where the *rabbi* eats ham, transgresses the Sabbath, and violates all the Torah "rituals." Rosen contrasts the "rabbi" and his congregation with the "Jews for Jesus." To attract confused Jewish youths, the Rosen group will put on the facade of eating kosher food, wearing yarmulkes, observing the Saturday Sabbath, and conforming to other Torah laws. If the Rosen Christian-missionary cult is not Jewish, where does that leave the temple in suburbia? Christian missionaries believe in God, in prayer, in messianic redemption, and in ultimate salvation. In varying ways, the other cults—the Moonies, the Buddhists, the Hindus, and the Hare Krishnas—do, too. If they are not Jewish, where does that leave the assimilated Jewish community and its "ethical-humanist rabbi"?

The *mitzvot* were given by God as a unity. They succeed in developing a holy nation only when they are observed as a unity. Without the Torah, the very notion of "morality" or "ethical conduct" is meaningless. What is morality? Is it immoral to eat people? In parts of Africa, cannibals consume human beings and see nothing wrong with their actions. Why should it be wrong? They have allegiances and "ethics" and "morals." Yet, they see nothing wrong with eating people.

During the Crusades, Christian hordes massacred Jewish communities for "the glory of Christ." Was that "ethical"? At the time, the popes said it was the "Christian" thing to do. To this day, the Vatican reveres men like Saint John Chrysostom.[6]

What are "ethics"? What is "morality"? Plato, the Greek philosopher, devised a system which would have destroyed the concept of the family unit.[7] The highly rational Germans invented crematoria and gas chambers. A systematic consideration of Marxist societies reveals wholesale bloodshed and murder being sanctioned as a means to effectuate a "workers' paradise." In the summer of 1977, an electrical failure in New York City generated widespread looting and vandalism; the participants in the day-long anarchy maintained, in interview after interview, that their actions were justified.

Ultimately, morality and ethics are highly subjective terms. Different societies, faced with different needs, evolve their own appropriate value structures. The Torah alone provides a totally objective "moral-ethical" system. To the extent that Western society has been influenced by the Torah's value structure — via the Christian scriptures, which "borrowed" from Judaism everything from the "golden rule" to the ban against eating the limb of a live animal — an excellent basis for morality and ethics has been established. The very values of "ethical culture" societies emanate from the laws given by God to Moses.[8] How ironic to find individuals practicing atheistic "ethical humanism"! Although rejecting God's laws and even denying His existence, they nevertheless praise and live by His ethics. Without God serving as an objectively removed arbiter who stands above mankind, how do we arrive at the "ethics" of our society? Is killing or outright murder unethical? The ancient Greeks and Romans, whose gods reflected their own values, worshipped deities who committed the most heinous of crimes — often as playful pranks. Greek society produced lofty works of literature, but no less cultured a man than Sophocles wrote of a society which could produce an Oedipus — whose life began with his noble father leaving him to die.

The Greeks and Romans were the most sophisticated men of

their eras. The Church was the most enlightened institution of its time. The Germans of the 1930s extolled science and the pursuit of reason. Yet, each of their societies created barbaric horrors. Their very failures illustrated that, without God, man is incapable of constructing a truly moral-ethical paradigm. Were it not for the Torah, the "ethical culture societies" would be non-existent. It is no surprise that the movement's founder had been trained as a Jewish clergyman. Man is too subjectively steeped in his society to conceive an all-encompassing system of what is "just"; Plato's *Republic*, which sought to define that very notion, serves as a potent illustration. Only God could devise a meaningful moral-ethical paradigm.

The Torah is anchored in the principle of justice: "Justice, justice shall you pursue."[9] Those who have, en route to the melting pot, attempted to portray the laws given at Sinai as archaic or as obsolete would do well to consider whence emanated their *own* concepts of morality. Consider the nineteenth chapter of the book of Leviticus, which commands the Jewish people to respect their parents; to provide for the needy; not to steal, deal falsely, or lie; not to curse the deaf or put a stumbling-block before the blind; to judge in unprejudiced righteousness; not to go from person to person as a talebearer; not to stand idly by the "blood of your neighbor"; not to hate one's brother (i.e., fellowman); not to seek vengeance or bear a grudge; to love one's neighbor as oneself; to treat a stranger justly; and to conduct one's business affairs piously.

The laws of Leviticus 19 alone would put the behavior code of "ethical humanism" to shame. What a grand and magnificent chapter it is! As the word of God, it challenges the Jewish people to rise above the basest human instincts—indeed, to rise above the values of the surrounding "civilized" society—and to sanctify themselves for their holy mission. Anyone can talk about the importance of being ethical and moral; Jews, however, are commanded to act. Every religion can devise—or borrow from Torah—the "golden rule." Jews alone are obligated not to mouth platitudes but to act tangibly and consistently in accordance with its demands.

"Do not stand idly by the blood of your neighbor." Such a law transcends morality and ethics. It obligates the Jew to personally sacrifice his own comfort for the sake of his endangered brother. What an awesome obligation! Anyone can write letters or sign petitions for the victims of persecution abroad. Anyone can donate money to "benevolent causes." The Jew is obligated to personally intervene on behalf of the oppressed and persecuted, even at the expense of his own wants. In the words of the Talmud:

> When the community is in trouble, let not a man say, "I will go to my house, and I will eat and drink, and all will be well with me . . ."
>
> Rather, a man should share in the distress of the community, for we find that Moses our teacher shared in the distress of the community, as it is said: "But Moses' hands were heavy, and they took a stone and put it under him, and he sat on it" (Exodus 17:12).
>
> Did not Moses have a bolster or a cushion to sit on? Hence, this is what Moses sought to convey: "As the people of Israel are in distress, so shall I share with them. He who shares in the distress of the community will merit to behold its consolation."[10]

It is not accidental that the Jewish people have traditionally taken leading positions in every human-rights cause in history. The moral-ethical basis of the Torah is so deeply rooted in the hearts of the Jewish people that even the most assimilated and alienated of Jews carries this ideal with him. And, for those Jews who remain loyal to their heritage, the bounds of humane involvement truly know no limit.

What better example of this commitment to the "golden rule" is there than the world Jewish community's united efforts to free Soviet Jewry from indescribable horrors? In New York City alone, public demonstrations have attracted hundreds of thousands of Jews to rally behind the banner demanding: Let My People Go! A memorable testimonial to the Jewish involvement on behalf of their brothers in the Soviet Union appeared in a newpaper column written by William F. Buckley. Commenting on the unrelenting efforts of American Jewry to free their co-religionists in the USSR—and contrasting that with the virtual silence in the American Christian community over the oppression of Soviet Christians—Buckley expressed his hope that the Jews of America would one day see their goal realized and that Soviet Jewry would be permitted freedom. But then he added a final thought. It would be nice, he concluded, if the Soviets would keep one Jew behind. If the Christian world would not be there to protest, at least the Jews would have a motivation to continue focusing the spotlight of world opinion on the oppressive regime in the USSR.

There is nothing so deeply rooted in Judaism as the commandment to live ethically and morally. No one expressed this thought better than the Talmudic sage, Hillel. On one occasion, a non-Jew approached him and said, "Convert me to Judaism in such a way that you will teach me the entire Torah while I stand on one foot." Hillel calmly responded, "What is hateful to you, do not do to your neighbor. That is the entire Torah—the rest is but its commentary. Go and learn it."[11]

How does one begin to convey the overwhelming spirit of humanity embedded in the Torah's words? One might begin with the acts of Abraham who interceded with God on behalf of the people of Sodom and Gomorrah.[12] What Abraham began, the Jewish people have never ended. While others have amused themselves over the centuries with gladiator matches, public burnings, bullfights, duels to the death, sadistic animal hunts, and such "civilized" forms of entertainment as boxing contests, the Jews have stood out as a "light unto the nations."[13]Among Jews who have lived their lives by the Torah, such practices as drinking, gambling, betting on horses, and wife-beating have been unknown. The common notion that "Jewish men make better husbands" did not emerge from a vacuum. That stereotype is the outcome of millennia of Jewish moral-ethical history.

How does one begin to catalogue Judaism's overwhelming commitment to ethical and moral behavior? By quoting from the Talmud or from the Bible? Where does one begin? God commanded the Jews to give of themselves and their possessions to assist the poor. The Hebrew word for charity is *tzedaka*, etymologically rooted in the Hebrew word for "justice." And that is what "charity" is to the Jewish people: justice. A Jew who gives to the needy in accordance with the dictates of the Torah does not hold a press conference before handing over his check. He does not accept any public recognition for his contribution, and he shuns the notion of being awarded a plaque for his donation. A Jew does not give "charity." A Jew enacts justice. He gives not because he is nice but rather because God commanded him to give. All the world belongs to God;[14] that which man has is only his by Divine grace.[15] It is a Jew's *obligation* to uplift the needy, to provide for the poor:

> If there be among you a poor man, one of your brethren,
> within any of your gates in your land which the Lord
> your God is giving you, you shall not harden your heart,
> nor shut your hand against your poor brother. Rather shall
> you open your hand wide to him, and shall surely lend him
> sufficient for his need, in what he lacks . . . You shall
> surely give him, and your heart shall not be grudging
> when you give to him, because for this thing the Lord
> your God shall bless you in all your activities and in
> all that you put your hand to. For the poor shall never
> cease out of the land. Therefore, I command you,
> saying, "You shall open your hand wide to your brother, to
> your poor, and to your needy in the land."[16]

God promises no plaques. He offers no thanks for "generosity." Helping the poor is not "charity"; it is justice. Such a concept towers above the best in "ethical culture" and "Christian charity."

The Torah obligates the Jew to contribute tithes to *levi'im* (Levites) and twenty-four different types of donations to *kohanim*, who perform the special priestly duties of the "nation of priests." It sets forth laws of every kind to assure that justice will be accorded not only the needy but also the widowed, the orphaned, and the stranger living in the land. The Talmud expands upon the Written Law, and the record of the Jewish people to this day testifies to the impact these laws have made—even upon those assimilating. Ethical and moral conduct is the Torah's legacy to the Jewish people, and it is the Jews' contribution to mankind. It is part of the witness borne by the Jewish people: "Give thanks to the Lord, call upon His name, make known His deeds among the people."[17]

God's commandments are imbued with variegated purposes. *Tzedaka* is not only a nice act of benevolence; it is a *discipline*. It teaches the Jew to control his desires, to harness his inclinations. He has some money, and he would like to spend it a certain way, but he cannot—because he is commanded to give. He collects the produce of his field, and he accidentally drops a few grapes. He would like to pick them up, but he is commanded to leave them for the needy. While he is working, he might just as well reap the corners of his field, but he is forbidden to do so. The corner of his field is for the needy. His gifts to the *kohanim* and *levi'im* are not optional acts of philanthropy; they are mandatory deeds required by God. It is so much easier to be a part-time philanthropist than to be a full-time Jew. The reward is not in the plaque or in the banquet honoring donors; it is in the deed —and in the knowledge that God has promised an eternal reward:

> These are the things of which a man enjoys the fruits in this world, while the principal remains in store for him in the World to Come: honoring his father and mother, practicing kindness, early attendance at the house of learning in the morning and evening, providing hospitality to wayfarers, visiting the ill, dowering the bride, attending the dead to the grave, devoting himself to prayer, and bringing peace between his fellow-men . . .[18]

Justice. Kindness. Piety. These are not acts of lofty benevolence—these are Jewish obligations. They are ordained Torah rituals, part and parcel of the 613 commandments given to the

Jewish people by God. A Jew who scrupulously performs *other* Jewish rituals but neglects the rituals governing personal moral-ethical conduct is no more a "religious" person than his counterpart who would perform these rituals only and ignore the other moral-ethical laws (including *Shabbat, kashrut,* and *taharat hamishpacha*). Of such hypocrites did Isaiah speak:

> Bring no more worthless offerings; incense of abomination are they to Me. On the New Moon and Sabbath to call holy assemblies — I cannot bear iniquity and solemn meeting. . . .
>
> And when you spread forth your hands [in entreaty], I will hide My eyes from you; though you make many prayers, I will not hearken. Your hands are full of blood.
>
> Wash, make yourselves clean. Remove the evil of your doings from before My eyes. Cease to do evil. Learn to do well. Seek justice. Relieve the oppressed. Judge the fatherless. Plead for the widow.[19]

Clearly, Isaiah was not conveying a message to all Jews to cease observing New Moons and Sabbaths. Rather, he was attacking the hypocrites of his time who would "piously" observe the festivals and holidays — but trample on the spirit and letter of the Torah laws. He was telling them that God has no need for their festivals and their other observances, if such "religious" activities are conducted in an atmosphere of spiritual bankruptcy and theological mendacity. A Jew must live by all the Torah laws — not just a select few — if his actions are to have any real meaning in the eyes of God.

In this vein, it is ironic that Isaiah's call for spiritual honesty and Jewish authenticity has been reinterpreted by Christianity — and, in turn, by American Jewish assimilationists — to mean that he was announcing that Jews need no longer observe the Sabbath, the New Moons, and other such occasions. Nothing could be farther from the truth. Isaiah was addressing a community which so carefully dedicated itself to the fulfillment of the Sabbath and other such laws that it was unnecessary to rebuke them regarding their performance of those commandments. The same assimilationist "rabbis" who would interpret Isaiah 1:13 to mean that they may violate the fourth commandment of the Decalogue given by God at Mount Sinai nevertheless extol the importance of "family worship" at the temple, despite Isaiah 1:15 which declares, "though you make many prayers, I will not hearken." Clearly, Isaiah was neither annulling prayer, nor was he announcing the termination of the fourth commandment. On the contrary, Isaiah clearly states: "Thus says the Lord: Keep justice and do righteousness, for My salvation is near to come and My righteousness to be revealed. Fortunate is the man who does this, and the son of man that holds it fast: *who guards the Sabbath from being desecrated* and guards his hand from doing any evil."[20]

The source of the Jews' moral-ethical values, then, is the Torah. In fact, the Torah has provided these values to all of Western civilization and to the Islamic world. Although these laws have come to seem sensible to mankind, it is significant that man did not evolve these concepts—in their unity and totality—on his own. The morality of man is subjective and is barbaric when viewed by his descendants; the perfection of God's objective moral-ethical code is evinced by the lofty spirit with which it imbues modern man today, thousands of years after the original Divine revelation at Mount Sinai.

All of the Torah is infused with sanctity. Consider the laws of *kashrut*. *Kashrut* was never meant to provide man with a healthy diet, devoid of trichinosis. The laws were never intended for that purpose; nowhere in the Torah is there any such explanation for the commandment that Jews eat kosher food. Rather, the laws of *kashrut* were given for two major reasons: to strengthen the self-discipline of the nation chosen by God and to remind the Jewish people that they have been called upon to perform a task which sets them apart from all the other nations that have passed through history and which exist today on the face of the earth. "Holy shall you be, for I the Lord your God am holy."[21] That is the Torah's underlying purpose for commanding the Jews to fulfill its laws.

The Written Law sets forth only part of the dietary obligations of the Jew.[22] It lists the animals, birds, and seafood prohibited to the nation of Israel. Expanding on the Pentateuch, the Oral Law discusses *shechita* (ritual slaughter) and the various other facets of the regulations governing Jewish eating habits. *Kashrut* extends far beyond the prohibition against consuming pork: A Jew may not eat dairy and meat products at the same meal. After a meal at which meat is served, a Jew must wait a minimum period before partaking of any comestibles having a dairy content. He may not eat any meat or fowl which has not been slaughtered in accordance with the humane practice of *shechita*.

Why are there so many laws regarding food? Why are so few meat products in the United States actually permissible according to the Torah laws of *kashrut*? Why can Jews not eat in the vast majority of restaurants in America? The reason is clear, and it has nothing whatsoever to do with trichinosis prevention. The Torah wanted to create a special holy nation, one whose every action would be imbued with an aura of sanctity. The act of eating, being a purely physical matter, can be performed in a manner which degrades the very essence of man. A Jew—chosen by God for a holy mission—cannot permit himself to fall below the level of sanctity. He must discipline his instinct to consume food. He must uplift himself spiritually.

If a person is hungry, he can grab anything he sees. Hot dogs are available everywhere for eating, and beer is always on tap for drinking. He need not think twice before purchasing his frankfurter and consuming it. He is hungry so he eats at once to satisfy his need. Not a Jew. A Jew must think before he eats. Is this food permitted by the Torah for Jewish consumption? Was it slaughtered in the humane style prescribed by the Oral Law? Whether the answers to the questions are yes or no, the very act of asking sanctifies the eating process. If the food is not permissible, then the Jew understands that he must bear his hunger and wait. Sometimes for a matter of minutes, sometimes for hours. Before satisfying himself, he must come to terms with his hunger and live with it for a brief period of time. He must understand that his spiritual sanctity supersedes his urge to fill his stomach. Such a task requires thought. It requires understanding. And it requires the discipline of self-sacrifice. The Jew may not eat every animal that moves. He may not stuff himself with lobsters, crabs, or shrimp. He must control his appetite and understand that food is holy and man's need to eat can be a sacred action.

While the laws of *kashrut* discipline the Jew, they simultaneously liberate him. He is liberated from slavery to his cravings. He is freed from his animal instincts. He is empowered to rise above the base aspect of man, to reach the level of sanctity. When he smells food, he can survive without it for the time being. He is not a slave to his need to eat. Rather, he forces food to serve him. And on his terms.

In affluent America, the inability of millions to control their eating habits has helped generate a multi-million-dollar "dieting" industry. People lose control of themselves, allow their waistlines to expand like balloons, and suddenly realize that they are killing themselves. Desperately, they turn to any of a number of diets. Atkins does not permit the ingestion of carbohydrates. "Weight Watchers" allows some carbohydrates but strictly rations the total food intake by setting maximum calorie amounts which may not be exceeded. Some diets restrict fat intake; some simply forbid the consumption of saturated fats. Some permit nothing but a vial of liquid protein; some require minimum amounts of bran and other forms of natural-food fiber. Each of these diets is strictly structured; violaters are warned that they will not achieve their desired goals. And millions of Americans, despite the rigors imposed on them, agree to abide by the diet rules. To them, it makes perfect sense.

Kashrut is a diet for the soul, a spiritual diet. No one has ever died from this diet. Its regulations were conceived by the Lord God who created the universe. Not by doctors looking for instant fame, glory, and guest appearances on television talk shows. Not by subjectively motivated individuals. But by God.

Carbohydrates are permitted. Saturated and polyunsaturated fats may be ingested. Protein may be consumed. Calorie intake is not measured. And, of course, certain foods may not be eaten. Pigs are taboo. So are chocolate-covered ants and roaches. (There *are* such candies, and they are considered to be delicacies in certain parts of this hemisphere.) Even those animals which are acceptable may not be eaten when improperly slaughtered.

Is the diet restrictive? Really, it is not more restrictive than most diets tried by millions of Americans annually. The difference is that this diet was handed down to the Jewish people by God. For the Jews, it is a spiritual discipline, a sanctification process worthy of a holy nation.

Moreover, it reminds the Jew that animal life is not to be treated cheaply. The animal kingdom was also created by God. He gave man dominion over the animals, and, as a concession to man's needs, He eventually expanded on the laws presented to Adam and Eve and permitted man to eat meat. Nevertheless, He wanted man to remember that the animal world is part of Creation, too. An animal may be eaten, but only because God permitted its consumption. Were it not for God's grace, man would have no right to lay his hand on another aspect of Creation. And, in light of the special consideration given man, it is his obligation to spare the animal excessive pain in the slaughtering process. The laws of the Torah strictly defend the rights of animals; nothing is as repulsive as the notion of "the American sportsman" who spends his Sunday afternoon destroying God's world with his shotgun.

And, finally, *kashrut* serves to remind the Jew of his roots. It reminds him that he is not like everyone else; rather, he is under special obligation to God to conduct his life as a Jew should. The Jewish accountant who wishes to take a client to lunch must carefully choose a kosher restaurant; he cannot eat at the first place he passes. He must select a restaurant which will suit his spiritual needs, not necessarily his business requirements. The Jewish student who sees the advertisement for the class wine-and-cheese party knows he cannot imbibe the wine nor partake of the cheese. So he cannot go to the wine-and-cheese party — or he can go and stand out as the individual not taking part in the "tasting." Where does that leave him? It reminds him that he is a Jew and that his obligations to God transcend his partying needs. He can search through the school paper, hoping to find the local Jewish students' organization sponsoring a *kosher* wine-and-cheese affair — but he cannot attend one under any other auspices. The initial sacrifice is easily overcome, and it builds within him the discipline to overcome temptations which may confront his Jewish commitment later in his school years. The chances that he will intermarry are almost non-existent. The possibility that he will join a foreign cult is absolutely out of the question. He achieves a personal sense of liberation — he can be the Jew he is, and he can fulfill his obligations to God without constantly falling prey to personal cravings. He reaches a plane of sanctity. He is ready not only to serve God but to serve his fellow man by living a life based on genuine Jewish values. And he builds within himself a greater moral-ethical structure. He is not an animal which fills its belly instinctively; he is a thinking human being whose mind participates in the process of personal nutrition. He understands the sanctity of human life and the importance of conducting himself with respect towards animal life.

Such a Jew does the Torah seek to create, a person whose actions are truly befitting a member of a "kingdom of *kohanim.*" The table on which he eats is an altar to God, and the blessings he recites before his meal and upon its conclusion constitute the devotional service.

And he could not care less whether or not the United States Department of Agriculture has determined that properly treated pork is trichinosis-free. Yet he smiles at the Jewish assimilationists all the same, as he considers the insight offered by the authors of *Eight Questions People Ask About Judaism:*

> The assumption that Kashrut is a health measure raises an interesting question. How do the people who believe that the prohibition of eating pigs saved Jews from

death by trichinosis account for the Jews anticipating the negative effects of eating pig thousands of years before physicians knew about it? They must concede that either the Bible was written by God or by veritable supermen who made medical discoveries thousands of years before anyone else. In either case, persons holding such beliefs should adopt a more respectful attitude towards the laws of Kashrut, insofar as they might be based on other medical knowledge that the modern world does not yet know. We, of course, do not look to Kashrut as a source of medical benefits but as laws leading to moral sensitivity and holiness.[23]

Much like *kashrut*, the laws of *taharat hamishpacha* have been subjected to analyses which attribute to them a systematic *raison d'être* which has absolutely no basis in Jewish thought. *Taharat hamishpacha* is a central aspect of the Jewish value structure. As a distinctly small minority trying to survive in a hostile environment, the Jews have always had to rely on the power of the strong family unit to imbue in successive generations the overwhelmingly uplifting spirit of authentic Judaism. During a child's youth, before he is confronted by the alien thoughts and bizarre "religions" of the non-Jewish world, he must be trained by his parents not only to act like a Jew but to think like a Jew and to conduct his every moment as a Jew should. The lessons he learns at home during his early years must last him a lifetime; they must strengthen his resolve to withstand the pressures imposed by external cultures and by assimilationist elements present within his own community.

The Jewish home is not just a motel or rooming house where, coincidentally, one man, one woman, and two or three children live. It is a sacred unit, the quintessential core of Jewish existence. Throughout the Bible, the Jewish nation is referred to as the "House of Jacob,"[24] with God representing the absolute Parent and all of Israel being sons and daughters. Jewish life emanates from the home, and it is the family unit which serves as the wellspring of Jewish values from which the child draws spiritual sustenance sufficient to serve him a lifetime.

If the home is the core building-block of the Jewish community, then the husband-wife relationship is the fundamental institution in Jewish life. It is the ultimate foundation on which the Jewish family unit is built. In scientific terms, the Jewish home is the atom which serves as the basic constituent of Jewish existence; the father and mother, together with God, are the protons, electrons, and neutrons of Jewish survival. In the home, the Sabbath is observed, the laws of *kashrut* are brought to life, and the study of Torah is begun. There is absolutely no institution in Judaism which rivals the family unit in terms of religious significance.

The husband-wife partnership is sacred. And, yet, modern society has seen it debased. A world of "romantic" literature has arisen which depicts the glamor of adultery. Books, movies, and other forms of entertainment portray heroic men who sleep with their neighbors' wives and married women who sleep with other men. And the literature merely reflects the social values of its authors and readers. Men who have risen to the presidency of the United States have been implicated in extramarital affairs; scandals involving senators and congressmen have become even more commonplace. While current bestsellers compete to arouse readers with explicit details of inappropriate sexual adventures, major "men's magazines" report enormous profits as they compete to publish the most suggestive photographs. Prostitution, topless bars, and massage parlors are so acceptable in some cities that pedestrians are subjected to a non-stop barrage of open leafleting promoting the institutions. Even homosexuality — deplored as an "abomination" by God, if not by the "Union of American Hebrew Congregations" and other such bodies — is gaining public acceptance as a "viable alternative lifestyle."

The problem even affects intra-marital relations. The scandal of wife-beating has become so pronounced in the United States that *Newsweek* magazine reported in 1978 that "at least 28 million wives have been beaten by their husbands, and that

4.7 million of these cases involve serious injuries."[25] In turn, American wives have begun retaliating. One woman shot her husband three times in the chest and twice in the head, while another simply pumped him with a shotgun, wrapped his body in plastic, buried it in the smokehouse of the family farm, and then set fire to the smokehouse.[26]

Even the husband and wife who live in peace and fidelity do not necessarily reach the heights of sanctity as conceived by the Torah. The Christian "Gospels" have always tainted sexual intercourse with an aura of "dirtiness" and "ungodliness." Jesus never married. Popes and other clerics in the Catholic hierarchy are expected to remain celibate throughout their lives. Pious women are urged to pledge abstinence and to become nuns. Protestant theology, as well, has always pictured man's sexual needs as "dirty."

It is not difficult to understand the negative imagery. The sexual need—in fact a function of man's reproductive system—is not an intellectual act so much as it is a purely physical one. As are wild animals, male and female human beings are sexually attracted to each other. Pigs reproduce, horses reproduce, and humans reproduce. Superficially, the sex act is "dirty," "animalistic," and an "ungodly craving of the flesh."

Not so in Judaism. The Torah was given to the Jews to spiritually uplift them, to raise them to the heights of a holy nation. Just as *kashrut* imbues the act of eating with a sense of sanctity, so do the laws of *taharat hamishpacha* raise the sexual act to an elevated level. The Talmud teaches that the husband-wife relationship is a union conceived in heaven and that it is the highest form of interpersonal love: "Rabbi Tanchum stated in the name of Rabbi Chanilai, 'A Jew who has no wife lives without joy, without blessing, and without goodness . . .' Rab bar Ulla added, 'And without peace . . .' "[27]

And, in the Talmud's most famous statement on the subject of marital harmony, the rabbis taught that a man should "love his wife as himself and honor her more than himself."[28] As Maimonides explained, a man is required to speak softly and kindly to his wife, never treating her with anger or causing her sorrow.[29] Perhaps the clearest expression of the contrasting attitudes of Judaism and Christianity towards marriage and marital relations was the statement by the Talmudic sage, Rabbi Chama bar Chanina, who taught: "When a man marries, his sins are buried."[30]

Marriage is a sacred institution to the Jewish people, and the love between a husband and wife is a pure and wonderful love. There is no "dirt." No shame. No guilt feelings or hang-ups. Rather, Judaism extols that love in consonance with the word of God: "It is not good for man to be alone."[31]

The holiness of the marital relationship is created by the Torah's laws of family purity. These laws raise a bodily function from the depths of beastliness to the heights of sanctity. They uplift the morals and spirit of the people of Israel by imbuing their relations with the aura of Divinity. Like the *kashrut* code, they teach the Jew to discipline himself and his bodily lusts, to liberate his mind and his bold human spirit from perpetual enslavement to his cravings. *Taharat hamishpacha* is a Divinely ordained discipline incumbent only on the Jewish people. No other nation is expected to live by its guidelines because no other nation has been chosen by God as His "treasured people."[32]

A full discussion of all the laws of family purity would be extraneous to the scope of this study. In short, the Torah extols the husband-wife association. Extramarital affairs are antithetical to the moral values of the Jewish people. A holy nation, chosen by God, does not live out the fantasies of Jacquelyn Susanne. Homosexuality, likewise, is looked upon as the misappropriation of the great gift of sexual pleasure which God bestowed upon man.[33]

With marriage, a husband and wife may engage in marital relations until the time of month when the woman menstruates. Seven days after the woman's menstrual flow ceases (but not before the twelfth day since the beginning of the period) the Jewish woman goes to a *mikveh* (a pool of water meeting the requirements of the Torah) and immerses herself in the natural

waters three times. After her fulfillment of this commandment, she and her husband may once again engage in physical
relations.

Such a law may seem strange in a society which extols "free
sex" and "swinging," among other "virtues." Yet, such a law
has served to uplift the Jewish people for thousands of years.
While Minnesota police detectives flock to New York City to
locate runaway teenage girls working for Times Square pimps,
the Jewish family which conducts itself in a manner consistent
with the values of the Jewish people reads about the phenomenon with astonishment and repugnance. While television
newscasters report on boy-prostitution and child-pornography,
Jewish children raised in homes imbued with the uplifting
values of their people look on in bewilderment. How ironic it is
to hear "progressives"—who have created a society in which
three-year-old children are regularly rented to film producers
for the purpose of being sodomized on camera—offer their
critiques of the Torah's concept of *taharat hamishpacha*!
American society today is so "liberated" that nary a month
goes by without a news report being published on the problem
of rape. Twenty-four-hour-a-day "rape hotlines" are in effect
throughout the country, while female karate and self-defense
groups are busy training potential victims to protect themselves from the neighborhood rapist. And telephone companies
advise women not to have their first names listed in the local
phone book.

Where genuine Jewish values proliferate, instances of rape,
prostitution, and homosexuality are virtually non-existent.
Taharat hamishpacha disciplines the Jew's cravings; it uplifts
the animalistic sexual function to a sublime experience. It
forces the Jewish man and woman to talk to each other, to
relate in non-physical ways, to respect each other as thinking
human beings and not as cheap sex-objects. Husband and wife
have to develop meaningful ways of expressing love, affection,
and appreciation which transcend the mere physical. Sexual
relations become meaningful and fulfilling, devoid of the "dirt"
connotations suggested by the "Gospels." There is no shame in

the "desire of the flesh" because, every month, the Jew over-
comes the animalistic aspect of his drive; therefore, he knows
for himself that his act of marital lovemaking is not a
repugnant beastly urge but an elevated expression of affection
for his wife. Both husband and wife derive pleasure, then,
without shame or the need to apologize to God for enjoying their
relationship with each other. To a Jew, the act of celibacy is
folly. It is also unnatural, and it is spiritually degrading when
compared with raising a family in accordance with the values of
the Jewish people.

Taharat hamishpacha, moreover, serves to rejuvenate the
marriage experience on a monthly basis. In a generation which
has seen the act of divorce elevated to a virtual sacrament of
secular society, this aspect of the Jewish family laws cannot be
overly stressed. Two weeks (approximately) of every month see
husband and wife abstaining from physical relations. Rooted in
God's word, the family laws serve a unique purpose: the ab-
stention gives rise to a longing which intensifies daily, as the
wife patiently counts the days she must wait till immersing
herself in the *mikveh*.

The longing for a renewal of the marital union's physical
expression gives way on the day of immersion to an experience
which parallels the original "honeymoon." Ironically, then, it
may be said that observant Jews are society's ultimate "ro-
mantics" — honeymooning some twelve times a year in contradistinction to the surrounding society whose burgeoning divorce
rate might best be underscored by the legendary American
refrain: "Darling, it's nothing personal; it's just that I've gotten
bored."

Certainly, this "honeymoon effect" is not the reason that
the laws of *taharat hamishpacha* are fulfilled. Rather, the laws
are fulfilled in deference to the word of God as articulated in
His Torah. Were there no "honeymoon," *taharat hamishpacha*
would still stand before us as a Divinely ordained discipline,
sanctifying the husband-wife union in a uniquely constituted
bond of meaning, elevating that male-female relationship from
one of animalistic cravings to one of pure love. Nevertheless,

the "honeymoon effect" is a happy by-product of the Torah commandment, a unique experience in a society which sees even the most glamorous starlets of Hollywood divorced by husbands looking for "new excitement"—"something to rekindle the flame."

The purpose of the laws is to discipline, not to create ascetics. Hare Krishnas may have marital relations only one time every month—and, even then, only after reciting the mahamantra for six hours. Buddhists and other Hindu cultists are urged to seek celibacy. Moonies are regularly separated after marriage, with the husband and wife being sent to different branches of the Unification Church. All these practices are absurd to Judaism. God gave man sexual pleasure as a gift; asceticism is repugnant to the Jewish people. But discipline is important; it is essential for a people chosen by God.

Just as the *kashrut* laws have been misinterpreted as defenses against trichinosis, so have the family laws been ludicrously described as "sanitary aids." The *mikveh* is not a bathtub, replete with soap bubbles. It was never meant as a "hygienic" exercise, and nowhere in the entire Torah is such a preposterous reason given for its existence. The *mikveh* is an instrument through which a Jewish woman may acknowledge her devotion to God. Another interesting description of the *mikveh* experience was offered by a young Jewish woman who, coming from a non-religious background, decided to try living her married life in accordance with the *taharat hamishpacha* guidelines:

> . . . Once at the *mikveh*, I found a very clean and modern facility . . . I also found complete and detailed instructions on how to prepare.
> I enjoyed the preparation immensely and still do. Never in my daily life do I allow myself the luxury of a half hour in the [bath] and complete attention to my physical self from the top of my head to the soles of my feet . . . How happy I was to rediscover myself! When I

went into the *mikveh* the water was warm, friendly and accepting of my body. I said the *beracha* [blessing], submerged myself a second time, and came out, feeling really renewed. The only shock was the chlorine in the water, a necessary (I guess) modern intrusion.

The ritual of going to the *mikveh* had the hoped-for effect on our marriage. We each have two weeks free from sexual pressures and demands. I find that during this time I feel closer to God, meditate more often, study more easily. The together time is really together, precious because it won't last forever, treasured by both of us. During that time, I feel closer to the material human world and seem to have more energy for all people— not only my husband. The result of the whole cycle is a de-emphasis of the sex-object aspect of the relationship between men and women.[34]

What *kashrut* and *taharat hamishpacha* have in common is that they are both "ritualistic" commandments which go far beyond the purposes attributed to them by uninformed observers of the Jewish faith. They uplift the spiritual fiber of the Jewish people, elevating the nation of Israel to the heights expected of them by God. Not all of God's 613 laws are "sensible" to man; some appear puzzling, without any overt explanations. And, yet, the Jewish people are expected to fulfill the laws' dictates in conformity with the will of God. There is a danger in always seeking to find "new reasons" for every law. While it is natural and justified for intelligent people to seek out an understanding of God's purposes in commanding particular actions, it is vitally important to proceed with intellectual honesty and caution. Those who would define *kashrut* as a dietary aid to health and *taharat hamishpacha* as a guide to personal hygiene would, in effect, strip these commandments of their deeper meanings, thereby erroneously—and tragically—relegating them to obsolescence at the time they are most valid and vital. It is certainly important for a Jew to seek to understand God's path,[35] but he should

approach such a study with circumspection. Otherwise, he runs
the risk of evolving "theories" like the one offered by the rabbi
of the Mayfield Hillcrest Synagogue in Ohio for the reason that
Jews usher in the Sabbath every Friday evening with the
kiddush prayer, recited over a cup of wine:

> We have always encouraged sipping wine. In moderation
> of course. At the Sabbath table, with Kiddush. At the
> Yom Tov table, with sanctification. We raise the cup of
> blessing when the child is born and when the child is
> married. Hardly an occasion passes when wine does not
> grace the family table . . .
>
> Our praise for the grape and its juice is now augmented
> by no less than researchers of the Canadian Depart-
> ment of Health and Welfare in Ottowa who report the
> medicinal value of grapes and wine. In a report to the
> Journal of Applied and Environmental Microbiology, the
> researchers tell us that grapes kill viruses! In the test
> tube, grape juice and wines revealed antiviral activity!
>
> We are delighted with the discovery. Our appeal to
> make Kiddush at the Shabbat table is now documented to
> be both good for the body as well as the soul.
>
> We Jews always knew this secret. The microbiologists
> are now validating it . . .[36]

The fact is that we Jews *never* knew this "secret." If the
purpose for *kiddush* were to prevent viruses and other diseases,
we would recite the sanctification over a cup of cough medicine.
We recite the prayer over the fruit of the vine because it has
always carried with it an aura of special sanctity.[37] Even to
the non-Jewish world — especially to Christianity — wine is recognized for its special quality of holiness. Undoubtedly, this
rabbi sought to present the *kiddush* ceremony as an enlightened event in the Jewish week, but his effort — though well
intentioned — cannot be countenanced. Just as erroneous interpretations of other Jewish laws provide assimilationists with
added leverage in downgrading the Jewish obligation to
observe Torah "rituals," so can such a "theory" cheapen the

kiddush ceremony. If the reason for *kiddush* is to prevent viruses, then why not recite it daily? Why not recite it at *any* time of the day? Why not pronounce it over mouthwash? And what will the good rabbi tell his congregants if another microbiologist publishes a carefully documented study refuting the findings of the Canadian scientists? One shudders to consider the possibilities: "We Jews always knew this secret, too—but we decided to keep it a secret."

A Jew *should* attempt to use all the tools of intellectual inquiry at his disposal to come to an understanding of God's purposes. The reason Judaism never opposed science (as did the Church) is that Judaism was too busy encouraging science. Every new star and planet that is charted adds to our awareness of the awesome wonder of God's creation. Understanding how men breathe, how animals utilize their environments and their special properties to survive, how plants take root, and how every other aspect of the universe functions adds to man's appreciation of God. Maimonides has noted that man's love for his Creator directly correlates to his knowledge and understanding; the more one learns about God's ways and reasons, the better he can serve Him.[38] But one should proceed with care:

> "For My thoughts are not your thoughts; neither are
> your ways My ways," says the Lord. "For, as the heavens
> are higher than the earth, so are My ways higher than your
> ways, and My thoughts than your thoughts."[39]

The commandments were given to the Jewish people to uplift them beyond the planes they could have reached had they simply relied on human wisdom. They preserve peace between men, sanctify the mundane, provide the discipline necessary to enable man to liberate himself from subjugation to his cravings, maintain the special purpose of the Jewish national entity, and even keep Jews in constant touch with their roots. The Torah may seem demanding, but that is because it was conceived as a blueprint for the development of man's ethics and morals to their ultimate peaks of sanctity.

American women seeking to look like "that Cosmopolitan girl" will assume upon themselves excruciating disciplines to reach their goal. They will starve themselves daily, exercise ferociously, and subject themselves to near-ascetic deprivations. But, to them, it is worthwhile because the goal of achieving ideal physical womanhood is utopian. Similarly, when Farrah Fawcett-Majors became America's leading pin-up model, millions of women—some middle-aged—spent substantial sums of money to "look like Farrah." News reports showed women subjecting their hair to intensive steaming procedures in order to style their locks in a manner similar to those of Farrah. Those interviewed confessed that their efforts cost them a good deal of money and, frequently, quite a bit of pain—but, to look like Ms. Fawcett-Majors, it was worth it all the same.

In 1979 a hit-movie catapulted Bo Derek to instant fame as one of America's most glamorous actresses. The movie was titled "10," and the title's implication was that Bo Derek, when rated on a scale from one to ten in terms of physical beauty, scored a maximum "10." In the movie, Ms. Derek sported hair braided in a manner similar to the "corn row" hairdo then popular among many American Black women.

Overnight, from coast to coast, women of all sorts dashed frantically to their hairdressers to braid their hair "like Bo Derek." Fat women. Skinny women. Rich women. Poor women. Pretty women. Ugly women. In the words of one Detroit hair stylist: "There are a lot of 5's around here trying to look like 10's."[40] Ladies' salons, eager to cash in on this latest craze, charged up to $300 for providing this special hairdo. Women prepared to pay the price were informed in advance that the styling procedure could be painful and could lead to an actual loss of hair; moreover, the very process of braiding the hair could take up to six hours to complete. A New York dermatologist warned that the hairstyle could lead to "balding at the edges" within a few years.[41] These warnings stopped no one. Women with short hair underwent treatment in which hair extensions were woven in. At New York's exclusive Pierre

Michel salon the cost for the styling was as high as $500. And yet business was brisk. To look like Bo Derek, it was worth it.

If the goal is "worth it," then the need to assume special burdens in order to reach the goal is "worth it" as well. Jews do not seek to emulate Robert Redford or Racquel Welch. They seek to emulate God. They seek to reach the spiritual heights of Abraham and Sarah. The *mitzvot*, then, are not an oppressive burden but a wonderful gift to the Jewish people. God does not need the Jews to perform His commandments, but in His love for the descendants of Abraham and Sarah, He bestowed upon them His Torah. Just as in his love for a woman, a man will go to the greatest lengths to please her, so do Jews lovingly perform the *mitzvot* commanded them by God.

The Shabbat, for example, is not seen as a day on which "you can't do this, and you can't do that." It is a unique moment during which you *can* communicate with the world of nature in a special way. It is not only a day of physical rest but of indescribably sublime spiritual relaxation—and growth.

> The Shabbat is a day of rest, of joy, of pleasure, of prayer. It is the day on which we are commanded to refrain from doing—and to *be*; the twenty-four-hour period in which the Jew drops his facades, discards his artificial worries and sophisticated headaches, and exists—serves—responds to the all-enveloping quiet of the Shabbat. It is the day given over to contemplation, to spiritual rejuvenation, and to the regeneration of the tender responsiveness which is so visibly absent in our week-day lives. The Shabbat is the day on which man exists in a perfect balance with nature, neither creating nor destroying, and thereby experiences himself as a part of the Almighty's creation. During the week, we become completely absorbed in our daily occupations. We tend to see ourselves as supermen—doing and accomplishing, planning and executing those plans. On the Shabbat, we are made aware of our dependence, of our fragile nature in a cosmic order we do not pretend to fully comprehend. We

renew our bond with the Almighty and spend a twenty-
four-hour span living the spiritual superconsciousness
which that relationship confers upon us.

On Shabbat we exert a conscious effort to recapture our
perfect harmony with nature by switching off certain
habitual behaviors and by learning new ones. We attempt
to live one whole day without acting upon our
environment but letting it act upon us.[42]

From Friday evening (beginning an hour before sunset) until
the stars appear on Saturday night, the Jew observes his Sabbath. He does not perform any of the thirty-nine types of
actions prohibited by the Oral Law for that day. Not only does
he refrain from participating in standard business undertakings
but he also abstains from using vehicular transportation, from
cooking food, from using electricity,* and from doing many
other things so "essential" to human survival. And he survives.

The wondrous Shabbat is ushered in by the Jewish woman,
whose privilege it is to light the Shabbat candles. The candles'
brilliant glow radiates, reflecting off her face and spreading
luster throughout the home. Upon her husband's arrival from
the synagogue, the family turns to the beautifully arranged
table. They circle around it and welcome the Shabbat by
singing *Shalom Aleichem*. The father puts his hands on his
children's heads, and he blesses them; his wife follows by
blessing the children, too. He recites the *kiddush* prayer,
praising God for having chosen the Jewish people of all the
nations in the world to inherit the Sabbath legacy, and he
recites the blessing sanctifying the wine, the symbol of joy.[43]
After the cup is passed around, the entire family proceeds to
wash their hands in accordance with the ritual, as a spiritual
preparation for the Shabbat meal.

Seated at the table, the family then enjoys its most splen-

---

*One may, however derive benefit from electricity turned on before
Shabbat. Likewise, an electric timer may be set prior to Shabbat,
thereby making it permissible to derive benefit from electricity being
turned on and off automatically during the course of the Sabbath.

did meal of the week. Long, twisted loaves of bread, *challa*, adorn the table and add a special flavor to the repast. And the most precious ingredient of all—family love and warmth—brightens the table. There is no mad rush to finish the meal. The children will not be doing homework because they are forbidden to write on Shabbat, nor will they be running off to the television because they are not permitted to use the electrical devise on the holy day. The father will not be on his way to the TV for the same reason, nor will he be leaving for a night of card-playing or bowling "with the boys." (Money may not be handled on Shabbat.) The mother will not flee from reality to the television either,[44] nor will she be on her way to the pursuits which normally occupy her evenings. The parents won't be doing their children's homework—no writing—and no one will take refuge at the family telephone (not used on Shabbat).

What does the Shabbat do to people? It makes them people. They learn to talk to each other, to take an interest in each other, to share with each other. If *taharat hamishpacha* brings the husband and wife together into a meaningful relationship, Shabbat allows the children to join. Not rushing to finish supper, the family can come to enjoy each other's company. *Zemirot*, special Sabbath songs, are sung in unison by the entire family, in-between courses. They can sing it on-key, off-key, or beyond-key. It makes no difference. The important thing is that the whole family actually sings together. Grown parents sing with their children—every week. They talk. About school. About interesting moments in their week. About the portion of the Torah to be read in the synagogue the following day. They learn to share ideas with each other. To share feelings. To share love.

What an awesome day Shabbat is! How sharply it differs from the Christian Sunday! It is a day reserved neither for football games nor baseball double-headers nor horse races. Children do not seek sanctuary in their local movie theater, and women do not run to their friends' homes scheming to get their husbands away from the television sets before the post-game show begins. Shabbat belongs to the entire family, and everyone celebrates it together. It is not just a "day of rest"; it is a day of spiritual awakening. On Shabbat, man transcends the mundane and actually links himself with God, who also rested on the seventh day.[45] (It is not surprising that Jewish youths raised in homes where Shabbat is so observed do not run off to meditating gurus like Maharishi Mahesh Yogi in order to attain unity with God; such a oneness is theirs every Shabbat — and they don't even have to pay for a mantra.)

On this day, the Jew is not only at rest. He is at peace. He is free from all the headaches which manage to find their ways into the average "day off." He does not worry about his business affairs because he is forbidden to contemplate any business matters on Shabbat. He is liberated from the world of technology, and he has an opportunity to reflect on his role in the universe. What is man? Where does he stand in relation to the rest of Creation? The day of Shabbat is reserved for other-worldly contemplation, for the spiritual meditation accomplished by studying the words of the Torah.

How can Shabbat be described? It is not a day of which we can conceive; it is a day we must experience. Not only *avoda* (physical work) but *melacha* (creative toil) is absent from this day. So wonderful is the Sabbath to the Jew that, from the moment it is over, he literally counts the days till the following week's Shabbat: "Today, Sunday, the first day till Shabbat"; "Today, Monday, the second day till Shabbat . . ."[46] The rabbis of the Talmud caught the spirit of Shabbat when they engaged in this famous "exchange":

> Rabbi Yochanan said in Rabbi Yossi's name: "He who delights in the Sabbath is given an unbounded heritage . . ."
>
> Rabbi Judah said in Rav's name: "He who delights in the Sabbath is granted his heart's desires . . ."
>
> Rabbi Yochanan said in the name of Rabbi Shimon bar Yochai: "If Israel were to observe two Sabbaths according to its laws, they would be redeemed immediately . . ."[47]

Such is the awesome meaning of the Sabbath to the Jewish

people. Although celebrated every single week, it stands out in the Jewish calendar together with Yom Kippur as the most holy of days. It is a Torah commandment which disciplines the Jewish people to rise above their human weaknesses and to seek holiness. For a full day, Jews divest themselves of all the worldly technological "survival kits" and find that human meaning can emanate from the Divine spirit within them. They live in harmony with nature, neither putting the earth to work (because sowing seeds — though not arduous physical work — is prohibited on the Shabbat) nor putting animals to work.[48] Instead, the Jewish people join hands with all of Creation, resting in memory of the "six days which shook the world."

The Shabbat, then, is not a mere ritual; it is an event imbued with sanctity. It is a day which molds the moral and ethical character of the Jewish nation. And, it might be noted, it is a day which creates the kind of Jew who will not abandon his people and heritage.

As Shabbat differs from the Christian Sunday, so do all Jewish festivals and holidays stand apart from Christian counterparts. How does one begin to list the differences between the secular "New Year's Day," which has become immortalized by lampshades and alcoholic beverages, and the Jewish Rosh Hashanah, a day on which the Jew celebrates his hope for a happy new year by dipping apples into honey and by eating other sweets — while he also reflects on his deeds of the previous twelve months? The Jew spends his New Year's Day in solemn prayer, seeking to hasten the day when God's glory will appear before all mankind. As for the secular "New Year's Day," by the time the big ball has been lowered in New York's Times Square, most Americans are lucky if they can contemplate driving home safely.

The differences between the Jewish observances and the Christian ones extend to the least intense of the respective holidays. Purim is one of the "lighter" Biblical occasions commemorated by the Jewish people. Based on the Book of Esther's account of the salvation of the Jews under Persian rule, the Purim holiday is a rather robust occasion. During the

reading of the *megillah* (i.e., the Book of Esther, in its traditionally inscribed form), congregants are encouraged to
"whoop it up" on every occasion that Haman's name is mentioned. Noisemakers of all sizes (and sounds!) blast through the
evening in the festive synagogue. After the reading—which is,
of course, accompanied by special blessings praising God for
having provided salvation for the Jews whom Haman sought to
exterminate—gala parties are held in Jewish communities
everywhere. The Talmud set forth a guideline for the Purim
party-goer: "It is the duty of a man to mellow himself with wine
on Purim until he cannot tell the difference between the words
'Cursed be Haman' and 'Blessed be Mordechai.' "[49]

In other words, a Jew's ostensible "duty" on Purim is to get
inebriated!

Now, it does not require any great amount of imagination to
predict how such a rabbinical dictum would be interpreted—and enacted—by the kinds of religions which gave
America the "New Year's Eve" party. But how is this law
regarded by the traditionally sober Jewish community? A
perusal of post-Talmudic rabbinic literature provides a glimpse
of what kind of people the Jews are, and it boldly illustrates the
ennobling impact of the Torah on this "kingdom of priests."
Every single commentator reacts with bewilderment to this
ruling: Can it be that a Jew—who has been chosen to epitomize
sanctity—is required to get drunk on Purim, the great joy of
the holiday notwithstanding? It is impossible to believe so, say
the commentaries. Maimonides interprets the dictum to mean
that one should drink a bit more than usual and then go to
sleep, so that—while asleep—he will not be able to discern
between "Cursed be Haman" and "Blessed be Mordechai."[50]
Since every letter in the Hebrew alphabet also represents a
numerical value, other rabbis comment on the curious fact that
the letters which spell the words "Cursed be Haman" (*arur
Haman*) tally to the same total of 502 as do the letters which
spell "Blessed be Mordechai" (*baruch Mordechai*). Accordingly, they assert that the rabbinical dictum does not encourage
drunkenness but simply enough giddiness so that the

mathematical coincidence of the two expressions happening to each add up to 502 would not occur to the celebrant by party's end.[51]

How gallantly such devices speak for the Jewish people! They have before themselves an open license to imbibe freely, and they seek to re-examine it and to carefully ponder its intent, incapable of conceiving that, on even one occasion a year, the Jewish nation would be permitted to get drunk.[52] In the end, what matters is not which rabbi's opinion wins out,[53] but the very fact that such a dispute develops in the first place.

Of equal significance is the nature of the Purim custom to "give gifts one to another."[54] Every Purim day Jews prepare small packages of gifts of food (usually including cookies, candies, and other sweets) and bring the presents to their friends. Uninvited, they knock on their friends' doors, say "Happy Purim," and present their neighbors with gifts of food. To add to the fun, children dress up in all sorts of costumes before delivering the various bags and packages of "goodies." That is how Jews celebrate Purim. How different it is from the Christian world's "Halloween"—rooted in pagan super-stitions—on which occasion children are encouraged to knock on doors and to *ask* for food! On both holidays, children masquerade (though Jewish boys and girls do not dress up like witches and devils), but how different are the lessons they bring home with them! The child who celebrates Purim learns what it means to *give*. He brings a present without any forewarning, and he beholds the smile of pleasant surprise which greets him upon his arrival. He knocks on the door and neither threatens a "trick" nor requests a "treat." He smiles shyly, and then he presents an unsolicited gift to his neighbor. He cannot stay for long because he has to stop at a number of other homes as well, leaving a gift at each house.

Such religious obligation is not a "ritual"; it is a lesson in giving and sharing unparalleled in any other society. He is not "advised" to give or "urged" to give. He is *obligated* to give. He learns at a young age that "it is more blessed to give than to receive"—not by hearing others mouth lofty platitudes but by being obligated to perform tangible deeds. How very sharply does his upbringing differ from that of his non-Jewish generational peer, who learns at the same youthful age the antithetical principle and lesson embedded in the Halloween excursion known as "trick-or-treating"! (Need it be added that Purim is a thoroughly spiritual experience, while Halloween often degenerates into an excuse for vandalism?)

The more closely Judaism is analyzed, the more successfully it substantiates the prophecy of the Torah: "Keep, therefore, and do [the commandments of God), for this is your wisdom and your understanding in the sight of the nations which shall hear all these statutes and say, 'Surely, this great nation is a wise and understanding people.' "[55]

Every one of the 613 laws God gave the Jewish people is rooted not only in sanctity but in practical wisdom. And they all emphasize the underlying principle of Judaism: words are not enough; talk is cheap. What counts are *deeds*—solid, tangible deeds. Anyone can speak about the "golden rule." The Jew must practice it. So certain were the rabbis of the Talmud that the *mitzvot* of God are inherently saturated with wisdom and justice that they urged those who were not psychologically prepared to perform the commandments for the right reasons (viz., in recognition of the fact that they were commanded by God) to nevertheless perform the deeds. "For Rav Judah said in the name of Rav: 'A man should always occupy himself with Torah and good deeds, though it be done not for their proper sake—for, out of doing good for the wrong reasons, one comes to do good for the proper reasons.' "[56]

The deed is Judaism's central ethic. Every goal and ideal is meaningless until actualized by the performance of the deed. The Torah commandments obligating the Jewish male to don *tefillin* every morning and to wear *tzitzit* throughout the day are not mere "rituals." They are constant, physical reminders: Do deeds. The *tefillin* consist of two parts, each including a small cube in which are contained miniature parchments bearing specially designated Torah verses. The *tefillin* are put on in a manner such that one cube points to the heart while the other rests on the head; the actual deed of putting on *tefillin* binds the heart and mind of the Jew together and seeks to remind his emotional center and his intellectual base that his day is meaningless unless it is accompanied by the performance of deeds.[57] Wrapped in devotion to God, the Jew begins his morning by solemnly communicating with Him through prayer. He proceeds through his day wearing *tzitzit*, strings attached to a four-cornered garment. Wherever he goes, he carries with him a reminder:

> And it shall be to you for a tassel, so that you shall look upon it and remember all the commandments of the Lord, and do them; you shall not turn astray, following the desires of your hearts and your eyes, after which you lust. It is in order that you shall remember and do all My commandments, and be holy to your God . . .[58]

Surrounded by constant reminders throughout the day, the Jew learns to discipline himself and his desires. Wherever he goes, whatever he does, he is surrounded by God. On his body, he wears *tzitzit*. For his meals, he must seek out strictly kosher food. He must pray three times daily, at designated times in the morning, afternoon, and evening. As he wakes up, he is reminded by his prayers that God gave him his life. During his busy day, despite the building pressures of his business as the afternoon wears on, he stops to express his devotion to God and to remind himself that, whether he financially succeeds or fails, all his actions are in the hands of God. At night, exhausted from a hard day's work, he summons the strength to thank God for having given him the day. His prayers are not televised sermonettes, sterilized to fit in with the late-night movie. Rather, he pours out his soul in prayer, in devotion, and—most importantly—in gratitude.

Such a Jew is a holy person. He is not an ascetic, for that would be degrading to his character, and it would signal a rejection of all the wonderful pleasures and joys so abundantly evident in God's Creation. But he is a disciplined person. He can stand up to his temptations and his cravings and overcome them. He can enjoy a fabulous meal, but he will not allow himself to be ruled by food. He can derive the greatest pleasures from his marital relations, but he will not allow himself to be enslaved by his lusts. His home is a sanctuary where God dwells every moment. His doorposts are reminders of his obligations as a Jew, for they are adorned with *mezuzot*, each one bearing within it the scriptural passages reminding him of God's presence and of his duty to serve God.[59] He is, of course, human and he may yet err, but his humanity is uplifted to its greatest heights, as the rabbis of the Talmud have written:

> Beloved are the Jewish people, for the Holy One, blessed be He, surrounded them with precepts: *tefillin* on their heads, *tefillin* on their arms, *tzitzit* on their garments, and *mezuzot* on their doorposts . . .
>
> Rabbi Eliezer ben Jacob said, "Whosoever has the *tefillin* on his head and on his arm, the *tzitzit* on his garment, and the *mezuza* on his doorpost is securely guarded from doing evil, as it is written: 'And a threefold cord is not quickly broken.' "[60]

A threefold cord is not quickly broken by "Jews for Jesus" Christian missionaries, by Moonies, by Buddhists, by Hindu gurus, or by Hare Krishnas. It is not quickly broken by the temptation to marry someone who is not Jewish. In short, that cord has not been broken for nearly four thousand years.

Judaism is a discipline of liberation. It liberates the Jew to fulfill his manhood or her womanhood to the fullest potential. Backing up that claim are four millennia of history, culture, and knowledge. After fifty years of American bar mitzvas, Christmas trees, "New Year's Eve" parties on Friday night, *sukka*-mangers, astrology classes, pulpit exchanges, inter-burials, Tisha b'Av carnivals, "Jewish social service" interfaith summer programs, and Federation-sponsored lectures on horses and Gospel music, American Jewry finds itself at its time of severest social crisis.[61] Millions of dollars have been funneled into the pockets of analysts hired by Federations to "investigate and study" the crises of Jewish alienation and assimilation, and to seek out the "root causes."[62] Millions more have gone to highly regarded professionals, whose advice has been solicited for suggestions as to how the problems posed by the cults and intermarriage might be effectively countered, if not neutralized. Hundreds of thousands of dollars have been transmitted to Jewish lay leaders, in the hope that their full-time efforts might stem the tide of communal decay plaguing American Jewry.

Rabbis in a growing number of "Reform" and "Conservative" temples bemoan the decay. Consider two representative sermons, the first by a Reform clergyman, the second by a Conservative one:

> Shouldn't we be facing up to the fracturing of our Jewish families, the collapse of the home as the generating source of Jewish identity and celebrations? Shouldn't we be confronting the waning of Jewish practice, the loss of Shabbat and Festivals, the erosion of Jewish consciousness, the hodge-podge we call Jewish education, the drifting away of our college youth, the needs of our growing legion of singles, the confusion of our young, and the ignorance of adults?
>
> The trouble with Reform Judaism is that we do not take ourselves seriously. The historic task of Reform was to renew and reshape Jewish options and traditions. Its mandate was to vitalize Jewish life. Yet we have allowed that precious trust to degenerate in our hands . . .
>
> Reform . . . for many has become an excuse for doing nothing . . . for many it has become an apology for not knowing a kiddush from a kaddish, or Torah from Haftorah. . . . Tragically, "I am a Reform Jew" has come to mean for many "I don't keep Shabbat, I don't go to synagogue, I don't study, I don't wear a yarmulke or tallit" . . . a whole series of "don'ts" adding up to zero Jewish commitment.[63]

Does the average Conservative Jew truly reflect the image of an authentic Jew? Can the future of Judaism be

guaranteed by the religious patterns of Conservative
Jews? These are questions that of late have been
bothering me. As I view the typical Jew affiliated with
a Conservative synagogue I find myself doubting the
Jewish image that is reflected, and losing confidence in
the fact that through his/her religious behavior patterns
Judaism's future is secure. . . .

It is a problem that stems from the commitment or lack
of it by those who have chosen to label themselves
Conservative Jews. Among Conservative Jews I do not
find the degree of observance as I would among the Jews to
the right of us. I do not find the fervency of commitment
and dedication to Yiddishkeit within Conservative Jewish
ranks that I see evident among the Orthodox.
Conservative Jews do not seem prone to observance. Areas
such as Shabbat, kashrut, holidays, daily worship at
home or in the synagogue, putting on of tefillin, keeping
the proper yahrzeit date, even observing the period of
shiva, seem compromised in observance or not
observed at all. How can there be any guarantee for a
Jewish future when I find so many Jewish parents
rationalizing the mixed marriages of their children! There
can be no future for Jews who in their lack of knowledge
cannot understand why a Conservative Rabbi should not
be permitted to officiate at a mixed wedding — "After all,
rabbi, you're not Orthodox!" There is only one way that I
can see Judaism surviving and that is only by devoted and
diligent observance . . .[64]

Yet, despite hired analysts, despite professional consultants,
despite full-time lay leadership, despite sermons from temple
clergy, and despite all the many studies, reports, and
probes—the problems persist. Unsolved. Uncountered. Un-
stemmed. Never in American Jewish history has there been a
better time to mull over the words of Psalm 78 than today:

For He established a testimony in Jacob and set forth a
law in Israel, which He commanded our fathers to make

known to their children: that they might set their hope in God and not forget the works of God, but keep His commandments. And that they might not be as their fathers, a stubborn and rebellious generation, a generation that set not their heart aright, and whose spirit was not steadfast with God.[65]

It is time for American Jews—old and young alike—to return to their roots and to the lofty values of their people. There has never been a better time to be liberated.

Notes

1) Exodus 24:7. For a fuller consideration of the subject, see also chapter one above.

2) In addition to those events discussed in chapter one, see Norman Cohn, *The Pursuit of the Millennium* (N.Y.: Oxford University Press, 1970) for a scholarly, detailed account of the gory realities of Christian practice during the early centuries of the Church.

3) Cf. Perry Davis, "Corruption in Jewish Life," *Present Tense*, vol. 5, no. 2 (Winter, 1978), pp. 19-24.

4) Tractate *Yoma* 86b.

5) Exodus 19:6.

6) See chapter one.

7) Plato, *The Republic* (N.Y.: Oxford University Press, 1971), pp. 155 ff.

8) Felix Adler, the founder of the Ethical Culture Society in 1876, was the son of "Rabbi" Samuel Adler of New York's Reform Temple Emanuel.

The temple sent Felix to Germany, where he was to study for the rabbinate, in preparation for the job of succeeding his aging father. When he returned to the U.S. in 1873, he expressed his feeling that the Jewish religion was no longer useful. He thereupon founded the Ethical Culture Society. See Nathan Glazer, *American Judaism* (Chicago: University of Chicago Press, 1972), p. 49.

9) Deuteronomy 16:20.

10) Tractate *Taanit* 11a.

11) Tractate *Shabbat* 31a.

12) Genesis 18:17-33.

13) Isaiah 49:6.

14) Psalms 24:1.

15) *Ibid.*, 115:16.

16) Deuteronomy 15:7-11. See also Proverbs 21:13, "Whoever stops his ears at the cry of the poor, he too shall cry and not be answered."

17) I Chronicles 16:8.

18) Tractate *Shabbat* 127a.

19) Isaiah 1:13-17.

20) *Ibid.* 56:1-2.

21) Leviticus 19:2. See also *ibid.* 11:43-45: "You shall not make yourselves abominable . . . for I am the Lord your God. You shall therefore sanctify yourselves, and you shall be holy, for I am holy . . . For I am the Lord who brings you up out of the Land of Egypt to be your God. You shall therefore be holy, for I am holy."

22) See Leviticus 11 and Deuteronomy 14:3-21.

23) Dennis Prager and Joseph Telushkin, *Eight Questions People Ask About Judaism* (Simi Valley, Calif.: Tze Ulmad Press, 1976), p. 46.

24) See, for example, Isaiah 2:5.

25) *Newsweek*, 1/30/78.

26) *Ibid.*

27) Tractate *Yevamot* 62b.

28) *Ibid.* 62b.

29) Maimonides, *Mishneh Torah, Hilchot Ishut* 15:19.

30) Tractate *Yevamot* 63b.

31) Genesis 2:18. Cf. *ibid.* 61b.

32) Exodus 19:5.

33) See Leviticus 18:22; 20:13; Tractate *Sanhedrin* 54a-b; Maimonides, *op.cit., Hilchot Issurei Biah* 1:14.

34) *Lilith* (magazine), vol. 1, no. 2 (Winter 1976-77), p. 8. The modern *mikveh* is quite a bit more elegant than the stereotypes depicted in anti-Jewish literature. Nowadays *mikvehs* are as modern as any health club's facilities might be. They are tastefully decorated and spotless, replete with fashionable mirrors, blow-dryers, and other such basics. A new solar-heated *mikveh* in California, like some other new ones elsewhere, includes a sun-deck and the like.

35) Maimonides, *op. cit., Hilchot Teshuva* 10:6.

36) *Jewish Post and Opinion*, 5/20/77.

37) In a sermon delivered at New York City's "Jewish Center," Rabbi Norman Lamm of Yeshiva University offered a far more insightful analysis. Commenting on Genesis 14:18, which tells of Malkitzedek the Priest honoring Abraham with bread and wine, Rabbi

Lamm noted that those two food items share a common trait: they are the "perfected" versions of their ingredients. Bread is the "staff of life," uplifted from the raw grains which go into its making. And wine is the richly improved form of the grape which, in itself, is but another fruit. Just as these two foods represent the process of perfection (in a symbolic way), so did Abraham's rescue of Lot mark the perfection of his spirit, as he merged *deed* with *theory*. Likewise, it might be noted, the Sabbath marks the perfection of the week, as it imbues it with a special holiness otherwise absent from Sunday to Friday. (See also footnote 43 below.)

38) See footnote 37 above.

39) Isaiah 55:8-9.

40) *Newsweek*, 1/28/80.

41) *Ibid.*

42) From "Setting the Mood," an article by Linda Fisch, published in 1974 by the Lincoln Square Synagogue of New York City.

43) See the discussion in Tractate *Pesachim* 105b ff. See also the commentary of Tos'fot (*ibid.*, 106a) which notes that we fulfill the requirement to "*Remember* the Sabbath" (Exodus 20:8) by sanctifying the wine because wine is scripturally associated with the act of remembering (e.g., Hosea 14:8; Song of Songs 1:4). See also *Orach Chayim* 271:3 and *Mishna Berura ad loc.*

44) The role of one television-free day weekly should not be underestimated. In 1978, West German Chancellor Helmut Schmidt called on the people of his country to adopt "one television-free day each week." In Schmidt's words: "We are not talking enough with each other. That goes for married couples, parents, children, and friends." (*New York Times*, 5/22/78)

45) Genesis 2:1-3.

46) In Hebrew, there are no names for the days; rather, they are counted on the basis of their proximity to the Shabbat. At the conclusion of every morning's prayers, a special psalm is recited for the day; at that time, the countdown takes place. See, for example, Philip Birnbaum (trans.), *Daily Prayer Book* (N.Y.: Hebrew Publishing Company, 1949), pp. 139-147.

47) Tractate *Shabbat* 118a-b. The section quoted is not an actual exchange; rather, it is a compilation of aphorisms dealing with the same subject, the Sabbath.

48) Exodus 20:10; Deuteronomy 5:14.

49) Tractate *Megilla* 7b.

50) Maimonides, *op. cit.*, Hilchot Megilla 2:15; Cf. commentary of *Rama* and *Mishna Berura* on *Orach Chayim* 695:2. See also *Aruch Ha-Shulchan Orach Chayim* 695:2.

51) See the commentaries of *Magen Avraham* and *Ba'er Heitev* on *Orach Chayim* 695:2.

52) Note that some commentaries completely discount the dictum, which had been pronounced by the Talmudic scholar Rava. See, for example, the commentaries of *Bet Yosef* and *Bach* on *Tur Orach Chayim* 695:2, both of which cite the teaching of Rabbi Ephraim (as quoted by the *Ran*) who taught that Rava's dictum was not to be interpreted literally. Cf. *Aruch Ha-Shulchan Orach Chayim* 695:3-5, as the author deeply investigates the dilemma posed by Rava's dictum.

53) The accepted interpretation of Tractate *Megilla* 7b today is that one should drink more wine on Purim than the amount to which he is normally accustomed—but that he should by no means get inebriated.

54) Esther 9:19.

55) Deuteronomy 4:6.

56) Tractate *Pesachim* 50b; *Yoreh Deah* 246:20.

57) For Biblical sources, see Deuteronomy 6:4-9 and 11:13-21. See also Exodus 13:1-16.

58) Numbers 15:39-40.

59) Deuteronomy 6:4-9; 11:13-21.

60) Tractate *Menachot* 43b. (The verse quoted by Rabbi Eliezer ben Jacob is found in Ecclesiastes 4:12.)

61) See the shocking study published by Elihu Bergman, assistant director of the Harvard Center for Population Studies, in the October 1977 issue of *Midstream*, pp. 9-19. Bergman summed up his meticulously detailed study of the effects of intermarriage and assimilation on long-term prospects for American Jewish continuity in this bluntly worded opening paragraph:

"When the United States celebrates its Tricentennial in 2076, the American Jewish community is likely to number no more than 944,000 persons, and conceivably as few as 10,420."

In Bergman's analysis, "The decline is in progress because, in its meteoric rise to eminence, American Jewry has neglected to establish the sort of roots that would sustain it as a viable community. If present trends are not arrested or reversed, the American Jewish community faces extinction as a significant entity, and by its own hand, during the first half of the 21st century. . . The disaster is in the making."

62) See, for example, *Jewish Life* (Summer 1974), p. 30.

63) *Jewish Post and Opinion*, 2/1/80.

64) *Ibid.*, 12/21/79.

65) Psalms 78:5-8.

CONCLUSION

An analysis of the impact of religious cults on young Jews must inevitably lead to disquieting conclusions. That Jewish youths would join foreign religious groups disturbs us because the decisions they make in choosing to leave their people and faith reflect failures on our part. Having been failed in homes bereft of Jewish authenticity, having been failed by "Talmud Torah" or Hebrew school "educational programs" which provide neither quantitative nor qualitative Jewish knowledge, having been failed by a community which does not adequately provide meaningful Jewish substance — the youths who turn away from Judaism symbolize, more often than not, the decaying fabric of American Jewish life.

Tragically, the crises and implications run deeper than we might superficially infer. For every American Jewish youth who leaves his people to join an alien theological phenomenon like the Unification Church or the International Society for Krishna Consciousness, there are countless more who simply opt for social neutralization: they desert their four-thousand-year heritage and quietly assimilate into the society around them. Whether their departure from the Jewish fold takes the form of defiant alienation, subtle assimilation, or intermarriage, theirs is a shattering action, not less devastating to American Jewish vitality and continuity than that of their generational peers who flee to Korea and India.

Their decisions do not emanate from a vacuum. Rather, they are the inevitable offspring of years and years of spiritually barren life. A Jewish youth who grows up without knowing a real Shabbat is left that much more Jewishly deprived as he reaches the adolescent years during which his major conceptions begin to develop. If his sole brush with Jewish knowledge is a meager Sunday school "education" and a year-long undertaking to memorize a *haftora* from a record (also available in cassette tapes and 8-track cartridges), then his Jewish bankruptcy will take him spiritually to the same destination that financial bankruptcy would take him economically. A bar mitzva or bat mitzva is not enough. Sunday morning bagels-and-lox breakfasts will not suffice. A summer visit to the Catskills or a winter journey to Miami Beach won't do. Not even the distinction of birth in a hospital named Maimonides, Mount Sinai, or Beth Israel will guarantee a young Jew's life-long affiliation with his people. Without the real tools for Jewish growth and development, one might just as well be born in the maternity ward of the local Catholic hospital.

The cult phenomenon, then, is not a curse but a culmination. It is a symptom, not a cause. And, perhaps most importantly, it may yet be revealed to be a blessing in disguise.

Before Guru Maharaj Ji, Maharishi Mahesh Yogi, Prabhupada, Sun Myung Moon, and "Moishe Rosen" emerged, scant attention was focused on the breakdown of Jewish authenticity in the American Jewish society. Such a neglect was tragic because, while young people were not then joining foreign theological communities, they were nevertheless rejecting Judaism and leaving the Jewish fold en masse. Intermarriage was already skyrocketing in the 1960s; alienation was more than evident on the American campuses of that decade. If a generation of Mark Rudds, Jerry Rubins, and Abbie Hoffmans were not attending Unification Church retreats or *Bhagavad-Gita* classes, neither were they dreaming of the day when they might contribute to the United Jewish Appeal.

Had it not been for the emergence of the bizarre and alien religions of the 1970s, American Jewry would have continued to allow precious time to pass by without undertaking a comprehensive program to revive Judaism for the young. As it is, the responses to the challenges posed by the cults have been less than adequate to meet the needs of American Jewish youth. But, at least, responses have been made. It is a beginning.

It took the American Jewish Committee three-quarters of a century to call for the intensive Jewish schooling of our young, but the call has, at least, finally come. Not till the end of the 1970s did any meaningful segment of the American Jewish community challenge the established priorities of the Jewish Federations (the perspicacious Agudath Israel of America being a notable exception). Other than the few dissenting voices emanating from sources outside the American Jewish main-stream—including those of the Jewish Defense League, the Jewish Student Movement, and others—few actually advocated giving more money to Jewish educational insti-tutions than to "Jewish" medical facilities. By the end of the Seventies, on the other hand, such calls were coming from the prestigious American Jewish Committee, the New York Metropolitan Coordinating Council on Jewish Poverty, and leaders of such diverse Zionist organizations as the United Zionist-Revisionists of America and Hadassah. Of even greater significance has been the increasing regularity at which such criticism has been heard within the very study committees established by the local Jewish Federations for the purpose of muting communal criticism.

The road ahead will be difficult. But, in terms of American Jewish survival, it will yet prove to be that road "which is long but short." The restoration of Jewish *substance* to American Jewish life will bear great fruits. It will assure continuity. Undoubtedly, there will remain obstacles and pitfalls along the way. Some will seek to circumvent the growing calls for greater support for Jewish education by attempting to fund "edu-cational programs" bereft of meaningful content. Perhaps it must be expected that those who have opposed substantial Jewish schooling for decades will fight for time by focusing their "reassessed" allocations on such forms of "Jewish knowledge" as classes in Israeli dancing, Jewish art, modern Hebrew poetry, and other subjects which do not revolve around the study of core Torah texts.

Time will be wasted. But it is in the very nature of bu-reaucracies to move slowly. "Responsible" individuals do not restructure communal priorities overnight. Or over a decade. Such things "take time."

And that is why the emergence of devastating religious aberrations like the Hare Krishnas and the Moonies, who suck the very souls of our young people from their bodies and from their people, may yet prove to be American Jewry's greatest blessing. The cults — even more than the iconoclasts of the 1960s — will force the Jewish communal bureaucracies to deal with the need for increasing Jewish education in the United States. More than the gallant efforts of such figures as Rabbi Shlomo Riskin, Rabbi Avi Weiss, Rabbi Moshe Sherer, Rabbi Shlomo Carlebach, the Lubavitcher Rebbe, Rabbi Avigdor Miller, Rebbetzin Esther Jungreis, and all the other rabbis, rebbetzins, and Jewish laymen who have been voices in the wilderness for so long, it will be the Reverend Sun Myung Moon, Guru Maharji Ji, Swami Prabhupada, Maharishi Mahesh Yogi, Reverend "Moishe Rosen," Sri Chinmoy, and all the other alien clerics who will impel American Jewry to restore meaning, substance, and authenticity to their slowly vanishing community in the United States.

Sometimes it takes a curse to bring a blessing. The blood which was shed on the British gallows fertilized the movement for Jewish independence in Eretz Yisrael. The tragedy of war in June 1967 revived the Jewish people throughout the world. The oppression of Soviet Jewry led to the emergence of a liberation movement in the United States which brought renewed life and vigor to segments of American Jewry which had all but assimilated into spiritual oblivion. Tragedy brings the Jewish people together, much as it does any family.

So, if the cults have been a tragedy, let us make of them a blessing. Let us look within our community and restore ourselves as of old. Let us face up to our crises and respond by returning to the cherished values which bred Jewish greatness for millennia. By meeting the challenges in a bold and united fashion, we may yet see the day when every American Jew will return to his people. Then to his faith. And, finally, to his land.

Such a day will come when we will it.